Mr. Ramsey,

Listen carefully! We are a group of individuals that represent a small foreign faction. We ~~do~~ respect your bussiness but not the country that it serves. At this time we have your daughter in our posession. She is safe and unharmed and if you want her to see 1997, you must follow our instructions to the letter.

You will withdraw $118,000.00 from your account. $100,000 will be in $100 bills and the remaining $18,000 in $20 bills. Make sure that you bring an adequate size attache to the bank. When you get home you will put the money in a brown paper bag. I will call you between 8 and 10 am tomorrow to instruct you on delivery. The delivery will be exhausting so I advise you to be rested. If we monitor you getting the money early, we might call you early to arrange an earlier delivery of the

money and hence. d earlier
~~delivery~~ pick-up of your daughter.
Any deviation of my instructions
will result in the immediate
execution of your daughter. You
will also be denied her remains
for proper burial. The two
gentlemen watching over your daughter
do particularly like you so I
advise you not to provoke them.
Speaking to anyone about your
situation, such as Police, F.B.I., etc.,
will result in your daughter being
beheaded. If we catch you talking
to a stray dog, she dies. If you
alert bank authorities, she dies.
If the money is in any way
marked or tampered with, she
dies. You will be scanned for
electronic devices and if any are
found, she dies. You can try to
deceive us but be warned that
we are familiar with Law enforcement
countermeasures and tactics. You
stand a 99% chance of killing
your daughter if you try to out
smart us. Follow our instructions

and you stand a 100% chance
of getting her back. You and
your family are under constant
scrutiny as well as the authorities.
Don't try to grow a brain
John. You are not the only
fat cat around so don't think
that killing will be difficult.
Don't underestimate us John.
Use that good southern common
sense of yours. It is up to
you now John!

                    Victory!
                    S.B.T.C

WHO WILL SPEAK FOR JONBENÉT?

A New Investigator
Reads Between the Lines

Andrew G. Hodges, M.D.

Village House Publishers
P.O. Box 530312
Birmingham, Alabama 35253

Library of Congress Cataloging-in-Publication Data

Hodges, Andrew G.
Who Will Speak for JonBenét?
Summary: An analysis of the JonBenét Ramsey murder investigation

1. True Crime 2. Psychology (Subconscious Mind) 3. Criminology
4. Psycholinguistics

Cover photo: Judith Phillips
Cover design: Jon Thompson
Book design: Scott Fuller Graphic Design

ISBN 0-9617255-2-4

Village House Publishers

(205) 328-4364
Visit the author's Web site: http://www.aghodges.com

1st edition

Printed and bound in the USA

To my mother and father
who love truth as much as they do people

TABLE OF CONTENTS

Foreword xi

Introduction xiii

Acknowledgments xix

PART I: What They Had
Method, Motives, and Messages

CHAPTER 1: A New Method.. 3

CHAPTER 2: The Motive for Murder 13

CHAPTER 3: The Best Detective—Patsy Ramsey 19

CHAPTER 4: The Ransom Note 31

CHAPTER 5: Uncovering the Smoking Gun
and the Motives.. 43

PART II: What They Did with What They Had
A Blind Investigation and a Mixed Media

CHAPTER 6: One Closed Mind—Deputy District Attorney
Michael Kane 69

CHAPTER 7: Switching Sides—Lou Smit 87

CHAPTER 8: Leaders Who Don't Lead—Alex Hunter
and Mark Beckner 101

CHAPTER 9: Getting the Word Out—The Media 107

CHAPTER 10: Reporters Who Don't Report 117

CHAPTER 11: Split Decision—Chuck Green 135

PART III: Where the Truth Can Be Found
Between the Blaming, Shaming, and Slips of the Tongue

CHAPTER 12: Following John and Patsy's Thoughtprints 147
CHAPTER 13: John and JonBenét—True Confessions 171
CHAPTER 14: Friends and Family Talk 187
CHAPTER 15: Burke Draws Attention to the Truth................ 203

PART IV: When Darkness Touches Light
Gullibility, Guilt, and Grace

CHAPTER 16: One More Death of Innocence 219
CHAPTER 17: In a Fog—The Ramseys Put on Piety 231
CHAPTER 18: Truth and Consequences—
    An Open Letter to John and Patsy Ramsey 243

APPENDICES

APPENDIX A: The Ransom Note
    An Overview, Outline, and Additional Insights 249
APPENDIX B: The Official Report to Michael J. Kane........... 257
APPENDIX C: The Christmas Letters 325
APPENDIX D: Biographical Information................................. 329

BIBLIOGRAPHY

FOREWORD

In Dr. Hodges's forensic analysis, he argues that without an understanding of the ransom note in the JonBenét Ramsey murder, the killers will go free. In this important work, he provides a "profile decoding" of the ransom note in order to identify the killers of JonBenét Ramsey. Dr. Hodges refers to this as reading "between the lines" in order to identify the "thoughtprints" of the murderers.

For Dr. Hodges, the ransom note identifies the murderers, explains the criminal motives present, provides details of events leading up to the actual murder, and tells how to apprehend the murderers. He believes it is the "smoking gun" in this case because no one can contaminate it. Dr. Hodges's work is the result of seeking the identity and nature of the author of the Ramsey ransom note by revealing his or her "thoughtprints" through decoding and clarification.

The profile decoding used in this important work is not to be confused with handwriting analysis or graphology techniques used in the past. Rather, this decoding is based upon the work of psychiatrist Robert Langs who discovered "super-intelligence" in his patients in their subliminal perception and communication. Dr. Hodges refers to this as "thoughtprints." He argues that these "thoughtprints" are far more perceptive than our conscious mind, as well as being incredibly honest. He indicates that virtually every action we take has an underlying reason or motive and that the subtext of communications identifies our unconscious mind, which speaks between the lines of such communication in identifiable "thoughtprints" that reveal reason and motive.

This important book is a new, cutting-edge forensic approach to document analysis. This pioneering effort to utilize Dr. Robert Langs's theory of the unconscious mind through profile decoding of hidden communication is applied with great clarity and precise analysis as Dr. Hodges builds a criminal case against the killers of JonBenét Ramsey.

This new technique of profile decoding as explained by the author will result in criminal offenders "speaking" through their deeper encoded unconscious messages and revealing their motives and true identities when written or spoken messages are decoded. Acceptance and application of this new forensic technique to written documents and oral communications will greatly contribute to the law enforcement arsenal of criminal investigation in the future.

Dr. Steven A. Egger
Criminologist and Professor of Criminal Justice
University of Illinois at Springfield

INTRODUCTION
Where It Stands

The Boulder, Colorado, authorities are certain they know who murdered JonBenét Ramsey on December 25, 1996—yet the murderers remain free. The grand jury, after more than twelve months of deliberation, was unable to indict the two most likely suspects: John and Patsy Ramsey, JonBenét's parents. Why? Patsy herself knows why. As she told the public after the grand jury's decision, it was due to the closed-mindedness of authorities. Their biases blinded them to the truth.

The Story: "Insufficient Evidence"

"Insufficient evidence." That is the excuse the Boulder authorities and the media have given to explain why JonBenét's murderers are still free. Almost everyone has heard or read that story, but few have heard the real story—the one much closer to the truth.

It's not that the authorities and the media are lying. But they aren't admitting that they are avoiding the most crucial piece of evidence—the ransom note. Everyone agrees that the ransom note is the pivotal piece of evidence in the case because it is the one piece that no one can contaminate. The ransom note provides sufficient evidence not only to indict, but also to convict Patsy and John Ramsey for the murder of JonBenét.

The author of the ransom note, one of JonBenét Ramsey's murderers, tried to tell the authorities all they needed to know: 1) who assaulted the little girl, 2) why they did it, and 3) how to catch them. The authorities ignored the author's clues because neither they nor the experts they called in to help with the case knew how to read the clues hidden between the lines of the ransom note. And the murderer didn't stop with the note—she repeatedly has given the authorities one clue after another in multiple public communications. But the authorities have missed each and every clue because they are unable to—or refuse to—"see" or "hear" what she was saying.

The key to "seeing" the incriminating information provided in the ransom note is knowing how to "read" it. That's where my two experienced forensic colleagues, clinical psychologist Dr. Patrick Callahan and psychoanalyst Dr. C. Jess Groesbeck, and I can help.

As experienced communication analysts, we examined the ransom note and applied a new method of document analysis—a breakthrough in reading and analyzing communication. After completing our exhaustive analysis, we are convinced that the ransom note is the "smoking gun"—the most convicting piece of evidence. This handwritten note details the events leading up to the murder, the murder itself, and the motives for the murder. And it indisputably ties Patsy and John Ramsey to the murder.

Other than calling in handwriting experts, who could not conclusively identify the author of the ransom note, the Boulder authorities essentially ignored this most crucial piece of evidence. Basically they didn't know what to do with the ransom note because their handwriting experts and linguistic specialists are not specifically trained in how the human mind communicates and how to read the "between the lines" communications. The prosecution's handwriting and linguistic experts reported that the ransom note did not contain sufficient evidence to identify the murderer or murderers, and the grand jury got the message. The jury's verdict of "insufficient evidence" mirrored the prosecution's presentation of the ransom note itself.

Sadly, the prosecution never took its best shot. Callahan, Groesbeck, and I uncovered overwhelming evidence in the ransom note, enough evidence to convict the murderers in a court of law, evidence intentionally left by the author/murderer for that very purpose. In a case that without the ransom note has admittedly thin evidence (as Deputy District Attorney and trial consultant Michael Kane told me, it's "not the strongest case"), it is criminal to pass up an opportunity to present such overwhelming evidence of the murderers' identity and motives. Callahan, Groesbeck, and I uncovered existing evidence contained in the ransom note by analyzing the author's "thoughtprints," specific communications from the murderer who wrote the note.

Patsy and John Ramsey continue to "clue them in" about the case. In desperation over the authorities' abject failure to make any use whatsoever of her clue-filled ransom note and other communications, the murderer made yet another attempt to get them to listen when she made the following public statement, released just hours after the grand jury announced they didn't have enough evidence to indict the Ramseys: "Experienced detectives were removed from this investigation in 1998. It is our [Patsy and John Ramsey's] request that this investigation be renewed by returning those skilled investigators to authority. This crime cannot be solved by those who close their minds to any lead that is inconsistent with their biases." In fact, Patsy suggested that the best way to find JonBenét's murderer was to engage someone like a profiler who reads crime scenes between the lines. Indirectly Patsy was hinting that the key to solving JonBenét's murder was to search for hidden messages at the crime scene, a clue that clearly points to the ransom note. In addition Patsy was hinting that if the authorities confronted the one person who knows all about the murder with the compelling evidence hidden between the lines of the ransom note, that person—who is Patsy herself—would break down and confess.

Drs. Callahan, Groesbeck, and I know the ransom note contains indisputable evidence that identifies the murderers, explains the motives for the crime, details the events leading up to and the actual murder itself, and tells how to apprehend the murderers. The police and most of the media don't believe or at least aren't admitting that they believe the ransom note contains any hard evidence.

The media and the prosecution want you to buy the story of "insufficient evidence." The media's embellished version of the "insufficient evidence" refrain focused on additional forces that compromised the investigation: infighting between the police and the district attorney's office, the passivity of District Attorney Alex Hunter, Patsy's and John's failure to cooperate with the investigation, and, above all, the authorities' failure to convincingly establish the motive to explain why two loving parents had murdered their beautiful young daughter—and on Christmas Day, no less. The prosecutors could never get the grand jury to look past the lack of evidence (which was caused by an initial contamination of the crime scene) and the lack of motive, along with what authorities felt was an unprecedented betrayal by one of their own detectives, Lou Smit, in mid-investigation.

But the real story of "ignored evidence" is much closer to the truth. By and large the prosecution and the media have failed to do their job of thoroughly investigating the crime and utilizing the latest breakthrough in communication. Breakthroughs take time to be accepted and widely used, but in the JonBenét Ramsey case, we don't have a lot of time to apprehend the murderers. Either we use the new method of analyzing the key piece of uncontaminated evidence, the ransom note, or the investigation dies. Despite bold statements from Police Chief Mark Beckner and District Attorney Alex Hunter, the prosecution has little hope of ever getting an indictment, much less winning the case, unless they present convincing evidence to a grand jury.

After the grand jury was dismissed, the jurors told reporters that "insufficient evidence" had prevented them from making any indictments in the case. Although both Police Chief Beckner and District Attorney Alex Hunter admitted that "insufficient evidence" had carried the day, Beckner still holds out hope that as-yet undiscovered evidence will bring JonBenét's murderers to justice, and Hunter insists that the case isn't closed.

Between the Lines

Callahan, Groesbeck, and I have consistently seen that thoughtprints contain wise advice and clear truth. We have also seen in hundreds of different situations how our deeper intelligence "sees" reality in a far deeper way than our conscious mind. Our deeper intelligence expertly assesses our deepest motives and tells us about them through thoughtprints.

We are all familiar with the subliminal or unconscious mind, particularly in its applications in police work. Police often hypnotize witnesses to obtain more information. Crime-scene investigators note how the unconscious mind of killers "speak" and leave valuable information at the crime scene, even when the killers are consciously trying to deceive the police by "staging" crimes. Over and over again investigators observe how criminals cannot stop themselves from unconsciously "confessing" and leaving clues.

Since we knew from experience with our patients that a person's brilliant deeper intelligence can unconsciously pick up and communicate truths about reality, we suspected that a murderer's deeper intelligence would pick up and communicate in thoughtprints his or her deepest motives and the details about the murder. Applying these tested principles, we analyzed the ransom note for the author/murderer's thoughtprints, and we did it in as unbiased a way as possible. When we started, we knew very little about the case. Our goal was to look for thoughtprints and see where the evidence took us.

The key to "reading" between the lines is to understand the subliminal or unconscious mind and to apply the recent discovery of a deeper intelligence we all possess, the way it communicates through thoughtprints. This deeper, truer part of our mind is light years ahead of our surface, conscious mind in its ability to observe what is going on around us and to communicate, often in symbolic ways, what it observes.

Once you "see" the thoughtprints in the ransom note, you "hear" the author/murderer not only confessing to the crime, but also elaborating on her motives in great detail: She tells about the horrendous, deep pain that started eating at her long before the murder and the shocking event that triggered her rage the night of the murder. The author/murderer makes it clear that this was a rage killing, an impulsive act in a chaotic family scenario that simply got out of control.

If you listen closely, as Patsy suggests in the opening line of the ransom note, and have an open mind, you will "read" about the family dynamics that precipitated the murder of JonBenét the night of Christmas Day 1996. You will also "see" the crime scene and the actual murder. And you will "hear" firsthand what drove two loving parents to murder their beautiful, much-beloved six-year-old daughter.

We Need To Speak for JonBenét

The murder of JonBenét Ramsey is a fascinating story in and of itself. In a moment of family chaos, two all-American parents who have it all—money, power, beautiful children, beautiful town, beautiful life—mortally injure their beautiful young daughter, their "trophy" child, and then cover up their crime by murdering her a second time. These are twists and turns worthy of Shakespeare, but the murder itself is only the first half of the story.

The other half of the story is how the all-American prosecution and many members of the all-American press have failed to do their basic investigative jobs. They have failed to recognize uncontaminated, incriminating evidence, the author/murderer's thoughtprints in the ransom note, and they have failed to use that evidence to indict and convict Patsy and John Ramsey for the murder of their daughter, JonBenét.

It's really quite a story when you think about it. The perfect mother and father in the perfect family kill the perfect child in the perfect town and create the perfect cover-up. And between the lines of the bogus ransom note, the mother's perfect conscience, her soul, really makes the perfect confession, wanting us to know how much her heart aches that she failed so horribly. She pleads with us to understand the pressure she was under, to understand why she lost it and went into a rage that night. She begs the authorities to whom she has written the letter to speak for the daughter she still loves and to bring her, the once-perfect mother, to justice, something she can't do by herself.

When a beautiful, helpless six-year-old little girl asks you to speak up for her when her voice is gone, you need to do everything you can to hear her whispers. And right now the JonBenét Ramsey murder case needs one thing more than anything else: somebody to do what the author/murder requested in the ransom note—to speak for JonBenét.

Who will speak for this murdered child? Who will listen to the voices between the lines? I plan to keep on speaking for JonBenét until she is heard. I believe you can hear her voice, too, and ultimately I believe she will be heard by "we the people."

ACKNOWLEDGMENTS

I am indebted to my two forensic colleagues, psychologist Patrick Callahan and psychoanalyst Jess Groesbeck, who appreciated my original work with the ransom note and were instrumental in our delivering a detailed report to the Boulder authorities—which they encouraged me to disclose in the appendix. They are a big part of the story I am telling here. Without my brother Greg this project would not have been attempted, and I likewise owe a special debt of gratitude to John Harrod, Norma McKittrick, Steve Pincus, and Joyce Farrell, who believed that this was a story worth telling. Tanya Dean helped pull things together with her editorial skills. There are many others whom I have met along the way, who have inspired me in their desire to speak for justice and for JonBenét, such as the housewife who wrote a daily Internet column with style and wit under the pen name "Mrs. Brady" and served as a major resource center on the case. As usual, my wife Dorothy provided the nurturing environment a writer needs. I am also deeply appreciative of the validation of my work by several other colleagues, as well as other forensic experts. Finally, the new approach to document analysis my two colleagues and I presented would not have been possible without the work of Robert Langs. I remain convinced that one day the history of psychology will fully recognize his genius.

PART I
What They Had
Method, Motives, and Messages

CHAPTER 1
A New Method

"The ransom note is the case. The ransom note is the whole case."
Patrick J. Callahan, Ph.D., Forensic Psychologist

Every day advances are made in the field of medicine, in the study and treatment of the human body. Likewise, there are advances in the understanding of the human mind, as well. This is as it should be. Life is psychological. Every moment, from birth to death, whether asleep or awake, we are psychological creatures. Our minds are the most unique features about us. They give us the power to rule the world over any other creature. This is where our genius lies, where our creativity and intuition are found. This is the place our plans are hatched, where our dreams and wishes grow. Our minds possess extraordinary potential for bringing about achievements we can scarcely imagine. Everything unique that mankind has accomplished had its start here.

But all our evil deeds have begun here, too. Our minds can be our glory—and our shame. Here we find not only the bright lights of goodness and genius, but also the darkness of hatred and destruction, our shadow side. Whether for good or for bad, we find the very center of our motivations here. Virtually every action we take has an underlying reason, a motive. However spontaneous or happenstance our behavior may appear, we don't do anything without a motive. Motives, then, are always psychological. Motives have everything to do with the mind.

If our behavior is *what* we do, then our motives are *why* we do it. How often, after doing something that got us into trouble, did we hear the question, "Why did you do that?" Sometimes we know exactly why—but other times, we aren't so sure. Our conscious mind isn't always aware of the reasons for our actions. But recent work with patients shows that some part of the mind—a deeper part—always knows. And part of its job is to tell the truth.

The Deeper Intelligence: Thoughtprints

Bottom line: We know more than we think we know, and we tell more than we think we are telling. Psychiatrists and psychologists have been aware of the subliminal or unconscious mind for quite a while, and in a variety of situations. Research studies show that people do indeed pick up on subliminal messages—messages just under the threshold of the conscious mind. Parents recognize this when they see kids paying more attention to what adults *do* than to what they *say*.

Many times people use their unconscious in dreams to intuitively solve problems. Parents subliminally picked up on things about their children, and their subliminal mind can communicate these observations in dreams. For example, a mother dreamed she was walking through a forest of poison ivy with her teenage son. She remembered her dream after she woke up, and she realized that poison ivy reminded her of marijuana, which led her to investigate and discover that her son was indeed using drugs. Her perceptive deeper intelligence communicated to her in a way that enabled her to "see" the situation, helping the truth she already knew deep inside cross over the threshold to a place where she could recognize the situation. As a result, she could get her son the help he needed.

Along these same lines, a major breakthrough to the unconscious mind occurred in 1973 when psychiatrist Robert Langs discovered that patients in therapy unconsciously picked up on far more than anyone else had realized and told therapists about it "between the lines." While therapists were familiar with the idea of unconscious or subliminal perception and communication, no one until Langs realized just how brilliant everyone's deeper (unconscious) mind was. In short, Langs discovered that therapy patients possessed a "super-intelligence" in their unconscious, which I have called the deeper intelligence. While the fields of psychiatry and psychology have largely overlooked the breakthrough—typical for new discoveries in any discipline—nevertheless we now realize the human mind possesses extraordinary capabilities, often untapped. Unquestionably, this will be the cutting edge of the psychology of the 21st century.

The practical effect of this discovery on therapists is enormous. The discovery of the deeper intelligence has led to improved listening techniques in therapy. As a result, psychiatrists have realized that a patient's deeper intelligence constantly picks up on what is really bothering him or her—thus, in therapy sessions the patient himself or herself unknowingly guides the therapist to help the patient understand himself or herself. As Drs. Callahan, Groesbeck, and I have watched peoples' deeper minds at work, we have learned that the perceptiveness of our deeper intelligence is utterly brilliant. Numerous times our patients have unconsciously come up with excellent, creative solutions to their own problems, and they have communicated their ideas to us through unconsciously patterned thoughts—what I call "thoughtprints."

We have learned that people intuitively know what is best for them, and they will consciously know what to do when they truly "listen" to what their deeper intelligence is communicating through their thoughtprints. For example, sometimes when a patient decides consciously that he or she no longer needs therapy, his or her deeper intelligence, knowing that the person needs to continue for some reason, prompts the individual to think and talk repeatedly about unfinished business, stories such as: "My daughter needs to continue her piano lessons;" "my husband hasn't finished the room he's building onto our house;" "my son still has more courses to take before graduation." The patient's deeper intelligence uses these thoughtprints to "tell" him or her that he or she also has unfinished business, that there's more work to do. In short, a person's deeper intelligence encodes a central message—here "an unfinished business" code—by repeating thoughtprints.

In some other cases, when a patient asks for medication but his or her deeper intelligence advises against it, the unconscious mind patterns the patient's thoughts (thoughtprints) and prompts him or her to tell stories about people who were too dependent on chemicals (alcohol or drugs) to solve their problems. In this case, the thoughtprints form the encoded central message, "I really need to be more independent and handle the problem myself."

Sometimes when a patient thinks it would be a good idea to include his or her spouse for part of a therapy session, his or her deeper intelligence advises against it by patterning thoughts and prompting stories about third parties who disrupt one-on-one interactions—an "unwanted threesome" code.

The bottom line is that in psychotherapy we have discovered that the deeper intelligence is a phenomenal guide, far more perceptive than our conscious mind, and is incredibly honest, always insisting on the truth. It intuitively knows that wholeness comes from owning the truth about ourselves. Because a person's deeper intelligence is always a part of his or her mind—"always with him or her"—we can now utilize this deeper intelligence in selected cases, such as the Ramsey case where the killer left behind a ran-som note.

Now we can study the ransom note to see if the killer's deeper intelligence left behind clues, trying to tell us what was really bothering her or him, as invariably the deeper mind is inclined to do. Applying this new approach to the mind, we find that the killer did tell us the story behind this crime. We've all heard parents, particularly mothers, say something like, "If that kid screams one more time, I'll lose my mind." According to the thoughtprints found in the Ramseys' ransom note, that's similar to what happened to Patsy Ramsey the night of the murder. We will investigate this further in Chapter 4, page 31.

Right and Left Brain

Before going further, a familiar analogy will help you grasp the two ways the mind observes and communicates. Then you can understand what the ransom note writer is really saying (and what both the Ramseys are often telling us between the lines elsewhere). Most of us have heard of the idea of left and right brain. By analogy, the conscious mind represents the left brain, which utilizes literal, straightforward communication—"just the facts." On the other hand, the unconscious mind or deeper intelligence represents the right brain, which utilizes symbolic (or intuitive) communication. Going back to the examples from therapy above, a patient's left brain can tell them one thing, e.g., "I don't need any more therapy," while his or her right brain can tell the patient the exact opposite, by patterning a series of thoughts about "unfinished business." In short we have discovered that our right brain is far more perceptive than our left brain in any given situation. While this is not an exact version of how our left and right brains work, the analogy demonstrates how our mind works on two levels at the same time. Thus, we can examine the ransom note or any other communication from the Ramseys for both left- and right-brain messages. Listening in two ways to their messages is the key to the case, because their right brain indeed speaks between the lines in disguised but discernible thoughtprints. And it's telling the truth.

The Courage To Look Deeper

It isn't easy to look in deep places. We don't know what is waiting for us there. We tend to fear the unknown. It isn't surprising, then, to understand that the information Drs. Callahan, Groesbeck, and I provided to the Boulder authorities wasn't welcomed or used to help them. When listening to the deeper intelligence of others, we often must face some uncomfortable truths of our own. I have learned that we innately tend to avoid looking at our deeper motives, simply because we are human beings. We really don't like to get down to the "bottom line," to the raw emotions and dark truths about ourselves that can throw us out of control. But part of our minds wants us to know, needs us to know, in order for us to be whole people.

Leeza Gibbons brought this home to me after I had appeared on her show, *Leeza*, to discuss the case and the ransom note. Afterward, she told me, half-jokingly but obviously uncomfortable with the idea she had an unconscious mind, "Dr. Hodges, I don't want you reading any of *my* letters." In a way, she simply spoke for everyone, especially those involved in the case, because to open ourselves to the hidden messages in the ransom note means that we all have to acknowledge a deeper intelligence that is reading us (and others) like a book. And sometimes it wants to read out loud.

A major reason people fear the deeper intelligence is that dark secrets are often there—our shadow side, the side we want no one to see. To keep that part of us from emerging, we put on masks and we make sure they stay securely in place. But the deeper intelligence—aware of so much more—wants the masks to come off, wants the truth to be told. Still, we keep them on, and we want others to keep theirs on, too.

Case in point: How could loving parents murder their child? Many people struggle with the question, including the Ramsey defenders Lou Smit, Michael Tracey, and several in the media. Leeza Gibbons again spoke for many, including the Boulder authorities, when she continually resisted the idea that parents could harm their children, despite evidence that hundreds of parents kill their children each year, and thousands more abuse their kids, coming within a heartbeat of killing them. We believe that a major part of what happened to JonBenét was that she was in an abusive situation that went too far.

The problem is that everyone wants to bury his or her shadow side. Otherwise a loving mother, like Leeza Gibbons, would have to face the fact that, at times, she feels raw emotions and hostility toward those she loves. And not just her—these emotions are universal in everyone, including the Ramseys. Human beings are capable of great good and of deplorable evil. To refuse to believe that is to live in the deepest form of denial. We want only to consider that we are "good" people.

The Ramsey case makes us look at some powerful issues—things we cringe to even think about, let alone talk about. Issues like incest and death. People don't talk about sexual inclinations and curiosity among family members (even though it is quite common). Incest is one of the greatest taboos. Death, in its own way, is often just as taboo a subject to discuss—as I have often seen in my work as a physician and psychiatrist. We can say, "Death doesn't bother me," but we'd probably be out of touch with the truth. We will see that the Ramseys also were keeping these and other things hidden—fear of death, incest, discomfort about aging, jealousy, just to name a few.

To face our shadow side is a kind of death in and of itself. But our ideal, "only-good" selves must die. The masks eventually must come off, particularly for the Ramseys who need to confront their fear of what lies hidden rather than to continue to see themselves in the greatest light possible: the loving mother/beauty queen, the CEO, and the perfect family with the beautiful daughter. As a physician and psychiatrist, I know that what you don't know about yourself *can* hurt you. Alternately, it is also true that the truth shall set you free. For better or for worse, the Ramsey saga confronts us with this truth.

A Hornet's Nest: Investigators and the New Method

In any ongoing investigation, the authorities rely on experts to help them solve their cases. No one can be an expert at everything, so many people, each with his or her own area of expertise, are called upon to provide insight and theories. As experts in motives (the deeper intelligence), my colleagues and I brought to the Boulder authorities the understanding that, more often than we like to think, we all do things for reasons (motives) that are initially unknown to us. This is never more true than in the case of something a
s powerful as a rage killing. We also brought with us a knowledge and

expertise in dealing with the deeper intelligence, that part of us that knows us like a book, that understands our deeper motives because it can see them moment by moment.

The authorities in this case are experts in their own areas, but they know nothing about this recently discovered deeper intelligence; therefore, they can't possibly know how it communicates. We came along to help them find out if the killer's deeper mind had expressed its viewpoint, particularly in the ransom note left at the scene. Specifically, we were looking for thoughtprints—patterned communications from the killer's unconscious mind—because we knew they might be there. If the investigators were not looking for something and didn't know it was there, they weren't likely to ever see it. As experts, we could see the hidden messages and analyze what the killer's deeper intelligence was trying desperately to tell the authorities. Nowhere would this be more evident than in the three-page ransom note.

Here is our premise: Above all, the ransom note is psychological. Whoever wrote that note did so for a psychological reason. Obviously the killer wrote the note to cover up the crime. Very few believe—other than the Ramseys (and their supporters) with their vested interests—that this crime was an actual kidnapping gone wrong. Everything points away from a true kidnapping. For instance, the killer molested and strangled the child on the premises. The killer lingered in the home long enough—at least thirty minutes—to write an elaborate ransom note using materials (pen and paper) from inside the victim's home. (There is also strong evidence that the killer had even written some "practice" notes before completing the final one.) In the note, the killer asked for an extremely small, specific, and odd ransom amount, and then never carried out the kidnapping. The ransom note was extraordinarily long, unlike a typical ransom note. Crime scene specialists agree on one thing: The ransom note was part of the staging of the crime.

Obviously, the killer had definite motives in writing that note. Consciously, the killer wanted to throw the police off and to get away with the crime. The major question is whether or not the killer had *other* motives in writing the note—deeper motives that wouldn't be apparent, even to the killer herself or himself. Does the killer reveal his or her psychology in that note? Can we come up with a psychological profile of the killer from that note? We provided the Boulder authorities affirmative answers to both questions.

Unfortunately, this powerful case presented the authorities with powerful issues of their own—ones they'd rather not deal with. They are human and have the same fears the rest of us have. We knew by presenting our findings that we would not be held in great esteem, mainly because we were experts capable of pulling back the covers of their lives, too. When Patsy Ramsey exposed her deeper, shadow side in the ransom note, she stirred up a hornet's nest for those involved in the investigation. It is not surprising to us then that when it comes to understanding the ransom note, those involved are looking the other way.

Law enforcement authorities in general resist dealing with psychological issues, particularly when the issues involve the unconscious mind. Like many other people, law enforcement agents feel uncomfortable or even frightened of psychiatrists and psychologists because we represent the unknown in both them and others. Over the past three decades Drs. Callahan, Groesbeck, and I have helped our patients overcome their fears of the unconscious and therefore to experience the value in understanding and tuning in to their deeper intelligence. We tried our best to help authorities overcome their fears and resistance to a new way of thinking, as well, but we have not yet been successful. We haven't given up on them. Sometimes new methods take time to be embraced.

From our observations, the Boulder authorities have come to the conclusion that "psychology" can be more or less what an individual wants it to be. They do not seem to see how an approach using the deeper intelligence makes it much more scientific. Thus, they have no real way of determining which approach to the psychology of the killer is best. As a result, they have basically followed the assumption that there is no best way. Because the authorities are unfamiliar with precisely how the unconscious mind communicates and how its messages can be validated, they have completely discounted any psychological motives in the Ramsey case. This is a grave mistake.

One of the primary problems in this case is that these men and women simply cannot deal with their own powerful emotions. This includes the police, the district attorneys, and, by and large, the media. The problem in this case isn't that we don't know who killed JonBenét—it is that the answer hits too close to home. It is just too powerful. That explains why, when the authorities were presented with a breakthrough method to understanding the killer's mind—one that sheds enormous light on the case—they rejected it. By acknowledging that we had a method for looking at the killer's deeper mind, these individuals would have to admit that someone could look below the surface at theirs. For professionals trained to be in control at all times, this was unthinkable.

Most people don't realize that the police struggle with powerful emotions. Not long ago, as a result of my involvement with the JonBenét case, I was one of sixty professionals chosen by the FBI to participate at a week-long conference at the FBI headquarters in Quantico, Virginia. The topic: Suicide and Law Enforcement. The FBI had the courage to confront a major problem in law enforcement—how dedicated men and women are prone to run from their own powerful emotions, a condition known as the "agent's disease," namely, depression and suicide. The tremendous pain, trauma, and violence that law enforcement personnel face on a daily basis conditions them to avoiding painful emotions. This kind of "shut down" can lead to suicide—all because they don't, or won't, face themselves. On the surface, suicide may look macho. But it isn't. In reality, it is running—running away from the painful emotions. The first step in helping these brave men and women who defend us daily is very simple: They need to know it's okay to be afraid. It's okay to feel overwhelmed. It's okay to be honest about the painful feelings. And it's okay to be human.

Embracing the New Method

Either we have a deeper (unconscious) mind or we don't. Either we have a brilliant deeper intelligence with far more ability than our conscious mind or we don't. Either the killer intuitively communicated through patterned "thoughtprints" or she didn't. My colleagues and I believe we do—and she did.

In thousands of clinical situations over the years, I have been guided and corrected by this special intelligence everyone possesses. Like others, I have resisted it, been blind to it, and made more than my share of errors. But I eventually learned about the remarkable abilities of our deeper mind and accepted the wisdom of submitting to it. I have seen wonderful emotional healing take place when someone heeds the advice of his or her deeper intelligence. In fact, I am convinced the ransom note writer herself, in that very note, was seeking a healing, however painful it would be. However much we all despise what she—and her partner in the crime—did, we can have great sympathy for her, for the emotional pain that she carried both before and after the crime, pain she still carries today.

We must have the courage to face these issues head-on. Certainly, no one likes the idea of someone intruding into his or her life, so we mistakenly experience the search for deeper messages as "reading someone's mind," intruding on their privacy, telling them what they are thinking, controlling them. But the truth is that people send *themselves* messages using their own marvelous deeper intelligence. And the truth in the Ramsey case is that we are only listening to the killer's own communications—at the killer's urging—and then simply following her instructions. Patsy Ramsey was secretly reading her own mind in a deeper way, and she was encouraging us to do it with her in order to bring about justice and wholeness. If we listen to Patsy and John Ramsey, in their various public communications, we will hear that they are really pleading with us to help them tell the truth so that ultimately they and their family can find peace.

Did the killer intend for the investigators and the jury to hear her messages? I think she made them plain enough that a good jury with adequate input from expert witnesses could come to a reasonable verdict that the killer had spoken for JonBenét and, in doing so, had spoken to them. In the following chapters, you the reader can evaluate for yourself the evidence from the ransom note and decide who was listening to JonBenét, who was listening to the messages between the lines.

In this book, I will also apply the same listening method to others—investigators, media personalities, prosecutors—who were and are involved in this case, because no matter who they are, deep down they want to tell the truth. Their very roadblocks to this breakthrough in listening to the deeper intelligence tells us that they recognize what they are doing. We need to hear what they are telling us, too.

CHAPTER 2
The Motive for Murder

"The heart of the sons of men is full of evil, and madness is in their heart while they live."

Ecclesiastes 9:3

Motive is how I got involved in the JonBenét case. Basically, I am an investigator. As a psychiatrist specializing in analyzing communication, I spend my entire working day in the land of the mind helping people understand themselves. Everyday I see eight to ten people with problems, people who possess clues about what's going wrong but they don't know they have these clues. My job as an investigator is to allow them to talk and present the clues, and then I use the clues to put the picture together for them—actually showing them how they are arriving at solutions to their own problems without realizing it. As such, I am a motive expert, someone who helps people understand themselves, to sort out real motives from superficial motives, to figure out what's really bothering them.

Because of my experience, I have learned that motives are tricky. Motives frequently aren't what they first appear to be. In fact, I have found that the more powerful the motive is, the more a person tries to hide it. Consistently, people want to settle for superficial motives—more palatable, "gentler" motives—when in truth, their passionate deeper motives are actually driving them. If people want to understand themselves, they have to go where the power is. We must do exactly the same thing in analyzing the motive behind JonBenét's murder—go where the power is, find out who had the powerful motives, who possessed the murderous rage and acted on it. Fortunately, we have never been in a better position to understand motives, particularly in a case like this. The killer made a huge mistake when she left a three-page ransom note, a document filled with motives. But, as in those deeper motives that people try to hide, we must look between the lines where the motive is planted, waiting to be read.

To say that motive is a crucial question in the JonBenét Ramsey murder case would be the grossest of understatements. In a case where no eye-witnesses have come forward, a case largely involving non-physical, circumstantial evidence, the motives of the accused—the Ramseys—take on even greater importance. This is what the grand jury struggled with.

Lack of motive has always been the Ramseys' theme song. Since the very beginning, Patsy and John Ramsey have vehemently proclaimed their innocence and have continually offered the persuasive defense, "We loved our daughter and had no reason to kill her." Over and over they tell us, "We had no motive." The Ramsey defenders all passionately adopt the same party line. Reporters agree and inform us that they have uncovered nothing in the Ramseys' past to indicate they could be murderers (as if this is a true gauge of guilt or innocence). The public also asks the same question, "How could loving parents like these kill their child—on Christmas Day of all times?" At first glance, the Ramseys make a strong case. But not if you really understand motives and the mind, because secretly they both were in enough pain to spin out of control and commit such an act.

If this case ever goes to trial, at the heart of the defense's case will be the claim, "But, ladies and gentlemen of the jury, the accused had no reason to murder this young child, no reason whatsoever." And if they say it once, they will say it a thousand times, "If the motives don't fit, you must acquit." Of course, the defense will have other tactics: The DNA doesn't match; the shoe print in the basement doesn't match; the window was broken. But when all is said and done, the case will almost certainly come down to motive. Even if the police find new DNA evidence or something equally convicting, the Ramseys' high-priced lawyers will vigorously attack, and like in the O.J. trial, DNA might not be enough. The case would undoubtedly come down to motive.

One thing is certain: Whoever killed JonBenét Ramsey had a motive. Once you know the motive, you know who the murderer was. Boulder DA Alex Hunter and his deputy prosecutor Michael Kane, along with Police Chief Mark Beckner, all had a chance to see the motive staring them in the face, a motive straight from the mind of the killer. But they were blind to it because they weren't trained to see it. As you will see in *Part II: What They Did with What They Had*, these authorities had such low regard for the killer's mind (and, in essence, psychology) that they believed whatever they knew about psychology was enough. Unfortunately, that is not true.

My colleagues and I know that people have a tremendous need to tell the truth, because deep down we all desire to be whole and want to own up to who we really are. This drive never stops being a part of us, even when we desperately want simultaneously to cover up and confess to what we have done. Thus, whoever wrote the ransom note did so for conscious motives and for deeper motives. If this is true, then the ransom note and our analysis of the deeper motives found in it are keys to solving this case.

Does the Ransom Note Reveal the Killer's Motives?

Boulder District Attorney Alex Hunter desperately wants to find the smoking gun in the Ramsey case. He has said, "I don't care who it [the smoking gun] points toward." Larry King is still pleading, "Would somebody please tell me a motive?"

And all along, the motive has been right in front of them. The three leaders of the JonBenét Ramsey homicide investigation—Alex Hunter, Michael Kane, and Mark Beckner—have seen the ransom note. But they have failed to see in that note the murderer's eyewitness account of the events of the night, the motives for the murder, and the identity of the murderers.

The ransom note exposes the smoking gun, and it establishes multiple motives. Dr. Patrick Callahan, Dr. C. Jess Groesbeck, and I want to help the investigation by showing the prosecution's team how to open their eyes and minds to the evidence in the ransom note.

Callahan, Groesbeck, and I, as well as others who are familiar with how patients use their deeper intelligence, have learned that the clinical setting provides the best microscope for studying motives. During therapy sessions we get the most accurate look at the issues of the heart, and we can then take that knowledge and apply it to situations outside of therapy. This new understanding of the mind gives us two advantages in the Ramsey case. First, it enables us to look past externals with the knowledge that deeper motivations often control us, particularly frightening emotional events we've experienced that exert their influence long after they seemingly are over. Second, this new understanding of the mind enables us to listen to the author/murderer's thoughtprints in the ransom note.

Up to this point Kane, Hunter, and Beckner, as well as Detective Lou Smit, have demonstrated significant resistance to understanding how the mind works. Part of their resistance comes from the Boulder prosecution team being overwhelmed by a deluge of unsolicited offers of help. Kane told me he personally had received hundreds of letters. These men have been exposed to a multitude of different opinions on the Ramseys' possible motives and have worked with professionals on their own. Still, they resist the expertise provided by professionals in a breakthrough method of analyzing motives.

Motives, specifically deeper motives and deeper instincts, are what this case is all about. Dr. Callahan, Dr. Groesbeck, and I examined the note to see if it contained such motives, if thoughtprints from the killer's deeper mind were in that note, telling us how the killer saw the crime. We believed the motives were there, for a number of reasons. First, the sheer length of the note suggested the killer's deeper intelligence had truly taken over and had pressured the killer to elaborate. No matter how crafty the killer thought she was being in writing the note, her deeper intelligence appeared to have gone into overdrive. From the moment we picked up the ransom note, we had one basic question: Were the killer's thoughtprints in that note? The central question in this case remains, "Why did the killer write the ransom note?" We believe the killer told us. We believe that the killer's deeper instincts took over and confessed. (For more detailed explanation of the clues left in the ransom note, see Chapter 4, page 31 and Chapter 5, page 43.)

Too Good to Kill?

Certainly no one wants to believe that two "normal" parents could kill their child, especially in such a horrific manner. But if we think about it logically, if the Ramseys were involved, then we must think about the possibility of deeper motives. If we look only at superficial motives, then it is an impossibility they (or any other "nice" people) could have committed this crime—because on the surface they had no motive. However, if we face the fact that human beings have a "shadow side" and deeper, hidden motives, then we will be dealing with the killer's motives much more realistically.

I told the whole story of JonBenét's murder in my book *A Mother Gone Bad: The Hidden Confession of JonBenét's Killer*, and Drs. Callahan, Groesbeck, and I told it again in the comprehensive report on our forensic analysis of the ransom note that we sent to Deputy District Attorney Michael Kane. As I listened to the major talk shows after the grand jury's declaration of "insufficient evidence," it struck me that there wasn't a motive specialist—someone who is trained to look for deeper motives—in the crowd of experts. Two and a half years into the investigation, I heard Larry King say, "I wish somebody would give me a motive if the Ramseys did it." Patrick Callahan, Jess Groesbeck, and I have given Larry King and everyone else not one motive, but at least two motives—a time bomb motive and a trigger motive—for why Patsy and John Ramsey murdered JonBenét.

King's statement reveals the media's difficulty in assessing motives. Larry King and many others are fooled by the "external" Ramseys, these nice successful people with no prior record of acting out. To their credit, some media professionals, including Denver television reporter Carol McKinley and radio talk-show host Peter Boyles, did investigate the concept of thoughtprints in the ransom note. Other radio talk-show hosts around the country also did their job of thoroughly investigating the case and accepting a new form of evidence. Syndicated radio talk-show host and psychologist Lori Roth said our explanation of the crime was "the first thing that makes any sense." And Mrs. Brady, a self-described "average Philadelphia housewife," who became the leading Internet force for justice in her daily Web page column said that my book *A Mother Gone Bad* provided the missing motives in the case.[1] (For more information about the media's treatment of our analysis, see Chapter 10, page 117)

The law enforcement authorities have their own particular difficulties in assessing motives, and quite often they take their best "guess." In the Ramsey case they guessed that Patsy lost control and hit JonBenét in a rage over a bedwetting episode, even when this motive makes no real sense psychologically. Certainly some parents do hit their children over bedwetting, but not these parents on this night. Something far more powerful threw Patsy Ramsey into a murderous rage on Christmas night, and she tells all about it in the ransom note she wrote to cover up the murder.

---

[1] Mrs. Brady is the pen name of a Philadelphia housewife who became involved in the search for justice for JonBenét via the Internet. Eventually she formed her own Web site, which became the most comprehensive site on the Internet for information about the case. "Mrs. Brady" arises at 5:30 every morning to prepare her daily site, which is read regularly by many, including the Boulder authorities. Her current site is holoworld.com/mrsbrady.

CHAPTER 3
The Best Detective–Patsy Ramsey

"A wonderful fact to reflect upon that every human creature is constituted to be that profound secret and mystery to every other."

Charles Dickens, 1859

One detective on the Ramsey case has the extraordinary power to accurately observe people and determine their motives at their deepest level. Her name is Patsy Ramsey, and her on-the-scene work has contributed greatly to the fields of criminology and psychiatry. While Patsy currently is best-known as the mother of JonBenét Ramsey and as a primary suspect in the little girl's murder, eventually she will be most remembered for her brilliant dissection of the murder case and for providing the smoking gun.

Brilliant forensic detectives like Patsy Ramsey don't come along very often because, unlike Patsy Ramsey, most murderers don't leave written evidence that details the how and why, the means and motives, of their crimes. Patsy Ramsey the murderer/detective did all that and more. She wrote a masterpiece (the ransom note), filled with deep insights about the murderers and the victim, the circumstances leading up to the murder, the murder itself, and the way to bring the murderers to justice. Patsy also keeps following up with additional clue-rich written and oral communications, including an interview with CNN a mere seven days after the murder.

Patsy is not consciously aware of her brilliant detective work, but I am, because every day in therapy sessions I encourage my patients to use their brilliant deeper intelligence to analyze their behavior, to discern their deeper motives, and to come up with creative solutions to their problems. The key to making use of the revelations of the brilliant deeper intelligence is knowing how to listen. And the key to making use of Patsy's brilliant detective work in "solving" JonBenét's murder is to listen carefully, something Patsy herself repeatedly tells us to do in the ransom note. (See Chapter 4, page 31.)

Unfortunately the Boulder law enforcement authorities neither know how to listen nor seem willing to let experts help them listen carefully to the observations of Patsy's deeper intelligence. They have ignored her brilliant detective work, and they could really use her help.

How different the prosecution's brain trust summit on June 1, 1998, would have been if Patsy's evidence had been included. Boulder Police Chief Mark Beckner and his detectives; District Attorney Alex Hunter and his key staff members, including Michael Kane; Bill Hagameir of the FBI's Child Abduction and Serial Killers unit; psychiatrist and consultant Dr. Steve Pitt; and special consultants and former O.J. Simpson dream-team members Dr. Henry Lee and Barry Scheck gathered after eighteen months of investigation to review what evidence they had, what it told them, and if they had a case. For months prior to the summit meeting, the Boulder Police Department and the DA's office had been at war. Rampant distrust and polarization had hampered the necessary sharing of information until Beckner, the former lead detective and commander of the investigation, became police chief and managed to bring about rapprochement between the divided forces of the prosecution team.

However, the peace Beckner achieved was tenuous, and a scant two months after the June summit, on what would have been JonBenét's eighth birthday, August 6, the alienation erupted into a full-fledged public war when Detective Steve Thomas resigned in protest over what he perceived to be gross mishandling of the case by the DA's staff. On September 24, the DA's ace investigator, Detective Lou Smit, returned the salvo when he publicly pronounced Patsy and John Ramsey innocent and claimed they had been falsely persecuted, which implied the ineptness of the Boulder police force in solving the crime.

Smit, who had come out of retirement at Alex Hunter's request to help with the case, saw absolutely no motive for either Patsy or John to have murdered their daughter. Although the Boulder police investigators were uncertain about Patsy and/or John's motive(s), they believed enough circumstantial evidence pointed to the Ramseys to warrant presenting a case against them to a grand jury. The prosecution staff had come to a consensus that Patsy had murdered her daughter in a rage killing, most likely over a bedwetting incident. But since they had not found a "smoking gun," they were on shaky ground about the motive. As indicated previously, Alex Hunter told *The New Yorker* months before, "I would like there to be a smoking gun, and I don't care who it's aimed at."

Other experts, most notably distinguished prosecutor emeritus Vincent Bugliosi, recognized the prosecution's dilemma. Bugliosi believed the prosecutor and his staff were like fish out of water. Since the prosecution didn't have either overwhelming circumstantial evidence or a clear, strong motive, they didn't really know whom to charge with what.

Besides struggling to determine the motive for the murder, the Boulder police investigators still had a number of unanswered questions, such as:

(1) What happened the night of the crime and who did it?
(2) Which came first: the head injury or the strangulation?
(3) Was JonBenét sexually abused?
(4) Why did the murderer write such a long ransom note?
(5) How could the murderer(s) be brought to justice with such a lack of evidence?
(6) Which detective was right about the parents' innocence: Steve Thomas or Lou "the Fox" Smit? Had they failed to do their job by focusing so much on the Ramseys?
(7) Was there any hope of finding a smoking gun, something that would irrefutably tie the murderer(s) to the crime?

Despite the grand jury investigation, which began in September 1998 and continued well into 1999, the investigators' questions have remained unanswered.

Still Patsy, the brilliant detective, is trying to help them see the answers she has already provided, and she continues to provide more. Every time Patsy makes a public statement, her deeper intelligence gives more clues about the murder. Besides the ransom note, one of the best places to see Patsy's continued efforts to communicate the truth is in the interview she and John gave on CNN a week after their daughter's murder. The powerful clues she revealed in that interview show her deeper intelligence at work and help us "see" even more clearly the clues she left earlier in the ransom note.

Patsy and John's Interview on CNN

On January 1, 1997, seven days after JonBenét's murder, Patsy and John Ramsey were interviewed by CNN's Brian Koebel in Atlanta, where the Ramseys have a second home. John had placed a phone call thirty-five minutes after "finding" JonBenét's body to make the arrangements to fly to Atlanta, but the Boulder police delayed his trip a few days. While refusing to grant interviews to the Boulder or Denver press, Patsy and John had sought out a nationwide television interview of their choosing, a pattern they would repeat in their effort to control the media and the outcome of the murder investigation.

My colleague Dr. James Raney, a Seattle-based psychoanalyst who has forensic experience, noted that the moment the Ramseys took to the airways and began granting interviews to the media, they were inviting the public in on the case by essentially saying, "We want you to take a look for yourself and see if we are guilty of murdering our daughter or not." Just as serial killers unconsciously ask law enforcement authorities to catch them because they can't turn themselves in, Patsy and John are unconsciously using public forums to help the authorities catch them and bring them to justice.

A person's deeper intelligence always motivates her or him to tell the truth about every situation. So every time Patsy and John make a public statement or appearance, they give their unconscious deeper intelligence an opportunity to reveal the truth about the murder and their cover-up. This would be particularly true in their very first interview just seven days after the murder. The descriptive words and examples Patsy and John use, as well as their slips of the tongue, repeated thoughts, or denials are messages from their unconscious deeper intelligence.

The deeper intelligence often uses examples to slip the truth past the person's conscious mind, which tends to cover it up. At the very beginning of the CNN interview, Patsy gave some striking examples. When Koebel asked if the Ramseys believed the murderer was someone outside their home, Patsy truthfully replied, "There is a killer on the loose. I don't know who it is. I don't know if it's a he or a she, but if I were a resident of Boulder, I would tell my friends to keep your babies close to you. There's someone out there." Patsy could have simply said, "I don't know who it is," but instead she volunteered the information that the murderer could be either a man or a woman.

Given the facts that almost all kidnappings from someone's home in the middle of the night involve a man as the primary perpetrator and that most people would automatically think of such a kidnapper as a man, Patsy's example stands out as unusual. Her unconscious deeper intelligence was communicating: "Keep in mind that the killer could have been a woman as well as a man." (The Boulder mayor quickly made a statement a few days later to counteract Patsy's hysterics, saying, "There is no killer on the loose here.")

Next Patsy made one brief straightforward comment before giving another striking example. In response to Koebel's comment that it must be sickening to know that talk shows invariably would focus on Patsy and John as suspects, Patsy said, "You know America has just been hurt so deeply with the tragic things that have happened. The young woman who drove her children into the water, and we don't know what happened with O.J. Simpson. I mean America is suffering because they have lost faith in the American family. We are a Christian, God-fearing family. We love our children. We would do anything for our children."

In responding to Koebel's comment about people considering her to be a suspect, Patsy chose the amazing example of Susan Smith, the mother who deliberately drowned her children and then tried to cover up her crime. Patsy tried somewhat to distance herself from Susan Smith by seeming not to remember Smith's name, but unconsciously Patsy's deeper intelligence motivated her to talk about Susan Smith's crime. The message from Patsy's deeper intelligence was: "If you want to know if I am guilty, think of Susan Smith, a mother who murdered her children and tried to cover up her crime."

The unconscious deeper intelligence validates its communications by repeating itself and thereby leaving thoughtprints, which is exactly what Patsy's deeper intelligence did during the CNN interview. Patsy's first example communicated the message "a woman could have done it," and her second example validated that thoughtprint by presenting the clearest picture imaginable of a seemingly loving mother who killed not one child, but two, and then tried to cover up the murder, all while involving the media in the process.

By using the example of Susan Smith, Patsy's deeper intelligence was also revealing a murder motive. According to media reports at the time (which is what Patsy would have known), Smith's boyfriend didn't want the responsibility of raising children—they formed an unwanted third party. So she murdered them. Watch how the pieces line up: Patsy was strongly suggesting that a woman murdered JonBenét, that the woman was JonBenét's mother, that the woman did it because JonBenét had become between her and her man (John), and that the woman covered up the murder just as Susan Smith did by creating a story and involving the media.

To further validate the truth of these thoughtprints, Patsy's unconscious deeper intelligence motivated her to use another example: O.J. Simpson, a celebrity who at first glance, like Susan Smith, appeared to be too good a person to be a murderer. But according to the civil court's ruling, Simpson, like Smith, did commit murder. He murdered his wife because he was losing her to a third party, and, like Smith, he also attempted to cover it up.[1] In her first few minutes on national television just seven days after the murder of her daughter, Patsy talks about these two seemingly solid citizens who murdered their loved ones over the threatened loss of a romantic relationship and then covered up the murders.

To validate the truth even more, Patsy's deeper intelligence motivated her to give one last subtle hint about who was involved in this crime: an American family whom people have lost faith in. This thoughtprint further reinforces the idea that both she and John participated in Jon-Benét's murder.

In summary, the messages communicated by Patsy's deeper intelligence during the CNN interview suggest that the truth about JonBenét's murder includes the following:

(1) The murderer was a woman like a mother who killed two children, which points toward Patsy as the murderer.

(2) The murderer was a man like a husband who killed a beloved family member, which points toward John participating in the murder.

(3) The murder motive involved a love triangle, which points toward a sexual relationship between John and JonBenét.

(4) The murderer was driven by a powerful sense of loss due to the love triangle, which points toward Patsy discovering the sexual relationship between John and JonBenét.

---

[1] Between the lines of his various communications, O.J. Simpson suggested his rage toward Nicole was immediately triggered by her involvement with another man. Several friends confirmed the story.

(5) At first glance the general public would least suspect the murderers because they appear to be solid citizens.

(6) The murderers attempted a cover-up and used the media to manipulate public opinion and the outcome of the murder investigation.

(7) Like O.J. Simpson, the murderers might be people who were used to being on stage and in the public eye.

Message: Patsy Ramsey Is Susan Smith

On Tuesday evening, October 25, 1994, Susan Smith strapped three-year-old Michael and fourteen-month-old Alexander into their car seats, drove to a boat ramp, stopped the car, stepped outside, closed the door, and then let the car roll down the ramp with her two boys trapped inside. She watched her car disappear into Long Lake in Union County, South Carolina, and saw it float for a few minutes before it flipped over and sank. One report said Smith watched her oldest son struggle for his life before the car went under.

For several days Smith made dramatic television appearances, publicly pleading for the boys' return and telling a convincing story about a young man driving off with her children in her car. Appearing to be a loving mother, Smith told a believable story, and her vulnerability inspired almost everyone to come to her aid as she related poignant memories of her children. Smith's ex-husband, David, believed her story so strongly that he joined her in television pleas for his sons' lives. Hundreds of her townspeople rallied around her in a huge manhunt, and church congregations prayed for the return of her children. Her car became the most-sought-after vehicle in America.

Smith willingly provided the police with a composite drawing of the kidnapper, and her reputation in her community remained solid. She had been voted "friendliest" in her 1989 high school senior class. *Newsweek* noted that her high school principal, Buddy Blackmon, said she was "the kind of student you want in your class." Her acquaintance, Darlene, said, "She was perfect. You've got your bad girls at high school, and you've got your good girls. She was your good girl."

When she was questioned about possible involvement in the crime, Smith responded with a seemingly heartfelt faith, "I know right here [as she pointed to her heart] what the truth is . . . the Lord and myself both know the truth. I did not have anything to do with the abduction of my children."

Neighbors unhesitatingly came to her rescue. As one person explained, "I think everything happened just like Susie said it did, because her and David are nice people. They never showed any hostility. They were friendly and all." Next-door neighbor Alice Valentine shared the same view: "I saw the love that they had for these children . . . and there would be no way that you would convince me that they had anything to do with what happened to these children."

When her story began to fall apart, Smith finally confessed, and all those who knew her were absolutely shocked. Following the revelation, *Newsweek* noted, "The transcript of her lachrymose performances should be required reading for juries. It demonstrates how easily even untrained people can lie when their own hides are at stake."

The murder of Susan Smith's children has striking similarities to the murder of Patsy Ramsey's daughter: an alleged kidnapping used to cover up a mother murdering her child(ren); a popular, friendly woman with a reputation of having been a "perfect student in high school;" a nurturing mother with no history of violence; a mother pleading on television to help find the alleged assailant; a mother who invokes God's name as a guarantee of her innocence; and neighbors who swear by her.

One last eerie similarity is the continuing disbelief that a mother could carry out such a crime. *Newsweek* ended its feature article on Susan Smith still expressing shock: "If what police say is true, Smith's crime was monstrous in conception. But still more horrible is the realization that it was composed of a series of discrete actions, each leading to a fatal result. The question we are left with is not just why Susan Smith killed her children. It is how she could have strapped them so carefully into those car seats for that last terrible ride."

Lawrence Schiller ended his bestseller on the JonBenét case, *Perfect Murder, Perfect Town*, with the following observation:

> What neither Thomas, Smit, Hunter, Eller, Hofstrom, nor anyone else connected with the investigation could explain was the use of the noose on JonBenét. The garroting did not connect to any other element of the crime. The FBI had no record of a young child being strangled with one, let alone by a parent.

After JonBenét's skull was fractured she would have slipped into unconsciousness quickly. It would have been just as easy to end her life by smothering or strangling her by hand. There was no explanation why anyone would even think of making a noose which takes time slip it around her neck, and use it to kill her.

Death by this method is gruesome and horrifying. It does not come quickly. The person pulling the cord and tightening the noose little by little around JonBenét's neck would not even have been able to look away. He or she would have had to eventually look into the child's face, to be sure that she was dead.

It was so merciless to that child.

If the Boulder law enforcement authorities would listen to the clues Patsy Ramsey provided in the CNN interview, they would know the answer to the question of how Patsy and John could have murdered their six-year-old daughter. As Patsy's deeper intelligence, the brilliant detective, could have put it, "If you want to know how someone could bash their child's head in or strangle her child with a garrote or watch someone else strangle her child, think of Susan Smith who tied up both her children with seat belt garrotes, pushed them into the water, and watched them slowly drown without lifting a finger to save them."

JonBenét Ramsey was murdered on Wednesday, December 25, 1996, just two years and two months to the day from Tuesday, October 25, 1994, when Michael and Alexander Smith were murdered by their mother. If one mother could murder two of her children, then two parents could murder one of theirs. Indeed Patsy's patterned thoughts revealed that there were two killers: a man and a woman, as in Susan Smith and O.J. Simpson—or Patsy and John Ramsey.

Not only did Patsy unconsciously give us a clear picture of how she could have done it by linking herself to Susan Smith and by linking John to O.J. Simpson, but she also clarified how a man could kill someone close to him in the chaos surrounding a love triangle. First John "killed" Patsy with betrayal, then he murdered JonBenét because of Patsy. Patsy's deeper intelligence suggested other similarities between her husband and O.J. Simpson, someone who was frequently out of control sexually. This fact further points to John Ramsey's possible sexual involvement with JonBenét. In addition, Simpson was a very successful businessman with a confident, self-controlled demeanor, just like John Ramsey.

Not surprisingly, in her next public interview, May 1, 1997, Patsy went one step further, stating that she and her husband believed *two* people murdered their daughter.

Parents Who Murder Their Children

More than 1,300 children are murdered each year by parents or close relatives. About two-thirds of these children are under ten years of age, with the youngest children being the most vulnerable. Men are the perpetrators only slightly more than women. Usually the murder of a child by a parent is not premeditated, but occurs when a parent suddenly loses control. More than half of the parents who have murdered their children have never been reported for child abuse.

Admittedly researchers know far less about why parents murder their offspring than why marital partners murder each other, but most agree that some type of stress is the culprit. After Susan Smith was apprehended for the murders of her two sons, *Newsweek* quoted Dr. Katherine Kaufer, of the Violent Injury Prevention Center in Chicago, who explained, "Any big-time stress—a job loss, a death in the family, eviction—can set people off."

Some experts called Susan Smith's murder of her children "murder by proxy" after she described driving around for hours before the murder ruminating about taking her own life. Richard Gelles, director of the family violence program at the University of Rhode Island, described such murders as involving a form of "boundary confusion" with the mother being "overly enmeshed in the lives of her children. She doesn't know where her life ends and theirs begins." These words could have been written about Patsy Ramsey and JonBenét. Some pictures of the two convey how much JonBenét was an extension of her mother, as does the crime scene itself. The heart the killer drew on the palm of JonBenét's left hand points strongly to Patsy Ramsey (see Chapter 12, page 147).

The Boulder authorities remain puzzled by the heinousness of the crime, the strangeness of the garroting, and the motive. They have yet to appreciate just how far ahead of them Patsy Ramsey's unconscious deeper intelligence is. She has been trying to clue them in from the moment she composed the ransom note, which not only elaborated on the powerful motive that triggered her killing rage, but also provided the deeper motivations that made her so vulnerable to exploding in rage the night of the murder.

The one-hour CNN interview and the three-page ransom note provide the answers to all of the law enforcement agents' questions about the murder of six-year-old JonBenét, beloved child of Patsy and John Ramsey. Unfortunately the Boulder authorities are still not listening to the most brilliant, insightful detective on the case, the only one who knows the whole truth—Patsy Ramsey. This explains why immediately after the grand jury chose not to indict the pair, detective Patsy Ramsey's brilliant deeper intelligence in another public letter told the Boulder authorities they had taken the best detectives off the case and had ignored leads—leads she unconsciously had carefully crafted.

CHAPTER 4
The Ransom Note

"A thorough analysis of an anonymous letter may greatly reduce the number of possible writers and may at once dismiss certain suspected writers. The use of a semicolon or the correct use of an apostrophe may eliminate a whole group of writers."

— Osborn and Osborn, *Questioned Document Problems*

I had studied the ransom note for well over a year before analyzing it jointly with Dr. Patrick Callahan and Dr. C. Jess Groesbeck for an additional 600 hours. From the first time I saw it, when it appeared in *Newsweek* as part of an article about the case, the ransom note gave me a unique perspective about the murder of JonBenét Ramsey. After studying the ransom note for clues, I began to see certain patterns and messages from the author/murderer until I felt certain I knew who had killed JonBenét—and why. The note itself kept taking me further and further, continually teaching me more. Eventually, in 1998, I wrote a book on the case, *A Mother Gone Bad: The Hidden Confession of JonBenét's Killer*, which was based on the ransom note, as well as other communications from the Ramseys.

After Callahan and Groesbeck (both of whom had extensive court experience) read *A Mother Gone Bad*, they suggested that the three of us write a definitive profile for District Attorney Alex Hunter's office. They felt the profile would be significantly different from and more official than my book. Both of them were convinced that the ransom note was the key to solving JonBenét's murder. They were also convinced that our profile could be admitted as evidence in a grand jury hearing, as well as in a court case against the murderer(s).

Rather than examining a number of communications from the Ramseys as I had done for my book, Callahan, Groesbeck, and I focused solely on the ransom note for our forensic profile. This narrow focus forced us to delve deeper into the mind of the note's author, and as a result, we saw far more clues in the ransom note than any of us had seen before.

The clues Callahan, Groesbeck, and I found during our intensive study of the ransom note convinced us more than ever that Patsy and John Ramsey killed their daughter. We developed a clear picture of what happened the night of the murder as we "read" the author/murderer's firsthand description in the note. All of us were awestruck by how much the author/murderer revealed in the note about herself, the family situation, and the crime.

The author, Patsy Ramsey, could have written a brief ransom note or could have come up with an entirely different scenario. Instead, she wrote a two-and-a-half-page masterpiece full of clues. Not only will Patsy's ransom note go down in the annals of both psychology and criminology as a remarkable document, but I also believe it will validate the existence of "thoughtprints" as an invaluable new method of document analysis, a tool that in certain cases can reveal vastly more information about a perpetrator than any other method. (For a detailed review of our analysis and how we came to our conclusions, see Chapter 5, page 43.)

The Author/Murderer's Thoughtprints

The thoughtprints we found in the ransom note communicate that:

(1) The author is a woman.
(2) The author is a cancer victim.
(3) The author committed the murder.
(4) The author identifies the unconscious deep pain/"time bomb" motive for the murder.
(5) The author identifies the "trigger" motive for the crime.
(6) The author caught John Ramsey sexually abusing the victim the night of the murder.
(7) The author had unconsciously encouraged the victim's sexual involvement with John Ramsey.
(8) Two people participated in the murder.
(9) Patsy Ramsey wrote the note, and she participated in the murder.
(10) The victim was dead before the ransom note was written.
(11) The ransom note is a confession.
(12) The murderers will be relieved to be caught.

(13) The author has artistic skills.

(14) Message markers in the ransom note serve as valid predictors of valuable unconscious messages from the author/murderer, and they provide rich, new information about the crime.

The deeper intelligence has a mind of its own and basically communicates by repeating ideas to form "a code" and tell a story. As we analyzed the ransom note, we looked for repeated thoughts that formed a coded "pattern" and the story "encoded" in the author/murderer's thoughtprints. This approach gave us a built-in check and balance—what scientists call a validating methodology. We let the ideas in the first paragraph of the ransom note suggest certain conclusions, and then we "tested" those conclusions by looking for thoughtprints, repetitions of the same ideas and, therefore, the same conclusions. By the time we had analyzed the entire note, we had found four major thought patterns from the deeper intelligence of the author/murderer that led straight to the identity of JonBenét's murderers and their motives:

(1) The author/murderer gives motives for the murder and thereby tells us that the ransom note is a confession.

(2) JonBenét was already dead when the author/murderer wrote the note, a conclusion that is particularly important in refuting claims that an intruder wrote the note prior to JonBenét's death.

(3) The author/murderer is an emotionally and physically damaged woman who is terrified she is dying of cancer and was ready to explode emotionally before the murder.

(4) John Ramsey's secret sexual misbehavior with JonBenét sent the author/murderer into a rage the night of the murder, and the author/murderer is angry with John Ramsey.

In the ransom note, the author/murderer implies the sequence of events the night of the murder, including the initial blow to JonBenét's head and the second "murder"—the strangulation. The first paragraph of the ransom note contains hints of all of these ideas, and repetitions of these ideas in the rest of the note validate these conclusions.

As Callahan, Groesbeck, and I continued to analyze the author/murderer's thoughtprints, it became clear to us that the ransom note was really a story—a powerful, firsthand story told by an eyewitness. Amazing as that is, it is even more amazing that the author/murderer tells the authorities how to apprehend her—and most amazing of all, she pleads with the authorities to do so. The author/murderer did not really write a ransom note to JonBenét's parents. Instead, she wrote a lengthy message to the authorities, giving them background information, motives, details of the crime, and instructions on how to bring the murderers to justice.

In the very first sentence of the note the author/murderer says to "listen carefully," which means to listen for deeper messages. The author/murderer repeats the word "instructions" four times in the note. At both the beginning and the end of the note, the author/murderer says "to follow the instructions to the letter" and JonBenét would speak again. Since JonBenét was already dead when the author/murderer wrote the note, she was saying that she was going to speak for JonBenét, as if from the grave, and reveal what had happened and why.

The author/murderer pleads for someone to understand her messages, because she is telling a powerful, believable story that unequivocally points to the murderers—and that's exactly what she did in the note. In essence the author/murderer's deeper intelligence said, "Watch what I'm going to do" and then did it in an impressive, remarkably specific way.

The author/murderer's unconscious deeper intelligence prompted her to make up a story to reveal her deepest motives and her secret actions. The author/murderer wrote almost three pages of fiction; there was no kidnapping, no ransom, and no foreign terrorist. The note is bogus, which means that the words came largely from the "right" or creative side of the author/murderer's brain—and that is exactly how the deeper intelligence communicates. As I noted earlier, the deeper intelligence communicates indirectly but distinctly in a "right brain" way by patterning key ideas. The key in listening to its messages is to pay attention to ideas, examples, and stories—not just to the literal "left brain" message.

Our knowledge of the deeper intelligence and the fact that the author/murderer's deeper intelligence would both long to confess and to guide the investigation gave Callahan, Groesbeck, and me an advantage over the handwriting experts, the linguistic specialists, profilers, and other investigators on the case. For years we have been decoding messages from our patients' deeper intelligence, and we brought our specialized expertise to the Ramsey case. We offered the authorities a new method of "psycholinguistics"—the study of language for psychological clues—using the brilliant unconscious mind to help them "see" the incriminating evidence Patsy had left for them in the ransom note.

Our Forensic Report

On April 14, 1999, almost six months to the day before the grand jury refused to indict Patsy and John on the grounds of insufficient evidence, Drs. Callahan, Groesbeck, and I presented our seventy-page analysis of the ransom note to Deputy District Attorney Michael Kane, a trial consultant who was working with District Attorney Alex Hunter. We titled our seventy-page forensic report *A Psychoanalytic Decoding of the Unconscious Content in the Ramsey Ransom Note*. The cover page stated: "This evaluation is submitted to Mr. Michael J. Kane, Deputy District Attorney for the City of Boulder, County of Boulder, State of Colorado, in the criminal matter of the death of JonBenét Patricia Ramsey, a human being." We sent the following letter with our report:

Dear Mr. Kane:

Enclosed please find our forensic assessment. We believe that it is possible that the sole piece of uncontaminated evidence is that which has been characterized as the Ramsey "ransom note." We are specially trained mental health professionals with a significant amount of clinical and forensic experience in both civil and criminal litigation. Our underlying theory and assessment of the aforementioned note is based on a well-accepted, peer-reviewed, and scientifically based methodology. Our method looks at the deeper underlying unconscious content of forensic documents and communication.

We strongly believe that this method has the potential in a variety of settings to decode or unlock the hidden psychological truth that is embedded by writers and speakers, and give valuable clues to police authorities and triers of fact in both civil and criminal cases. It is our hope that you and your team of prosecutors will give your utmost attention to our work. We have produced these documents only after a great deal of time was expended in their research and production. The document was produced specifically for your office.

Our purpose in providing this document to you is grounded in what Vernon Gerberth, author of *Practical Homicide Investigation*, states: "Death investigation constitutes a heavy responsibility, and as such, let no person deter you from the truth and your own personal commitment to see that justice is done . . . and remember, 'you're working for God.'" We would hope that our work will assist your office in finding the truth about the death of this innocent six-year-old child. While none of us personally knew JonBenét Ramsey, all of us have children (and daughters) of our own, and we would hope that any professionals with specialized knowledge would help us in solving a serious crime potentially involving our loved ones.

We believe this note in an unforeseen way is in part a final statement by the unconscious of the writer to give instructions to the reader to expose the murderer(s) of JonBenét. We firmly believe that this note points to the person or persons responsible for her death, and that the note is written as though the victim herself is now assisting in this investigation from her grave.

We are presently preparing for your reference a significantly annotated theoretical paper with an extensive bibliography. We expect that this theory paper will reach your office within the next two weeks.

After reading our assessment and the supportive letters from law enforcement, academia, and Dean Williams's scholarly treatise on expert testimony in light of Daubert and a recent Supreme Court decision, it is our hope that you present this material to the appropriate authorities. If you or your staff would like to discuss this further we are available to assist you.

Sincerely,
C. Jess Groesbeck, M.D.
Patrick C. Callahan, Ph.D.
Andrew G. Hodges, M.D.

Other Forensic Experts Endorsed Our Report

When we sent our letter and report to Kane, we included letters from a variety of other experts who urged him to utilize our work. Dr. Steven Egger, a professor of criminal justice at the University of Illinois, an authority on serial killers and the author of several books on the subject, including *The Stranger Among Us*, wrote the following to Kane:

> [This report uses a] new cutting-edge approach to document analysis. This pioneering effort to utilize ... the unconscious mind through encoding of hidden communication is applied with great clarity and clear analysis. It can now be said that in situations involving kidnappings and murder that the offenders will "speak" through their deeper encoded unconscious messages and reveal their motives and true identities when written messages are decoded.
>
> This work is the result of seeking identity and motive of the author of the JonBenét Ramsey kidnap note by decoding and clarifying hidden communication. Not to be confused with graphology or handwriting analysis, this new forensic technique will contribute greatly to the law enforcement arsenal of criminal investigation in the future.

In his letter to Kane, Parham Williams, Dean of the School of Law at Chapman University, wrote:

> As you present the results of the Ramsey investigation to the Grand Jury, I urge you to consider using the testimony of three experts who, utilizing the psychoanalytic methodology, have intensively analyzed the purported ransom note. The process and the results of this analysis are quite helpful to your case.
>
> When first asked by one of the experts, Dr. Andrew G. Hodges, to review the law governing admissibility of expert testimony of this nature, I frankly was skeptical. I wasn't convinced that the methodology met either the Frye "general acceptance" test or the broader formulation of Daubert. However, after reviewing the literature and considering again the principles of Daubert and its progeny, I have concluded that my skepticism is unfounded. I believe now that the methodology is scientifically valid and that it meets the standards of admissibility.
>
> After reaching this conclusion, I prepared a brief synopsis of the law and its applicability to the psychoanalytic methodology.

I enclose a copy for your consideration. The synopsis reviews the standards of Frye, Daubert, and several more recent cases including the March 23, 1999, Supreme Court decision in Kumho Tire Company, LTD v Carmichael. After tracing the development of the psychoanalytic methodology, the synopsis tests that methodology in the ways suggested in the case law. The result: The expert opinion testimony of the three experts should be admissible.

An experienced FBI agent had read *A Mother Gone Bad* before he read our report, and he had written to me asking me to consult on another case involving letters from a suspect. In his letter to me, he commented:

I have been an FBI agent for over 20 years and have studied numerous true-life kidnappings, hostage situations, and homicides. In addition, I have been the case agent on several kidnapping/homicide cases that were successfully prosecuted. The JonBenét case is by far the most bizarre that I have studied. . . . After reading your book I am now convinced that both Ramseys are involved. What's amazing is now, after my wife has read your book, she is convinced that both parents are involved. Originally, she couldn't imagine someone of Patsy's background and social stature would do such a thing to her own daughter.

I hope that the law enforcement and prosecutors in the Boulder area have taken your book seriously to help guide them to building their circumstantial case.

After reviewing our seventy-page forensic report, this FBI agent was even more convinced. He wrote Kane a personal letter that strongly endorsed our work as having significant merit.

My Prior Involvement with the Murder Investigation

Prior to working with Callahan and Groesbeck on our joint forensic report, I had already had some contact with the Boulder authorities. In December 1997 when I started writing *A Mother Gone Bad: The Hidden Confession of JonBenét's Killer*, Mark Beckner called me. Beckner had just taken over as commander of the investigation of the Ramsey murder for the Boulder Police Department and was calling me on the recommendation of another experienced FBI agent who had reviewed my early work and encouraged both the Boulder police and the FBI at Quantico to consider that there was a new way of obtaining valuable information from criminals or suspects from their writings or interviews. When Beckner and I talked, he listened politely to my analysis technique and findings with some interest, but he said he doubted that such work could be used in court.

Shortly after our conversation, Beckner began consulting with Steven Pitt, a forensic psychiatrist from the University of Arizona, and I heard nothing further from him. Pitt had a completely different clinical orientation and, to my knowledge, had no awareness of the recent groundbreaking work of using messages from the deeper intelligence as clues to understanding motivation and behavior.

By July 1998 I had completed *A Mother Gone Bad*, which I based primarily on my analysis of the ransom note and a comparison of it with written and oral communications from Patsy and John Ramsey. I had no doubt that Patsy and John were responsible for the death of their six-year-old daughter, JonBenét, and that Patsy had been the first one to attack the little girl the night she was murdered.

I felt certain that Beckner hadn't even mentioned my work on the ransom note to District Attorney Alex Hunter, so I sent Hunter a prepublication copy of *A Mother Gone Bad* just before it came out. Hunter's reaction confirmed my hunch that Beckner had not shared my findings with him. Almost immediately after I sent the book to Hunter, several media people connected to his office called me to ask for their own copies.

Several media people told me that Hunter and his team initially were impressed with my work. One of them, however, told me that the DA's staff liked the second part of *A Mother Gone Bad* better than the first. I found that interesting since the first part of the book contained my detailed analysis of the ransom note and other Ramsey communications. The second part of my book read like a novel, but the first half required the reader to follow the slow, painstaking process of looking for messages from the murderer's deeper intelligence and decoding the real story written between the lines of the ransom note—a task police might call "grunt work."

Hunter had difficulty accepting the concept of a deeper intelligence. He did not "see" the hidden but distinct and powerful clues the murderer unconsciously but deliberately left in the ransom note, clues left especially for the law enforcement agents so they would know the true story of JonBenét's murder and be able to apprehend the murderer(s) and bring them to justice.

A *Mother Gone Bad* received significant professional recognition. The book was endorsed by several of my peers, including Dr. James Raney, a psychiatric colleague and psychoanalyst with forensic experience. Raney saw a prepublication copy and wrote a very favorable review of the book for a professional journal. He praised my application of clinical work to a forensic setting. Raney felt so strongly that my "profile" had significant merit that he wrote the following letter to Hunter:

July 8, 1998

Dear Mr. Hunter:

I have just finished the galley proofs of Dr. Hodges's book *A Mother Gone Bad*. Dr. Hodges mentioned that he believes he has some expertise that may help you in prosecuting this case. I offered to write you directly, as I was very impressed with this book. His book could be a professional text on the psychology of women. His research and argument are sound.

In addition to my practice as a psychiatrist, psychoanalyst, university teacher, and psychotherapy supervisor, I have spent 23 years as a forensic expert in 200 or so cases. I can see that Dr. Hodges's perspectives as a physician and psychiatrist, as well as his impressive capacities in interpretation of the unconscious communication in various media, could bring considerable guidance and information to your case.

His arguments are scientific yet simple. He presents compelling evidence in this book, given the premises or contexts that appear to be well known. He works in his book as a good psychotherapist works, gathering evidence, making hypotheses, and then testing the hypotheses. This is also the sequence of good science and, I believe, good forensic investigation. His medical and psychiatric insights bring an important dimension to his investigation. He has done an immense amount of research on this case.

Dr. Hodges wrote a chapter for a book of mine 18 years ago. We have communicated since then and met several times at meetings.

I have always liked his work and his ideas. He is serious and personable. He writes and speaks in terms a layperson can understand. I think he could be a credible witness if you used him for that.

You should find Dr. Hodges very interesting and useful to you on this case.

Sincerely,
James O. Raney, M.D.

As Raney indicated, analyzing the ransom note and delving into Patsy Ramsey's deeper intelligence had given me deep insight into the female mind. In particular I had learned what ovarian cancer and its accompanying devastation looks like on the deepest level of a woman's mind—what she sees through her deepest eyes and what it really means to be a woman and have one's femininity challenged in such a primitive way. In the ransom note and other communications, Patsy Ramsey presents a vivid picture of what a woman's declining femininity looks like—and I "saw" that picture through Patsy's eyes when I decoded the note.

Hunter did not respond to Raney's letter or make any effort to utilize Raney as an expert witness or consultant, even though he had impeccable credentials. Nor did Hunter utilize me or the investigative work I had done on the ransom note. Instead he sought the help of different experts. He regularly discussed the case with a tabloid writer who himself consulted a professional educator who had a background in addiction and criminology. Months later, this educator called me and, after reading my book, endorsed my conclusion. She was impressed with the use of the deeper intelligence in psycholinguistics and acknowledged that her expertise in document analysis was considerably less than mine. Interestingly, Hunter had frequently sought her opinion through the tabloid writer.

By ignoring the breakthrough to the deeper intelligence and its application to the ransom note, Hunter ignored the plaintive cries of the killer for justice and her specific instructions to him. Any other approach to the ransom note that he ultimately uses—if any—will fall immeasurably short of what the killer's deeper intelligence is trying to tell him.

CHAPTER 5
Uncovering the Smoking Gun and the Motives

"Sex is the opposite of death."
—Irving Weisberg, Ph.D., psychologist, professor
Adelphi University (Garden City, New York)

If we are going to make a case against the killer, we must use the ransom note. It is the one absolutely crucial piece of evidence. If the case ever goes to trial, I am convinced in the final analysis the guilt or innocence of the killer will rest on this note. Whatever other evidence the authorities uncover will not be enough. The ransom note is where we first see the killer's thoughtprints, and it serves as the basis for understanding all the other Ramsey communications. Without understanding the ransom note, the killers will go scot-free.

Is there valuable communication and key evidence in the note? If so, the note must prove its mettle. If it's ever going to be used in a court of law it must make sense—common sense—to the jury. The ransom note writer herself uses this phrase when she advises John Ramsey to use his "common sense." One of her secret intentions in writing such a phrase was to remind the authorities (and eventually the jury) to use their common sense in reading between the lines.

Does the ransom note explain why JonBenét's killers acted as they did? If the Ramseys are the killers, the note must offer persuasive reasons explaining why two normally genteel parents exploded on Christmas Day and killed their beloved daughter. Clearly, the writer is telling us that the ransom note is an explanation, a story of what really happened. If Patsy Ramsey's conscience did indeed compel her to confess as she was composing the ransom note, then the note should contain a persuasive, detailed explanation of both how and why she assaulted JonBenét. And if Patsy intended that not only law enforcement authorities but also a jury of her peers read her confession and bring her to justice, then the story she tells about JonBenét's life and death should make reasonable sense to everyday people, as well as to police officials, detectives, prosecutors, and members of the legal system.

Since the killer intended for the investigators and the jury to hear her messages, I think she made them plain enough that a good jury with adequate input from expert witnesses in communication could come to a reasonable verdict that the killer had spoken for JonBenét and, in the process, had spoken to them. Is the killer speaking clearly between the lines? Do we find understandable motives? Dr. Patrick Callahan, Dr. C. Jess Groesbeck, and I strongly believe the note contains all this and more, as we "listened between the lines."

Among themselves, Boulder detectives agreed the ransom note was the most important evidence they had, absolutely vital to the case. Detective Steve Thomas described its importance in his book *JonBenét: Inside the Ramsey Murder Investigation*. In October 1997, on a ten-day trip, Thomas carried the ransom note and folders filled with Patsy Ramsey's handwriting samples to consult with experts in Michigan, Maryland, and Washington, DC. "No one ever took the possibility of car-jacking as seriously as I did in those cities, and I made certain that I always had quick access to my pistol. The two boxes I carried were more valuable than gold," says Thomas in his book.

He consulted six independent sources, all of whom thought Patsy wrote the note, but they felt they lacked courtroom evidence. The Speckin Forensic Lab in Okemos, Michigan, (coincidentally where John Ramsey finished high school) was prepared to testify that the odds on an intruder having handwriting so similar to one of the parents (Patsy) was "infinitesimal."

Thomas then tells us, "Taken together, the six opinions formed a strong body of evidence, but I wanted more—I wanted someone willing to stand up in a court of law and decisively declare who wrote the note. I had no idea where to find such a person."

Drs. Groesbeck, Callahan, and I thought we were those people. So did our legal adviser, law school dean Parham Williams, among others. We knew we had something far beyond handwriting analysis that revealed precisely the mind of the killer, her motives, and the spark that set her off that night. We felt strongly that the ransom note writer's own mind could persuade a jury, once they knew how to read it. Dr. Groesbeck had testified in the Juan

Corona serial murder case (and helped find the missing bodies using Corona's dreams) and would have made a creditable expert witness. Callahan, too, had courtroom experience.

Eventually Thomas settled for a handwriting expert of another type, linguist Donald Foster, whom the DA's office refused to use in court. Steve Thomas never saw our report, but it is doubtful he would have used it because he seemed determined to stick with a handwriting expert, even though such an expert would also have been challenged in court (as we would be) and provided him with far less information, particularly the "missing motives." As his book reveals, Thomas had a limited understanding of motivation, otherwise he would have seen that the killer's motives were staring him in the face. That was the real gold he had in his possession.

Reading Between the Lines

When Dr. Callahan, Dr. Groesbeck, and I began decoding the bogus ransom note written by Patsy Ramsey, we saw that the note not only describes the actual murder, but also explains the family dynamics leading up to the powerful event that triggered Patsy's killing rage. We also saw that Patsy's confession "hidden" between the lines makes sense and is consistent with the facts of the murder case, as well as with Patsy's, John's, and JonBenét's personal histories. Furthermore the note clearly points to Patsy and John as the murderers. It reveals not only that Patsy wants to be caught, but also how the authorities can catch and convict her and John.

Patsy opens the note ("Listen carefully!") by urging the reader to pay close attention and listen to this note for deeper messages. At the beginning and the end of the note, the writer repeats the command to follow instructions to the letter, strongly implying that clues are hidden between the lines. The deeper intelligence often communicates by repeating ideas, and the repetition of this and other ideas in the ransom note helps validate that it is a communication from Patsy's deeper intelligence. This part of her mind "sees" reality with intense clarity and communicates truths about reality in a variety of ways, including the use of repetition.

I will start by analyzing the end of the note, although it was the last thing we understood. This is the most puzzling part of the note because the communication is overtly encoded. Patsy closed the bogus ransom note with "Vi ctory ! S.B.T.C ." Once we decoded this final word and closing, we realized that it matched other thoughtprints in the note, validating that Patsy, the author of the note and one of the murderers, was indeed speaking for JonBenét. By putting this encoded message at the very end, Patsy was telling us to look for hidden messages throughout the note, which reinforces her opening words, "Listen carefully!" Patsy creatively disguises the same message of "Victory" in "Listen carefully!" by making the "lly!" of "carefully!" looks like "Vy!", suggesting an abbreviated version of "Victory!" including the exclamation point.

Patsy is an artist at communicating both literally and figuratively, as the deliberate space between "Vi" and "ctory" in the closing illustrates. When read by itself "ctory" suggests "story," and the *c* of "ctory" has a long flowing extension (unlike any other *c* in the note) that makes the letter look like a reverse *s*, which further suggests the word "story." While the spacing of letters or misshapen letters are not the most common ways the deeper intelligence communicates, the spacing in this word is so impressive that it can't be merely coincidental. This is exactly why Patsy told us at the beginning of the note to "listen carefully!" She wants us to closely observe every nuance in every word.

"Vi" is commonly used in Roman numerals vi or VI and means "six," which suggests that the ransom note is a "six story" or the "story of six-year-old" JonBenét. (As we will see Roman numerals had a very special place in Patsy Ramsey's life.) Thus, in a disguised but simple way, Patsy used the last word of the note to emphasize that it is JonBenét's story. This is the reason for focusing on the signature first. It underscores in a striking way that the ransom note is a story. The question is: Who is going to decode JonBenét's story as Patsy tells it in the bogus ransom note so they can then bring her and John to justice? That will be the real victory.

The real story in the still unsolved JonBenét murder case is not the "Perfect Murder" but rather the "Perfect Confession," something Deputy District Attorney Michael Kane's own deeper intelligence recognized. In a conversation with me, he confessed that deep down he knew the ransom note was a work of art. (See Chapter 6, page 69.)

Patsy Tells JonBenét's Story in the Ransom Note

Patsy begins the ransom note by stating that she intends to speak for the victim, JonBenét, in this ransom note ("we . . . represent a small foreign faction"), and then she strongly hints that discovering John Ramsey molesting JonBenét (bussiness [sic]) was the immediate catalyst for the murder. Among several clues, her slip or misspelling "buss-iness" suggests buss/kiss/romance/sex. Next she alludes to what was really eating at her deep down: She was a physically and emotionally damaged woman who felt tremendously threatened, perhaps by a severe health problem or another form of physical or emotional assault.

In the second paragraph of the note, Patsy confirms that prior to the murder she had been under great stress from a life-threatening disease that affected her female organs, causing her to feel extremely inadequate as a woman and to greatly doubt her femininity. The words Patsy used in the note suggest that she had a virulent female form of cancer, and indeed she had been diagnosed with stage IV, the most advanced, ovarian carcinoma, in July 1993. (Roman numerals from this moment on were associated in Patsy's mind with life-or-death issues, which explains the significance of "Vi" in the closing, "Victory.") Deep down Patsy is certain she is going to die. She sees herself having a "99% chance" of dying, as she states in the note. Although Patsy was almost 100 percent certain she was going to die from her cancer, she desperately tried to deny the probability of death, and she spent inordinate energy maintaining her denial of the probable outcome of her illness. By Christmas 1996 Patsy had precious little, if any, emotional reserves left. She was stretched as thin as possible. She was at the breaking point.

In Patsy's vulnerable emotional state it didn't take much to cause her to erupt into a killing rage. Her bogus ransom note indicates that she discovered John Ramsey sexually abusing their daughter, JonBenét, turning her into a "pickup," and prostituting her. In the note Patsy describes the brief but explosive psychotic rage she felt when she saw an obviously sexually aroused John with JonBenét. She confesses that she lashed out at JonBenét, striking her in the head. Patsy, whose feminine identity was already extremely fragile, explains that she momentarily saw JonBenét as a rival, a "fat cat," who had moved in on her territory. We believe the writer is also talking about JonBenét (and not just John, who was also a fat cat) because this was where the writer clearly became the most overtly viscous toward JonBenét and said that killing her would be easy.

Patsy regained her self-control immediately after striking her daughter, and in the ransom note she describes the subsequent sequence of events that ended JonBenét's life. Patsy and John knew that JonBenét's head injury was very serious and that she would soon die if she didn't get medical help. But instead of calling the paramedics, Patsy and John, "two gentlemen," decided to cover up the crime. They planned to make the "accident" look like a kidnapping/murder by an intruder and to create a cover-up story about a foreign terrorist group who had a grudge against John's company for doing business with the United States government. But Patsy and John needed a body for their cover-up story, and this meant one or both of them had to end JonBenét's life so there would be "nothing but remains" ready for burial. John strangled JonBenét so that he and Patsy, JonBenét's own parents, would have the body they needed for their cover-up story.

The story Patsy tells in the ransom note matches everything we know publicly about the crime scene and the autopsy. Patsy not only tells a believable story of the events surrounding JonBenét's murder, but she also explains how two loving parents who were overcome with their own pain lost control and lashed out at the daughter they loved. In the ransom note Patsy hints that eventually one of the two murderers will break down and confess, and she implies it will be Patsy herself. She also gives numerous clues about her and John's identities and how they can be caught and convicted.

How Patsy Communicated These Ideas

Below are the words of the ransom note followed by the thoughts Patsy was unconsciously communicating. (For a more in-depth analysis of the ransom note, see Appendix A and B, pages 249 and 257.)

Mr. Ramsey,

Listen carefully! We are a group of individuals that represent a small foreign faction. We ("don't" crossed out) respect your bussiness [sic] but not the country that it serves. At this time we have your daughter in our posession [sic]. She is safe and un harmed [sic] and if you want her to see 1997, you must follow our instructions to the letter.

(1) *What Patsy was unconsciously communicating:*

"I am giving you a huge clue by starting this note with 'Listen carefully!' I want you to listen carefully for the clues I am giving you in both the words of this note and between the lines. I am giving you an additional clue in the word 'carefully!' Notice that I run together the lly! so that it looks like a 'Vy!' and strongly ties to the word Victory! at the end of the note. Listen carefully for my victory. Police, I'm talking to you. If you understand my victory, you will understand your victory—what my motives were, who I am, and how to catch me. Right off I'm telling Mr. Ramsey, 'Victory over you,' and I say it again at the end. Listen carefully as I tell you about my victory over John Ramsey and also my victory over JonBenét.

"By 'we are a group of individuals' I am saying that more than one person was involved in this murder, and I am also telling you that we can be broken into individuals. If you understand that I am writing this note as a confession, you will be able to split us apart. I could have written simply 'we represent' or 'we're a group,' but to help you catch us, I suggest that each of us is an individual and our group of two can be divided into individuals.

"Make no mistake about it, I/we indeed 'represent a small foreign faction,' in particular the little entity with the foreign name, JonBenét. I/we represent her as if I am her attorney speaking on her behalf. I will repeat these ideas several times so you don't miss my message. This note will reveal what happened the night of her murder just as surely as if she had written it herself.

"I am also using the words 'small foreign faction' in reference to the killer [cancer] that is chasing me. Part of the reason I lashed out at JonBenét the night of her murder is that I have a life-threatening disease and I fear for my life.

"Listen carefully to my two slips: 'We ("don't" crossed out) respect your bussiness (sic) but not the country it serves.' I am divided about John Ramsey's business. I do and I don't respect it. I am giving you a clue about why I don't respect John's business by misspelling 'bussiness.' A 'buss' is a kiss, and it implies romance and sex. In other words I am divided about John's romantic/sexual business. On the one hand, it's his private business, but when John became involved in 'serving his country' as in 'cunt ry' or 'cunt,' I don't respect his 'bussiness.' So I/we respect your [John's] 'bussiness' but not the count-ry/cunt it serves. I repeated the idea that a sexually related event triggered my rage killing by misspelling 'bussiness' and with the double entendre of 'count-ry/cunt.'

"I know my words and thoughts sound shocking and crude, but I wanted to shock you as I was shocked the night I found a sexually aroused John with

JonBenét. If you listen carefully for my thoughts as you read the ransom note, you will find much more of the same shocking crudeness. It is my way of telling you that I was overwhelmed when I discovered the sexual abuse. Sometimes I communicated between the lines of the note by using entire sentences, and other times I used a slight modification such as dropping a syllable or word and repeating ideas.

"Notice my next misspelling: At this time we have your daughter in our 'posession,' 'pose-ssion' instead of 'possession.' Read it now the way I meant you to read it: At this time we have your daughter in our 'pose.' I am confessing that we have placed JonBenét in some kind of pose. Since 'pose' refers to staging, which is often a key element in a murder, I am suggesting that we had already killed JonBenét and posed her body when I wrote this bogus ransom note (which was the second part of the staging). Of course we had been 'posing' her for years in her role as a beauty queen, and John had been posing her as his own little beauty queen. And possession suggests an evil force, a killer(s) controlled by his or her dark side.

"I emphasized that JonBenét is already dead by leaving a space between the syllables of 'un harmed' so the word doesn't hang together, which tells you that 'She is safe and un harmed' is a lie. The truth is that she was no longer unharmed. When I wrote this note, we had already harmed JonBenét. She was already dead, and we had posed her body.

"Read 'She is safe' as 'she is hidden away in a safe place, like a safe.' If you think about where safes or vaults are hidden away in homes, you might think of a basement. I am telling you that we hid JonBenét's posed body in a safe, a small room in the basement of our house.

"I wrote 'if you want her to see 1997, follow our instructions to the letter' to emphasize that *if you follow my instructions in this letter closely, I will speak for JonBenét as though she were speaking from the grave.* I repeat this message at the end of the note so that the opening and closing are like bookends to again emphasize that I/we represent JonBenét and speak for her in this note.

"This is the third time I have used an entire sentence to somewhat blatantly suggest that I have hidden vital clues in the ransom note. I am also somewhat blatantly detailing the events of the murder and stating motives that only the murderers would know. I am thereby proving that the ransom note is my confession.

"If you read every idea and thought I communicate in this note as part of me, you will have clues to my identify. The words I use in the ransom note describe what I personally am experiencing. I refer to bodily harm (safe and un harmed) and also to someone being controlled (disrespect, servitude, and being possessed) to help you understand that I am an emotionally and physically damaged person. I personally feel entrapped and threatened because something is threatening my life, and I use many feminine references (she, her, daughter, and country/cunt) to tell you that I am a woman.

"By the end of the first paragraph of the note, you can already see the powerful story I am telling begin to take shape. In the rest of the note I will not only confirm the facts of this story, but I will also answer crucial questions, such as why I didn't assault John Ramsey rather than JonBenét, and clarify the main source of the overwhelming stress I felt the night I assaulted our daughter."

The details in the next part of the ransom note are intriguing. Much ado has been made about the actual numbers here, but much more information is hidden between the lines. The actual note continues:

"You will withdraw $118,000.00 from your account. $100,000 will be in $100 bills and the remaining $18,000 in $20 bills. Make sure that you bring an adequate size attaché to the bank. When you get home you will put the money in a brown paper bag. I will call you between 8 and 10 am [sic] to instruct you on delivery. The delivery will be exhausting so I advise you to be rested. If we monitor you getting the money early, we might call you early to arrange an earlier delivery of the money and hence. [sic] a [sic] earlier ('delivery' crossed out) pick-up [sic] of your daug hter [sic]."

(2) What Patsy was unconsciously communicating:
"The second paragraph of my note starts 'Scene Two' of JonBenét's story. Lights, camera, action. I tell you who I am and what's happening to me by the action in the story. The scene is a bank and stern orders are given. Money, an unusual amount ($118,000), is suddenly withdrawn from a bank on an emergency basis. [Author's note: In the appendix we will see that all the numbers in the note have special significance for the Ramseys.] Pay attention to the main idea I am communicating: Valuables are being withdrawn

from a container. The picture is one of control, extreme detail, close scrutiny, and change.

"Two types of change are going on. First, the valuables are shrinking. The money is divided into smaller and smaller amounts until only remains are left. Second, the valuables are being constantly changed from one container to another, and the containers become progressively weaker from a bank/bank account to an attaché to a brown paper bag.

"I question the adequacy of the container (make sure attaché is big enough) to reveal my fears of inadequacy. I keep repeating the ideas that the container is changing and the valuables in the container are changing and the changes are all going downhill.

"I repeat two different words four times each, 'delivery' and 'early/ earlier,' to clarify my motives. My obsession with delivery is the key to the second paragraph and to my two motives: the deep pain that was eating at me and the trigger pain that ignited my killing rage toward JonBenét. The first time I use 'delivery' is the very first time I refer to myself in the note ('I'), to let you know that 'delivery' personally relates to me. Delivery, or delivering a child, is something only a fertile woman can do, and it represents the heart of my identity as a woman. Birthing a valuable child means you have a nurturing, life-giving container inside of you that holds the valuable fetus.

"I chose the picture of a container that is getting weaker and weaker with the shrinking valuables precisely to say that my container has changed, to tell you that I am going through 'The Change' (menopause) in a big way. The word 'delivery' confirms that my emphasis on containers relates to my femininity and my 'container.'

"I started the second paragraph with the stern command to withdraw the valuables (money) to let you know that my problem started when they had to suddenly and harshly withdraw this valuable part of me, the feminine bank within me. My own container (my uterus, my womb, and my ovaries) had become weak and damaged and had to be withdrawn.

"By telling you about the valuables in the container shrinking until only a remaining amount or remains are left, I am showing you how I experienced my hysterectomy and oophrectomy (removal of the ovaries). I could no longer create or hold valuable life within me. It makes no difference if I planned or wanted to have more children or not. I am reacting to the loss of my container because of all it symbolizes to me.

"I can't shout it loudly enough: I want my femininity, the heart of my identity as a woman back! I want to feel like a vibrant powerful woman again, capable of giving life and birth, rather than face the terror of shrinking and dying and becoming nothing but remains. I am hinting at the terrible disease that directly attacked my femininity and emotionally and psychologically attacked my feminine identity. [Author's note: The container is the perfect image of a woman's femininity. Think of women holding babies in their arms, a mother holding or comforting a child, a woman holding the home together and making it a nest for the family, a mother serving as an emotional container for her child's unpleasant emotions. Banks also have a distinctly feminine connotation—containers where "nest eggs" are kept. A woman's purse is a similar symbol. Biologically the mother contains the egg and sperm, which become the fetus she contains and nurtures for nine months.]

"I use the idea of delivery in another important way at the end of this paragraph by making a gigantic slip of the pen and crossing out the word 'delivery.' If you put my three-page note up on a board with the pages side by side, from twenty feet away you can see that this crossed-out word is obviously the most chaotic word in the note. By this one crossed-out word I am telling you that this is where I lost it and why. This is the moment femininity, both mine and JonBenét's, is destroyed. This is when I/we killed her. I am emphasizing that JonBenét's whole bloody story is about damaged femininity.

"I also repeat the word and idea of 'early' meaning 'prematurely' and 'unexpectedly' to convey how badly I was caught off guard. First, I was caught off guard by my life-threatening disease, which attacked my femininity and left emotional pain eating away at me because I am certain not much is left of me, certain that I don't have much longer to live. I have been deeply assaulted as a woman, and I am terrified.

"Second, I was caught off guard when I saw John sexually abusing JonBenét. My fragile femininity was totally destroyed when I discovered that JonBenét had replaced me as John's sexual partner. I deliberately and chaotically crossed-out 'delivery' (to graphically illustrate my destroyed femininity) and substituted 'pick-up' (I 'accidentally' inserted a hyphen between 'pick' and 'up' to connect the two words and make them one word) to tell you plainly that the murder resulted from John turning JonBenét into a prostitute. I momentarily lost my sanity when I caught John 'robbing' her precious little female 'vault' and turning her into a sex object.

"I used numerous glaring errors in the sentence: a mid-sentence period, the chaotically crossed-out 'delivery,' inconsistent grammar ('an' earlier vs. 'a' earlier), 'daug hter' separated into two parts, and others to communicate my momentary chaos, madness, extreme shock, and out-of-controlness. Additionally, I used the word 'hence,' meaning 'conclusion,' to emphasize 'here is where the events of the night culminated in JonBenét's death.' I repeated the idea of 'unexpectedly' (early) four times for emphasis, and I told you that I caught John molesting JonBenét, getting something valuable from her little bank as I secretly monitored his misbehavior.

"Notice how the sentence reads originally with the most prominent slip in the note, the crossed-out 'delivery,' included: 'We might call you early to arrange an earlier delivery of the money and an earlier delivery of your daughter.' My slip makes both his guilt and mine plain. He is delivering both the money and the child, a confession that all along he has had the money and also has had the child and that we are covering up her murder.

"Witnessing a sexually aroused John with JonBenét overwhelmed me. I lashed out at JonBenét because, with my severely damaged femininity, I was already feeling insignificant beyond belief. (I will tell you more about why I lashed out at JonBenét instead of John later in the note.) I hit JonBenét and separated her from life itself, as the divided word 'daug hter' implies that 'here is where JonBenét came apart or undone.' I give you another more subtle clue of the same idea with the second syllable of the divided word 'daug hter': 'hter' suggests 'hit her,' as in 'hit her daughter.' I used the divided word 'un harmed' earlier in the letter and 'daug hter' now to emphasize that JonBenét was already dead when I wrote this note."

The ransom note continues:

"Any deviation of my instructions will result in the immediate execution of your daughter. You will also be denied her remains for proper burial. The two gentlemen watching over your daughter do ('not' crossed out) particularly like you so I advise you not to provoke them. Speaking to anyone about your situation, such as Police, FBI, etc., will result in your daughter being beheaded."

(3) *What Patsy was unconsciously communicating:*

"I validated that sexual abuse of JonBenét was the trigger that ignited my killing rage by mentioning that John Ramsey deviated from 'my' (not 'our') instructions with the result (which repeats the idea of hence/conclusion) that JonBenét is immediately executed. Notice that I subtly call John a deviant ('deviation').

"Pay close attention to this paragraph because this is where I detailed the sequence of physical injuries that resulted in JonBenét's death: (1) I suddenly attack JonBenét, resulting in the 'immediate execution' (the head injury); (2) JonBenét is unconscious and terminal, nothing but 'remains' as good as dead; (3) both of us 'two gentlemen,' her normally genteel parents, are watching over her unconscious body lying before us; and (4) she is strangled ('beheaded'), which is really an assault on the neck. Notice that the sequence I describe in the bogus ransom note fits the autopsy findings. Notice, too, how much I fear law enforcement catching onto my messages as I capitalize both 'Police' and 'FBI' (and later 'Law enforcement')." I know I have given them the evidence they need."

As the writer continues, the letter gets more intense:

"If we catch you talking to a stray dog, she dies. If you alert bank authorities, she dies. If the money is in any way marked or tampered with, she dies.

(4) *What Patsy was unconsciously communicating:*

"I have reinforced the idea that John Ramsey's deviant behavior is the immediate cause of JonBenét's murder by repeating three more times that his secret misbehavior 'could cause' her death (for a total of five times to this point in the note, and I will say it twice more). Unconsciously, in the back of my mind, I had been observing John's ongoing abuse of JonBenét, but I didn't want to admit it to myself, a fact that enables you to understand this sequence. Think of me as the police with whom he secretly communicates without realizing it. He tipped me off about his dirty little secret. He also 'communicates' with a lost little puppy named JonBenét, a 'stray' who wanders away from her usual place. Also think of me as the 'bank authority' who had been monitoring him fooling around with JonBenét's little 'vault.' John had 'tampered with' the valuables, JonBenét, symbolized by money that is to be exchanged for her."

The ransom note continues:

> "You will be scanned for electronic devices and if any are found, she dies. You can try to deceive us but be warned that we are familiar with Law enforcement countermeasures and tactics. You stand a 99% chance of killing your daughter if you try to out smart us. Follow our instructions and you stand a 100% chance of getting her back. You and your family are under constant scurtiny [sic] as well as the authorities."

(5) *What Patsy was unconsciously communicating:*

"I now tried to make crystal clear that the primary motive behind my loss of control was my cancer, which is driving me crazy. In the back of my mind, I am certain I still have it, certain I am dying. I am terrified. Fear causes people to get angry, and terror causes people to explode.

"Notice how I communicate the idea of cancer by mentioning a scanner that finds the slightest defect and you die. I reinforce the idea by mentioning countermeasures that fail, two survival percentages, being under constant scrutiny (and the desperate need for victory), all of which are cancer language. I confirmed this is the deepest motive behind my rage by linking 'follow our instructions' to survival percentages and thus to cancer.

"If you look back at the beginning of the note, you will see that I referred to cancer earlier by telling you that something destroyed my feminine organs, which led to a hysterectomy and oophrectomy, resulting in my deep sense of emptiness as a woman. Like the money and the containers that both keep shrinking, I see myself dwindling away to nothing, which is why I repeated the idea of remains/remaining—that's all I feel like I am. I also emphasized the role my cancer played in JonBenét's murder by writing about being monitored, being threatened by a small foreign faction, and feeling trapped and possessed."

Finally, the ransom note closes:

> "Don't try to grow a brain John. You are not the only fat cat around so don't think that killing will be difficult. Don't underestimate us John. Use that good southern common sense of yours. It is up to you now John!
> Vi ctory!
> S. B. T. C

(6) *What Patsy was unconsciously communicating:*

"I don't want anyone to forget that this is a very personal crime and that I have been deeply and personally wounded, which is one reason I repeatedly bring up John's first name in the last paragraph. He gets the big head ('grows a brain'), underestimates me, and acts like a 'fat cat.' But in my eyes at the time, so did JonBenét. I felt desperately insecure as a woman, which made me feel enraged when I realized she had replaced me as John's sexual partner. This is why I wrote the most brutal thing at this point in the note—killing her will be easy—to let you know how betrayed I felt by both John and JonBenét. Of course, it isn't rational to feel so betrayed by my young daughter, but when you're looking at life through the lens of cancer and imminent death, you don't see very clearly. If you're already terribly insecure as a woman, anybody you catch in bed with your husband is a rival, particularly someone who is as beautiful as JonBenét. And she kept becoming more beautiful every day while I keep deteriorating.

"That sexual scene was so utterly shocking that I wanted to shock you with crude sexual images to communicate just how offended and overwhelmed I felt. That's why I used the crudest expressions I could think of: 'don't try to grow a brain (a big head, an erection) John,' 'it is up . . . now John,' warning him about getting 'fat,' thinking about JonBenét as a 'pick-up' or a 'fat cat' (a fat pussy—I called her a cunt earlier), encouraging John to use his common or most base instincts, his 'southern' (as in below-the-belt) instincts, and calling him a 'john' three times to underscore how he prostituted JonBenét. Earlier I suggested that he was 'getting some' from JonBenét's bank. Subtly, I also suggested that I unconsciously encouraged his actions and helped turn her into a 'call girl' ('I will call you to instruct you on delivery' [of the valuables]).

"In the very last sentence of the note—'It is up to you now John!'—I tell you who strangled JonBenét. John did. It was up to him to take the life of our severely injured daughter so we would have a body to fit our cover-up story. By 'it's up to you John' I'm implying that 'everything is in your hands, John' at the very end of note. I am suggesting that he carried out the strangulation, the final act that resulted in JonBenét's death.

"I made my identity as plain as I could in the note. All you have to do is 'listen carefully!' to the ideas I communicated. I have told JonBenét's story, and I have also told mine. I desperately needed to find some 'victory' over the horrible circumstances of that dark night and over my cancer. I needed a 'victory' over John Ramsey and JonBenét, a 'victory' over the utter helplessness I felt when I saw them together, an utter helplessness that deep down reminds me of the far greater helplessness I feel because of my cancer.

"My soul cries out for justice, as I'm sure hers does even though we are her parents. I want to be caught so I can stop living this lie. There was no intruder, no kidnapping, no real ransom note. There was only a murder committed by us, the victim's parents, and my confession note."

There is another striking link between Patsy Ramsey and the last sentence in the ransom note. In describing her battle with cancer during a 1994 (December) interview with the *Colorado Woman News*, Patsy said, "What makes me so angry is that women get sonograms all the time for trivial things like finding out what sex their child is, and yet it isn't covered by insurance companies to help find this deadly disease (cancer)." She went on to say, "Insist that you have a sonogram in conjunction with a CA 125 blood test. If your doctor tries to talk you out of it, find a doctor who is more receptive . . . . It isn't up to them if you have a sonogram, *it's up to you*." The familiar phrase at the end of the ransom note, linked with a cancer victim's need for "Victory" and matching Patsy Ramsey's vehement connection with cancer on another occasion suggests "it's up to you" was Patsy Ramsey's thoughtprint.

The Story Told in the Note Fits Patsy

The story Patsy told in the bogus ransom note fits hand-in-glove with her personal history. She was at the peak of her adult femininity, a vibrant and attractive thirty-six-year-old former Miss West Virginia. She had just recently been a judge in the pageant she had once won when she felt a lump in her abdomen and was diagnosed with stage IV ovarian cancer on the July 4th weekend of 1993. Immediately she had a unexpected, emergency hysterectomy and oophrectomy and the sudden onset of menopause, followed by the hair loss and other physical changes brought about by cancer treatment.

Patsy's personal history suggests yet another strong link to the ransom note. Her country symbolized by a woman (the Statue of Liberty) celebrates its birthday every July 4th, a day that Patsy would forever link with the shocking trauma of discovering her cancer. No wonder she would have such mixed feelings toward women. On the one hand she was a grand and glorious woman, while on the other she was a despicable "cunt." This further explains Patsy's rage at JonBenét, who symbolized the same thing. In fact, Patsy's attack on and destruction of the beautiful JonBenét suggests Patsy herself is behaving exactly like the cancer that attacked her beauty. Surely Patsy, who discovered her cancer while she was judging a beauty contest, would have unconsciously and permanently linked "beauty" and "cancer" in her. It would not be a stretch to think that unconsciously she saw one causing the other, which would motivate her to destroy "beauty" because of its link to her cancer.

Being diagnosed with this insidious, life-threatening disease made Patsy constantly aware that she could die in a very short time. In addition her cancer attacked the very core of her identity as a beauty queen, the epitome of femininity. For years she had competed with other women for that identity, and she had won 99% of those competitions. Catastrophically losing most of her precious femininity in one fell swoop when they withdrew her uterus and ovaries overwhelmingly and understandably traumatized Patsy.

Even though her hair grew back, it served as a daily reminder of just how fast she could lose it again. She knew beyond a shadow of a doubt that her beauty could be gone in a heartbeat. Although she publicly proclaimed that she had been healed of her cancer through her faith in God, deep down she still feared because the human deeper intelligence has a "mind of its own." It sees reality in a sharper, clearer way.

Patsy's cancer also robbed her of her ability to give life, a part of her femininity that she depended on for self-esteem. Her empty-nest syndrome arrived like "a total and unequivocal nightmare," as she told the *Colorado Woman News*. Her annual family Christmas letters reveal that she keeps playing the role of super-mom, all the while desperately concerned about her children losing their teeth, leaving home, going to school, and growing up rapidly.

On Christmas night 1996, the night of the most special day of the year, a time when she least expected something bad to happen (even though she still felt that she was holding onto life by the tips of her fingernails), Patsy walked into JonBenét's bedroom and found her husband and her beautiful young daughter in an explicit sexual act. Suddenly Patsy saw her daughter not as a little six-year-old girl but as a powerful woman who was just coming into her full beauty while Patsy was dying and who had replaced Patsy in bed with her man. Furthermore this was the one man she counted on to boost her cancer-deflated feminine self-esteem, as well as her feelings of sexual inadequacy due to frigidity (feelings so strong that she had even discussed them with her housekeeper). Patsy's daughter and her husband had hit her right where it hurt the most, and as the ransom note and the autopsy findings suggest, this blow was powerful enough to ignite a psychotic rage, a mercurial rage that her friends had witnessed to a lesser degree at other times. But this time Patsy erupted into a killing rage that dealt JonBenét a life-threatening blow to her head.

The police paid a high price for refusing to think psychologically and to really listen to the killer's mind. Patsy Ramsey clearly laid out her deepest motives in the ransom note as she revealed how completely devastated she had been by her cancer and how it left her on the edge of exploding. Even so, Detective Steve Thomas speculated in his book that her cancer could have stressed her, but he never understood that the killer was specifically confirming his hunches in the ransom note. Certainly a jury would be impressed to hear this from the killer's own mind—and then to be shown how well it matched her history. Otherwise, Thomas barely made mention of Patsy's cancer in his book, and he failed to comprehend the depth of her pain.

But why should the police understand the powerful deep motives of the psyche without training? The first thing you learn as a psychiatrist in doing therapy is there's a universal tendency for therapists to move away from emotional pain because they are human beings, too. It is no coincidence that Thomas had significant emotional pain in his own life concerning loss, particularly death issues because of his mother dying when he was very young. I saw the same avoidance in other investigators who had similar pain of their own.

The Story Told in the Note Also Fits John

The events leading up to JonBenét's death that Patsy describes in the bogus ransom note also fit the other "gentleman," John Ramsey, who actively participated in the murder that Christmas night. For most people Christmas symbolizes life in all its fullness: families, friends, togetherness, nurture, gifts given and received, joy, music, delicious foods, memories often captured on film, all of which tend to maximize the nurturing potential available in human relationships. But Christmas can also symbolize loss and pain as vivid memories of loved ones who have died rain on the parade of togetherness like an unexpected, unwelcome, devastating storm. The greater the loss, the more striking the pain, particularly on this day when emotions can swing about as far as humanly possible in all directions.

People who have lost a child often find Christmas particularly painful for many reasons. That is the most painful loss a parent can experience. For one, it's the most unexpected loss. Parents are expected to die before their children. Losing a firstborn child compounds the pain because no matter how conflicted the parent-child relationship might become in later years, the birth of the first child affirms the parent's identity as a man or woman like nothing else. The loss of a child, particularly a firstborn child, guarantees that Christmas Day will never be the same, that grief will color every Christmas no matter how long you live. And if, horrors upon horrors, a parent loses a child on or around December 25th, that loss will become the grief that keeps on grieving.

John Ramsey lost his firstborn child, his oldest daughter Beth, when she and her fiancé died in a horrible automobile accident on January 8, 1992, two weeks to the day after Christmas 1991. It is only five short years from December 25, 1991, to December 25, 1996, when JonBenét died. And evidently John was still grieving for Beth at Christmas time 1996 because he had a copy of *Dealing with the Loss of a Child* next to his bed. Also, in his first public interview on CNN one week after JonBenét's murder, he talked about the pain of losing his oldest daughter. We can rest assured that at the very least in the back of his mind John thought about Beth on Christmas Day 1996.

Events in 1992 and 1993 magnified the grief John felt over Beth's death. In the spring of 1992, three months after losing Beth, John lost his father, a powerful, domineering figure he emulated in many ways, not the least in demeanor and interests. Both John and his father were pilots, and both were cold and iron-willed. So in the short span between Christmas 1991 and Christmas 1992, John suffered major losses in two out of three family categories, his child and his father, an event alone which Freud called one of the most significant in a man's life. And before Christmas of 1993 arrived, John suffered a third "death" when his wife, Patsy, was diagnosed with a very aggressive ovarian cancer and given a poor prognosis. As Patsy told us later in their book, when she got sick John was still reeling from his losses. John's world had come crashing down about as hard and fast as it possibly could, and he was in the throes of life-sapping grief, just as he had been when he lost his mother to cancer a number of years earlier.

It's three short years between Christmas 1993 and Christmas 1996, quite short if you're going by a cancer calendar and you're in the middle of a wait-and-see five-year survival test, the basic standard for cancer patients. But in addition to experiencing grief over Beth's and his father's deaths and Patsy's battle with cancer during these three short years, John also experienced his own cancer scare. Sometime in 1996 a medical test suggested prostate cancer, and John reportedly was alarmed enough that, without telling Patsy, he flew to the Mayo Clinic to be evaluated. Eventually John was given a clean bill of health, but Patsy was very upset that he had kept it a secret until the scare was over, even though he was following his established code of not discussing traumas. Also during this time, John was dealing with tremendous business and financial success, which on the surface is a very positive thing. But deep down this success always means danger, including the threat of death because of envy on the part of others and self-guilt, to name just two of the common reasons people find success scary.

However much joy John felt on Christmas Day 1996, the night when JonBenét was murdered, significant grief would also have been with him that day before the murder. He couldn't have prevented the grief; he could only have been aware of it, and given what we know about John's personality, we can assume that he probably wasn't consciously aware of the extent of his grief.

Grief can take a variety of forms, but people who are pilots and successful risk-taking businessmen tend to cover up grief with action, particularly action that gives a temporary sense of power and a temporary victory over powerlessness. To say that John Ramsey would be especially reminded of his helplessness because of his guaranteed Christmas Day grief would be an understatement. If nothing else, that day he would have been especially prone to action, to finding some way to get back his power. Maybe that's why John had planned a family airplane trip and vacation to Orlando and Disney World's Fantasyland for December 26, 1996. But maybe that wasn't enough for him. Maybe he had been needing and finding temporary releases from his grief and powerlessness at home by other actions.

In attempting to undo the pain of loss, some people feel the urge to bond, and many times this urge to bond is expressed sexually. Sexual relationships tend to get complicated if your spouse is sick, weak, dying, less appealing because of body changes, and experiencing frigidity. A man who experiences losses in relationships with women can easily develop the idea that getting close to an adult woman spells danger, and he can also just as easily suddenly develop the urge to look elsewhere, maybe even take a risk, if that is his nature, to seek out someone who would temporarily meet his needs for power without having to run the risk of true intimacy or the risk of losing her to a devastating disease or to an automobile accident. The man would be inclined to pick the healthiest available woman and the closest substitute for his spouse.

John's heart really ached, and his sexuality would have been a grand weapon for coping with losses. He may have begun looking elsewhere for a woman, preferably a safe young woman with all her vitality, who would be the farthest thing from loss and danger. John may have discovered that perfect person right in his own house, the perfect substitute for the daughter he had lost as well as the "perfect substitute"/closest reminder for his wife. Patsy herself implies this is exactly what happened in a Christmas letter she wrote immediately before the murder, and she implies that she had been aware of John's sexual relationship with JonBenét for some time. As we will see in her Christmas letters of 1995 and 1996, Patsy refers to John as a playboy and noted that he had set aside his old boat for a new boat—his real love—a boat dressed up to look old when it was really new (young).

John is a risk taker, and if the pressure he felt was great enough and the potential pleasure seemed enough, he would at least be tempted to bond sexually with JonBenét. Then he wouldn't have been just "Daddy" anymore— he would have been Superman. She would have been in such awe of him and his affections that she would almost be spellbound. John and JonBenét would have had a unique relationship, and the secret, as well as the secret pleasure, would have made it even more special, almost as special as the "little" girl he had lost.

The potential would have been exciting and, in some ways, it couldn't have been safer. JonBenét would never reject John. She would always love him, and the two of them would share a very special bond. And if Patsy did die, JonBenét would be the closest substitute he could possibly find. In several interviews after the murder, which we will explore later, John unconsciously explains his over-attachment to JonBenét and how he used her to rescue him from his pain. And a friend will tell us about JonBenét's overly close relationship with her father when she was clearly outside the boundaries as a daughter. (See Chapter 13, page 171 and Chapter 14, page 187)

In addition to meeting his sexual needs, JonBenét would be a perfect vehicle for relieving his anger at Beth for "leaving him" and at Patsy for "threatening to leave him" by death. Grief produces enormous anger at the person who left us no matter how innocent their departure.

When Christmas Day 1996 rolled around, John Ramsey was surrounded by grief or distinct reminders of grief, and unconsciously he was primed for action to overpower his deep sense of helplessness. If he had already developed an addiction to his daughter JonBenét, he would have had the strongest of urges to continue it—on that day particularly—because that's when the grief would have been the strongest, that's when he would have needed a victory over his helplessness the most.

Looking below the surface, we find that both John and Patsy had been under horrendous stress for a number of years before JonBenét's murder the night of Christmas Day 1996. They were two potential time bombs ready to go off, and they went off, just as Patsy described in the bogus ransom note. Both the murder and the cover-up bear the signatures of Patsy and John Ramsey.

How Patsy and John handled the tragic results of their explosive actions verifies the pain and anger they felt the night of Christmas Day 1996. When they saw JonBenét's unconscious, helpless, severely injured body lying on her bedroom floor, their grief again became too much to bear, and they handled it with action. Patsy and John Ramsey then got busy and channeled their energies into a battle with the authorities—looking for another victory, another fix, anything to kill the pain.

Once again we can see how an understanding of the mind and of stress could have helped the authorities. They were continually puzzled about the motives and chose to speculate using almost exclusively autopsy and the crime scene findings, while ignoring the psychological messages in the ransom note. Steve Thomas, again a good example of such thinking, never heard the ransom note writer tell him how John Ramsey's sexual abuse of JonBenét was the immediate trigger for her rage and how this led to John's participation in the murder. If he had known how to listen for the messages, Thomas or any other investigator could have understood why John Ramsey would be motivated to get involved in such a heinous act and to continue the cover-up.

Furthermore such an understanding of the mind would enable an investigator to see the tremendous pain in John Ramsey's life, pain which was there all along and which made him vulnerable to sexually abusing his daughter. An investigator who knew how to listen would be prepared for any communication from John Ramsey that confirmed the sexual abuse. By remaining ignorant of the recent advances in the psychology of the mind (as opposed to biology, e.g., brain chemistry studies, etc.), Thomas ended up where all the other investigators did—applying his own theory. Sadly, he came to the conclusion that John Ramsey was not involved in the crime and that "the woman" had done it all. In the end, he failed to comprehend either John's or Patsy's motivations for this crime. Thomas would have been left at best with going to court with a weak motive—a bedwetting battle—which a jury would have a hard time buying. It would be even more difficult for them to believe that Patsy then strangled her own daughter. If Thomas had listened to the right consultants, he would have heard Patsy Ramsey pleading with him to speak for JonBenét, fully arming him for battle at the same time.

The Real Victory for JonBenét: Bringing Patsy and John Ramsey to Justice

Both Patsy and John Ramsey continue to need a victory over their feelings of helplessness, which murdering JonBenét only intensified. The inadvertent ineptness of the law enforcement authorities gave them a big victory over the prosecution. Now they apparently have a new scapegoat: They are suing the tabloids for the stories about them and the murder case. How long will they be able to continue before they have to look themselves in the mirror and see themselves as the "gentlemen" who murdered their own daughter?

Of course, they can keep justifying their cover-up by telling themselves, "We've suffered enough. What good would a confession do? What good would a prison sentence do? We're not going to kill again. We have to live with the fact we killed her. What business is it of yours? She was our daughter. Do you want to inflict more pain on her brothers and sister, particularly twelve-year-old Burke? Do you want to further embarrass our family? When is your pound of flesh enough? We have enough grief with losing one daughter and accidentally killing another."

However, when Patsy and John rationalize their actions, they forget about JonBenét and Burke. And they forget that the only real salve for grief is truth.

PART II

What They Did with What They Had

A Blind Investigation and A Mixed Media

CHAPTER 6

One Closed Mind—Deputy District Attorney Michael Kane

The idea of hidden messages shouldn't be foreign or unacceptable to law enforcement authorities because forensic investigators constantly look for the hidden messages they believe criminals leave behind. For example, when a murderer leaves a blanket over a victim or places a body where it can be easily found, forensic profilers "see" the criminal as someone who cared about the victim and was emotionally invested in the deceased. The profilers see the blanket, the place the body was left, and other subtle clues as symbolic, encoded messages from the murderer. Profilers "decode" crime scenes, and they fully recognize that the encoded clues they find come from the criminals' unconscious mind. Criminals are not consciously aware that they leave these messages—they just do it.

Profilers and experienced law enforcement agents know that criminals have a natural inclination to leave clues behind. In fact, stories about criminals making unbelievable mistakes as a way of getting themselves caught are legendary, such as a bank robber who gives the teller a note plus his driver's license. Profilers talk about a criminal leaving his or her "signature" at the crime scene. They also note that criminals often inflict on their victims the pain they themselves are feeling. For example, abusers often have been abused themselves. In many crimes the criminal's unconscious mind will reveal the truth. As our forensic analysis of the ransom note shows, Patsy Ramsey revealed the truth about what happened and why.

When Dr. Callahan, Dr. Groesbeck, and I sent our forensic analysis to Deputy District Attorney Kane, we were asking him and his staff to take the next step in profiling by looking for the symbolic, encoded clues the author/murderer had left in the ransom note. We made it easy for them to take this next step by giving them an in-depth analysis that guided them word by word, sentence by sentence, and concept by concept through the ransom note. All they had to do was follow the clues we detailed in our analysis, and they too would "see" the murderers' signatures at the crime scene.

The thoughtprints the author/murderer left in the ransom note are as authentic and convicting as fingerprints. Just as a criminal unconsciously leaves encoded clues at a crime scene, a criminal also leaves unconscious encoded clues in a ransom note. So even while the author/murderer was trying to disguise her identity, she unconsciously used words and communicated ideas that were on her mind. In the Ramsey case the author/murderer left a highly unusual and lengthy ransom note, encoded clues unconsciously intended to reveal her identity, as her own personal signature on the crime. The ransom note also provided evidence that the murderer had inflicted the pain she herself was feeling on her victim, JonBenét.

Michael Kane's Response to Our Forensic Analysis

Deputy District Attorney Michael Kane and his staff, as well as the other Boulder law enforcement agents on the Ramsey case, are familiar with forensic profiling concepts. Our forensic analysis asked them to apply these concepts at a deeper level by "reading" the messages the murderer unconsciously communicated in the ransom note. Our analysis decoded words and ideas that came straight from the murderer's mind, so Kane and his investigators didn't have to guess or intuit the murderers' motives as they did in other cases. In the Ramsey case they could "hear" the murderer herself describe not only the murder, but also the motives and the events leading up to the murder. But Kane rejected our psychological approach.

I believe Callahan, Groesbeck, and I are closer to the mind of the murderers than anyone on the Boulder district attorney's staff. Other forensic experts who read our analysis thought so, too. They included experienced FBI agents, an acclaimed criminologist and authority on serial killers, and the leading special agent in psycholinguistics at the FBI Academy; each highly praised our work—one even called it "compelling." As mentioned previously, several experts personally wrote to Kane, encouraging him to use our expertise in apprehending and prosecuting the murderers.

These experts saw that author/murderer Patsy Ramsey had unconsciously written the ransom note specifically to the district attorney's staff, begging them to work for justice on JonBenét's behalf. Since Patsy had written the ransom note immediately after murdering JonBenét, she was consumed by guilt. Patsy was almost shouting to the authorities and specifically to Michael Kane, "Please, please follow the hidden instructions in this note and speak for JonBenét. It's your job to tell a jury this story so they too can speak for JonBenét!"

Kane admitted that he had sensed to some extent that the ransom note was a sort of story written to the investigators, but he couldn't say exactly what the story was. Obviously he didn't see the real story in the ransom note, the one written by the mother who had just killed her child, the story giving him and others on the prosecutor's staff clear instructions to speak for JonBenét. If Kane had seen that story, he would have followed Patsy's "instructions," and at the very least he would have convinced the grand jury to indict both Patsy and John for the murder of their daughter.

From the very beginning of the investigation, the Boulder investigators knew that the ransom note was not only key evidence, but that it was also some of the only uncontaminated evidence, and Hunter indicated that he was aware the ransom note contained hidden clues. Surprisingly, however, the authorities did not welcome our forensic analysis of the author/murderer's thoughtprints. Kane basically said, "Thanks, but no thanks."

When Dr. Callahan called Kane to make sure he had received the comprehensive, seventy-page forensic analysis we had sent him, Kane said, "Yeah, I got that thing," a response that spoke volumes about the close-mindedness Patsy Ramsey later referred to in her public statement after the grand jury's failure to indict her and John (See "Introduction" on page xiii.) Callahan, Groesbeck, and I had spent a collective total of more than 600 hours analyzing the ransom note and compiling "that thing," and we had provided it to the Boulder authorities without charge. In addition, we have more than ninety combined years of clinical experience, and two of us are experienced, expert courtroom witnesses. We had put our professional reputations on the line when we sent him "that thing."

Our report provided not only the identity of the murderers and their motives, but it also undermined the testimonies given by the defense's major witnesses, detective Lou Smit and profiler John Douglas—testimonies that had irreparably weakened Kane's case against Patsy and John. Our analysis particularly refuted Smit's testimony. This famed, folksy-mannered lawman, who was known as the Old Colorado Fox, had grandiosely claimed that he understood the case better than anyone, but our analysis showed how badly he was mistaken. (For more on Lou Smit, see Chapter 7, page 87.) Callahan, Groesbeck, and I believe it was a travesty of justice for Kane not to have presented our evidence to counter Smit's emotional proclamation of the innocence of his friends and employers, Patsy and John Ramsey.

Helping Michael Kane See and Understand the Truth— About Himself and the Ransom Note

Kane's personal reaction to our seventy-page forensic analysis gave Callahan, Groesbeck, and me a sterling look at what is going on inside the mind of the leading prosecutor in the Ramsey case, a man whom Alex Hunter specifically hired as a consultant. In our conversations with Kane, he revealed that deep down he has indeed heard Patsy Ramsey's messages.

Kane also revealed some of the real reasons he backed off from our forensic analysis of the ransom note—and in a way he offered hope that, as he put it, "down the road the report may be useful." This suggests that Kane not only realizes but also admits that he could be wrong about the note, and he wants the next prosecutor on the case to know that the report will indeed be useful to any prosecutor who has the courage to pick up the ball and run with it after Kane had dropped it. In essence Kane told us that the man or woman courageous enough to "listen carefully" will be the one who speaks for Jon-Benét, and he encourages his successor to do just that.

Even though indirectly Kane admitted that he knew he was making a huge mistake, he steadfastly refused to really read our report, to look into the author/murderer's mind, and to present this uncontaminated evidence to the grand jury. He told us to come back in thirty years after all the research had been done on applying this breakthrough to the deeper intelligence as it relates to document analysis and psycholinguistics. Then he "might" read our report and listen to our expert advice. Meanwhile he has no use for any "encoded" messages from the author/murderer, even though the author/murderer had written the ransom note specifically to him, and it spelled out both the motives and the sequence of events of the crime.

Despite the wise message from the author/murderer's unconscious mind to "listen carefully," Kane decided to follow his own mind—he would determine on his own how the murderer's mind worked and the motives for the crime. Kane felt sure that he knew enough about document analysis to immediately spot any new worthwhile approach. He was the expert on the case, and he wasn't about to move over for any other expert, even if it meant ignoring the author/murderer's specific written instructions and losing the case.

Kane's own deeper intelligence picked up on how badly he was mistaken, just as many of my patients pick up on mistakes they are about to make. And like my patients, many times when Kane was talking about others, he was—without realizing it—talking about himself. For example, Kane told me that many times members of a jury really don't listen to experts— just as he wasn't listening to Callahan, Groesbeck, or me.

Of course, you must be very careful any time you attempt to read another person's deeper thoughts. But in very clear-cut situations when you know precisely the issue that unlocks the thoughtprints and when the thoughtprints are clear enough, it sheds enormous light to be able to hear a person's deeper intelligence speaking. In this situation the issue was crystal clear—Michael Kane was rejecting the author/murderer's messages to him. Deep down Kane, like the rest of us, wants the truth to come out, which is why I believe he talked to me for an hour and revealed so much about his deepest motivations, what he was really thinking. Kane's deeper intelligence knew he was making a terrible mistake in rejecting our analysis and tried to tell both of us so that the truth would be told. This explains Kane's statement that our analysis "might be useful down the road."

During our conversation Kane told me that "juries make up their minds in the first ten minutes of a trial," "first impressions are lasting," and "when a jury gets a case, they make up their mind early, follow their first response, and most people want confirmation of their own beliefs." He added, "It takes a lot of evidence to prove a case" implying that juries can be difficult— another disguised reference to himself. Along with his other thoughts, Kane suggests deep down he realized how resistant he was being.

Kane commented that psychiatry was on the low end of the scale as far as respect was concerned, and he then told an insulting joke about psychiatrists. He further suggested that I take his joke with a grain of salt and mentioned that there were lawyer jokes, too. Kane's hostility so clearly linked us and his repeated thoughtprint about "jurors who decide too early" that they clearly fit hand-in-glove with the way he treated our forensic analysis:

Kane was the jury who had to vote on our analysis. He strongly demonstrated his close-mindedness by informing me, "You're not going to change my mind."

By presenting a series of ideas about impulsive decisions, Kane was also conveying his deeper awareness that his decision to reject our analysis was hasty. He added the idea that initially jurors stuck with their first impressions but that "there were no five-minute verdicts"—because "jurors take their roles seriously and can spend two days going back over things," thereby suggesting to himself that he should give up his first-impression bias and reflect further on our analysis. To underscore these ideas Kane noted that "sometimes juries see things that professionals don't" and "sometimes psychological profiles are admitted into evidence."

When we're making a major error in judgment, our deeper intelligence will often try to help us in two ways— first by bringing to mind a series of thoughtprints (ideas) that address our blind spot and second by presenting a model of a better way, which is exactly what Kane did at this point. He kept mentioning juries making premature decisions, and then he presented a model of ideal behavior—spending time reflecting.

Kane repeated his thoughtprint and advice to himself "to take more time to think over the report" by making several references to teaching situations. He told me that if we did go to court, we would have to make sure after a couple of hours that the jury understood the ransom note as well as we did. He talked about having to teach the police that this was not an easy case, that their ideas of a quick verdict were wrong, which added even more weight to the wisdom of taking time and having to learn. Kane also spoke about the "untrained eye" not seeing the messages in the note and hinted at training jury members to see the evidence in the ransom note.

Kane really wanted our forensic analysis to be "completely rational"— he wanted no mention of indirect or encoded messages, no unconscious mind and no deeper intelligence. At one point Kane came surprisingly close to seeing the truth of the ransom note. As previously mentioned, he told me that he believed the ransom note was a message and a story from the killer. (Earlier, he had told detectives to review their notes on the case because they could have picked up valuable information they hadn't yet consciously realized—another suggestion from Kane on how to use the unconscious mind.) However, he did not stay with this line of thinking.

What Kane failed to see was that as long as he insisted on completely "rational," straightforward communication he had no case against the Ramseys, people who straightforwardly denied the crime and did not appear, rationally speaking, to be likely culprits. This crime calls for an irrational motive to explain how seemingly rational, caring parents could murder their daughter. All Kane left himself open to was somehow to figure out Patsy's and John's irrationality and hope that a jury would see it. Maybe he could eventually get a confession out of Patsy and/or John if he was lucky. Or maybe he would get lucky in another way and find a witness who had heard the Ramseys say something incriminating. Kane has not yet accepted the very real probability that Patsy has already confessed in the ransom note.

During our conversation Kane made an even more striking reference to the deeper mind by comparing teaching the jury about the ransom note to an art professor trying to teach people about a beautiful painting with many hidden symbolic messages that were over the heads of his audience. Although he consciously used the analogy in a negative way, the analogy itself speaks volumes, and along with his other idea of people being taught (a professor who teaches) here and elsewhere, he contradicts himself. This suggests that Kane recognizes that the ransom note is a work of art—it is extremely valuable and filled with crucial messages, word pictures of the crime. This again strongly implies that he was in denial and had made up his mind too early—and that a jury could be taught to see the messages and motives in the note itself.

Even Kane's negation that our report doesn't make "common sense" suggests the identical idea the ransom note writer suggested to the authorities and to the jury: "Use your common sense" In other words, consider the ideas in the ransom note, see if they fit the Ramsey family, and if they explain how fine, upper-class parents Patsy and John lost control. The ransom note does all of these things, which is precisely why it is indeed a work of art.

Kane also revealed in other ways that deep down he saw the potential in our forensic analysis of the ransom note. He emphasized that sometimes "juries lap up things professionals don't" and raised the possibility that "you guys could be twenty years ahead of your time." He also mentioned that trials were sometimes like "NBA playoffs, and whoever got hot could win," which suggests that at first what seems like a long shot could in fact win out. In short, Kane was hinting that the ransom note presented to the jury in the right way would be extremely powerful—even to the point of being "lapped up by a mesmerized jury."

Michael Kane also revealed to me that he was clearly being governed by deeper motives as he talked about why he wasn't going to use our report as a way to decode the note and reveal the killer's motives. He passionately told me, "My instincts as a prosecutor tell me not to use that report."

While strongly insisting that his instincts as a trial attorney told him not to use our report, Kane was inadvertently suggesting using a deeper part of his mind—his instincts. The deeper intelligence is, simply speaking, our "deeper instinct," the place where we all have an incredible ability to determine the truth of a matter. He followed these thoughts with an even clearer picture of accessing his whole mind when he talked about a jury trial requiring an "out of body" experience for the attorney in terms of anticipating a jury's needs and tendencies. By mentioning instincts and using the striking image of a lawyer needing to be able to have an "out of body" experience to try a case, Kane was strongly suggesting using another part of his mind, one outside his "normal" mind, i.e., his deeper mind. His deeper intelligence was prompting him to think about the enormous capability of the mind that he was already familiar with and to apply it to this case. He was telling himself, "Pay attention to your broader mind."

In many ways Kane is no different from any other human being—he fears what he doesn't know. Therefore, one of his central problems is an inability to trust his deeper mind, the killer's mind, or our minds. If he trusted the killer's messages and trusted in his deeper instincts, he would have seen the impressive messages left for him in the ransom note. Then he would have gone to court fully armed.

Most striking is the difference between Kane's superficial instincts and his deeper instincts. Deep down, Kane believed we were right. Deep down his deeper intelligence recognized the ransom note was an invaluable communication—truly a work of art. His deeper intelligence tried to tell his conscious mind that he knew he already held the case's smoking gun. But it all came down to his lack of awareness of how the human mind worked and his distrust of psychology.

When Michael Kane and the other investigators minimized the killer's communications, they missed the motives behind the crime. Without understanding the ransom note writer's mind, they will never understand why JonBenét Ramsey was murdered, nor will they be certain who killed her. If they ever want to understand the most powerful motives in the criminals they deal with, they must learn how the mind really works, specifically the deeper intelligence, so they can readily hear the messages criminals are sending them. Investigators must embrace the fact that in the right hands, psychology is a wonderful tool—able to provide revelation and guidance.

When our deeper intelligence is at work we don't feel it, and we won't even notice it—unless we know it's there and know to look for its messages. Unless we realize how limited, in comparison to our deeper mind, our conscious mind's ability is to give us accurate feedback, we won't pay it any attention. Thus Kane didn't realize his own comments applied to him—that he was talking about his own major blind spot.

I understood Kane's need to maintain credibility with the jury. But because I teach people on a daily basis how to overcome their reluctance to trust their deeper intelligence's ability to guide them, I knew that this reluctance could often be overcome. I explained to Kane that psychotherapy was basically teaching, and I knew that once people got the hang of it, it was very persuasive for them to realize their own mind was teaching them. In the JonBenét case, I believed that once the jurors understood that the killer herself was actually speaking for JonBenét in a disguised way and providing the motives that reading those messages would be a powerful experience for them.

During some talks I had given, I had already seen several lay people respond well to the conclusions I'd made. Others had similar responses after reading my book, *A Mother Gone Bad*. A sterling example was "Mrs. Brady," a self-described average housewife who had an Internet site for the JonBenét case (see footnote, page 17). For over a year and a half she couldn't conceptualize how people of the Ramseys' stature could have been involved in the murder. She credits my analysis of the ransom note in my book for providing her with the missing motives in the case and for moving her "off the fence."

Kane Recognizes His Blind Spots

All of these references ("out of body," instincts, teaching, reflecting, training, symbolic paintings) were message markers from Kane's own mind, trying to help him see there was another way. These are key words signifying communication when someone unconsciously is trying to emphasize a key message. He was advising himself to listen differently, as in "listen carefully."

Kane unconsciously recognized his resistance when he spontaneously told me, "The law never allows anything that makes it easy—like lie detectors." Along with his earlier comment that it took an inordinate amount of evidence to convince a jury, he was suggesting deep down that his resistance to accepting our report was excessive and, in that sense, that he wasn't telling himself the truth. A spontaneous reference to a lie is often a crucial message marker in therapy. Here it came on the heels of Kane's beautiful image of the ransom note as an amazing work of art.

Deep down Kane was telling himself, "The ransom note is a work of art filled with key messages. Go back and try to see them; quit being so unreasonably demanding." Our experience with the recently discovered deeper intelligence reveals it understands everything. If the ransom note was truly valuable to the prosecution, and if the killer was talking to law enforcement, Michael Kane's deeper intelligence would have recognized it in a heartbeat. In an indirect way, Michael Kane offered impressive validation of his own that indeed the ransom note was invaluable—like a treasured work of art an artist had diligently and brilliantly created.

In short, Kane would want to confess to his blind spot—just like the ransom note writer had to confess, because (also like the killer) Kane wanted to see justice done, more so at a deeper level than he did consciously. I believe that Michael Kane is such a fine attorney that by talking to me for an hour he was attempting to break through his own resistance in order to listen to his own deeper instincts/deeper intelligence. I also believe in his heart of hearts he wants this story told because it's the only way the ransom note is going to be used effectively in this case. Secretly, Michael Kane hopes another prosecutor has the courage to do what he couldn't: to use the killer's mind in a court of law.

More Resistance Comes

All evidence to the contrary, Kane could have convinced the grand jury to indict Patsy and John—if he had used the incriminating evidence we uncovered in the ransom note. Over the next few months, Dr. Callahan, Dr. Groesbeck, and I each followed up with Kane to answer his questions about the report, hoping to convince him at least to read our forensic analysis and to consider our findings. In fact, I spoke with him on June 30, 1999—three and a half months before the grand jury's decision not to indict.

Each of us spoke with Kane by phone at different times. During each conversation he showed significant hostility toward our work. In addition to referring to our professional, in-depth forensic analysis as "that thing," he frankly admitted, "I don't know what this stuff is about." Other than those comments, Kane acted gentlemanly and likable during our conversations, but we found reasoning with him to be tricky. He first told Callahan that he couldn't consider using our forensic analysis because I had written a book, *A Mother Gone Bad: The Hidden Confession of JonBenét's Killer,* which focused on the Ramsey ransom note. Kane's insisted that my authoring a book on the subject had contaminated our forensic analysis and had rendered it useless as a prosecution tool. This seemed ludicrous, especially when considering that ex-FBI profiler John Douglas testified before the grand jury on Patsy's and John's behalf and he was not only an author of several books on profiling that he was actively promoting, but he also worked for the Ramseys.

Callahan, Groesbeck, and I had anticipated this objection and had consulted with former prosecutor and law school dean, Parham Williams, who told us that he saw no major problems with my having written a book about the ransom note. Furthermore, our suggestion to Kane was that either Callahan or Groesbeck be the expert witness to testify in court because of their experience: Both of them had previous experience in murder trials. Regardless of my authoring a book on the subject, the ransom note remained uncontaminated evidence and yielded invaluable, incriminating clues.

Callahan, Groesbeck, and I realized that the real concern wasn't about my book—it was about our methodology. Kane and the other investigators questioned whether we were right, "really right," in applying what we knew about the unconscious deeper mind to analyze the ideas communicated in the ransom note. Was our new way of analyzing communications a valid method to use in extracting crucial information from a note left by a murderer? If our methodology was valid, then the fact that I had written a book about the ransom note could not discount the validity of our forensic analysis—the truth would stand on its own.

Kane further resisted our analysis, stating that he couldn't get our "profile" of the murderers admitted in court because our methodology lacked scientific basis. We had also anticipated this objection, and again we had asked Dr. Williams whether our forensic analysis was evidentiary in the eyes of the court. Williams stated that in his opinion there was a better than even chance that a reasonable judge would allow our report to be entered as evidence. But Kane ignored Williams's understanding of the legal climate.

The week after a short follow-up conversation with Kane, Callahan received a phone call from an attorney named Bass who claimed to be from Kane's office. Bass inquired in great detail about the scientific basis of our analysis, but, as it turned out, he wasn't working for Kane. Apparently someone working for Patsy and John Ramsey had gotten wind of our analysis and called pretending to be from Kane's office. Kane later denied any knowledge of the phone call and was certain it didn't come from his office. Kane also said he was unconcerned about the matter. Four months after Bass called Callahan, Chuck Sullivan, a Denver private investigator working for Patsy and John, persistently pursued me trying to obtain a copy of our analysis, which Callahan, Groesbeck, and I had presented at an international forensic meeting after Kane declined to use it as evidence. At first Sullivan tried to make it sound as if he was a forensic expert who had heard about the conference, but eventually it came out that he worked for the Ramseys. When I refused to provide a copy of our forensic analysis, Sullivan made it plain that he was authorized to buy it from me, but I still refused to give it to him. How ironic that the Ramsey camp was willing to pay us for our forensic analysis, which provided evidence of Patsy's and John's participation in JonBenét's murder, while Kane and other members of the prosecution team wouldn't give us the time of day.

Groesbeck followed up Callahan's phone call to Kane, and in their conversation, Kane reviewed his strategy for discounting our forensic analysis, again focusing on the lack of a scientific basis. Groesbeck, Callahan, and I came to the conclusion that Kane's real reason for not accepting our analysis was that he didn't understand it and he didn't want to look foolish in court using an unfamiliar methodology. As my experienced forensic colleague Callahan observed from his vantage point of innumerable courtroom experiences, Kane didn't like it one whit that the JonBenét Ramsey murder case had boiled down to being an expert's case, rather than it being one that depended exclusively on his own investigative abilities and interviews with eye witnesses. He didn't want to take this case to court and have to present that the real truth was "between the lines" in the ransom note. He didn't want to tell this to the jury because he didn't have any expertise in dealing with the unconscious mind and its brilliantly clear observations of reality.

Next I called Kane to try to reassure him of the scientific nature of our work and to convince him of the uniqueness of the Ramsey ransom note. During my conversation with Kane, I realized that he was not even aware that we were basing our analysis on a new scientifically solid method, nor was he aware of our academic credentials. Obviously he had not even read Dean Williams's brief that we had included, which made it plain that we had met scientific criteria. Furthermore, Kane expressed surprise that my book, *A Mother Gone Bad*, had received a positive, substantiating review in a professional journal.

Once I pointed out the scientific method we had used, Kane switched to complaining that my having written a book was the reason he couldn't possibly use our report. He added, "I'm not being critical," a tip-off considering all his comments that he really was being critical. He then told me about the time he tried a difficult murder case against defense attorney Larry Posner. At the beginning of the trial Kane had said to Posner, "This is what your client did," and Posner had replied, "No, you must prove this is what my client did." Kane talked about how that was a defining moment for him as an attorney—and how ever since then he had focused on "proof."

Kane again vehemently insisted that his instincts as a trial attorney told him not to use our forensic analysis, and he kept mentioning my book, *A Mother Gone Bad*. He acknowledged that he had read my book, and he referred to it when he said that if he "put the evidence in front of a grand jury, some of your conclusions would be off the charts." He added, "They would tear your credibility to pieces." In the final analysis, my credibility wasn't what he was concerned with—Kane was worried about his.

Pressure to Maintain the Status Quo

The more I have thought about our conversation, the more I believe Kane was confessing that he never gave our forensic analysis his full attention and that he was unfairly tearing our credibility to pieces—destroying it by not really reading it. I think this was why he immediately called it "that thing" and why he said he didn't "know what this stuff is about." I had written my book nearly a year before Dr. Callahan, Dr. Groesbeck, and I collaborated on our forensic analysis. I had learned far more about the ransom note and the murder in the intervening time, and our forensic analysis was a better-organized, more cohesive picture of the ransom note. I agree with Kane that some of the ideas I presented in *A Mother Gone Bad* were a stretch for readers who were not experienced psychiatrists. In retrospect I realize I should have left these ideas out of the book—and Callahan, Groesbeck, and I did leave them out of our forensic analysis. I understood the note better after studying it for another year, and our report reflected it.

None of the forensic and legal experts who had read our analysis thought a grand jury would "tear our credibility to pieces," although all of us knew any defense attorney would surely try. Kane's comment about my book actually describes how he himself had reacted toward our forensic analysis: He didn't understand it, and he thought it was a stretch. Then, when he got our analysis, he gave it a cursory read while essentially sticking with his original impression, justifying his lack of support by saying a jury wouldn't accept it.

I was particularly struck by the violent nature of the references Kane made during our conversation, beginning with his story about being involved in a murder case that was hard to prove. In essence Kane murdered our forensic analysis. While he would have previously been involved in murder trials, his bringing up anger spontaneously when he could have used other examples suggests he was also talking about himself. Another example he chose to use seemed to confirm his anger. In response to my question about the possibility of jurors who themselves understood the messages in the note convincing other jurors, Kane talked about "Twelve Angry Men," a story about one juror who was able to convince the other eleven and help them become appropriately angry. He thought such an occurrence was possible but "rare." I began to wonder why "anger" and "murder" were so much on Kane's mind—also reflected in his comment about people tearing our credibility to pieces—when I talked with him about our forensic analysis.

During our conversation Kane explained that he wanted to be perceived by the grand jury as "completely rational" and that he couldn't use our analysis because it "doesn't make sense to the average person." I tried to emphasize the importance of motive and that our analysis established motive based on the ransom note. While Kane agreed that establishing "a provable motive is very important," he felt that a jury wouldn't buy psychology or a psychological profile—as if motives had nothing to do with psychology. Finally he acknowledged that juries could understand motives like "jealousy," but there had to be "objective facts." He thought that an "untrained eye" might not see deeper motives. He said that he wanted "scientifically controlled experiments to prove" our analysis was "right." He added that if "fifty deans of medical schools said, 'This is valid,' I might accept it," but concluded "that's probably not going to happen." (Fifty deans of medical schools couldn't agree on anything. Experts can and will disagree, but we thought, as the ransom note writer did, that the jury could decide which experts were right.)

Every time I seemed to be making some headway with Kane, he brought the conversation back to my having written A Mother Gone Bad and my "profiting from the book." He seemed to be fixated on this, which made no apparent sense to me, nor to Callahan, Groesbeck, or our legal expert Dean Williams. I began to wonder if Kane's obsessive preoccupation with my having written a book unconsciously had to do with jealousy. If he wanted to, he easily could have "rehabilitated my credibility as a witness" if he had emphasized that I had printed the book at my own considerable expense after spending countless hours investigating the case and that my goal was not only to pursue justice but also, as a teacher, to explain to law enforcement and to the public a new way of using the mind to bring about healing for society as well as individuals. He also could have pointed out that Callahan, Groesbeck, and I had collectively spent 600 hours—at no expense to the Boulder authorities—analyzing the ransom note and preparing our forensic report. He could have underscored that the profits from the book were minimal and had not in any way begun to compensate me for the time I had spent analyzing the ransom note and preparing the forensic report. He could have even thrown in that we live in America, where we have the freedom to earn money by writing and publishing books. Finally, he could have pointed out to the jury that I should be allowed the same freedom to write books and still testify that John Douglas had been allowed—and I didn't work for anyone involved in the case like Douglas did.

I can understand why Kane might feel jealous. It's perfectly human to envy outside experts who come into your territory carrying the keys to a very difficult case. This would explain why Kane believed a jury might understand a motive of "jealousy." On one level, he was talking about what he understood. It's an old story, and ground-breaking inventors have a name for it: "Not Invented Here." Many times earlier successful inventors had their ideas rejected because they were not part of the "in-house team."

The ideas Kane expressed during our conversation provided significant clues about the real reasons he was rejecting our forensic analysis: experts being ignored, people wanting to decide on their own, people being overly sensitive to information "being forced down their throat," and jealousy. He had a difficult, high-profile case and very limited evidence. Furthermore, the key evidence in the case—the ransom note—demanded that he trust outside experts to make his case. Using the key evidence depended on expertise that was foreign to him. Since he is a "conscious/left brain mind" kind of person, Kane has trouble with symbolic encoded messages that are out of his normal way of functioning. They were "things" and "stuff" that he'd rather not have to try to understand. Kane's comment to me that "if I put one of you guys on the stand for a couple of hours, when you're done the jury better understand it as well as you do" summed it all up. A jury, of course, would never understand a subject as well as an expert witness in any field, but that is acceptable. What they needed was enough information to make a reasonable decision. Even so, Kane's comment said it all: He wanted to know as much as we did about the mind so he would feel comfortable trying this case. We can understand his wish, and we can see how it would lead to a type of jealousy. But the circumstances of the case were what they were, and Kane failed to adapt to them.

Although Kane's response disappointed Callahan, Groesbeck, and me, it didn't really surprise us. We know that when experts are presented with new information that asks them to look at things in a new way—in a sense to move over and make room for new knowledge and new expertise—they usually guard their turf as if it were a gold mine. Callahan, Groesbeck, and I realized that we were asking a lot of Kane for him to be willing to take a new approach to a case. But breakthroughs do ask a lot of people, and even more importantly that is exactly what the author/murderer was asking Kane to do.

Even though a number of highly respected, experienced forensic experts, including a fine lawyer (himself a former prosecutor) and legal scholar had read our report and had personally urged Kane to use our findings to his advantage, it was all to no avail. Ultimately fear of the unknown, his sense of territorial expertise, and his close-mindedness held Kane back from following the wise counsel of his unconscious intelligence and using our report to win his case and bring Patsy and John Ramsey to justice.

One final and equally powerful explanation of Kane's defensive hostility is that he had suddenly come into national prominence from out of nowhere. Six months prior to JonBenét's murder, no one had a clue who Michael Kane was, and suddenly he was the primary trial strategist for the prosecution, and in that sense, he was leading the investigation. Kane was feeling the same kind of incredible pressure that L.A.'s prosecuting attorneys and Judge Ito felt—they were "no names" until the O.J. Simpson trial, and I believe the horrendous pressure caused by their sudden fame and notoriety undermined their potential success in the courtroom. Kane told me that he "might not be the one to try the case if it comes to trial," which sounded as if he might be trying to retreat from center stage. When I told him the ransom note would one day be an incredibly famous document in forensics and psychology, he immediately responded, "It already is." That's not totally true, but I think he was primarily referring to his own sudden fame and saying that he'd already had enough.

Success brings enormous pressures—as I noted with the Ramseys. For instance, it often creates a powerful "lonely at the top" syndrome, which might have been too much for Kane to handle. Success also often creates the "if I'm on top, everyone will shoot at me" fear, which contains more than a little bit of truth. If he had gone to trial, his opponents would have tried to destroy his case. The pressure of success and the fact that Kane would have to try this case differently, having to depend more on experts than he would like, left him vulnerable and anxious—which again explains his defensive attack on our report.

Kane was responding to powerful pressures. The ex-district attorney and famed prosecutor Vincent Bugliosi once described a major trial as a heavyweight fight in which the winner is the one who gets off the floor last. Dr. Callahan thought that if the Ramseys had to go to trial, it would be the battle of a lifetime—with Kane up against John Ramsey and his expensive attorneys. But Callahan and Groesbeck were confident Kane would win—if he used the smoking gun. That is why we wrote our forensic analysis of the ransom note in the first place. Unfortunately, Deputy District Attorney Michael Kane refused to use the keys that would unlock the truth about who killed JonBenét Ramsey.

CHAPTER 7
Switching Sides—Lou Smit

Is it possible than an experienced detective with high moral values could deceive himself so badly that he could undermine a murder investigation, falsely accuse his peers of biased investigation, claim moral superiority over them, and then enable two murderers to go free—all in the name of God? And could he do this secure in the false knowledge of self-righteousness and detective acumen?

Detective Lou Smit's personal story is amazingly similar to the Ramseys': hidden pain, hidden fear, hidden (and not so hidden) anger, hidden guilt, and cover-up. Emotional pain leads to all kinds of distorted thinking and behavior problems. Sadly, Smit's only accountability is his own judgment. We have a saying in medicine: "A doctor who treats himself has a fool for a patient." Smit took things into his own hands with disastrous results.

From the beginning of the investigation Lou Smit began crossing investigative boundaries by rationalizing his role as "the good cop" in the well-known investigative strategy of "good cop/bad cop." Police inter-rogation tactics often include using two interviewers, one being the confrontational "bad cop" and the other acting as the nurturing "good cop" at the same time. Smit's strategy was to befriend the Ramseys while investigating them. Maybe that had worked well for him in solving other crimes, but it didn't work with the prominent, personable, media-savvy, pseudospiritual Ramseys. And it didn't work at this particular point in Smit's life when personal circumstances made him vulnerable to manipulation.

Instead of maintaining the professional objectivity so crucial to the investigation, Smit immediately bonded with Patsy and John. Reportedly Smit the investigator was first thrown offtrack by Patsy's grief. For a few weeks, Patsy emotionally regressed to the point of extreme withdrawal and help-lessness, often having to be helped to the bathroom and needing someone to comb her hair. When he learned how grief-stricken Patsy appeared to be after JonBenét's murder, he strongly questioned whether she could have been involved. But what Smit and many others seem to have overlooked is that Patsy was experiencing "triple" grief. First, she truly grieved the loss of the beautiful, vivacious JonBenét herself, a loss that would provide enough grief for any mother. Second, she grieved the loss of the daughter who was an extension of herself and to whom she was overly attached because of her own terror of dying from cancer. JonBenét's death brought Patsy closer to her own death—and the related grief over all her losses, particularly the loss of her femininity, which she had never properly grieved. And knowing that she herself had murdered her own beloved daughter provided a third level of grief. Patsy privately felt ashamed and grief-stricken about her murderous rage. Because of her crime, Patsy was also facing the shame of public humiliation. The idea of undergoing a public trial was unthinkable, and even if she got away with the murder, people would never forget. Losing her All-American self image would create unspeakable grief for someone who depended on being a former Miss America contestant.

In actuality Patsy's extreme grief strongly suggests that she was involved in the death of her daughter because, as painful as it is to lose a child, her grief was excessive even for that untenable reality. But Smit could not reconcile how someone as grief-stricken as Patsy could have written a lengthy ransom note immediately after the crime. He underestimated the fear of being pronounced guilty and going to jail. He forgot that in a crisis, a dysfunctional person often rises to the occasion and then collapses later. This is doubly true if the person possesses an iron will, as Patsy does. Patsy's friend Judith Phillips publicly pointed out on several occasions that Patsy had the absolute strongest personality of any person she has ever known. Later, during the Ramseys' largely contrived television interview with Michael Tracey (see Chapter 10, page 117), Patsy's body language told us just how hard it was for her to write that letter, evidenced when she winced excruciatingly as John mentioned the killer writing the note.

Patsy herself showed Smit her iron will and skilled manipulation when (according to Lawrence Schiller in *Perfect Murder, Perfect Town*) fewer than six months after JonBenét's murder, she called and asked him if he would check on their house in Boulder while she and John took Burke on vacation to Charlevoix, Michigan, at the end of the school year. Patsy was playing on Smit's sympathy, and Smit, thinking this was an opportunity to get close to the Ramseys as the "good cop" willingly agreed to monitor the house in their absence. But when Smit drove up to the Ramseys' house on June 6th, Patsy and John "just happened" to meet him. Soon they were all sitting in Smit's van chatting, and Patsy insistently told Smit that neither she nor her husband were involved in the murder and expressed the strongest of wishes that the murderer be caught. Following Smit's suggestion, according to the Ramseys in their book *The Death of Innocence*, they held hands and prayed for God's blessing on the investigation. While Patsy and John were out of town, Smit checked on the house where JonBenét had been murdered, and he prayed every day.

It's not that Smit was mistaken about following his Christian beliefs, but he forgot that the Bible repeatedly warns about the deceitfulness of human beings, particularly when they are scared and in a corner. Smit's devout Christian faith set him up to become the Ramseys' pawn and from that time on, he demonstrated excessive sympathy for the Ramseys, always rationalizing it with his Christianity, as his peers noted.

Smit also bonded with the Patsy and John because they shared the common bond of being victimized by cancer. Smit's wife was battling cancer during the time he was investigating cancer-victim Patsy. The terror of cancer prompts people not only to cling to each other, but also to quickly give up healthy boundaries of individuality.

Bonding with Patsy and John led Smit to ignore evidence, including the ransom note, which pointed toward them. He focused instead on evidence that supported an intruder theory: an unexplained Hi-tec shoe print near the body, an unidentified palm print on the cellar door, a partial palm print on the ransom note, pieces of glass on the suitcase near the broken basement window, and a scuff mark on the wall below the window. And to explain the "unexplained" bruises on JonBenét's body that could be seen in photos taken in the days before her death, Smit raised the possibility that the perpetrator had been involved with JonBenét for some time and had used a stun gun to keep her quiet when he was molesting her. He even suggested that JonBenét's body be exhumed to see if the bruises verified his stun-gun theory, which his peers considered to be unfounded speculation and which forensic pathologists debunked. But he derailed the investigation, providing more confusion for a already tentative, to say the least, district attorney's office.

Unfortunately for the prosecution team, Smit not only ignored key evidence in the case and created "wild" theories to explain JonBenét's murder, but he also deliberately sabotaged the case against Patsy and John Ramsey by persuasively testifying on their behalf at the grand jury hearing.

Smit's Quit-and-Switch Move

Smit served on the Ramsey case as a prosecution consultant for a year and a half before resigning and going to work—on behalf of Patsy and John. In his resignation letter, Smit himself explains why he made such a dramatic switch:

September 20, 1998

Dear Alex [Hunter]:

It is with great reluctance and regret that I submit this letter of resignation. Even though I want to continue to participate in the official investigation—and assist in finding the killer of JonBenét, I find that I cannot in good conscience be a part of the persecution of innocent people. It would be highly improper and unethical for me to stay when I so strongly believe this.

It has been almost 19 months since we talked that day in your office and you asked me to assist in this investigation. It has turned out to be more of a challenge than either one of us anticipated. When we first met I told you that my style of approaching an investigation is from the concept of not working a particular theory, but working the case. Detectives collect and record information from many sources, analyze it, couple that with their experience and training and let "the case" tell them where to go. This process may take days, weeks, or years, depending on the direction the case tells you to go. Sometimes you must investigate "many paths" in order to find the killer. It is not a political speed contest where expediency should outweigh justice, where "resolving" the case is solving the case.

Alex, even though I have been unable to actively investigate, I have been in a position to collect, record, and analyze every piece of information given to your office in the course of this investigation. I believe that I know this case better than anyone does. I know what has been investigated and what hasn't. I am a detective with a proven record of successful investigations. I have looked at the murder of JonBenét through the eyes of age and experience and a thorough knowledge of the case. At this point in the investigation "the case" tells me that John and Patsy Ramsey did not kill their daughter, that a very dangerous killer is still out there and no one is actively looking for him. There are still many areas of investigation which must be explored before life and death decisions are made.

When I was hired I had no agenda one way or the other, my allegiance was to the case, not the Police Department nor John and Patsy Ramsey. My agenda has not changed . . . I only desire to be able to investigate the case and find the killer of JonBenét and will continue to do so as long as I am able. The chances of catching him working from the "outside looking in" are very slim, but I have a great "Partner" who I'm sure will lead the way. There is no doubt that I will be facing a great deal of opposition and ridicule in the future, because I intend to stand with this family and somehow help them through this and find the killer of their daughter. Perhaps others who believe this will also help.

The Boulder P.D. has many fine and dedicated men and women who also want justice for JonBenét. They are just going in the wrong direction and have been since day one of the investigation. Instead of letting the case tell them which way to go, they have elected to follow a theory and let their theory direct them rather than allowing the evidence to direct them. The case tells me that there is substantial, credible, evidence of an intruder and lack of evidence that the parents are involved. If this is true, they too are tragic victims whose misery has been compounded by a misdirected and flawed investigation, unsubstantiated leaks, rumors, and accusations.

I have worked in this profession for the past 32 years and have always been loyal to it, the men and women in it, and what it represents, because I believed that justice had always prevailed. In this case, however, I believe that justice is not being served, that innocent people are being targeted and could be charged with a murder they did not commit.

The law enforcement Code of Ethics states it very well. My fundamental duty is to "serve mankind: to safeguard lives and property; to protect the innocent against deception, the weak against oppression or intimidation, the peaceful against violence or disorder. To respect the constitutional rights of all men to liberty, equality and justice." This applies not only to JonBenét but to her mother and father as well.

I want to thank you and the others in the office for the wonderful support and treatment I have received. You have a great DA's office and the men and woman who work with you are some of the most honest and dedicated people I have ever met. My life has been enriched because of this memorable time together. I have especially enjoyed working closely with Peter Hofstrom and Trip DeMuth, who also have dedicated so much of their lives to this case. I have never met two more fair, honest and dedicated defenders of our system.

Alex, you are in such a difficult decision. The media and peer pressure are incredible. You are inundated with conflicting facts and information, and "expert" opinions. And now you have an old detective telling you that the Ramseys did not do it and to wait and investigate this case more thoroughly before a tragic mistake would be made. What a double travesty it could be; an innocent person indicted, and a vicious killer on the loose to prey on another innocent child and no one to stop him.

History will be the judge as to how we conducted ourselves and how we handled our responsibilities. Shoe, shoes, the victim's shoes, who will stand in the victim's shoes?

Good luck to you and your fine office and may God bless you in the awesome decisions you must soon make.

Sincerely,
Detective Lou Smit

Smit, nicknamed the Old Colorado Fox, wielded inordinate power in both muddying the waters of the investigation and in testifying on behalf of Patsy and John. Imagine yourself as a member of that grand jury. If an old detective, who has a John Wayne-like reputation and was called in from retirement especially by District Attorney Alex Hunter just to solve this case and who seemingly has no ax to grind, testifies that based on his vast experience he is certain Patsy and John Ramsey didn't kill their daughter— what would you think? How impressed would you be if Smit went on to tell you that he felt so strongly about the prosecution's mishandling of the case and persecution of the Ramseys that he resigned and, regardless of the criticism, is publicly breaking ranks to speak out about this ungodly injustice? You would be inclined to admire his courage and find his testimony to be inordinately powerful and persuasive. Who could doubt the motives of a distinguished, respected law enforcement agent who would stand up to his peers and tell them they were wrong? Smit reeks of integrity, and his testimony was devastating to the prosecution's case against Patsy and John.

So, who could refute Lou Smit's testimony—apart from some of his fellow detectives who disagreed with him? We need more. We need someone who sees further into the human heart than Lou Smit consciously does. And we have the perfect investigator, Lou Smit's own brilliant deeper intelligence, which sees his heart of hearts and tells us how mistaken he is in mistakenly protecting the Ramseys. Just as the ransom note writer confesses to the crime between the lines of the ransom note, Lou Smit confesses to his misdeed between the lines of his resignation letter. In the back of his mind, Lou Smit knew how phenomenally tricky—"deceitful" to use his own word—his mind could be.

Human beings do things for all sorts of reasons, and powerful hidden motives frequently drive everyone—particularly when people behave out of character. Simply because they are human beings, loving parents like Patsy and John can sometimes explode and kill their children. And capable detectives like Lou Smit can explode without realizing it and murder the truth. Smit's deeper intelligence reads his deepest motives like a book and describes in vivid ways just how far out of line he was. Smit left plenty of evidence that he had exploded in his public letter of resignation to Alex Hunter. Smit dealt Hunter the most devastating blow a detective can inflict on a prosecutor by his unprecedented crossing over from investigating the two prime murder suspects to befriending them, then publicly defending them, and finally stating that his professional colleagues were at best confused and at worst devious.

Smit's deeper intelligence in his public letter of resignation reveals that he was wrong about Patsy and John's innocence and that he knows he deceived himself and the public. Like the author of the ransom note writer and Michael Kane, the Old Colorado Fox's deeper intelligence tells a far different story from the one he consciously intended.

Helping Detective Lou Smit See and Understand the Truth—About Himself and the Ransom Note

The thoughtprints Detective Lou Smit left in his resignation letter reveal the real reasons he befriended Patsy and John and testified for them against the prosecution. He wrote, "Alex, even though I have been unable to actively investigate, I have been in a position . . . to analyze every piece of information given to your office in the course of the investigation. I believe I know this case better than anyone does. I know what has been investigated and what hasn't, what evidence exists and what doesn't . . . I am a detective with a proven record of successful investigations." Smit's deeper intelligence is suggesting that his overestimation of his abilities and training caused him to believe he was the most informed detective on the case—but he ignored the ransom note.

I know Smit heard about my evaluation of the ransom note, and I assume he was around when the district attorney's staff discussed the prepublication copy of my book, A Mother Gone Bad, which included an in-depth analysis of the note. I also know that he gave it no more than a passing thought. Consciously Smit honestly believed he had thoroughly analyzed the case, but he has no background in document analysis or the new methodology Callahan, Groesbeck, and I had used. He didn't know what evidence the ransom note contained, yet he claimed to have more knowledge in criminal communication than anyone, expertise that he really doesn't have.

Very simply Smit can't tell us the truth—however much he thinks he can—because he doesn't have the expertise to see the whole truth. Intuitively he recognizes this and states in his note, "I have been unable to actively investigate." When people are mistaken and know it, they have a strong urge to confess, which Smit does in his resignation letter. While appearing to be talking about others, he is really talking about himself—projecting onto others who he really is deep down. His comments reveal how badly he was mistaken and why. Smit repeatedly talks about investigators who make the terrible mistake of having an agenda before a case starts and who don't really pay attention to the evidence. Interestingly, he first links his training to the idea of investigators who stick to a theory: "My style of . . . investigation is . . . not working a particular theory, but working the case.

Detectives collect . . . information from many sources, analyze it, couple that with their experience and training, and let 'the case' tell them where to go." Since Smit's training in this kind of communication analysis by definition was insufficient, he is intuitively explaining his bias. Consciously he thought he was being objective, but he wasn't.

The problem was Smit's style—the belief that he knew the best way to investigate this case and that he didn't really have to consult an expert because he was the expert. Nevertheless, he holds up the ideal model: A good detective should let the evidence direct the case, exactly as the author of the ransom note, Patsy Ramsey, encourages.

The repeated thoughtprint of "people with biases or agendas" underscores Smit's problem. He accuses the Boulder Police Department of "going in the wrong direction and have been since day one of the investigation. Instead of letting the case tell them which way to go, they have elected to follow a theory and let their theory direct them rather than allowing the evidence to direct them." Those words are self-incriminating. The ransom note is evidence and leads investigators, but Smit refused to allow the ransom note to direct him. He points another finger at himself when facts reveal that he came quickly to the opinion that Patsy and John weren't involved in JonBenét's murder. Smit's claims that when he was hired he "had no agenda" and that later his "agenda has not changed," blatantly suggest someone who is protesting to the point that he is actually shouting, "Can't you see? I had the biggest agenda imaginable!"

Smit starts confessing his guilt in the very first paragraph of his letter: "It would be highly unethical for me . . ." Smit's misguided pride has led him to think he would be unethical for not going public with his knowledge about the case based on his vast experience when, in fact, his behavior in undermining the investigation is abominable. He further describes his unethical behavior when he talks about "victims [John and Patsy] whose misery has been compounded by a misdirected and flawed investigation, unsubstantiated leaks, rumors, and accusations." While Smit is describing what he believes to be police victimization of Patsy and John, he is actually describing how he himself made his peers—the members of the prosecution team—his victims through leaks, rumors, and accusation. Whatever evidence Smit thinks the police haven't substantiated pales in comparison to his own accusations and unsubstantiated leaks in his resignation letter. Certainly the investigation is flawed—partly because of Smit's own limitations and poor judgment.

"My fundamental duty," continues Smit, "is . . . to protect the innocent against deception, the weak against oppression or intimidation, the peaceful against violence or disorder." JonBenét was all three, but the Ramseys were none of the three. Blinded by his friendship with Patsy and John, Smit himself has deceived his unsuspecting and, in many ways, innocent peers, has tried to oppress and intimidate them, and has acted in a violent and disorderly way by discrediting vital information.

Notice how destructive Smit really is. He sets himself above all his colleagues ("I understand this case better than anyone"), insisting he is the only truth-seeker while at the very moment he is trying to destroy the truth. He can't even go quietly off into the sunset upon retiring, but drags all the authorities through the mud in a blatant effort to discredit them, even as he violates a fundamental principle of law enforcement and completely loses his objectivity. As Jesus once put it, Smit can't see the log in his own eye because he's too focused on the speck in his peers' eyes. Given the Judeo-Christian distaste for pride—the fundamental basis of all sin according to the Bible—Smit takes it a step further. He does his dirty work in God's name, telling us, "The chances of catching him [the killer] working from the 'outside looking in' are very slim, but I have a great 'Partner' who I'm sure will lead the way." Above all the others on the case, Smit has access to God, Who he's confident will help him solve the case. It never occurred to Smit that maybe God was trying to speak through the ransom note and the conscience/deeper intelligence that He gave Patsy Ramsey.

Toward the end of his resignation letter, Smit confesses yet again to what he is doing to his friend, Alex Hunter: "Alex, you are in such a difficult decision. The media and peer pressure are incredible. You are inundated with conflicting facts and information, and 'expert' opinions. And now you have an old detective telling you . . . ." Smit is applying peer pressure, and he himself is the "expert" who inundates Hunter with conflicting information. And at the very end of his letter, Smit talks about and to himself when he counsels Hunter to "investigate this case more thoroughly before a tragic mistake would be made . . . an innocent person indicted and a vicious killer [still] on the loose."

The Old Colorado Fox

Sixty-seven-year-old Smit came out of retirement to help with the case. One key to Smit's blindness to the truth in the Ramsey case is his preoccupation with aging: "an old detective," "I have looked at the murder . . . through the eyes of age and experience." He also states that "a dangerous killer is still out there and no one is actively looking for him. There are still many areas of investigation which must be explored before life-and-death decisions are made." Smit recognizes that he has not investigated—that he is not consciously aware of—frightening matters involving life and death. In short, he suggests he has ignored powerful personal threats to his well-being and is trying to avoid a destructive force that threatens his life—or the life of someone close to him. Smit suggests that, like Patsy and John, he didn't want to look at the powerful threat to his wife's health, the dangerous killer that is still out there: cancer. Of course, he was acutely aware of his advancing age, seeing himself following not far behind his wife in death.

No one really wants to talk or think about death, and even those people who say, "I'm not afraid of dying," are only speaking for their conscious mind. Communications from both Patsy and Smit reveal that they, like most other people, are reflexively trying to push thoughts of death out of their consciousness. As a physician I have seen more than one person overtly do it in a crisis[1] and as a psychiatrist I have seen virtually everyone demonstrate hidden fears of annihilation and death.

But another fear accompanies death, a fear many people never talk about, but a fear Smit reveals in his resignation letter. Like most old people, at least in the back of their minds, Smit is preparing to meet his Maker. "History will be the judge of how we conducted ourselves," he wrote, and he ends his letter with "God bless you," which confirms Who is on Smit's mind. A devout Christian like Smit would take the idea of a day of reckoning seriously. Between the references to God and being judged by "history," Smit asks an unusual question about "who will stand in the victim's shoes." The idea of standing in someone's shoes fits closely with the idea of Judgment Day—as reflected in the old saying, "I wouldn't want to be standing in his shoes on Judgment

---

[1] In *The Deeper Intelligence*, I told about a time when I was an intern and had to inform a mother that her child had just died. The mother continued to ask me to give her deceased child something for his cough—she couldn't consciously accept his death.

Day." (Christopher Darden addressed this very issue on the back cover of his book on the O.J. Simpson case in essence saying, "I take comfort knowing that one day Simpson will face a Higher Court.") Maybe Smit, as people are prone to do under such circumstances, already felt deep down that his wife's cancer represented a type of punishment.

Smit may appear to be a man at peace; this is not necessarily true if he has hidden sins he hadn't yet admitted to himself—such as the destructiveness, self-righteousness, and false pride he reveals in his resignation letter. In fact it is quite likely that Smit's shadow side bothers him terribly. As he gets older, his guilt haunts him. When he talks about the police being forced into a "speedy" premature judgment, a killer being on the loose, and the persecution of the innocent, on one level he is alluding to the terrible aggression he has just inflicted on his peers when he attacked justice and tried to destroy their case. Accordingly, because he doesn't wish to be tried and found guilty for his own faults and wrongdoings, he can't find the Ramseys guilty either.

Surrounded by his wife's health problems and his own aging Smit feels like an innocent victim, and like many victims he inflicts his pain on others. Smit inflicted his own pain on his colleagues—much as Patsy and John Ramsey inflicted their own terror of death on JonBenét. And so unconsciously Smit joins the Ramseys in covering up their failure—and his.

Given Smit's own grief, fears of entrapment, and his feelings of being stunned by the discovery of his wife's cancer, he understandably bonded with the Ramseys. Patsy, John, and Smit were suffering similar pain, and they all used their Christian faith at moments in manipulative ways to deny their pain. From the get-go Smit's preoccupation with "biased investigators who ride a one-horse pony" fits him like a glove, because early on he himself inappropriately bonded with Patsy and John.

Considering the capability of his brilliant deeper intelligence to critique his deepest motives, it's no wonder that a man like Smit, who prides himself on his good judgment and his character, would not be open to knowledge to the contrary. He would not be willing to listen to investigators who came forth with a new way of looking at the psyche, a psyche that speaks powerfully about deeper motives. Smit had to destroy knowledge like that, which explains why he would ignore the ransom note writer's deeper intelligence. If author/murderer Patsy told the truth on herself, then Smit would have to accept that his mind possessed the same potential.

We have recognized that from the beginning Smit was out of bounds in claiming expertise he didn't have regarding the most crucial evidence in the case, and we have listened to his brilliant unconscious mind provide us with a striking critique of his deeper motives as to why he sabotaged the case. The testimony of his fellow detectives particularly stands out, further testifying to Smit's destructiveness. As Detective Steve Thomas describes in *JonBenét: Inside the Ramsey Murder Investigation*, Smit made his mind up in the first seventy-two hours on the case without even reviewing the massive files of evidence on the case. He quickly fell in love with an intruder theory (of an assailant who used a stun gun), ignoring substantial evidence to the contrary.

These examples are reminiscent of the 1991 murder of Heather Dawn Church when the police were set to indict a family member, but Smit discovered a missing fingerprint that identified another killer outside the family. He became an instant hero. As is so often the case, success went to his head and subsequently in the JonBenét case, he got lost in the past, trying to recreate another hero role for himself.

This led Smit's protection of the Ramseys in almost of unheard of ways: praying with them, providing them inside information about the detectives' conclusions, going over evidence with them, discussing his intruder theory with them in depth as though they were allies, and prompting them as to how to respond publicly, as well as making suggestions for their public relations campaign. Reality be damned, he was going to recreate the scenario of his choice. Given the tremendous stress he was under, the all-conquering invulnerable hero role was too enticing to give up.

Patsy, Kane, and Smit Agree on How the Investigation Should Be Handled

Striking agreement exists among three of the primary investigators in the Ramsey case. Smit echoes Kane's idea that investigators need to put aside their biases and let the evidence speak. And these are Patsy Ramsey's exact words following the grand jury's failure to indict her and John. Their thoughtprints match about how to handle the investigation.

Smit's deeper intelligence had brilliantly suggested that the investigators had to "be completely open-minded to wherever the evidence leads," but his conscious mind took him only so far. He had no way of recognizing the limitations of his conscious mind, including those times when he was unknowingly violating his own recommendation. He knew nothing about deeper intelligence and thus failed to appreciate the evidence left by Patsy Ramsey's deeper mind in the ransom note and other communications, including personal conversations with him.

In a seemingly strange way (although not so strange once you understand the human mind's need for truth), the prayer to find JonBenét's murderer—a prayer that Smit, Patsy, and John said together—was already answered. But Smit, a man of faith, lacked the faith to see the truth even when it was staring him in the face. Smit poignantly echoed author/murderer Patsy's plea for someone to speak for JonBenét when he wrote, "Shoes, shoes, who will stand in the victim's shoes?" His own blindness to the truth kept him from being the man to do just that.

CHAPTER 8

Leaders Who Don't Lead— Alex Hunter and Mark Beckner

Every investigation has its leaders. These are the individuals who take the point, who think creatively, who plow into whatever it takes to get the case solved. When the major evidence in the case begs to be utilized, they do everything they can to take advantage of it. If the tried-and-true isn't working, then they break new ground. They do the hard thing if they have to. These leaders step outside the box and become open to new possibilities. Bottom line: They never stop investigating, and that includes investigating new methods, not just new evidence. Unfortunately, the two major leaders of the Boulder investigation—District Attorney Alex Hunter and Police Chief Mark Beckner—didn't lead like this.

District Attorney Alex Hunter's Response to Our Forensic Analysis

Alex Hunter consciously knew the case would come down to the ransom note. In addition to repeatedly stating how crucial the ransom note was, way back in February 1998, he declared that the investigation would ultimately come down to a "linguistics case," meaning the linguistics in the ransom note. Ironically, Hunter agreed with my colleague Patrick Callahan's assessment that the case would come down to being an "expert's case."

Hunter called on linguistic expert Dr. Donald Foster, who had attained some notoriety for his academic work in identifying overlooked works of Shakespeare and later for identifying the anonymous author of *Primary Colors*. Based on his comparison of Patsy's handwriting with the ransom note, Foster told Hunter that Patsy Ramsey had written the letter. But Foster as it turned out, had badly compromised himself as an expert witness when, early in the case, he had spontaneously written to Patsy to tell her that his initial opinion was that she was innocent. Not long after that, Foster had also staked his reputation that an Internet personality by the name of Jameson was really John Andrew (John Ramsey's son), and that he felt John Andrew was behind the murder. These two factors came to light later after Foster had changed his mind and decided Patsy had written the note. But by then, the damage was done, essentially rendering useless Foster's 100-page report on the ransom note.

It is to Hunter's credit that he sought out someone with some expertise in document analysis to help him uncover the evidence hidden in the words of the ransom note. If he had just taken the next step—considering other ways of gleaning information from the ransom note, such as the methodology Callahan, Groesbeck, and I used—he could have seen the messages Patsy left for the prosecution. But when Hunter received our forensic analysis, he ignored it.

If only Hunter had taken his statement "this case is going to come down to a linguistics case" one step further to "this case is going to come down to experts who can show me hidden information in the ransom note that links it to the murderer," he would have had the incriminating evidence the prosecution needed to both indict and convict Patsy and John Ramsey for the murder of their daughter. If only he had been open to the new way of doing psycholinguistics, which emphasizes the psychological aspects of language—particularly for unconscious meaning—and brings some psychological teeth to the definition of "psycholinguistics," Hunter would have been able to effectively use the evidence in the ransom note to successfully prosecute Patsy and John Ramsey. Even Donald Foster admitted in a *New York Times* interview that he saw the value of applying "psychology" to language, but he admitted he was a neophyte in doing so.

One other if only: If only Hunter had asked his wife, who is a gynecologist, to help him understand the female psychology that is at the heart of the ransom note, he would have heard Patsy describing the overwhelming fear she felt as an ovarian cancer victim. He then would have grasped the explosive rage Patsy felt when she realized that JonBenét had replaced her as her husband's lover. Dr. James Raney, a noted psychiatrist and forensic expert, had tried to point Hunter in that direction, but Hunter failed to follow through on his suggestion. (See Chapter 4, page 31 .)

Alex Hunter was so close, but so far away, so open-minded on the one hand, yet, as Patsy herself pointed out, so closed-minded on the other. (See

Introduction, page xiii.) His conscious mind kept telling him to listen to the author of the ransom note—but he just quit listening

As a result of his failure to listen to author/murderer Patsy Ramsey, Alex Hunter didn't have sufficient evidence to convince the grand jury to indict the Ramseys for the murder of their daughter. Tom Miller, a former Denver attorney and handwriting expert who was quite involved with the case in his own way, insists that Hunter could have gotten an indictment. Miller and a few other handwriting experts have no doubt that Patsy wrote the note and have said so publicly. Miller says that even more experts who have not gone public also believe that Patsy is the author. But Miller recognizes that this fact alone would not be enough evidence for the grand jury to indict the Ramseys. According to Miller, Hunter didn't think he could win the case, so he most likely allowed his buddy Hal Haddon, the Ramseys' attorney, to convince him not to push for an indictment. It was common knowledge that Hunter and Haddon were buddies from way back, even having made financial deals together. Throughout the case, Hunter was constantly criticized for sharing far too much information with the Ramseys' attorneys.

It is helpful to know that all of the district attorneys in the five counties surrounding Boulder are elected. Not surprisingly, all are Democrats and Haddon is a preeminent figure in the Democratic Party and once served as Gary Hart's former campaign manager. According to Miller and others, behind the scenes Haddon pulled a lot of strings and had uncommon influence with Hunter who didn't want to look foolish. Miller says he still feels Hunter should have tried the case. But Hunter is known to be a plea bargainer more than a challenge-driven trial attorney, and waging such a battle went against his grain. Unconsciously, he also easily could have been influenced by politics.

Even Alex Hunter's conscious or superficial intelligence told him the case would come down to the ransom note, but he quit listening. Sadly everything comes back to Hunter's failure to listen to his own mind and get the expert help he needed to hear Patsy tell all about the murder, the murderers, the victim, and the motives—all available in the ransom note.

Police Chief Mark Beckner's Response to Our Forensic Analysis

Like Michael Kane and Alex Hunter, Police Chief Mark Beckner also failed to appreciate the clues Patsy Ramsey's deeper intelligence left specifically for the investigators. Instead of following up on the motivations Patsy describes in the ransom note, Beckner wasted time tracking down other leads that led nowhere. On one occasion he spent a significant amount of time talking with an elderly lady in South Georgia whose only exposure to the case was television and who had a wild theory that John Ramsey's former mother-in-law, Irene Wells (who later became his stepmother), was the murderer.

On the other hand, Beckner did not take the time to talk with me about Patsy Ramsey's extremely revealing 1997 Christmas letter, which she wrote shortly after Beckner and I had our first conversation. I had written Beckner in late December 1997, telling him that the "Ramsey Christmas Message," which had just been released to the public, contained many "thoughtprints" that matched the ransom note. But he refused to talk with me, even though I was trying to help him see that Patsy's Christmas letter contained messages specifically for him as the chief law enforcement person on the case.

Beckner believed a direct, traditional approach needed to be taken in examining the ransom note, and he selected consultants who would investigate in the usual way. All the while, the killer's hidden messages were staring him in the face. Initially Beckner had an eagerness about him, and on the surface was likable, patient, and attentive. He called me on the first day he took over as the commander of the investigation (even prior to becoming police chief) and went to the trouble to track me down. Unfortunately, he just didn't catch on to the power of a new method of investigating and eventually became disinterested, moving along to investigate the next lead. "Detective" Patsy Ramsey had nailed it right on the head—he ignored leads. He wrote off the possibility of using new information too quickly. In the end, he couldn't distinguish crucial communication from meaningless chatter.

Beckner told me that he didn't think my "profile" would be admissible in court even though the messages from the note were strikingly clear early on. Eventually when my colleagues and I submitted our official report on the ransom note our legal expert, law school dean Parham Williams, stated unequivocally that it should be admitted into a court of law. This shows that if Beckner had continued digging, he would have had the evidence he needed. His uncertainty about whether my "profile" was admissible in court should have served as a red flag to Beckner, a tip-off to investigate further. A good investigator would have sought several opinions and explored further, particularly after being encouraged to do so by an FBI agent experienced in kidnappings and ransom notes.

Perhaps Beckner was looking for ways to discount a new method of forensic analysis. Even if he didn't think he could use all the information in court, he still could have made far greater use of the ransom note than he did in his investigation. Instead of guessing at the motives, he could have had hard answers. His interrogation of the Ramseys would have been far more effective when they finally agreed to talk. I tried to show him how helpful this method would be for interrogations—which is basically what I do all day long—but who was I to tell him?

Ultimately, Beckner's close-mindedness prevented him from utilizing the help offered by outside experts who pointed to the invaluable help the killer/ransom note writer was trying to be. Although Beckner tried to remain noncommittal, his comments revealed that he thought the Ramseys were guilty, which only makes his refusal to accept a new forensic methodology all the more telling. Like Hunter and Kane, he was so close but so far away. Part of him tried to tell himself, "Think about using this 'profile' in court" but he wasn't listening.

Distrust Blocks Investigation

My colleagues' and my own experiences with Beckner, Hunter, Kane, and other members of the Ramsey case investigative team made me realize that law enforcement agents have a significant distrust of mental health professionals. Like everyone else, police initially want literal communication because that's what we all know and trust. Whenever people are presented with new way of communicating or thinking, they have to trust another person to teach them, and law enforcement agents in particular have problems trusting others because their experiences on the job often reinforce how untrustworthy other people can be.

This distrust of other people, especially psychiatrists and psychologists, contributed to Hunter's, Kane's, and Beckner's close-mindedness and prevented them from hearing Patsy speaking for JonBenét in the ransom note. They relied on conventional experts who used only tried and familiar methodologies, experts who unfortunately didn't have the expertise to "read" the clues Patsy had left specifically for the prosecution team in the ransom note. As a result, the prosecutors didn't use the key piece of uncontaminated evidence that is "sufficient" to both indict and convict Patsy and John Ramsey for the murder of their daughter.

CHAPTER 9
Getting the Word Out—The Media

The last bastion of an investigation gone bad is the media. The media doesn't have to get it exactly right, and it doesn't have to be completely scientific, but it does have to be able to smell the truth—especially when official investigators have missed it. The media is the sergeant-at-arms, the one who brings order from chaos, who holds the plumb line. It must be able to filter out the truth from all the subterfuge that comes its way. And in the JonBenét case, when not one of the primary law enforcement investigators is speaking for the victim, nor is anyone of them using the key evidence, the media must do so. To do their job, the members of the media have to be able to listen and be open-minded, almost to a fault, so they don't miss anything. If they aren't sure, they must investigate—and keep investigating until one way or another they *are* sure. Sadly, it would appear that they don't make reporters like they used to—and even some of their own have told me this is the case.

Some Media Masters

In studying the ransom note, I met many of the major participants in the case, some directly and a few indirectly—not only Michael Kane, Mark Beckner, and Alex Hunter, but also many reporters who discussed the case in the media. Among these was leading Denver radio talk-show host Peter Boyles of KHOW, on whose show I appeared several times. Cyril Wecht, noted pathologist and author of *Who Killed JonBenét?*, and I discussed our findings on ABC's *The View*. Denver attorney and former prosecutor Craig Silverman, a frequent commentator on the case, appeared with me on *The Crier Report*. On another occasion I discussed the case during a radio interview with Patsy Ramsey's friend and former schoolteacher, Linda McLean who wrote her own book, *JonBenét's Mother*, on the case. I also appeared on a national television show with Patsy Ramsey's sister Pam, who was a call-in guest. In short, in addition to talking with the prosecution, I got to see how others, including the Ramseys' friends and relatives, handled the murder.

But unquestionably I spent more time with one type of media investigator than any other. I had significant contact with the primary reporters on the case: Denver television reporter Carol McKinley, Dan Glick of *Newsweek*, Charlie Brennan of *The Rocky Mountain News*, and Chuck Green of *The Denver Post*. I also had many discussions with writers from the tabloids, and tabloid-writer-turned-mainstream writer Jeff Shapiro read an early version of my book manuscript, *A Mother Gone Bad*.

I also appeared on *Leeza* with investigative author Steven Singular (*Presumed Guilty*) and with the Ramseys' chief protagonist, Michael Tracey, the producer of a major pro-Ramsey documentary. All in all, I had a firsthand look at how the media investigated the murder. And it was eye-opening.

Those Who Embraced Our Forensic Analysis

In a sea of media darkness, some lights did shine. These individuals embraced the possibility that the ransom note contained vital information, key messages that needed to be decoded. *Dateline* producer Patrick Corbett was one of those lights. He spotted *A Mother Gone Bad* in New York on the desk of his immediate boss, Bruce Hagan, and was intrigued. Hagan himself didn't grasp the book (or the ransom note), but he quickly granted Corbett's request to borrow the book.

Patrick Corbett took to the deeper mind like a duck to water. After completing the book, he immediately called me, and we had several extensive discussions. Like a good reporter, he inquired about the scientific basis for my work and the clinical method I had applied to the note. He was curious about the newness of the method, those who used it, its acceptance, and its usefulness clinically—all good, thorough questions. After studying the note himself and utilizing our method, he believed I was onto something. In short order, he told me he wanted to do a story based on my book for *Dateline*. As an assistant producer, all he could do was submit a proposal—and he wasted no time coming up with one. He composed a thorough proposal, including a full script, and submitted it to his boss, hoping to gain his approval.

Corbett, in a nutshell, explains:

"Probably the majority of people believe the parents were involved in some way, and if they were, the extreme guilt they must feel could certainly result in a confession at some point. According to psychiatrist Andrew G. Hodges, this has already happened—and we just need to look and listen more carefully to the ransom note the killer left and what the Ramseys have said and done since the death of JonBenét. Therein lies the confessions, says Hodges . . . ."

Assistant producer Patrick Corbett expected some resistance to the idea—and he wasn't disappointed. His senior producer, Bob Calo, turned him down, but not because he disagreed. In fact, his boss said he thought I was right about the ransom note pointing to Patsy Ramsey and her motives. It made sense to him. But he wanted to wait until an indictment had been handed down before doing the show and felt *Dateline* would be accused of trying the Ramseys unfairly in the media.

The general public hasn't heard of our work, not because it isn't true, and not because it was over peoples' heads. Rather, it was because of a lack of courage and perhaps a misguided sense of justice, as well as a fear of the Ramseys suing the network. In the end, *Dateline* lost sight of its role to present the facts. Thus, the media overprotected the Ramseys at crucial moments (despite the Ramseys' complaints about media harassment). On the other hand, the Ramseys vociferously defended themselves on the airways, and producer Michael Tracey defended them in a one-sided television documentary which was produced in Britain and aired primarily on *The Arts and Entertainment* cable network. Unfortunately, the television media couldn't simply report the facts that professional communication specialists had determined that the ransom note pointed unequivocally to the Ramseys.

As my colleague Dr. James Raney pointed out in his journal review of my book, several members of the media missed the Ramseys' distinct invitation to them to discuss the matter. He says, "Their [the Ramseys'] public denial/disclosures, however, are further violations of the family frame of privacy and confidentiality. The disclosures are the license and invitation for an outsider, whether police detective, news analyst, or psychoanalyst, to investigate and make a hypothesis."[1]

By going public, the Ramseys were first saying, "Let's discuss this matter publicly." From there, they clearly invited the public to study them, to see if

---

[1] Raney, James O., M.D., "Who Killed JonBenét Ramsey? A Review of Andrew G. Hodges's *A Mother Gone Bad*," *International Journal of Communicative Psychoanalysis & Psychotherapy*, Vol. 11, Nos. 3-4, 1997, pp. 43-44.

they were lying, by making such statements as: "We have nothing to hide;" "here are our reasons for not talking with the police;" and "here are the reasons we couldn't have done it." The Ramseys asked to be examined and believed the public should respond if asked.

When the Ramseys brought their case to the American public, they in effect charged people with the responsibility of determining if the Ramseys were truthful. Each environment (family or public) demands integrity. If a person keeps a matter private, it remains private. However, once a person enters the public arena, claiming integrity and using the media to present his or her viewpoint, then the public has a right and responsibility to find out if the person is being truthful.

We see the same invitation in the ransom note. By leaving a written document at the crime scene, JonBenét's murderer (Patsy Ramsey in disguise) implicitly said, "See what you make out of this;" "see if you can figure this out;" "catch me if you can;" "these were my motives;" and " find me if you can, because I am taking a citizen's life." To keep the public from the information presented about the ransom note by available experts is to ignore the writer's and the Ramseys' public requests.

But Patrick Corbett had given me hope. Despite the ever-present obstacles the media created to prevent the truth from surfacing, some individuals from the media caught on. I remember the first night of my trip to Denver in August 1998 when my book initially came out. I had a few radio and television interviews scheduled, but nothing like I had expected. I was surprised at the lack of response, considering I was a professional who was presenting a new way of "profiling" and was making serious claims that the ransom note—the most crucial evidence—revealed the killer's identity. My publicist had arranged for a few interviews, and one reporter in particular, who himself had been interviewed on several national television shows as a local media expert, called to give me the lay of the land. He informed me that a significant battle was going on in the Denver/Boulder media and that those who leaned toward the Ramseys being guilty were coming under heavy criticism. Particularly, Peter Boyles, KHOW-AM talk radio show host, was among those being criticized.

The reporter further warned me that many would be resistant to what I had to say. Foremost among those were Lisa Rykman of *The Rocky Mountain News* and Daniel Glick, the *Newsweek* writer at the Denver bureau, both of whom to this day loudly (albeit indirectly) proclaim the Ramseys' innocence. The television reporter told me to forget about the largest paper in town, *The Rocky Mountain News*, because they weren't interested in anyone who thought the Ramseys were guilty. (Reporter Charlie Brennan, who had tried to remain balanced, had just gone on leave from the paper to work on Lawrence Schiller's book about the case, *Perfect Murder, Perfect Town*.) He also noted that Channel 9, KUSA, was distinctly pro-Ramsey. So much for objective journalism.

Many citizens of Denver, and especially of Boulder, were embarrassed by the continued publicity that had lasted for well over a year and a half by this time. Several Boulder bookstores refused to even carry my book, and the main Boulder paper, *The Daily Camera*, wouldn't interview me. People in Boulder wanted the case simply to go away. They didn't like anyone tarnishing their image of Fantasyland of the Yuppies, where the air was the cleanest in America.

In covering this hot national story in July 1998, the media was confused not only about how to evaluate new information, but also about its role. The overprotective media, who refused under any circumstances to see the Ramseys as guilty, had mixed the citizens' shame of such a crime occurring in such a "perfect town" with their opposing colleagues' sense of fair play into a powerful cocktail. Using "tabloid bashing" as a ramming force, pro-Ramsey factions had put some of the most reputable journalists on the defensive. Michael Tracey played on this in his pro-Ramsey documentary, and he coaxed statements out of these reputable journalists saying the tabloids had often gone too far. This implied that the media had totally victimized the Ramseys. As a result, the media was far too tentative and, therefore, ineffective.

Undeterred, Peter Boyles relentlessly publicized his observations about the Ramseys' strange behavior, often discussing their ongoing attempts to avoid interrogation even well over a year after the murder. Boyles had no hesitancy about inviting me on his show, and we finally met in person on my trip to Denver that summer. Likable and engaging, he was one of the few reporters who quickly grasped the essence of my work. He understood some fundamental things about how the mind perceives things in deeper ways. For example, we once discussed how dysfunctional married couples often find each other like radar, reading each other on deeper levels. Boyle understood that this was the same "radar" (deeper awareness) that the ransom note writer used to tell us her story, "radar" she didn't know she had. Of course this "radar" was her perceptive deeper intelligence, which not only picked up on her deepest motivations, but also communicated about her findings—in a sense sending out her radar to the public for them to pick up on her messages.

While I was in Denver, John Ramsey's presence, with all his money and power, was constantly lurking in the background. Word was out that John Ramsey intended on suing for libel as many people as he could if an indictment wasn't forthcoming. Many in the media were anxious. It was a very unsettling time. Carol McKinley, who was with the local Fox affiliate and who was the most prominent television reporter on the case, didn't back off (although her network did). She interviewed me during my stay in Denver, and later told a colleague she was impressed with my work. Word got back to Fox national, and they scheduled another interview for their national news. Eventually, as I found out later, the Fox legal department in New York canceled both of my interviews. The interview McKinley conducted never did run, and my national interview was "bumped" that day.

The concern over litigation is puzzling. According to the law, the Ramseys had clearly made themselves public figures, which meant they supposedly could be discussed in an open forum. As a citizen, I or anyone else could say what we wanted to about them as long as we didn't intentionally libel them. But the Ramseys obviously wanted the media to go down a one-way street. As long as the media would spin its party line, everything was perfect, but if it included other messages that contradicted the party line, it was slander. Sadly, the courts too often let money talk. This seems, in the Ramsey case, to have created an overly cautious media. The law itself is clear in defining the difference between slander and free speech, but the court's interpretations of that law aren't always so clear—or fair.

After my interview with Carol McKinley, another television reporter discovered my work and sought me out. After our interview, the reporter told me that "every reporter in Denver ought to be knocking your door down, but they won't because you're an outsider." Once again I had the ambivalent experience of hoping our findings would get out, but also of being discouraged by the overall lack of interest and exclusivity of the Denver media. Where, I wondered, were the real journalists who would report the whole story to the people? Almost everyone understood that the ransom note was the key to the case. Despite my professional qualifications, these findings about the note were being silenced.

Many reporters avoided dealing with the killer's deeper mind in the ransom note. If they acknowledged that the killer had a deeper mind that could be read, then they would have to admit that they did, as well. Unfortunately, this bias keeps the media from reporting the facts. I remember one young reporter who not only misquoted me, but who also had made up his mind from the beginning that he wanted nothing to do with the unconscious mind, all because he "didn't like people telling him what he was thinking." When reporters are more concerned about "the danger of reading minds" than about a killer's deeper mind communicating messages he or she wants to have heard, these reporters cannot hear a killer's secret confession and cry for justice. If they refuse to accept the way the killer gives them the smoking gun, they won't ever see it. If they refuse to look at a new understanding of the mind, they will continue to have a limited understanding of motivation, which goes to the heart of their work as investigative journalists.

Before I left Denver, I got a call from former Judge Catherine Crier's producer who asked me to appear with Denver attorney and former prosecutor Craig Silverman on her national show, *The Crier Report,* by remote from Denver. A reporter explained to me that either Fox wasn't worried because Crier was a lawyer or that since her show was considered to be more interview than "hard news," libel suits were less of a possibility. During the show, Silverman showed little interest in my evaluation of the ransom note, assuming that since the evaluation wasn't "hard science," it couldn't be used at all. (In our report to Kane, a legal expert would declare that our report could indeed be used in court.)

A year later, in the summer of 1999, Carol McKinley flew to Los Angeles, where my colleagues and I were presenting our new method of forensic document analysis—of gleaning hidden messages from communication such as letters—at an international forensic meeting. (As we mentioned then, we believe that our approach can be applied to communication in general, such as interrogations or 911 calls.) She came to interview me for the Fox national news, seemingly now allowed to because the media felt safer with the official stamp of academia on our work.

But John Ramsey was not shy about using his influence with the media. The director of a major television outlet in Atlanta told my publicist that he believed my work was accurate, but that he couldn't take the chance of offending the Ramseys, who were now living there. So he refused to interview me. Ironically, here I was—an Atlanta-trained psychiatrist (I completed my residency at Emory)—and the Atlanta media, by and large, wouldn't talk with me. However, John Ramsey, who must have had connections with Atlanta-based CNN, had quickly arranged to be interviewed by them immediately after the murder. Larry King's show was carried on CNN and many have wondered if this had something to do with his consistently overly sympathetic panel who regularly discussed the case. Dan Glick and Lisa Rykman, both clearly biased, were two of the three regular panelists.

The Tabloids: Closer to the Truth

For all the bashing the tabloids took, they unquestionably did the most thorough job of investigation. Even Chuck Green of *The Denver Post* said, regarding *The National Enquirer*, "They're good people." They put in the man-hours and had more people consistently on the case than anyone. I spoke with three different tabloid writers: Don Gentile at *The National Enquirer*, Joe Mullins of *The Globe*, and Art Dworken of *The National Examiner*. They were all straight with me, and all of them did articles about my book or our work. They checked out their stories, like good reporters should.

Not surprisingly, the tabloids were interested in my book. They were willing to explore cutting-edge approaches in print, though not completely for unselfish reasons. Nevertheless, they showed interest and courage by keeping an open mind. Even there, I ran into resistance at first. *The National Enquirer* canned Don Gentile's article about my early work on the case. But Joe Mullins (*The Globe*) wrote an outstanding article, accurately and creatively summarizing my findings. Later the *Enquirer* broke the story about my book coming out. A year later they were the print journalists who broke the story about our detailed report to Michael Kane.

We and the tabloids were indeed strange bedfellows. Here were my colleagues and I, with significant professional and academic credentials, presenting our findings on the ransom note—the smoking gun—and only a tabloid initially would publish them. Still, cutting-edge work must find exposure where it can. Of course, we knew that much of what the tabloids produce is sensationalistic. That's their market. But sometimes the truth is sensational and cutting-edge advances in any field almost always appear "far-out" at first. A major paper would be unlikely to admit a tabloid beat them to the punch, so publication in such a newspaper only increases mainstream media's desire to avoid whatever the tabloids have presented, whether the information is true or not. In their sometimes arrogant zeal to trash the tabloids, the media missed the heart of the JonBenét murder, while the tabloids at least reported it. Rarely did the media even show the people that the ransom note itself was the smoking gun.

Granted, this fact didn't come so easily for the tabloids either. I quickly discovered that the different writers all had their biases and were prone to consider themselves experts on—rather than reporters of—the case. Most of the writers had their own pet theories, which made it hard for them to really hear the killer in the note. Even though Joe Mullins of *The Globe* wrote as fine an article on my work as I could have hoped for, he never totally bought the new approach. In the end he was convinced I had simply read "the writer of the ransom note is a female cancer victim" into the note because I knew Patsy Ramsey had had cancer. Mullins did not fully understand how I had let the writer of the note guide me, and he disregarded my scientific method of investigation even though I carefully described to him how my colleagues and I use this open-minded approach on a daily basis in our clinical work. I continually waited on the writer of the note to repeat her ideas. In the end, like other investigators, he stuck with the ways of investigating that he already knew.

The media is a place where people should be able to turn for unbiased information—an impossible standard, but one the media should continually strive for. Unfortunately, when it came to looking at a breakthrough to the mind and to motivations, the media had no more interest in changing its ways of working than law enforcement did. This is simply because they are human beings. It is my hope that the investigative journalist of the future will maximize the understanding of motivation that the discovery of the deeper intelligence brings to the table.

CHAPTER 10
Reporters Who Don't Report

Most of the major reporters on the case walked all around the major evidence (the ransom note and the various Ramsey communications) and, like the police, missed the killer's deeper messages. Ironically, the investigators, men and women who specialize in language, didn't understand the killer's language. We tried to teach them to understand the special language of the killer's deeper intuition, and then pointed them toward crucial areas to investigate. Those writers who understand that language can have two meanings, literal and symbolic, shouldn't be shocked by this approach. They themselves us it every day. Sometimes reporters use literal examples, and sometimes they use symbolic examples. Very simply, we told them that the killer's symbolic examples revealed who she was. The problem wasn't that they couldn't grasp the idea; the problem was that they didn't like where the ideas led.

Dan Glick: *Newsweek*'s Man

In September 1997, a copy of the entire ransom note was published by *Newsweek*, the first major publication to do so. The note was accompanied by a lengthy article written by Dan Glick. Reading that issue of *Newsweek* started my involvement in the case, and I then began studying the ransom note for deeper messages from the killer. I wanted to see where these messages led, completely uninvested in who the killer might be. Because *Newsweek's* copy of the ransom note was directly responsible for my work, I turned to Dan Glick in February 1998, when I began to run into police resistance. I had hoped Glick would appreciate the ransom note's importance and be interested in our new way of investigating. Glick initially was responsive. After checking me out, he returned my phone call, and we had an extensive discussion. He was extremely personable, listened patiently for well over an hour, and seemed to welcome my expertise as he told me that

Newsweek had printed the letter over police objection for just this reason: "We were hoping people like you would come forward." In addition, I found out that Glick's father was an obstetrician, which encouraged me even further because I thought Glick would be open to hidden medical terms—particularly the disguised female psychology that is at the heart of the ransom note. Also, with his background in literature, he was well-acquainted with symbolic messages and even expressed a familiarity with the concept of the shadow side of man, which told me he was open to looking below the surface. I thought he could see beyond the Ramseys' continual propaganda that they were exclusively nice people who didn't possess a shadow side, who had no capacity for harboring painful emotions, including terror and rage. He seemed genuinely interested and agreed to look at my early evaluation, which I immediately sent.

After reviewing my work, instead of using it to show the public the hidden messages in the ransom note, Glick told me that he wanted "just the facts" and couldn't use it. We talked about the innovative approach I was presenting, which led to a discussion about science and about where criminal law and psychiatry intersect. He echoed the long-standing resistance to new ideas in science stating, "The system is weighted against innovation." Now Glick's deeper mind was trying to tell me the truth. Without realizing it, Dan Glick was talking about himself by confessing, "I am not open to new ideas." (The exact thing Patsy Ramsey herself confronted the Boulder authorities about.) But if science, which prides itself on innovation, isn't open to new ideas, then who will be? Glick intuitively showed us the problem with applying an innovative approach to document analysis on the ransom note: "The system" is against it. And what is this "system"? Law enforcement, district attorneys, and the media. Glick, in essence, was saying, "Forget about it. The system's going to ignore your work."

Glick went on to tell me that he could never write an article that would say, "This is who did it," and that it was "not my job to try any person." Finally he told me, "I will not use the hallowed pages of *Newsweek* to try anyone in the press." But I wasn't asking him to try anyone in the press or for him to say, "This is who did it." What I was asking him to do was to report the news—to merely say, "Dr. Hodges, a seemingly unbiased psychiatrist, says the ransom note tells us who did it." Glick easily could have checked out my approach with several experts around the world, and thus could have added, "And backing up Dr. Hodges's innovative claim of being able to use a criminal's own mind to reveal his or her motives are psychiatrists Dr. so and so, etc." I wasn't asking Glick to try anyone in the press. However, I *was* asking him to do what the ransom note writer asked him to do: to speak for JonBenét by showing the public how well the motives in the ransom note pointed directly at the Ramseys.

Reporters don't try cases; they report the facts as best they can. No matter what any reporter says, the killers will have their day in court. But Glick got his role confused and tried to be a lawyer—and, as it turned out, a document analyst—and in the process he totally abdicated his role as a reporter. He ultimately took on the role of a destructive gate-keeper, of one who didn't allow potential evidence to enter the public domain. He hid evidence in the face of the Ramseys' invitation to bring it out—as Dr. James Raney pointed out in his review of my book. (See Chapter 9, page 107.)

One of Glick's central problems, I believe, is common. On one hand, he was just too nice a guy. He was overly concerned about judging another human being. He thought he was on the jury, when he was a member of the press. He knew it was his job as a journalist to heighten awareness and to confront potential blind spots, but he misinterpreted this as voting for a conviction. But while being a person of integrity in his own eyes, he failed to use his power as an investigative reporter and appropriately inform the public. In actuality, he impeded the investigation by not reporting potential truth crucial to the case, particularly in light of law enforcement's failures and blind spots.

Glick repeatedly appeared on *Larry King Live* as a panel guest, and his demeanor was that of a low-key, somewhat laid-back but "show me" sort of person. His theme song was that the evidence wasn't impressive enough to point toward the Ramseys. He stated that there was nothing in their background to hint at such hostility (such a blanket statement is simply poor reporting). Both of the Ramseys had skeletons in their closet as far as their temperament went. Patsy had a mercurial temper, and John could be ruthless and cold at times. At the very least, Glick had made an incredibly naïve comment, especially coming from a reporter who claimed to understand that everyone possesses a shadow side. Even the public is no longer shocked to find that hundreds of times a year, parents with no prior criminal record or histories of violence kill their children.

But it wasn't that Glick was simply afraid of judging others—he was also afraid of being judged. In particular, I believe his behavior showed that he was afraid of the hostility inside of him. Years ago, Carl Jung wrote about "anima" and "animus," the two sides of man. One is whom we appear to be and the other is the rest of ourselves, which we hide. Often, Jung noted, our shadow side is the exact opposite of our external demeanor.

It's not hard to see Glick's hostility if we look closely. Glick stated that he just wanted the facts, but, of course, he meant the facts as he wanted them to be. As a journalist, he had to judge whether the ransom note contained facts or not. He did not consider the deeper mind patterns, thoughts, and the analysis of the particular thought patterns themselves in the ransom note to be facts. He wasn't a scientist who "had to wait" on fifty years of studies to definitively declare what the facts were. He was a journalist, a reporter, who merely had to look at the evidence presented in the thought patterns and tell us either: "They seem like facts to me" or "they don't." Once he was told about the existence of an innovative approach, Glick had to at the very least examine the existing evidence more thoroughly.

Instead, while appearing to be open-minded, Glick made a choice against the facts that several of my colleagues and I had established. He set himself up as judge and jury of our findings in the case, and quietly destroyed them—by failing to report them at all. While protesting against being judgmental, he quietly but ruthlessly judged those who disagreed with him. It later became common knowledge that Glick had mostly made up his mind about the case months before he ever talked to me. He had decided that the police lacked evidence, and he quickly bought into the idea that the police had made up their minds prematurely that the Ramseys were guilty. This became even more true when he was offered access to the Ramseys themselves and certain information, such as the ransom note, with the unspoken stipulation that he maintain his bias. Thus, when I came forward and told him what he didn't want to hear, he rather quickly ignored me without further investigation. In the end, Glick unwittingly spoke in defense of the very people who killed JonBenét—and he hid behind a smug self-righteousness, a false pride in being open-minded.

In this way, Glick displayed his shadow side. Good guy, family man, serious reporter, smart man, doctor's son—Dan Glick's shadow side has the capacity to destroy the truth, particularly truth he doesn't like. And so does every single human being in the world. But not everyone is a reporter, supposedly trained to be unbiased and to report events and findings, regardless of personal beliefs.

Newsweek should have responsibly reported our findings—an amazing story that reveals the greatness of the human mind we all possess. We also believe *Newsweek* could—and should—speak for a helpless six-year-old girl who was tragically murdered, especially when no one else will. This is what real journalists do. But Dan Glick never saw it—because his own shadow side was in the way.

Denver's Newspaper Reporters

Of course, *Newsweek* wasn't the only major national magazine on the case. *Time* magazine didn't give the case the pre-eminence *Newsweek* did. Not surprisingly, their national reporter on the case, Richard Woodbury, with whom I had minimal correspondence, had no interest in our work or in reading between the lines of the ransom note. Nor did *The New York Times'* major writer on the case, James Brooke, whose office was in Denver. Even so, his newspaper published a major article on linguist Donald Foster, whose involvement in the case proved to be unhelpful. Even when Foster told them he was a neophyte in psychological motivation and pointed them in the direction of document examiners who had expertise in motivation, Brooke looked no further. Glick's comments about "the system" not catching on to new knowledge continued to prove prophetic.

When *Newsweek*, *Time*, and *The New York Times* drop the ball, there's little hope that the local Denver and Boulder reporters would do any better—and for the most part, they didn't. In the end, three primary local reporters covered the case: Charlie Brennan (see below) and Lisa Rykman of *The Rocky Mountain News* and Chuck Green of *The Denver Post*. All of them frequently appeared on national television in various capacities, off and on for three years.

I had no contact with Lisa Rykman, who appeared to be the most overtly biased of the three. Rykman made plain in several comments that she had no use whatsoever for psychology or reading between the lines, and she continually demonstrated on national television an extreme inability to think psychologically. Everything to her was literal, and early on she was married to the idea that the Ramseys were mistreated by the press and that the evidence was too thin; therefore, she defended them. She couched her bias in "objective journalism," but if she was objective, she would have checked out our findings and would have told the public how well the Ramseys fit as suspects in such a case. Rykman was often referred to by many as the media princess of the pro-Ramsey faction. Like many in the case, she had a superficial view of motivation, and continued to be resistant to the possibility of the Ramseys' guilt.

Charlie Brennan and Lawrence Schiller: A "Perfect" Pair

My association with Charlie Brennan was short but extremely revealing. Brennan represented the largest paper in town, *The Rocky Mountain News*, and for the first year he was the most prominent reporter on the case. He was extremely well-connected to Alex Hunter's office, evident when I heard from him within a week of mailing my pre-publication book to Hunter. When Brennan called to inquire about my book and profile on the killer, he couldn't reveal his sources about how he'd heard of me. It wasn't difficult to figure out when, the same day, I got a call from Peter Boyles, who had also heard about the book. He called to ask me to be on his show and Boyles later revealed what I suspected—that Alex Hunter and his staff had been discussing my book.

Brennan had just gone on a leave of absence from his newspaper to work with Lawrence Schiller on *Perfect Murder, Perfect Town*. I agreed to send Brennan the book and, in return, I simply asked him to give me some feedback—good or bad. I never heard from him again, and he wouldn't return my phone calls. It is clear to me that Brennan avoided talking with me because he had already made a commitment to work on what was supposed to be the biggest book on the case, written by a noted author who had also written a huge book on the O.J. Simpson case. He believed in the project enough to take a leave of absence as a reporter covering one of the biggest murder cases in history, certainly the biggest case he would most likely ever work on. As he once admitted, outside of Denver he had been an unknown and now he was nationally known. Now he had had an opportunity to do something even bigger—the book. Then, out of nowhere, comes someone who claims that this was far from a perfect murder and states that the killer has confessed.

If my allegations about the ransom note were right, what would that do to Brennan's plans? Under the circumstances, how receptive do you suppose he would be to the new information? Certainly, this might explain his complete avoidance of me and his refusal to even communicate with me—after he gave me his word he would do so. It seems that he quickly discounted my work.

So here was Charlie Brennan, who had my book *A Mother Gone Bad*. I wonder if it didn't prove useful to him—but not as I had intended. He maintained a professional association with Lawrence Schiller, whose plans for a big book on the case panned out better than he could have hoped. It became a bestseller and was later adapted for television. Interestingly, Lawrence Schiller never referred to my book in his massive work on the case, but he mentioned virtually everybody else who had any connection with the case. Certainly, Brennan would have discussed my book with Schiller. In fact, it became quite obvious that Schiller knew of my work.

Prior to my work with the ransom note, no one had noticed the numerous cancer references in the note. I found it interesting that one day after his book came out, Schiller commented on the reference (which I had already made) to survival percentages in the ransom note, to its possibility of pointing to cancer victim Patsy Ramsey as the author. Did Schiller come up with this on his own? If he believed that the writer would unconsciously give herself away by the use of certain phrases and ideas, then why didn't he consult with an expert in unconscious communication? And why didn't he allude to other cancer images in the ransom note? If he was interested in hidden messages in the ransom note, particularly about cancer and motives, don't you suppose he would be interested in a book such as mine? He even put the ransom note in the front of his book (just as I did), indicating its importance.

Understandably, Schiller was hell-bent on reporting one thing: a perfect murder. The last news he wanted to hear was that the killer had left a "perfect confession." Patsy Ramsey would have stolen most of his Schiller's thunder. And that would have exposed his lack of expertise. (Actually, I am indebted to Schiller because his book with O.J. Simpson was instrumental in showing me how criminals will confess between the lines and this eventually spurred me to get involved with the ransom note.)

Schiller reacted as someone typically does when he has turf to protect: He marginalizes anyone who disagrees with him. In no way did the author of *Perfect Murder* want to draw any attention to *A Mother Gone Bad: The Hidden Confession of JonBenét's Killer*. Schiller's style, it seems, is to keep the stage for himself, evident as he refuses to go on a show with any another person (author, investigator, etc.) besides the interviewer.

In addition, many reviewers of Schiller's book have commented on his failure to come to any clear conclusions, that he simply reported what most people already knew, albeit adding interesting details. He left the reader and the case up in the air. That's sad when there's evidence going overlooked that brings the killers down to earth.

Jeff Shapiro and Frank Coffman: Two Men in Over Their Heads

Reporter Jeff Shapiro also gained notoriety from the case. Initially hired by *The Globe* to do undercover investigating and reporting, Shapiro wormed his way into the case by alternately trying to befriend John Ramsey's son, John Andrew, and by feigning interest (as a Jew) in converting to Christianity in order to get closer to the Ramseys at their church in Boulder. Eventually he crossed over to mainstream journalism after berating the tabloids for their investigative excesses. Later, Shapiro wrote John Ramsey a personal letter, apologizing for his behavior in the case. The most amazing part of the letter, though, was when Jeff Shapiro assured John Ramsey that he believed he was innocent.

Shapiro saw a pre-publication copy of my book through Frank Coffman, a contact in Boulder, and reportedly told Coffman, "It's too psychological." Too much about deeper motivation. Too much from the unconscious mind. It is a typical reaction from an unpredictable twenty-three-year old who's in way over his head. But Shapiro put his finger on the problem when it came to psychology. The psyche—in particular his psyche—was too much for Shapiro to handle.

When Shapiro became uncomfortable with some of his journalistic tactics and for being overly zealous to convict the Ramseys, he did an immediate about-face, turning on *The Globe* in the same judgmental nature he had been using on the Ramseys, while grandiosely telling everyone he was certain of John Ramsey's innocence. With such wishy-washiness, how could anyone know when to believe Shapiro? Where did he suddenly gain the necessary investigative credentials and expertise in document analysis to declare anyone's innocence? Psychologically, it seems clear that Shapiro was out of control as an investigator, so he blamed his employer for his behavior, and then proceeded to demonstrate the same grandiose lack of self-control in another direction—obviously controlled by hidden guilt for being so destructive in the first place. Shapiro was "overdoing" in an effort to "undo" what he felt guilty about—a typical dysfunctional behavior.

Frank Coffman, my Boulder contact and part-time reporter, had the same problem as Shapiro. He made the national news when John Ramsey assaulted him in December 1998 outside a Boulder restaurant after Coffman took his picture. Previously, when I was researching A Mother Gone Bad, Frank had been very helpful in giving me the lay of the land in Boulder. But we reached a striking impasse when Coffman became overwhelmed by the possibilities of the human mind. He insisted that the deeper mind—in particular, the ransom note writer's mind—could not observe and communicate as I indicated it did. Without any training in psychology or having done one hour of psychotherapy, Frank Coffman felt he was qualified as an expert in psychiatry, psycholinguistics, and document analysis. Even when I tried to reason with him by referencing the latest literature, he remained closed-minded. Once again, psychology was too much for an investigator.

I have wondered if Coffman really didn't want me or anyone except the person of his choosing to solve the case. As a Boulderite, he felt a unique sense of ownership of the case and conveyed a touch of "detective envy." Another lay person, someone similar to Coffman, was honest enough to educate me about this phenomenon. As a member of the Internet community in another state interested in the case, this person went to a nationwide meeting in Boulder. There he likewise experienced the sense of others who were outside his particular Internet group as intruding on his case—and others in the group shared the same feelings. They later laughed at themselves, but their response spoke volumes about how human beings tend to think—even when it comes to solving the murder of a helpless little girl. But are these people different from Boulder's journalists, policemen, district attorneys, reporters, authors, or psychiatrists? Didn't many of them have problems acknowledging other experts? Our legal expert, Dean Parham Williams, was well-acquainted with the problem. When we asked him about re-approaching Michael Kane, he discouraged it and commented on how territorial district attorneys could get.

TV Talking Heads: Larry King and Geraldo Rivera

Two renown reporters each had difficulty hearing JonBenét's killer. Two and a half years after the murder, Larry King was still asking, "Would somebody please tell me a motive?" And the ransom note writer herself tried to tell him—on his own show with millions of viewers watching and listening. In September 1997, immediately after Princess Diana's tragic death, Patsy Ramsey called Larry King while he was on the air. She publicly berated the paparazzi, whom she insisted caused Diana's death. In the process, Patsy connected Britain's princess to America's princess, JonBenét (so proclaimed by Patsy). She felt compelled to call King's show to publicly blame someone for murdering a princess. Thinking like a reporter should, King should have been able to see the possibility that Patsy was unconsciously talking about herself—and confessing. But King is not used to thinking psychologically; he's not used to trying to read between the lines. He is in the business of getting the answer he needs by sharp questioning—but that's not how the mind works.

We in psychology now know that the way to effectively question people is to see where their examples or ideas go. This is particularly true of people who have a vested interest in denying the truth. Reporters must give up the myth that only sharp, aggressive, direct questioning produces the truth. Any reporter worth his salt would realize that if the Ramseys were guilty, they had a vested interest in hiding the fact. An astute reporter would listen for where their ideas and their examples go, because this is how a person's real conscience speaks.

But reporters aren't used to thinking psychologically. In fact, they aren't even trained to do so. This is why on a special interview Patsy granted just for his show, Geraldo Rivera missed all the messages from Patsy Ramsey, messages confirming her guilt. When special investigative reporter Jennifer Kay interviewed Patsy exclusively for Geraldo's show in November 1997, Patsy repeatedly confessed to the crime through a series of stories (and slips)—

even to the point of mentioning for the first and only time that she'd made an egregious error with JonBenét. If Geraldo had been educated about the mind, he could have easily read Patsy Ramsey between the lines. For example, as she spontaneously reminisced about how JonBenét could stand on her head, and how long she could hold the pose, Geraldo would have seen how Patsy was confessing that she and John Ramsey were themselves holding a pose and had turned the investigation upside down.

The Book Reviewers

Book reviewers are media insiders who attempt to capture the essence of a book and distill it for the general audience. Needless to say, like all other reporters—and human beings—their immediate perception is all too often colored by their own personalities. Even fine writers, like Joyce Carol Oates, are no exception. Oates reviewed my book, *A Mother Gone Bad*, for *The New York Review of Books* and characterized it as "the most idiosyncratic of the books" on the Ramsey case. While she felt my deconstruction of the ransom note was ingenious, she went on to call my book "overkill" and portrayed it as somewhat obsessive in its focus on the ransom note—particularly mocking the breakthrough on which the book was based. She minimized how Patsy's Christmas letters dovetailed with the ransom note and obviously had not done her homework as she focused on the most obscure and least convincing of the letters. Ultimately, she declared the book lacking in original thinking, comparing it to the works of a creative Canadian crime writer.

Clearly, Oates is resistant to new ideas to the point she can't see them—particularly ideas related to the mind (and her mind). My colleague Patrick Callahan laughed about her impression that the book lacked originality. All I was purposing (as we had proposed to Kane in our report) was that the killer's mind had secretly observed her deeper motives and told us herself exactly what happened at the crime scene, confessing between the lines.

Interestingly, while Oates wasn't impressed with Patsy Ramsey's repeated messages explaining the crime, she was impressed with my analysis about JonBenét 's recent problems with encopresis (soiling) immediately before the murder. Oates lapsed into a lengthy section on JonBenét 's bowel habits, clearly an anal (no pun intended) and obsessive focus on this trivial aspect to the case (in contrast to the genius Patsy Ramsey demonstrated in the ransom note). Without realizing it, Oates was also confessing to soiling my work, my colleagues' work, and most importantly Patsy Ramsey's desperate and brilliant work to solve the crime. Vividly, Oates portrays the typical resistance, showing how people—from reporters to district attorneys— treat new ideas that threaten them. They become anal and focus on unnecessary details in order to distract themselves. They, in essence, treat new ideas like s—. They attempt to marginalize and ridicule new ideas without ever investigating them further.

Another reporter made the same error. APBNews.com's Diane Freeman reviewed my book with two "far out" books, lumping us all under the heading, "Ramsey case produces books who [sic] skate near the edge." She included my work with a book by a former employee of John Ramsey who claimed to have consulted a medium and to have talked to JonBenét about the murder—along with a second book stemming from a discussion group made up of wealthy people who fly to exotic locations and explore a particular crime. Without once looking at the scientific underpinnings of my work or talking to any other professional familiar with the new work in psycholinguistics, Freeman simply characterized me as weird. I understand at first glance it seems strange to listen for deeper communication, but good reporters take more than one glance. They not only take a good look; they put things underneath a microscope. Both Oates and Freeman demonstrate the continued tendency to jump to conclusions that we've seen over and over again—and the failure of investigators to truly investigate

If they had investigated, they wouldn't have had to look far to run into my colleague James Raney's review of my book in a professional journal (see Chapter 9, page 107). Raney commented, "Hodges suggests that this method of scientific psychological investigation of the text and context of criminal actions can offer important dimensions to criminal investigation. If this book is an example, his case is quite convincing. The book reads like a good detective story. From the technical point of view, most therapists would find the approach interesting and useful. The theory and exposition of the grim psychology . . . of a woman in stress is illuminating."[1]

---

[1] Raney, James O., M.D., "Who Killed JonBenét Ramsey? A Review of Andrew G. Hodges, *A Mother Gone Bad,*" *International Journal of Communicative Psychoanalysis & Psychotherapy,* Vol. 11, Nos. 3-4, 1997, pp. 43-44.

A Bizarre Theory Sells: Steven Singular

Steven Singular, author of *Presumed Guilty*, presented a far-out theory of JonBenét 's murder. Singular's book, which received strong media attention when it appeared in 1998, took the media to task for its treatment of the Ramseys. His bizarre contention is that JonBenét had become involved in child pornography because her father wanted to further her pageant career. Child pornography was supposedly the price of admission to the upper echelons of the pageants. Singular speculated that John Ramsey had, without Patsy's knowledge but for her sake, tried to enable JonBenét 's career by allowing her to be photographed in sexual ways. Then, on Christmas night, a photographer supposedly had secretly taken JonBenét off the premises with her father's knowledge, and things had gotten out of hand. Singular further hypothesized that a kinky sex game resulted in JonBenét's death and her body was returned home, leading to the cover-up by the parents. Thus, Singular suggested that neither parent actually murdered JonBenét .

Singular's theory is based on nonexistent evidence. Even his colleague Michael Tracey confronted him on the *Leeza* show (see below), telling him he didn't have even half a leg to stand on. But Singular surely tells us that he was concerned with alleviating the Ramseys' guilt, that it wasn't murder, it was a mistake. Singular was preoccupied with people who were seemingly being victimized and with avoiding guilt. Prior to this he had written a book about O.J. Simpson that centered around what he believed to be police prejudice and mishandling of the evidence—another "somebody done somebody wrong" angle.

But there is another reason he wrote about JonBenét's murder. In a fascinating sequence toward the end of the book, Singular refers to the power of the unconscious mind and then, without realizing it, he talks about himself: "The unconscious mind seemed to be running amok . . . ," which he linked specifically to a prominent television talk-show host unknowingly enabling a corrupt author (in Singular's mind) to promote his book. Singular's example was Oprah Winfrey having the "evil" Mark Fuhrman on her show. Singular specifically chose this example himself, suggesting deep down that he realizes the media enabled him to exploit JonBenét's death in his own book when they should have ignored him. Shortly after that, Singular wrote, "We could use sex to promote or sell anything: razor blades, tires, or bottles of beer . . ." and books, as he just reminded us.

As if he couldn't say it enough, Singular immediately writes an extensive section about writers—tabloid reporters involved with the JonBenét story who exploit and destroy people with half-truths and inflammatory lies. Like other investigators, Singular intuitively knows his motives and suggests he wrote the book to sexually exploit the situation in order to sell books. A few pages later, he writes about Patsy Ramsey's failure to recognize her involvement in the sexualization of JonBenét .

Singular adds his voice to the choir that suggests investigators in the JonBenét case needed to be more thorough. But his is one more voice that, without realizing it, is talking about himself.

Bully on the Set: Michael Tracey

The biggest thorn in the side of the prosecution (as far as the media is concerned) was Michael Tracey, a transplanted British journalism professor at the University of Colorado in Boulder, who ended up producing the major documentary on the case so far. Several months after the murder, Tracey invited Patsy Ramsey to speak to his class about her experience with the media and offered her a non-threatening supportive environment.

Patsy Ramsey convincingly told her tale of woe to his class, the same version she and John Ramsey have tried to sell all along: "We're loving parents who could not possibly have had the slightest motive for killing our daughter. Can't you see we're fine upstanding citizens and Christian people who have had a perfect track record? The evil Boulder police just assumed we're guilty and the sensationalistic media particularly the tabloids have unjustly crucified us." And Michael Tracey bought it—hook, line, and sinker. I know because Tracey behaved with me almost certainly as the Ramseys' mouthpiece, showing his true colors.

We met on the set of *Leeza* in September 1999, one month before the grand jury's decision. Originally, my colleague Patrick Callahan and I were to appear together to discuss the report we had given to Michael Kane and to offer a counterpoint to Steven Singular. *Leeza's* producers reportedly were uncomfortable enough with Singular's perspective that they wanted another viewpoint. Eventually, *Leeza's* producers decided that if Callahan and I would appear together, it would look as though we were ganging up on Singular. The new plan called for Singular and me alone to discuss the case one-on-one.

When I arrived at Paramount studios (the company that owns *Leeza*) in Los Angeles, I was surprised to find that Michael Tracey was also there. *Leeza* had personally invited Tracey to appear with us, reportedly as a courtesy to him because I was going to use clips from his documentary to show how the Ramseys had confessed "between the lines." It seemed that *Leeza's* producers unwittingly were doing to me what they hadn't wanted to do to Singular.

The producer who was working with me informed me about the change in plans when she greeted me. I had first noticed Tracey in passing when I was backstage in the dressing room area, and I had wondered why he was there. But I figured that either he would be on our show or they were taping a separate show with him. It really didn't bother me initially. I didn't mind reasonable discussion and differing viewpoints, and I thought ultimately that Tracey had done the case a favor by capturing Patsy and John Ramsey on tape. I even had the fantasy that he might find it interesting to consider the possibility that the Ramseys were telling him valuable things he wasn't aware of, revealing personal information to him that they had done nowhere else. I wasn't naïve enough to think he would agree with me on national television, but I thought he might at least listen. But I quickly found out that listening was the last thing on Tracey's mind.

I should have suspected something given his behavior backstage. "My" producer had introduced me to Singular, who was cordial. It was after that when I first spotted Tracey. As the next moments unfolded, I saw that he and Singular obviously knew one another. They engaged in a lengthy conversation on one side of the gathering area outside our individual dressing rooms. Finally, just as we were going on the set, I stopped and introduced myself to Tracey, who was continuing to talk to Singular. His offered a clipped response, but had made no effort to meet me.

Tracey's documentary had painted the media and the tabloids in the worst possible light, which meant the Ramseys looked like poor victims for whom you would feel sorry. Many who follow the case closely now refer to Tracey's documentary as the "Ramsey infomercial." Tracey had managed to get British backing for the documentary, which first aired on British television in the summer of 1998. Eventually, the documentary was picked up in the United States and has repeatedly run on the A & E cable network. In a nutshell, it portrays the Ramseys as victims of the police and the media.

On *Leeza*, the plans had called for Michael Tracey to have a somewhat lesser role than Singular or I. For the first segment of the one-hour show, the producers placed him in the audience, while Singular and I remained on stage, discussing the case. Leeza involved the audience in her interviews, as is her style, and quickly included Tracey from the start.

I was prepared for give-and-take, even for strong emotions at times, but mostly I was prepared for rational discussion. However, I was *not* prepared for was *The Jerry Springer Show*. I reviewed for the audience the communications and confession my colleagues and I had seen. I pointed these out using an enlarged copy of the three-page note, one page each on three separate easels. When Leeza turned to Tracey for a response, his first comments differed from mine, as expected. But suddenly he began to vehemently and irrationally attack our work. Tracey erupted, "Junk science! Voodoo science!" and continued by making other hostile comments such as, "It's unconscionable to accuse people of murder on national television." His response continued like that for the rest of that segment. It took me a minute to get my balance.

For the second and third segments, Tracey was on stage between Singular and me, obviously placed center stage. He alternated between speaking sweetly with Leeza and attacking whatever I said. He showed no interest in listening, only in defending the Ramseys. He believed every rationalization the Ramseys presented, and then added some of his own. When I pointed out the Ramseys' deeper communications shown in his own documentary— their slips, their body language, their obvious anxiety, John Ramsey's communications indicating discomfort and guilt around the subject of sexual abuse, their preoccupation with cancer—it made no difference.

Tracey tried to portray me as someone who was intentionally persecuting the Ramseys. When I pointed out a legal expert thought our work was courtroom-worthy evidence against the Ramseys, he ignored the statement. But Tracey's most striking behavior occurred off-camera, between takes. There I saw firsthand what he was really about. He leaned over, and with an angry snarl, half-whispered to me, "You ought to be ashamed of what you've done. It's unconscionable." Then he showed who he really was when he said, "We'll see who's left standing when this is over. We'll see what happens." I knew he was John Ramsey's mouthpiece. It had been rumored that the Ramseys planned to sue anyone who pointed toward their guilt. It became clear who

Michael Tracey was speaking for. And it reinforced to me what kind of people the Ramseys had become.

As Tracey continued his diatribe against me and our work on-camera, I made plain we had no ax to grind and, pointing once more to the enlarged three-page ransom note to our right, I simply said, "The killer spoke in that note, and we went where the evidence took us."

Tracey's bias is inexcusable, but it may be understandable. He made the same error Smit and Kane had made: He claimed expertise he didn't have. He knew nothing about document analysis or psychology. Worst of all, he demonstrated unprofessionalism in his chosen career. A man who claims to be a media journalist, who presents a documentary designed to get at the truth, has a clear responsibility to his audience—to thoroughly investigate and impartially present the issues. And if he is a teacher of future journalists, he has an even greater responsibility. Most of all, he has a moral responsibility not only to present the truth, but to aid the cause of justice, first for JonBenét and then for the American people.

Michael Tracey not only shirked his responsibility to investigate thoroughly and open-mindedly, but he also failed his students as a role model. Journalism students who might have witnessed his behavior on the *Leeza* show would have seen a textbook case in how *not* to do it. Tracey couldn't tolerate anyone disagreeing with him and had no desire to look further at his own work, important work that revealed hidden messages and deeper meanings in the Ramseys' communications, information no one else had obtained. (See Chapter 12, page 147.) Sadly, he lacked the capacity to appreciate a new investigative method, backed by experts from several other fields including criminology, law, and law enforcement. As a teacher of future journalists, he bypassed an opportunity to be on the cutting edge of investigative techniques. Instead, he continued to claim expertise while simultaneously undermining justice and enabling two murderers to remain free.

The show never ran. According to *Leeza's* producer, Paramount officials canceled it for reasons unknown (perhaps due to the uncertain legal climate), which was unfortunate because the public would have seen the most overt of the Ramsey defenders unmasked for the inadequate investigator he was.

All along he tried to portray himself as simply a defender of the oppressed and a seeker of justice and fair play for the Ramseys. He insisted that he didn't know who committed the crime, and the issue was the media's completely unfair treatment of the Ramseys. According to Tracey, the court should decide their guilt or innocence and the media had no business commenting on guilt or making accusations. All this was under the guise of being a tolerant, open-minded investigator. But his actions on national television betrayed him. He wasn't concerned about justice, only in defending his false ideas about objectivity—and about the Ramseys' "innocence."

CHAPTER 11
Split Decision—Chuck Green

Of the three reporters, I had by far the most contact with *The Denver Post's* Chuck Green, with whom I spoke at length on several occasions. In the end, Green became an example of how stress and personal issues in a reporter's life can affect his reporting. In general, Green was a no-nonsense, sometimes cynical journalist—a Marine with a pen in his hands. Because of his strong suspicions about the Ramseys, I had approached him after Beckner's lack of response. Likable and forthright, he expressed interest in my early work, and in February 1998 agreed to review my "profile" of the ransom note and discuss it with me. As months went by, he was always too busy to look at it in depth, but kept assuring me that he read everything I wrote and wanted more time to explore the details.

By the time *A Mother Gone Bad* came out in July 1998, Green and I had still not talked at length. Then we had several short contacts by phone before finally having two lengthy discussions in late August. During our initial short conversations, Green told me that someone from the DA's office had said the second half of my book was better than the first, which I found interesting because the first half, where I focused on decoding the ransom note, was the key to the case. Certainly the second half was easier reading, but ease should have little to do with it—we were talking about doing detective work and uncovering motives. Green also talked about his recent experience, discussing the Michael Tracey documentary on an hour-long television special in Denver in which the media "argued over the evidence." In another brief conversation a week later, Green was more optimistic that JonBenét's murderer could be brought to justice after Detective Steve Thomas had confronted the DA's failure to aggressively prosecute.

From the beginning Green had difficulty with the idea of disguised messages from the killer's deeper intuition. I wasn't surprised by this because it's normal for someone with his "tough guy" reputation to want "just the facts." Green was a "left brainer" and particularly resisted using the "right brain."

But he slowly warmed to the idea that thought patterns, "thoughtprints," might exist. After all, as a journalist, he already knew that words could be used both literally and symbolically.

In our first lengthy conversation, Green initially made seeming small talk about the Clinton–Monica Lewinsky scandal and told me, "I don't know who to believe." Then he told me as far as my work went, he was "85 percent there" and he needed "to be persuaded." He primarily expressed doubts about my finding hidden messages—second-level communication—not only in the ransom note, but in everyday conversation. Green had difficulty with my contention that Patsy Ramsey's thoughtprints regarding her terror of cancer were there in her Christmas letters before the murder, as well as in the ransom note. Certainly, he insisted, cancer was a common topic in everyday conversation, one that, he said, most people mentioned "four or five times a day." He then told me about losing his mother to cancer twenty years prior when he was around thirty.

At that point, I walked him back through the distinctive thoughtprints in the ransom note and through all the Ramsey communications, showing him the consistency of their thoughtprints. After a period of significant discussion, he told me, "That's all I can take at this time," and we agreed to continue the conversation the following week. Within the next two weeks, we spoke two more times and reviewed in depth the ransom note and all the Ramsey communications, which clearly pointed to their motives. Finally, Green told me, "You've made a disciple out of me." Immediately, however, referring to himself as the devil's advocate, he once again questioned the significance of "trivial communications," such as a misplaced period in the ransom note.

Nevertheless, I felt he had begun to grasp how the killer had clearly communicated a second story in the ransom note. He ended our talk by telling me about how he had been struck by the Ramseys' response to a question in their second major public interview (one with selected media on May 1, 1997). A reporter had asked them, "Does JonBenét's killer deserve death?" John Ramsey immediately responded, "Yes." But Patsy began crying and couldn't speak. (Earlier, John's son John Andrew had said that his wish for the killer was "forgiveness.")

Two weeks later, in mid-September 1998, Green and I spoke again. He still had failed to write anything about the ransom note. As we began our conversation, he told me he couldn't talk for long because of his grief over the loss of "his producer," Bruce Hagan on *Dateline* where Green was a frequent guest. Tragically, Hagan had drowned in a freak sailing accident in New York. Green also was dealing with his dog's terminal cancer. Green and his wife had no children and were extremely attached to their keeshond, Gus, on whom they had spent large sums of money for chemotherapy.

Then he mentioned for the first time that he would like for me to discuss my work with ex-FBI profiler Greg McCrary in a three-way conversation. Green had once spent a long evening with McCrary, who had greatly impressed him as "insightful and methodical," and he thought McCrary and I would be useful to each other. He also told me that "McCrary, more than anyone, would give you weight with Alex Hunter." Green insisted, "I'm anxious to set up the conversation and let him listen to your theory," but in asking for this meeting, he had added another condition before he would write anything about my approach to the ransom note. He told me he planned to call McCrary in the next few days to "get all of us to go over the ransom note together." Overall, my continual strategy had been to let the ransom note speak for itself and to particularly demonstrate how it clearly identified the killer's motives for the murder. I still held out hope that Green would tell the writer's (and JonBenét's) story because he seemed impressed with how well the motives shown in the note fit Patsy and John Ramsey.

Two weeks went by without hearing from Green, so I called him again on September 29, 1998, immediately after Lou Smit had released his letter declaring the Ramseys innocent. In typical fashion, Green said, "Lou Smit doesn't mean a damn thing," and added that the prosecutor ought to call Smit before the grand jury and let him show what he knows. He was confident Smit would be discredited as someone who had become emotionally involved with the Ramseys because of their common interests and as someone who was "all hunches" and who had "no real evidence." Somewhat unconcerned, Green pointed out that "the Ramsey attorneys already know everything the DA's thinking anyway." He didn't think Smit would have a great effect on the case (which proved to be wrong and about which I disagreed with him more as the case unfolded). Green also told me that he had suggested to Peter Boyles that he have me on his radio show to discuss Smit's motives in light of my work on motives (which he did).

The normally tough-minded journalist further discussed his take on the case. Green felt that, in a case without strong evidence, the DA's best bet was to get the grand jury to charge Patsy Ramsey with first-degree murder and to isolate her in jail. Then, he thought, she might break. But he agreed with me that the DA's office was struggling with deciding whom to charge and he seemed convinced by my argument that only the ransom note settled the question of the primary perpetrator. Green went on to tell me about discussing my book with a prosecutor over breakfast. He didn't know how seriously the prosecution had considered it, but thought that they ought to "figure out a way to use it." He added that they wouldn't until they were convinced that they could get it into court. He said there was "a severe problem with evidence, and unless they overcome that—until it was a compelling case evidentiary-wise, the case would have no energy."

At that point, Green told me in no uncertain terms he would be interested in helping me get my work before Alex Hunter and his staff, stating, "It's *as strong or stronger than* anything else they have." Then he informed me that he still hadn't reached McCrary, emphasizing again that I could "help the police with the motive." Then he told me about discussing Lou Smit's letter himself on MSNBC and advised me to "cover quickly" the motives on Peter Boyle's talk show.

Over the next five weeks, I checked with Green on several occasions, but he never contacted McCrary. Along the way, the ransom note had become even clearer to me. Two more things emerged: how clearly the killer was asking the police to speak for her and JonBenét, and how clearly the note revealed the order of events the night of the murder. Green himself was particularly impressed with the order of events when I reviewed my findings with him, but again he wanted to see what McCrary thought. I stressed with him again the need to speak for JonBenét and the increasing possibility that the entire case might come down to whether or not he did, since no journalist was reporting the case despite the killer's instructions. Just considering that kind of responsibility seemingly made him nervous as he suddenly laughed in a high-pitched voiced and immediately replied, "Uh oh."

Green's responses varied greatly. At points, he would be entirely resistant to looking deeper at the ransom note, as if we were back at square one and he had never heard the first explanation of how the mind works and communicates on two levels. This unquestionably correlated with the continued decline of his dog. One night near the end, I called him at his home as we'd agreed upon and Green told me that Gus's head was resting in his lap, that the dog hadn't taken any fluids and was near the end. We talked about Gus's personality, comical and loyal. A few days later, Gus died and Green wrote a moving column about him—about what a perfect dog he'd been. He contrasted the advantages of having such a loyal dog with the troubles a child could cause, implying that people were better off having dogs than kids. More importantly, he conveyed that losing Gus was like losing a child (the child the Greens never had).

In the end, his pain was too much for Green. The grief over losing his dog, of never having children, of the painful loss of his mother to cancer, and the sudden death of his friend in the sailing accident buried him. He told me so himself. Despite his continued promises to follow up with McCrary, he never did so, and the few times I called him after Gus died, he became irritable when I tried to talk with him about the case. "I told you I'm not going to do anything until I talk to McCrary," he said. Later, referring to my work, he said, "I can't get this in 480 words [the length of his column]," and I was surprised when he informed me that readers got upset if he even mentioned JonBenét anymore. Clearly, the deep psychological truth about JonBenét was too much for Green, because his own pain was overwhelming him.

The absurdity of not being able to get an explanation of the killer's deeper messages in the ransom note in his column strains belief. Under normal circumstances, a passionate man like Green would never let readers keep him from speaking out for JonBenét if he felt the need. All he would have had to do was to write something like, "An unbiased psychiatrist with a new method of document analysis says the killer confesses between the lines of the ransom note by secretly providing motives. He's no kook; his work has been endorsed by several experts and FBI agents experienced in kidnappings. The ransom note writer, he says, tells us that she lost her mind when she discovered her husband, John Ramsey, molesting their daughter. I've seen his report, and it's stronger than anything the DA has thus far. Could we now have a reasonable explanation of the missing motives—and of why the Ramseys could have murdered their daughter? Is this the smoking gun the authorities are looking for? One psychiatrist thinks so. The question, he says, is does the ransom note writer speak for JonBenét? Stay tuned."

Green's reasoning ability was suspect in other areas, as well. Why did he need McCrary's approval? The best McCrary could do was tell Green my work was interesting. McCrary had no credentials or training in decoding forensic documents and, apart from reading crime scenes for non-verbal clues, was unfamiliar with how the mind communicated in two different ways. Every time I encouraged Green to consult with a recognizable authority in my field to validate my work, he would discount the suggestion. Even though Green repeatedly promised to finalize a joint meeting with McCrary (who he said was interested in talking with me), he never did. All the while, Green continued to express interest in what I was doing and even asked me to send him a more in-depth profile of the Ramseys that I had developed.

As Christmas 1998 neared, Green discussed with me his uncertainty over what he would write in his column on the two-year anniversary of JonBenét's death and when he would write it. He felt that writing about the murder on Christmas Day might be too much of a downer for his audience, so he thought instead he would write about JonBenét in his December 27th column. I encouraged him once more to speak for JonBenét, but when he kept talking about how painful the subject was for his readers, I later realized he was talking about himself.

Chuck Green never wrote a column telling his readers about the motives the killer made plain in the ransom note. Also, never to my knowledge did he truly attempt to set up a meeting with McCrary. I last talked to Green on December 24, 1998. He told me that he'd disagreed with Peter Boyles all along and thought that there was only a 50 percent chance of an indictment, and that "we'd never see Patsy Ramsey in an orange jump suit." He thanked me several times for taking the time to talk to him, but the leading reporter on the case was to never mention my work. His comment about Patsy Ramsey proved prophetic. When confronted with the biggest question his readers had—who did it and why?—Green was silent. But he also clearly told us why it was too much for him, too big an emotional issue to fit in his column, too much grief for his readers, the main one being himself.

Ironically, Green's pain, the grief, and the death that surrounded him were eerily similar to that which haunted the Ramseys and Lou Smit (and possibly to a degree Michael Kane, who had just gone through a divorce). The problem wasn't simply that these investigators didn't recognize the truth presented in our findings—the problem was that it was too much for them. About Green, in particular, I've wondered if he was unconsciously protecting Patsy Ramsey because of her cancer, which identified her with his mother who had suffered with cancer. I recall he initially objected strongly to hidden messages of cancer in the ransom note, mostly likely because of his own mother having been a cancer victim. Under those circumstances, it would make sense that he wouldn't want "her" to suffer anymore.

What Was Really on Green's Mind

"Reading Chuck Green's mind"—telling him what his real motives are—is not just a professional exercise to me. I feel it is important to remember that every time he and I spoke, he developed an increasingly powerful responsibility to speak for JonBenét, just as the ransom note writer demanded in the unspoken question, "Why aren't you speaking up?" His stories and spontaneous comments fit hand-in-glove with powerful emotional reasons he might have to avoid the issue. Green's spontaneous comments came entirely from his own mind and reflect his own intuitive analysis of the problem. Green is a good reporter, and deep down (like Michael Kane) he strongly wants the truth to come out. That is exactly why he talked to me. He told me that the killer's deeper intuition had made a believer out of him, and that this evidence was stronger than anything the DA had. Unfortunately, because of his pain, he forgot what he really believed, a response that is not unusual.

Once Green had been confronted with the evidence in the ransom note, deep down he knew in a second whether or not it made psychological sense. Intuitively it would have rung true with him, and in the back of his mind he would have been aware all along that he was neglecting the truth about the case and his responsibility to tell it. Thus, we can read his columns after July 1998—after he had been clearly exposed to JonBenét's killer—in a new light. He knows he's not doing his job. He mentions the idea over and over again, writing about others who aren't doing their job.

I'm convinced Chuck Green's deeper mind realized he was making a mistake. Over the next year, from August of 1998 to October of 1999, he repeatedly wrote about the authorities' failures as investigators. His columns focused on how the authorities (1) were not properly investigating, (2) were holding the case to too high a standard of evidence, (3) were ignoring a situation and hoping it would go away, (4) showed excessive passivity and lack of leadership while stating "the public needs to know," and (5) were too meticulous, restraining evidence instead of letting jurors simply hear it so they could establish probable cause. Green even wrote about others' failures (e.g., "our work ethic is declining"—linking it to the Ramsey case indirectly in his column) and humorously wrote about a spin-off drug from Viagra called Directa—a medication for men who fail to ask for directions. In many ways he behaved with me much like the people he criticized.

Perhaps his December 27th column—noting the two-year anniversary of JonBenét's death—was his most revealing. He and I had had extensive discussions leading up to this column about what I felt was crucial evidence in the case and whether or not he would write about it in his column—whether or not he would speak for JonBenét. Indeed he mentioned my book, but only in the negative, and proceeded to give his take on the evidence. He wrote, "It [1999] most likely marks the year that justice will be denied the little beauty queen . . . those closest to the investigation aren't suggesting that any new evidence, òr any new direction, has been charted." He noted that no one besides the Ramseys were suspects, "But there appears to be a shortage of evidence to directly point to either parent . . . ."

Green went on to tell us, "Many theories, but precious little evidence, swirl around the case about possible suspects or motives. At least four books have been published on the case . . . . Few in the media have followed the case more intensely than this writer," and early on "I concluded there would never be a conviction unless someone confesses. That opinion remains intact. If ever the public gets to fully view police conduct in the investigation, and the evidence in the case, it will be a sad and tragic portrait of police failures, political maneuvering and family belligerence." He added, "It seems possible that in the first critical hours of the investigation valuable evidence was lost. The crime scene was terribly contaminated and the integrity of incriminating evidence was irreversibly violated."

Subtly but clearly, Chuck Green was declaring that he had expertise as a document examiner and that he had determined the ransom note ultimately wasn't important—just as Beckner, Hunter, Kane, and Smit had done. But deep down he knew he was wrong. Green had heard far more about the evidence the killer herself had put in the ransom note than the grand jury had heard, so in this column his preoccupation with writing about evidence being lost is understandable. His comment about precious information being lost in the beginning of the investigation also harkens back to his initial resistance to feedback from the killer's deeper mind. Green, I believe, recognizes deep down that he never got over his inability to hear the killer's hidden messages in the ransom note, and as a result, his own investigation was compromised from the start. The fact that he linked this column so definitively to books about the case strongly suggests he was dealing with our talks. Clearly, he had chosen to refute what I was saying in his column, making plain his stand that I hadn't persuaded him. Instantaneously, however, his deeper intelligence caused him to confess and write about investigators who "lost valuable evidence."

The fact remains that his statements about there being "precious little evidence" or that "the integrity of incriminating evidence was irreversibly violated" were just untrue. Green was simply in denial about the evidence hidden away in the ransom note, waiting on the right investigator to expose it. Green unconsciously knew that in the ransom note he held in his hands was a confession from the killer, evidence that could not be contaminated. Unconsciously, he tells us this as he spontaneously talks about the killer confessing and about the only way the case will be solved—precisely what he and I had talked about for months. We repeatedly discussed how the killer had confessed in the ransom note, and how it was his responsibility to speak for JonBenét. In this light, Green's failure to at the very least try to take the case in a new direction is indeed "sad and tragic," particularly when he had once stated that our theory based on the ransom note was "as strong as or stronger than anything the DA has."

On October 14th, the day after the grand jury failed to indict the Ramseys, Green, in his column entitled, "So Now a Killer Walks," once again hammers away at the prosecution's error that led to the miscarriage of justice—but indirectly he's also once again talking about himself and his own failings as an investigator. He also suggests what future investigators hopefully can correct this. "The leads are exhausted. Every known piece of evidence has been examined and re-examined. Every known witness has been interviewed and re-interviewed. Every suspect has provided alibis and handwriting samples . . . ."

This is plain and simply not true. While holding up the ideal way investigators should behave—to examine and re-examine, to interview and re-interview—Green himself did not thoroughly examine the evidence, much less re-examine it, even following his own standards as an investigator. He never consulted the one other expert he trusted (McCrary) regarding the ransom note, nor experts who are far superior to McCrary. Even so, the first piece of evidence Green specifically refers to is the ransom note (handwriting), another unconscious recognition that this was indeed the most crucial evidence in the case. What kind of reporter feels there is a strong theory on a case, but never investigates it on his own nor consults other experts in the field for feedback? Perhaps the same kind of reporter who feels that someone is enough of an expert on motives that he recommends to the top local talk show host that he should be interviewed about Lou Smit's motives, but never mentions a word about this expert's take on motives in the most crucial evidence in the case.

In his inimitable style, Green attributes the murderers getting off to "luck." He wrote, "Boulder cops were less adept at investigating a homicide than Curly, Larry, and Moe. The murderer was lucky that the . . . establishment . . . has shown little interest in the incompetence of the city's police department." Amidst his dark humor, Green subtly points the way for a future investigator to pick up the ball—although he does it by excessive denial. "The case is lost; there are no promising leads for detectives to pursue; there is no reason to believe that critical evidence escaped the grand jury's grasp." Deep down, Green has heard the evidence and knows it's there, which is why he goes through such an elaborate denial to remind us that promising leads and critical evidence have escaped notice. This statement is in amazing contrast to one made by the FBI's leading expert in psycholinguistics— an agent who called my book and our work "compelling."

Chuck Green found himself in a key role as an investigative reporter in one of the biggest murder cases in recent American history. He took this role seriously, as evidenced by his words, "Few in the media have followed this case more intensely." Green has a lot to teach us. Unfortunately, he turns out to be another dedicated investigator who is undermined by his own personality and pain, both of which created a crucial blind spot. This blind spot was so large that he walked away from the key evidence in a case where evidence was already in extremely short supply.

Journalists, like policemen and district attorneys, have a lot to learn about the human mind. They must face the fact that despite their credentials, their investigative skills are sorely lacking in certain cases. Until they admit this and allow new methods and experts to join them in finding the truth, then the truth and justice they have been sworn to uphold or to report will be compromised by their blindness.

PART III

Where the Truth
Can Be Found

Behind the Blaming, Shaming,
and Slips of the Tongue

CHAPTER 12
Following John and Patsy's Thoughtprints

At the Access Graphics annual Christmas party in December 1995, one year before JonBenét was murdered, Patsy Ramsey spontaneously entertained the gathering with her rendition of Patsy Cline's famous song, "Crazy." People present were surprised and felt Patsy was inappropriate and attention-seeking. But Patsy was telling them far more than she or they realized. Her choice of songs is filled with the poignant words of a lonely woman who cries out about losing her man. He has abandoned her for "somebody new," and now she's doubting herself, wondering what she could possibly have done wrong, and the whole thing is driving her crazy. And, even in the song, she tells us that all along in the back of her mind, she knew it would happen. If a picture is worth a thousand words, then a song may be worth two thousand. The thoughtprints are clear: loneliness, crying, grieving, doubting yourself, going crazy over losing your man to another woman.

If John Ramsey was sexually abusing JonBenét, Patsy would have unconsciously known about it long before her conscious mind would ever have been aware. Our conscious minds have an extraordinary ability to live in denial while our unconscious minds never cease trying to tell us the truth, in order to get relief. Patsy Ramsey chose a song that precisely matches the story of the ransom note so well that we can be sure Patsy Ramsey unconsciously chose to sing this song on this day as a cry for help. Deep down, she knew the pressure of John's involvement with JonBenét was already driving her crazy. Patsy's inappropriateness in singing the song suggested not only that she was starting not to be able to contain the pressure, but it also reflected the inappropriate activity in the home itself and a kind of warning to John Ramsey she had tuned in to his secret. Earlier that year she had once again spontaneously sung the same song at a family talent show, suggesting she was preoccupied with betrayal as far back as the summer of 1995. As we will see, her Christmas letters that year and particularly the next made it plain that she had picked up on what was going on in her home.

Patsy Ramsey wasn't just feeling "crazy" because of a man—the pressure of death also hung over her. Patsy Ramsey also would have identified with Patsy Cline, a vibrant, young woman who tragically died young in a plane crash, because of her fate—and because of being her namesake. Patsy Ramsey saw, as the ransom note and her Christmas letters reflect, that her own "plane" was about to crash. The twin pressures of betrayal and death were overwhelming her. As the song said, "she knew." A brilliant professor of mine and a renown psychoanalyst used to say, "Everybody who's slipping knows it." Our deeper mind knows everything. The Ramseys' thoughtprints demonstrate that they saw the whole story—and all along they have tried to tell us about it.

Every day both Patsy and John Ramsey see the world through the eyes of that event on December 25, 1996, an event that will forever shape their lives. The day they murdered their daughter stands still in their minds. No matter how they try to block it out or even how well they may think they are doing (at any given moment), it looms large. They cannot escape their deed. On the huge level of the deeper mind, their powerful mind's eye is constantly looking at that day. Even sleep provides them no escape, because the unconscious mind is ever on the alert, looking at nothing but the truth.

For the moment, they may think they have escaped the consequences. But, as they saying goes, there is the prison of the mind. This prison is far greater and stronger than they know. Even when they think they are escaping, they can't. For them, as well as those whom they love and who really love them, there is only one way out: the door of truth. It might lead to another kind of prison, but it would be better than the psychological one they are in now.

Deep down, the Ramseys have a far different dream from any they have on the surface. They long to be free, and truer words have never been spoken for them: Only the truth will set you free. Truth, of course, would initially lead to more ridicule, not only for what they did to JonBenét, but equally (if not more so) for their cover-up. The cover-up led to another kind of murder in this case, the murder of the truth. Their efforts also led to the murder justice, even, at times, in the name of God. But justice and truth, when allowed to come forth, lead to real freedom, even beyond public ridicule—it is called peace.

The Ramseys found themselves out on the limb of the big lie, the limb that gets very slippery. Once they're committed to the lie, they find themselves getting further and further out, going from one limb to another until they are tangled in a veritable jungle of lies. All the while, in their soul they long to tell the truth and repeatedly do so when they unknowingly speak from their hearts, their deeper selves. Virtually every time they talk, the Ramseys reveal in some way that even when they are in denial or are perpetuating the cover-up, they are looking at life through the lenses of their deed and their guilt.

The Ramsey case is what we psychiatrists call a good teaching case. So many lessons are available. Above all, we can see who the Ramseys really are. We can see their shadow sides, and we can see their hearts' secret desire to tell the truth. That's where their thoughtprints come in. If Patsy and John Ramsey each possess a deeper intelligence (and they do) that is greatly inclined toward telling the truth and that has thus declared their guilt, we should find consistent communication from one situation to another: "thoughtprints."

In therapy, we call observing such consistent communication between the lines as following the "red thread." We can see the "red thread" of JonBenét's blood on the Ramseys' hands if we continue to listen carefully. They will make the case against themselves—we need only to follow the thoughtprints.

One of the first lessons we learn is this: Not only is our unconscious mind capable of brilliantly picking up on deeper issues and motives, but because of its superiority, our deeper mind can even anticipate the future, particularly when we observe powerful pressures building in us (as Patsy Ramsey did). By carefully studying the Christmas letters Patsy Ramsey wrote in 1995 and again in 1996—the last two weeks or so before JonBenét's murder—we can see powerful motives lurking just below the surface of her mind. The letters were clearly spontaneous, which gave her deeper intelligence another chance to speak. We can see what's on her mind.

When we are under great stress and are in denial, our mind wants to help us understand, because our deeper mind knows that knowing is better than not knowing, despite the initial pain. The tendency to deny our pain is universal and human, but in the end it can be very costly. What you don't know about yourself *can* hurt you.

Access Graphics Christmas Party: December 1995

Thoughtprint: going crazy, losing her man, he loves someone new. Patsy Ramsey richly communicates in song that she has picked up on the sexual abuse in her home. The song suggests that tremendous emotional pressure is building in Patsy and that she is not far from going off the deep end and exploding.

1995 Christmas Letter: Health, Husband, and Hype

(See Appendix C: The Christmas Letters, page 325.)

Thoughtprint: health concerns. In the 1995 letter, the very first reference is predictably to Patsy's health. She has been sick (with the flu), which caused the Christmas cards to be late. At the end of the first paragraph, she wishes everyone a "Healthy" (note the capital "h") New Year—two quick health references. In the third paragraph, she mentions Melinda is completing her Nursing Degree (capitalizing both) at MCG (Medical College of Georgia), and toward the end of the letter, Patsy tells us that she has had good checkups at NIH (National Institute of Health) in Bethesda, MD (her capitals suggesting a physician, not the state). I count seven health references, five of which are capitalized. She goes on to thank God for her energy, mentions her return to being able to raise a family, and asks for continued prayers for her health. She mentions the future twice, including "here's to 1996." Obviously, she is extremely concerned about her health and the future, fearing her cancer will return.

Thoughtprint: playboy. She mentions John Ramsey first among family members and indirectly refers to him as a playboy. ("All work and no play makes John a dull boy, so he leaves *plenty of time* for the latter.") Then she notes that Burke is into Boy Scouting, ever so subtly suggesting that she herself is secretly "scouting boys," namely the playboy, John. On the heels of her singing "Crazy," Patsy feels the pressure building. It will be much more obvious the following year.

Thoughtprint: "Stay busy and just win, baby." Certainly her health concerns and any other major stresses such as a husband who is a playboy explain why the letter has such a frenetic tone and pace to it. Patsy reflects non-stop energy and achievement. John's business is "going great guns," conquering Europe and spreading worldwide. John is winning sailing awards ("in our sloop Miss America"), Burke is the tallest on his team, JonBenét and Burke won ribbons in bicycle contests, and JonBenét won a Little Miss Colorado beauty pageant. Patsy uses the word "busy" four times, adds an unbelievable seventeen exclamation points, and describes impending trips to Dallas and Phoenix for more contests (football games), and then to Michigan and back to Colorado. By the end of the letter, the recipient is worn out just from reading it.

This is a classic "manic" letter, as Patsy Ramsey demonstrates how she handles her pain, her fear, and the helplessness brought on by her disease: by appearing to be strong, victorious, and indomitable. (This is the same sort of thing that explains manic-depressive disorder when people become "hyper" or "manic" to ward of the pain of depression.) Additionally, Patsy notes that John's successful business (she mentions "business" twice in the very first paragraph) "grew out of our garage," the container where it was born, a familiar birth image clearly connected to her.

Even in this early letter, striking similarities to the ransom note appear: a preoccupation with her disease, a manic-aggressive persona that covers her helplessness (shown by a preoccupation with victories and exclamation points), a striking birth image, a preoccupation with "John's business" mentioned up front in the first paragraph, and repeated references to "John" (four in this letter as compared to three in ransom note). Such thoughtprints match those in the ransom notes in many ways, and both letters tell the same basic story of attempting to cover the terror of dying and helplessness with aggressiveness and activity. Also, Patsy Ramsey suggests she is secretly watching ("scouting") John's playboy tendencies. We would expect this thoughtprint to continue if it is troubling her.

All in all, Patsy's simple 1995 Christmas letter provides us with a sterling look at her mind one year before JonBenét's murder. And even this early, we find the same basic thoughtprints that we will see later in the ransom note.

1996 Christmas Letter: Little Miss Christmas

Thoughtprint: more health concerns. Her 1996 Christmas letter offers us another wonderful opportunity of studying exactly what was on Patsy Ramsey's mind, this time only two weeks before JonBenét's murder. In many ways she picks up exactly where she left off. She immediately talks about a "busy" year, and time running out ("can't believe it's almost over"). The second paragraph contains three medical references: Medical College of Georgia, Pediatric ICU, Kennestone Hospital (all connected to Melinda), and in the last paragraph Patsy mentions "enjoying continued good health." Three times she alludes to looking forward to 1997. She also tells us that she has no "free time," implying that she is a prisoner to time.

Thoughtprint: "acute" changes. Patsy notes that Burke (a fourth grader) has lost his baby teeth and that JonBenét is in her first year of "real school," gone five full days a week, and is advancing rapidly. Patsy mentions that immediately after Christmas she will have her "acutual" [sic] birthday, her fortieth, suggesting this is her "acute" birthday.

A snapshot of Patsy's mind immediately before the murder reveals the following thoughtprints: time is running out, "can't believe it's almost over," a preoccupation with the future (four references to 1997), continued health concerns, an empty nest, the loss of her other child's baby phase, as well as losing "body parts (teeth)," and her "acute" birthday, which puts her officially over the hill. We see not only the specter of cancer hanging over her, but now she has been presented with two new, but related, stresses—both losses. She is losing her babies, her nest is empty, and she is headed over the hill of forty.

So how does Patsy cope? As she said in the beginning of the letter, when she thinks time is running out, it's time to start over again, to stay busy, to keep up the pace. If you're looking cancer and helplessness in the face, the last thing you can afford to do is blink or slow down. So you keep up the pace.

Thoughtprint: stay busy and keep winning/victory. Everything continues to move fast. Burke is "busy," JonBenét has been moved ahead in her fast-paced school, John is always on the go and is still racing sailboats, and Patsy has been on a whirlwind trip to New York City. Life is obviously moving very fast for Patsy.

Not only does the letter place an emphasis on parties, but it particularly emphasizes contests. Burke is competing for grades, is playing golf, is on a "basketball binge," and his team was number one in Little League. JonBenét won two beauty pageants. John Ramsey's company just went over "one billion $$ in sales" and he's still racing yachts. Patsy's Charlevoix (Michigan) vacation home was selected for the home tour and *Better Homes & Gardens*.

Patsy herself is bingeing on competition, and she knows it unconsciously. Patsy furthermore suggests she heavily is invested in her children's accomplishments because they give her a temporary sense of restoring her terribly damaged feminine identity, as if saying, "See what I produced (delivered)?"

Parties, trips, and contests are perfect, albeit temporary, antidotes for the terror of death and any other related pain. We must not forget that at the time this letter was written, Patsy Ramsey was just into the third of her five-year survival (a major benchmark, hopefully signifying cure) from ovarian cancer.

While Patsy continues to describe her usual manic way of coping (trips, races, and contests), there is a subtle but noticeable change in the energy level in the letter. Exclamation points are down from seventeen to nine, and this letter is clearly shorter. Comparing this letter with the previous one suggests Patsy is more depressed this year. Surely she has presented several reasons why this year was more difficult. Throw an empty nest experience and an over-the-hill syndrome into a psychic brew already overloaded with the terror of death, and you have one powerful cocktail of emotions.

But there was another major stress Patsy hinted at, and we find the same subtle thoughtprint we did in the last letter, this time even more striking. Patsy's competitiveness is so striking that we can see why she might end the ransom note with "Victory!"

Thoughtprint: John's real love. Patsy unconsciously demotes John from first position in the 1995 letter to the fifth position (and only mentions his name once in the letter contrasted with four times the year before). She mentions that he had to pull out of a yacht race (most likely with his old boat Miss America) because of a lack of power. She also tells us that he's not as interested in the old boat, but "his real love is the new 'old-looking' boat, Grand Season." A boat often symbolizes a woman, and a new boat made to look old could symbolize a young woman made to look older and suggests that Patsy was picking up that playboy John has a new girlfriend and that he has dumped the "old boat," namely Miss America (with whom Patsy would have identified), for a "young boat," JonBenét—exactly as the Patsy Cline song put it, "somebody new." Patsy Ramsey points to other reasons she would see herself as an "old boat," but if John Ramsey was sexually involved with JonBenét, it would move to the top of Patsy's list of assaults on her femininity and would become a category all its own, second only to cancer. If the deeper intelligence communicates through stories, then this is a striking one. It is simply too coincidental that this story about John's new boat (made to look older) being his real love and replacing his old boat fits so well with the identical story in the ransom note, as well as matching hints from Patsy's 1995 letter.

Patsy suggests this same scenario in another way by positioning John next to JonBenét in the letter, and thereby linking the two. (In the previous year John was mentioned first and JonBenét fifth.) Prior to mentioning John, Patsy told us that JonBenét is moving ahead, going at a fast pace, and had won two beauty contests, "America's Royal Tiny Miss" and Colorado's "Little Miss Christmas." Of course, all this communication is subtle and indirect, but the unconscious mind communicates indirectly, the only way it can. Patsy was revealing what she was picking up on unconsciously with her deeper intelligence, but she could not admit to herself what she saw going on. Nevertheless, the consistency of the story and the similarity of the thoughtprints suggest exactly what was motivating Patsy Ramsey and which were the powerful forces that had a stranglehold on her.

Thoughtprint: a birthday bash explosion anticipated. The title of "Little Miss Christmas" takes on a whole new meaning in light of JonBenét's murder on Christmas Day, which the ransom note writer emphasized in the note by stating, "I will call you tomorrow," and which the Ramseys stressed on her tombstone for all the world to see (as they noted, she died on December 25th). Patsy suggests in several ways that unconsciously she knew she was about to explode, most likely on Christmas Day. Her striking reference to the message marker "school" and her emphasis that JonBenét was in the Core Knowledge program suggests that Patsy Ramsey herself had core knowledge of what was going on between JonBenét and John Ramsey. Her reference to an outrageous (as in "outrage") birthday bash, followed by Patsy being on national television, in national magazines, and books linked to JonBenét are so coincidental that they suggest Patsy anticipated her explosion and all the attention that was sure to follow. Indeed she bashed in JonBenét's head on the most famous birthday of the year—and just four days before Patsy's birthday—and suddenly Patsy Ramsey was appearing on national television, in magazines, and in books. If she was threatened by JonBenét and was enraged with her and John Ramsey, Patsy would have sensed it. For a woman as competitive as Patsy Ramsey, someone so used to winning contests to bolster her self-esteem, it would be a defeat beyond belief to lose out to a younger woman at this time in her life. If her "radar" picked up that something was amiss in her home, her radar would also have known what she intended to do about it. The same deeper intelligence that can accurately describe our motives *after* an event can likewise see them building beforehand. This is how the mind really works.

Patsy Ramsey suggests that she is in so much pain that she is willing to sacrifice JonBenét and herself to gain a victory over helplessness. Surely, the stage is a familiar method of coping for Patsy Ramsey—and now she would have constant national attention beyond her wildest dreams and would become a household name. As she unconsciously thinks of all the books that are sure to follow—linking the idea of books to JonBenét (book reports)—Patsy would then see her deceased child producing books and attention that reinforce Patsy's power as a woman, temporarily undoing the experience of death.

All in all, the themes in the 1996 Christmas letter are the same as the previous year, only the pressure is picking up, time is running out, and there are three new stresses in one year: a full-fledged empty nest syndrome, an acute over-the-hill syndrome, and—worse of all—Patsy, Miss America, has been dry-docked, replaced by John's "real love."

Notice the thoughtprints of both letters connected to the ransom note: (1) message markers suggesting listening, learning, instructions, conclusions, core knowledge getting to the deepest level; (2) the baby phase being over and birthing images of businesses growing out of garages, of JonBenét delivering a report, of Patsy having produced—delivered—children who succeed, and a preoccupation with the idea "delivery;" (3) time running out, health concerns, and repeated specific references to the future—to 1997, at times questioning if someone (JonBenét) will see it; (4) and the repeated suggestion that John was involved "romantically" and sexually with JonBenét and that he became a "fat cat" whom Patsy rendered powerless.

January 1, 1997: CNN Interview—One Week After the Murder

Thoughtprints: people who murder family members, death/loss, cancer, JonBenét as rescuer and Daddy's girl. As we saw in Chapter 7, Patsy and John clearly confess and explain why they committed such a heinous act.

John's Public Letter to an Artist: April 1997

Thoughtprints: JonBenét as an object, spin/cover-up, excessive emphasis on "normal" ("protests too much"), JonBenét's small part. John Ramsey writes a public letter to a young Boulder artist who created an exhibit entitled "Daddy's Little Hooker," centering around JonBenét's murder. Ramsey rebukes the young man, but in his letter refers to JonBenét as "a thing." John Ramsey is aloof on several occasions, and does not even mention her by name, either directly or indirectly (i.e., just "did well in school, loved to go the beach"). Also, he overuses the word "normal," something he frequently does during his interviews—and not just when he's denying inappropriate sexual involvement with her, which suggests he is having to sell the public on the idea that there was nothing abnormal about his relationship with JonBenét. He makes reference to someone incorrectly portraying or mishandling "a small part of JonBenét" and overemphasizes the word "portrayal," as though he is trying to spin the story himself and at the same time owning up to what he's doing without realizing it. He also connects the idea of "deeply hurt" to JonBenét, indicating how she was treated. Obviously, the artist struck a major nerve in John Ramsey, who must immediately take to the press his position on the art display, insisting that he wasn't molesting his daughter. However, the messages between the lines suggest otherwise.

May 1, 1997 Interview

Thoughtprints: slip/sexual abuse, two people know murderer, case close to breaking, Patsy's confession, "V" is for "Victory." On May 1, 1997, the Ramseys agreed to an interview/press conference, which they typically attempted to control by allowing only seven hand-picked journalists to be present. Nevertheless, John Ramsey does the identical thing he did in the Ramseys' first public interview on CNN on January 1st. He spontaneously introduces the accusations of child molestation and, in his vehement denial, makes a telling comment. At the very moment he insists that he maintained proper boundaries with JonBenét, he makes a crucial slip that contradicts his denial as the states, "JonBen–I," then corrects himself to say, "JonBenét and I were close." His deeper intelligence was telling us how it really was—that he had merged with her in a way that the two became one.

During this interview, Patsy makes a comment: "There are at least two people . . . who know who did this . . . the killer and some other person. . . ." The very moment she uses the word "killer," it's like someone suddenly jerked John Ramsey's chain. Like a rocket, his head suddenly drops down and away from Patsy, though previously he had been steadfastly at her side, staring at her, and encouraging her clearly rehearsed lines. The thought of Patsy and the public "knowing the killer" obviously overwhelms John Ramsey, suggesting that he has to look away when the subject comes up and also can't bear to look at the one person who does know he is one of the killers.

For her part, after telling us in the CNN interview that the killer could be a man or a woman (or both), Patsy spontaneously introduces that she and John think there are two people who know about the murder—a primary assailant and a confidant—but she never gives one reason for this conclusion. Simultaneously, she unconsciously holds up two fingers for the two killers in a "V" for "victory" sign. Along with her comment about two people who know about the killing points, her gesture points immediately back to the ransom note with its emphasis on "Victory" and its "two gentlemen" kidnappers who are watching over JonBenét. Also in this interview, Patsy stresses that the case is only one communication (one phone call) away from being broken, suggesting that she is closer to being broken than anyone realizes and that an accurate reading of her messages will break her.

July 23, 1997: John Ramsey's Profile of the Killer

Thoughtprints: hidden self-profile, hidden profile of Patsy, "stopping life." Next, John Ramsey releases his own profile of JonBenét's murderer to the media. He consistently describes a male killer, but his profile in many ways matches a description of his wife, as well as himself: suffering from a major stress in the weeks and months prior to the crime; experiencing a triggering event in a personal relationship that caused the killer to vent anger at a female close to the killer and at John Ramsey; avidly reading about or watching television shows about it after the murder; appearing to be very religious and cooperative; and having been in his home. Most importantly, John Ramsey states the killer "must be brought to justice" and "prevented from stopping the life of another young child." The extremely unusual description of a murderer *"stopping the life"* (e.g., instead of "taking a life") fits much more commonly with the idea of stopping someone from breathing or their heart from beating, suggesting an indirect reference to strangulation.

September, 1997: Patsy Calls *Larry King Live*

Thoughtprint: guilt over killing a princess, attention-seeking behavior. Shortly thereafter, in September 1997, Patsy Ramsey impulsively calls *Larry King Live* to berate someone (the paparazzi) for causing the death of Princess Diana, suggesting yet another confession. Patsy finds a temporary depository for her guilt and is really talking about herself. This again is not difficult to decode. Patsy also continues to demonstrate her love for the stage, and she continues to use it to ward off her helplessness, and now, her guilt. She once again unknowingly reveals how she used JonBenét to ward off her helplessness, as she calls JonBenét "America's Princess," and equates her death with Princess Diana's death. Never does a princess shine so bright as in a premature death. Now we can see how unconsciously Patsy would have foreseen how JonBenét's death could bring Patsy world-wide attention, how Patsy could have envisioned JonBenét's death had all the ingredients the national media yearns for. And when you desperately need a stage to keep you alive, in the end you don't care what they call you—you just want to make sure they do call you.

Patsy's desperate need to be on national television, particularly reflected by her manipulative method of going through a night watchman at CNN headquarters to get through to the show (as she describes in their book), suggests that she was also making sure that she didn't lose the spotlight to Princess Diana whose death made the Boulder murder tiny in comparison. But never the shrinking violet, Patsy had the unmitigated gall to interject JonBenét into the biggest international story in the world, putting JonBenét—and therefore Patsy herself—on the same level as Princess Diana, without missing a beat. Patsy had to get back on top, and she wasn't about to lose out, even to the enormous media spectacle that Diana's death had become. Certainly this gives us a feel for just how competitive Patsy Ramsey is—underscoring precisely how she could turn on anyone, even JonBenét, who displaced her. And that is precisely why she made the phone call—for all to see.

Over and over we see Patsy Ramsey continuing to seek out a stage, large or small. JonBenét has not been in the grave long when Patsy is dragging people off the street in Charlevoix, Michigan, to show them JonBenét's room. She needs a stage as much as a heroin addict needs a fix because energy and showtime equals life. In order to survive, the "show" must go on. This was made vividly clear when, on the recommendation of a friend, I drove by the Ramseys' home in Atlanta while I was there visiting other friends. I was shocked to find their home was on East Paces Ferry Road, a main suburban thoroughfare on the same road as the Governor's mansion (on West Paces Ferry). Not only was it in a conspicuous place two houses from the Chattahoochee River, but the home itself was even more revealing. One would think the Ramseys would want maximum privacy, but the two-story house was not far off the road, had very few trees in front, and had large, curtainless windows with the rooms all lit up, allowing for easy viewing of every room on the front of the house. Oddly enough, next to their house was a side street and it was on this side where they had a gate and more privacy. Once again the Ramseys seemed to be saying, "Notice me" and "Don't notice me" at the same time.

November 1997: Patsy Goes on *Geraldo*

Thoughtprints: posing, wearing masks, Patsy's excessive love, clues to find killer, killer a pedophile, the hole in Patsy's heart. Patsy gives her first solo interview, this time on Geraldo Rivera's daytime show, providing perhaps her richest communication besides the ransom note, as she tells one story after another, the telling way the deeper intelligence speaks.

On *Geraldo*, Patsy first talks about JonBenét standing on her head for a lengthy period, suggesting she and John Ramsey have turned the investigation upside-down and that they are holding a pose. Patsy then tells a story about the mistake she made in loving JonBenét too much—the only error Patsy has ever admitted to publicly, a confession that behind the crime was her inability to let go of JonBenét. Later, she connects JonBenét's death to Halloween, suggesting she and John are wearing masks. Patsy then suggests the way to catch the killer is to find someone who is an expert in reading between the lines, the same unconscious instruction she presented in the ransom note. This resonates with her earlier idea that "one phone call, one communication" will break the case. She also suggests a pedophile was the murderer, another clue that sexual abuse was involved in the murder.

Finally, in the *Geraldo* interview Patsy says, "I did not have anything to do with it. I loved that child with my whole of my heart and soul." Obviously she wanted to say "the whole of my heart," but her deeper intelligence over-ruled her, instead suggesting "my hole of my heart" or "my heart had a hole in it" and I failed to love JonBenét.

In summary, Patsy has told us a lot. She and John have thrown the investigation off-track and are continuing to hold the pose; she made a ter-rible mistake and was overly attached to JonBenét and used her; she had another flaw, a hole in her heart, and her love for JonBenét leaked out; the two of them, Patsy and John, are wearing a mask and are secretly monsters; God knows the truth; and the way to catch her is to find experts who can read these messages.

Note, too, how much more vivid communication from the deeper intel-ligence is as she paints pictures with words. Instead of saying, "I am fooling the police," she says, "We have the investigation turned upside-down like a kid standing on her head." Instead of saying, "I am a monster," she says, "Think of me with a Halloween mask of niceness on, but when you take it off I am a monster."

December 1997: The Ramsey Christmas Message

Matching thoughtprints: preoccupation with birth/femininity, death/no hope, "hence," end is near. This Christmas message, clearly written by Patsy, one year after the murder has many similarities with the other two Christ-mas letters, as well as the ransom note. Patsy is preoccupied with "birth" or "birthday," mentioning it directly four times. In the key sentence in the 1997 letter, she uses the identical word "hence," meaning conclusion (as in the ransom note), and spells it out again that without a birth (or the ability to give birth), there is no hope of life and, thus, permanent separation from loved ones (no hope of ever being with them). Patsy again suggests the bottom-line conclusion that drives her: She views loss of femininity as total hopelessness, a life-threatening disaster, an idea that fits perfectly with how she perceived her cancer. Despite her open declarations that she had been healed of cancer, Patsy strongly implies that unconsciously she was constantly living under a death sentence. In this letter, she uses "Christmas" or "Christ" eight times and repeatedly connects it with "birth," suggesting a "Christ" equals "birth" equa-tion and, thus, an even greater preoccupation with femininity.

It's as if Patsy is saying to the world, "In case you missed it, I wrote the ransom note. See the similarities? And this time I put my name on it so you couldn't miss it." She also repeats the idea of things coming to a conclusion, as in "hence," "hearing the music," "the day approaches," "death approaching," "seeing the light," "eternal life." After this letter, the Ramseys are strikingly quiet for months after several people notice the similarities in her 1997 Christmas message and the ransom note with the use of "hence." Never again will they write a lengthy Christmas letter. Even so, they communicate extensively in other ways: interviews, letters, and finally their own book—revealing that guilty people will continue to find ways of confessing.

July 1998: The Ramsey Infomercial—Michael Tracey's Documentary

Thoughtprints: cancer, sexual abuse, how to investigate, God knows the truth. Despite a close-minded producer and their own best efforts to conceal the truth, once again the Ramseys confess and reveal more than ever, confirming their motives. The Ramseys repeatedly tell several stories that give them away, revealing between the lines who they are.

As the Ramseys continue to give interviews and continue to tell stories, their unconscious, creative "right brain" mind is given free rein. One of the most telling sets of communications occurs in the documentary they made with Michael Tracey, the journalism professor at the University of Colorado which ran on *A & E*. (See Chapter 10, page 117.)

Despite Tracey's blatant attempt to portray them as victims of the media and police, Patsy and John told stories that underscored and elaborated on the story Patsy told in the ransom note. Their slips of the tongue and body language pointed to their guilt.

Cancer Story Number One: First Patsy Ramsey told a story about the time she was undergoing chemotherapy for ovarian cancer. She explained that Burke was stand-offish, but JonBenét came right up to her, pushed the bag of blood connected to her chest tube (catheter) aside, grabbed the tube, and followed it all the way into Patsy's chest. Burke handled his fear by avoiding Patsy, but JonBenét grabbed onto her mother and "the tube of blood going straight into her heart," symbolically reconnecting the umbilical cord. While Burke avoided, JonBenét clung, and Patsy clung to JonBenét in an attempt to avoid her pain just as Burke was avoiding his.

In essence Patsy was saying that the way JonBenét and she handled their fear of separation was to cling to each other as tightly as they could, like "blood sisters," so close that no one could tell them apart. She held on tightly so death couldn't get them. Death is separation, and they wouldn't—couldn't—allow that happen. Amidst their terror, Patsy and JonBenét merged into one person, and in so doing, Patsy used JonBenét to ward off her fears of separation and death. In this story Burke and JonBenét actually represent two parts of Patsy: one who overtly tried to avoid her pain by looking away (denial) and the other who avoided her pain by clinging.

Patsy's story also connects JonBenét to blood, a hidden confession that she herself has JonBenét's blood on her hands. In addition, Patsy's story explains the heart she drew on JonBenét's left palm after she killed her. Patsy was emphasizing that in the face of separation—this time the utter, final separation of death—you cling, you grab, you remain blood sisters. Patsy didn't draw the heart on her dead daughter's hand solely as a confession or as a sign of her love. She drew it because the heart was her signature, her familiar way of attempting to block out her pain. Patsy was known to reassure JonBenét on other occasions by drawing a heart on her daughter's palm, telling her that she had her mother's heart in her hand and encouraging JonBenét to grab the heart and not be afraid. Patsy had taught JonBenét to grab when she was desperate, just as Patsy herself did. When Patsy and John posed JonBenét's dead body, Patsy clung to JonBenét by drawing a heart—by placing her heart in JonBenét's hand.

Cancer Story Number Two: When Michael Tracey asked Patsy if a battle over bedwetting could have triggered her murderous rage, she laughingly wondered how she could lose control over bedwetting when she was a stage IV ovarian cancer victim. Unconsciously, Patsy was saying, "It's the cancer that caused me to lose control." The question was about motive, and Patsy made it plain that a bedwetting battle did not trigger her rage. Rather, it was the stark terror of cancer that left her on the verge of exploding.

Patsy makes so much common sense. Any therapist worth his or her salt can tell you how a major emotional trauma sits in a person's psyche and eats him or her alive. Bedwetting as a trigger motive doesn't fit Patsy, usually a very poised former beauty queen, who had handled JonBenét's bedwetting for years without undue frustration. A bedwetting episode on Christmas night, when generosity was in the air, surely wouldn't send Patsy into a rage.

Something more powerful and completely unexpected had set off the cancer-related time bomb of fear and anger inside Patsy that night.

Cancer Story Number Three: John admitted for the first time that he and Patsy had never talked much about her cancer. Unfortunately the price a person pays for not talking about traumas, particularly a trauma as ominous as stage IV ovarian cancer, is that fear controls the person, which often leads to acting out.

John hinted that he helped push JonBenét into a teenage role through her beauty pageant participation so he would have a more adult substitute for Patsy, whom he thought he was losing to cancer. In her costumes, JonBenét looked and acted like a seductive teenager. This revelation fits the unspoken equation deep in the human psyche: Sex is the opposite of death. And John may have had his own way of escaping death—through sex.

Cancer Story Number Four: John said that "we have a cancer in our society" when he was talking about the evil forces in society that harm children. John was really saying, "The specter of cancer loomed over our family. Death consumed our family and this led to evil acting out." This is consistent with John's sensitivity to separation anxiety, which was related to having lost his mother to cancer, and the sudden deaths of his oldest daughter, his father, and potentially Patsy.

September 28, 1998: John Ramsey's Statement After Smit's Resignation

Thoughtprints: key expressions, need to confess to God. When Detective Lou Smit publicly resigned and sent Alex Hunter a letter of resignation, which clearly supported the Ramseys' innocence, John Ramsey couldn't contain himself. Immediately, he released another statement to the media, once again insisting on his innocence. While the ransom note is the crucial evidence, it is interesting to see how the human mind insists on confessing through other thoughtprints. Not surprisingly, John's own mind turns the tables on him.

"As you know, our family has not often spoken publicly in the past because so much of what surrounds our tragedy is used to entertain for profit. For my family, the loss of JonBenét was a *crushing blow* [italics mine] that left us crying out, 'Why did this happen to such a precious child? Why did this happen to a good family?' JonBenét's murder has inflicted the worst pain imaginable on my family and it is simply cruel to exploit her death for profit, as so much of the media has. . . ."

John's choice of words, especially the sequence that links the loss of JonBenét to a "crushing blow" to "us," is so striking, so beyond coincidence, and so early in the letter (the second sentence) that we can sense how badly he wants to confess. His deeper intelligence wants to make clear that the Ramseys were indeed connected to the crushing blow that took JonBenét's life. This comes right after he mentions that this is one of the few times he and Patsy have spoken publicly, as if to announce or underscore the importance of what he's about to say. Before he provides us with the self-incriminating description of the murder, he talks about people who just want to entertain for selfish gain. He follows his confession with the idea of how cruel it is to exploit JonBenét's murder. Once again, if he and Patsy are involved in the murder, he is talking about Patsy and himself, two people who shamelessly exploit JonBenét's murder, attempting to entertain us with their declarations of innocence. If a jury ever wanted to see what John Ramsey would say about himself if he were on that jury, here it is: "Cruel exploitation of the worst kind." (He is repeatedly extremely hard on himself.) We can also see that consciously John is still shell-shocked and puzzled about how things blew up in their faces that night. He persists in searching for an explanation, to ask "why?"

John Ramsey continues:

> "We have always expressed our eagerness to participate fully in a competent investigation of this horrible crime, but I have been unwilling to submit my family to what seems to be little more than a *lynch mob* [italics mine] hiding behind the authority of police badges. It is not true that you can buy justice in this country, but sadly, it does take money to protect your rights against abuse of the law by those charged with its application."

John Ramsey connects his second-most-telling description, "lynch mob," to the Ramsey family. The phrase is not coincidental, but is indeed connected to Patsy and him—one more confession that they were the "mob" that "lynched" JonBenét, implying strangulation. This indicates, as we have suspected all along, that the strangulation was their joint decision as "mob" hints at more than one person.

He then speaks of people who hide behind their authority and, in the next sentence, mentions his authority: money. Simply read, each sentence shows John Ramsey is talking about himself—just as his unconscious mind intends it. Finally, John states, "Our fight with the Boulder police started when they refused to release JonBenét's body to us for burial until we complied with their demands."

John's ideas are strikingly similar to the ransom note, which said, "Any deviation of my instructions will result in the immediate execution of your daughter. You will also be denied her remains for proper burial." In the ransom note, the main ideas are: (1) deviation from instructions results in immediate aggression and (2) denial of JonBenét's body for burial. In the press release, John Ramsey's ideas are eerily similar: deviation from their (the authorities') instructions results in refusal to release JonBenét's body for burial.

December 11, 1998: Patsy's E-mail Letter to Internet Supporters

A small group of devoted Ramsey supporters communicated with them on the Internet, and once again Patsy, driven by the anniversary of JonBenét's death, feels compelled to write a Christmas letter.

"To Jameson, Seal, August, Nebraskafriend, Cal, Lovelypigeon, Sunshine . . .

Thank you for your wonderful thoughts of encouragement. We, too, know that JonBenét's spirit lives on, both in eternity and as a memory here. Our goal is to do our best to insure that her short life on earth will have great meaning for goodness and love."

John and Patsy Ramsey

Thoughtprints: JonBenét lives on (speaks), life is short, eternity. In a very short "private" letter, Patsy obviously is trying to avoid the mistake she made in writing her last Christmas letters with their revealing slips. But Patsy once again makes a crucial slip "insure" (as in "insurance") instead of "ensure," suggesting "insurance" and eternity are on her mind. Just as impressively, even more so perhaps, Patsy Ramsey connects her slip "insure" to "short life on earth" to once again reveal how constantly she is troubled by thoughts of just how short her life really is. Deep down she knows her cancer could return at any moment and probably expects it because she knows she deserves punishment. Certainly her slip in this sentence demonstrates amazing consistency with the rest of the story to validate that we are looking at the thoughtprint, "I am about to die." Patsy once again makes reference to JonBenét living on, suggesting she is still speaking for her.

December 15, 1998: John Ramsey Attacks Boulder Photographer

"Behavioral thoughtprint": loss of control. Sometimes actions speak louder than words, often even in place of words, particularly in people like John Ramsey who don't frequently communicate verbally. At times we can see clearly the thoughts behind the actions. Because of the powerful time of year and the Ramseys' deep-seated guilt, we could predict that the Ramseys would in some way make another hidden confession, just as Patsy did in the 1997 Christmas message. Surprisingly, this year John is the one who overtly acts out his guilt by showing us, "Yes, I'm capable of losing control and attacking someone, particularly around Christmas time." After leaving a popular Boulder restaurant, Ramsey suddenly charged Boulder resident and occasional journalist, Frank Coffman, who was standing across the street photographing Ramsey. John Ramsey had been photographed many times before. He surely would expect this to happen if he went out in public, but for some reason he broke. He wrestled Coffman to the ground and tried to get his camera, spewing out words of hatred.

Upon reflection, a logical explanation surfaces: Here's John Ramsey back in Boulder, just before Christmas, a short two years after the murder. The memories would be storming back. The guilt and fear would be oppressive. And then came a sudden sign of exposure—a photographer—which he wasn't quite expecting that night. Photographer Frank Coffman symbolized some of John's many hidden fears: exposure, publicity, communication, being caught in the act, being recorded forever, "somebody's watching you." It was all too much for John Ramsey. We see how vulnerable he is to breaking, particularly around Christmas—and the anniversary of JonBenét's murder. Certainly John would be picking up on Patsy's constant vulnerability to breaking, which would greatly heighten his tension. These two people, John and Patsy Ramsey, are under tremendous pressure, pressure that continues to grow when one is trapped by guilt in the prison of the mind.

October 13, 1999: Ramsey Family Statement After No Indictment by Grand Jury

Again, immediately after they have been temporarily exonerated, the Ramseys cannot wait to make another indirect confession. Since this was a particularly crucial moment when the best-laid plans of their deeper intelligence had failed because of prosecutorial ineptness, we should expect not only a striking rebuke of the prosecutors but also more blatant hints as to how the prosecution can salvage its case. And Patsy Ramsey doesn't disappoint us.

"The following will be the only statement today by John and Patsy Ramsey and their lawyers.

After almost three years of intense legal scrutiny, with the aid of a grand jury of honest and responsible citizens, it has been determined that there is simply not sufficient information to indict anyone for the murder of JonBenét. We take no satisfaction in this result because a child killer remains free and undetected.

The Ramsey family lives in a nightmare. There has been no end to the public lynching and speculation which marred the case from the beginning. The public has been mislead by a constant stream of attacks and false information from people all too eager for a headline regardless of truth. Those persons who have biased this case by leaking false, incomplete or misleading information are as corrupt as those who report it. The time has come for an accounting of those responsible for this spectacle.

Experienced detectives were removed from this investigation in 1998. It is our request that this investigation be renewed by returning these skilled investigators to authority. This crime cannot be solved by those who close their minds to any lead which is inconsistent with their biases.

We thank our many friends and family members for standing by us during this terrible ordeal. We also extrend [sic] our thanks to the grand jurors who took so much time out of their own lives to assist the investigation.

There is still much work to be done. We remain committed to finding our daughter's killer. With God's help, we will succeed."

Thoughtprints: use the mind, clues/leads, overcome bias, numerous cancer images, "a lynching," and God will prevail. So it's all over but the shouting. And if the Ramseys are guilty, they will shout once more in the same way they always have. They give one more sterling clue to the authorities about how to solve this case: "Stop closing your minds to leads that are inconsistent with your biases." Again Patsy Ramsey tells them how to catch her—use the mind, be open-minded. The key to this case is the mind, the whole mind, the deeper mind. Patsy herself emphasizes law enforcement's primary problem—bias—the same bias my colleagues and I experienced.

This statement also exudes an enormous number of cancer images. In the very first sentence Patsy connects this letter to the ransom note: "After almost three years of intense scrutiny . . ." This is nearly identical to the ransom note's "you and your family are under constant scrutiny," which was written when Patsy had been closely scrutinized for cancer for nearly three years. At the end of the first paragraph we find, ". . . result . . . a [child] killer remains free and undetected." "Result," meaning "conclusion," was a favorite word of the ransom note writer. "Undetected," another highly unusual word, is used often in the medical field, and certainly "undetected killer" resonates with cancer—Patsy's greatest fear, that recurrent cancer (a killer if there ever was one) had gone undetected. She feared this would be the "final result."

In the second paragraph, we see Patsy living in a "nightmare" with "no end to the . . . speculation which marred this case from the beginning." The word "marred" is close to the words "tampered" or "marked" used in the ransom note and to "tainted" used in the 1997 Christmas message. It also fits well with cancer, as does "nightmare" and "no end to the marring." Later on Patsy refers to a "terrible ordeal" and "so much time out of their own lives" to suggest she is thinking herself about how much of her life will she miss out on.

Once again we find a fascinating connection between "nightmare" and "public lynching." Patsy finds another way of reminding us of JonBenét's strangulation, which certainly was an unequivocal horror associated with the very beginning of the case. Finally Patsy reassures us in a familiar way that God will help find the killer, and then Patsy shows us how He's going to do it in her final promise, "[with God's help] we will succeed. " This is eerily similar to "Victory !" at the end of the ransom note. Patsy Ramsey is shouting at us, "Look at the similarities in the thoughtprints! Can't you know that I wrote the ransom note?" Patsy Ramsey's deeper intelligence is so brilliant, it places the thoughtprint (of ultimate success) in exactly the same place as the same thoughtprint/idea in the ransom note.

In summary, hear Patsy Ramsey as she calls her communications "leads." If that's the case, then what should the authorities call them? What should a jury call them? Patsy Ramsey's deeper intuition and I are in total agreement about this case. The central question in solving it remains, "Will the police open their minds?'"

November 8, 1999: Ramseys Announce Plans for Their Book on WSMV-TV in Nashville

Thoughtprints: death of innocence, sexual deviation, affair with a blonde, being recognized, writing a book on acting, laying JonBenét, properly laying JonBenét to rest, desire to find killer, call for a new type of investigator. Less than one month after the grand jury's announcement of no indictment, on November 5, 1999 publishing company Thomas Nelson announced the impending release of the Ramseys' book *The Death of Innocence*. Three days later the Ramseys are interviewed on a Nashville television station. As we will see in Chapter 13, once again John Ramsey confesses while desperately trying to hide. He underscores as never before that he indeed sexually abused JonBenét and poignantly explains why.

During the rest of the interview, we can still see Patsy's and John's great need to confess as they continue to insist that they want to keep the investigation alive. The right kind of investigators will not only hear John confess to a sexual crime, but will also recognize Patsy's validation of John's confession when she used the word "hot"—as in a murder about "hot" sexual passion and about Patsy being on the "hot seat," as she continues to point to her cancer. Such investigators will even hear John's self-incrimination in his comment, allegedly about Burke, "[his] grades could be better." John is implying that deep down he recognizes he himself didn't pass the grade as a parent and a spouse. Over and over the Ramseys call for a new investigator.

March 17, 2000: The Ramseys' Book *The Death of Innocence* Released

Despite trying their hardest to cover up their crime, the Ramseys for the first time "speaking uninterrupted," revealing their guilt—once again, between the lines. Together they fill in many details and elaborate on their crime in new ways, as their thoughtprints in their book repeatedly match the same story they've now told us numerous times before. (See Chapter 16, page 219)

March/ April 2000: Series of Book Promotional Interviews with Barbara Walters, Katie Couric, Larry King, and Carol McKinley (Fox)

John and Patsy Ramsey continue to live out their vow to bring JonBenét's killer to justice. While they continue their cover-up and pick up the pace of their relentless media campaign, once more their deeper intelligence finds creative ways of confessing. Now to anyone willing to see it, they leave no doubt of their participation in the murder as they tell one invaluable story after another. (See Chapter 16, page 219)

The Future

From the beginning of the cover-up, starting with the ransom note, the Ramseys have been unable to conceal their guilt. Every time they communicate, they reveal the truth in some way. Taking all their communications as one, the mosaic becomes clearer and clearer as their thoughtprints continue to overlap, confirming the messages from their brilliant deeper intelligence. Very simply, they cannot stop themselves.

Undoubtedly there will be more thoughtprints to come as they fulfill their own predictions. They will find the killer "as God is their witness." The case is only one phone call—one communication—away from being solved. All that is needed is a new detective who will follow the leads that are already there. Without question, the Ramseys themselves have underscored the importance of thoughtprints—these are the leads. But who will hear them?

CHAPTER 13
John and JonBenét—True Confessions

One of the keys to getting the investigation of JonBenét's murder back on track is listening to messages from Patsy's, John's, *and* JonBenét's deeper intelligence. The stories each of them told before the murder, and the stories Patsy and John have told afterward, reveal that each of them knew what was going on in their family relationships—and where it would lead. At times, they even tried to warn themselves.

JonBenét: Distressing Symptoms

Although we have very limited communications from JonBenét, what we do have is enlightening. Kids in distress communicate in specific ways, and JonBenét was no exception. In the year before she was murdered, this child experienced escalating enuresis (bedwetting) and the onset of encopresis (soiling), both of which provide sufficient evidence of emotional trauma. Given what we know of her life, her messages were unmistakable: "Let me show you what I think about what's happening to me. I'm pissed off, really pissed off, and I think the whole thing is one big pile of sh—. And if you need me to say it any clearer, stay away from my bed and stay out of my panties. All of this stinks to high heaven."

JonBenét's body was speaking in other ways, too. She had frequent vaginal infections, and repeated visits to her doctor testify that she was breaking down under the horrendous pressure she felt in her family relationships. Sadly, her pediatrician, Dr. Beuf, missed the messages JonBenét's body was sending, and he continues to insist that twenty-seven doctor visits in three years is "normal." Most pediatricians—and I asked several—and mothers would strongly disagree. Did Beuf look out for JonBenét's best interest or, as a friend of the Ramseys, was he motivated to look the other way?

It's no accident that Lawrence Schiller opened his book, *Perfect Murder, Perfect Town*, with the fascinating story of JonBenét's interaction with the

Ramsey's gardener, Brian Scott. Writers often unconsciously pick up on the real story and try to tell us, just as writers Patsy and John Ramsey have done at key moments. In September 1996, three months before her death, JonBenét asked Scott, "Do roses know their thorns can hurt?" Such a ponderous statement from such a young child. Over a two-year period, the gardener represented to JonBenét a type of comfortable authority figure/therapist with whom she had often spontaneously talked as he was working in the yard. Given the deeper intelligence's need to tell the truth and solve problems, we can assume that JonBenét's beautifully powerful question had deep implications.

There are enough commonly known details about her life for us to know that this child beauty queen was tremendously burdened. She would need someone to talk to. The interactions between JonBenét and Scott were remarkably similar to one between a child and her therapist, in which an adult therapist gets a child to relax, be spontaneous, and communicate in some original way through playing with dolls, by drawing, by making up stories, or simply by talking. Scott once indicated that he felt as though he was in a counselor's role. The nature of JonBenét's question suggests that she was trying to unload her burdens by using her trusted friend, Scott, as a surrogate therapist.

Roses symbolize the purest of loves, so JonBenét was almost certainly alluding to being hurt by someone who loved her, probably a parent. JonBenét's personification of the roses and her questioning their being aware of causing hurt suggests that nurturing people very close to her were unaware they were causing her great pain—sharp, prickly pain, like the pain caused by a thorn. The "softest" of loves had become sharp and dangerous. Most likely JonBenét was referring to both parents and their blind spots, hinting that her parents' love had failed her by not protecting her. In short, JonBenét was trying to tell Scott that she was very confused over love, not only maternal love, but also romantic sexual love, which roses also symbolize (as evidenced by the link between roses and Valentine's Day). JonBenét could also have been talking about herself, about how burdensome her precocious sexuality was to her. Even child beauty queens get roses, and JonBenét may have been implying how much pain that role brought into her life.

Another powerful reference is possible: Something sharp and pointed has pricked her, causing her pain—a long, prickly stem with a red flower on the end, something soft and hard at the same time. It is not difficult to conceptualize a long-stemmed prickly rose as a phallic symbol—a hurtful phallic symbol. JonBenét subtly suggests she was deeply troubled over being abused sexually by a man who supposedly loved her. In essence she was asking if the "loving" man knew that his sexual attention was hurting her. The striking phallic image strongly suggests an adult male, most likely her father. This image fits well with the story Patsy tells in the ransom note, and it also can be connected to the heart on JonBenét's left palm and the heart image in the ransom note. (When she drew a heart on JonBenét's left palm after the murder Patsy was also saying that this murder was about a love triangle— the same message she left in the ransom note with a heart [See Appendix B, page 257].)

Like adults, children possess a deeper intelligence, a "right brain" that communicates through ideas. JonBenét's question about the thorns was not a simple one, and she had other thought-rich questions, too. She also asked Scott why (with the pine needles falling off the trees) trees dripped sap. At the very least, this image suggests that something strong and tall had changed, was seemingly breaking down and leaking. This implies that she was picking up on the breakdown in her family boundaries around her, that the strong, stable environment was leaking. Taking the image a little further we again find phallic symbols: pine needles and a long, tall tree dripping sap, something sticky and light-colored. JonBenét continued to be puzzled, as any sexually abused child would be. On the one hand, she would initially trust an adult and believe that there was nothing wrong with sexual abuse. On the other hand, she would know deep down that it was wrong.

In between her questions about roses and pine trees, JonBenét asked a question about time: "What is a year?" After Scott explained that it was the time it takes the earth to revolve once around the sun, JonBenét immediately linked it to how old she was: "So I've been around the sun five, nearly six, times." JonBenét was wondering how old she *really* was, how old someone was when she was five, nearly six. She seemed to want to make herself old, which is not unusual for any child, but would certainly be a strong wish for a child who was being sexually abused. It was as if she was saying, "I need to be older to do what I'm doing." Even the phrase "I've been around" implies worldly experience.

As Schiller reported, the last time Scott saw JonBenét was six weeks before she was murdered. He was raking leaves, and JonBenét insisted that he leave a pile of leaves for her to play in. Then she immediately connected the pile of leaves to her father: "Last year my dad and I did that." Suddenly she began crying and talked more about her father. "I really miss him. I wish he was around more . . . . Sometimes he goes away for a long time . . . . I really miss him a lot." Then JonBenét became somewhat "bratty" and started pulling the raked leaves out of the top of the barrel and throwing them back over her head. When Scott grabbed the barrel and ran toward the compost pile where he put it down, JonBenét chased him and dumped the leaves out of the barrel.

This picture tells a story: JonBenét was watching a father figure (Scott) holding his long rake, stroking the ground and suddenly she becomes demanding—wanting a treat, wanting to play in a carefree way without boundaries. The demand was triggered by her acute sense of separation from her father who goes away for a long time. The suddenness of her grief as she quickly lapses into tears tells us how much the pain of separation was constantly lurking in the back of her mind. This leads to an impulsive physical activity where she is demanding and outside the boundaries, recklessly dumping leaves everywhere. She suggests a pattern: playful, impulsive, almost reckless acts with her father where boundaries are momentarily suspended and where she feels very special undo a painful sense of separation—something her father encouraged. (She also connects the idea of a year with the playful physical activity with her father, as in "we did that last year.")

Such a pattern would explain precisely John Ramsey's sexual abuse of his daughter—that he was warding off separation and death by an impulsive act where any sense of boundaries was momentarily abandoned. Reckless play or impulsive sex translates as the exact opposite of the worst kind of boundary imaginable—death. JonBenét strongly suggests that all along she was picking up on the massive separation anxiety (fear of death) in the family and coming to everyone's rescue, including her own. This role would fit hand-in-glove with John Ramsey's repeated description of JonBenét as the family sparkplug (See below). Family rescuers and scapegoats—often one and the same—are phenomenally sensitive, and early on JonBenét must have sensed the enormous pain in her parents and tried with all her heart to make it go away.

JonBenét would have been inclined to go along with her father's inappropriate advances because of her own terror of losing him. As a bright five-year-old, JonBenét understood that her mother was suffering from a serious form of cancer and had a poor prognosis. Children with physically ill parents are vulnerable children, and under the circumstances JonBenét was exceptionally prone to experiencing fear over separation from her father, because he would be the only safe adult left, the only parent who wasn't going to leave her, the parent who wasn't going to die. Also, like any other daughter, JonBenét felt "natural romantic" impulses for her father, which would have been greatly intensified if she feared losing him.

As I previously noted, the sense of "our special little secret" often is a primary driver in sexual abuse. Under such conditions JonBenét also would have been more prone than usual to keep such a secret between her father and herself. She couldn't risk confessing and losing him because he was all she had since her mother had been so ill and remained under a dark cloud.

The onset of encopresis (soiling) not long before her death suggests she was also picking up on her mother's growing awareness of the abuse and growing anger. She would have sensed any change in Patsy. The encopresis also reflects the terrible bind JonBenét was in. On the one hand, she terribly needed to bond with her father and was determined not to give him up under any circumstances. On the other hand, she knew her very competitive mother, who had quite a temper on occasion, didn't like her special relationship one bit. Only such a bind can cause a symptom as severe as encopresis—which we must keep in mind doesn't just come out of nowhere. Something extremely troubling was going on in JonBenét's life—a fact investigators have largely ignored, but a fact which is a crucial part of the picture. Such turmoil would offer a logical explanation as to why JonBenét might wonder if roses know how much their thorns hurt those they love.

More Stories Confirm JonBenét's Role

During their interview with Brian Koebel on CNN one week after JonBenét's murder, both Patsy and John unknowingly confirmed that her death was indeed connected to their own pain of separation as they sponta- neously mentioned two major separations: the loss of John's older daughter from his previous marriage in a tragic car accident, as well as Patsy's cancer, which Patsy reminded us, "she (JonBenét) will never have to experience."

John consciously kept asking, "Why? Why? Why?" had JonBenét's death occurred, as he was obviously trying to understand Patsy's and his puzzling explosion that had led to JonBenét's death. However, with his next breath, he consciously answered his own question by making several references to the cloud of death hanging over them. John revealed that the tremendous grief he and Patsy were living with prior to JonBenét's death had led each of them to explode in his or her own way. Responding to the question of how he remembers JonBenét, John said (with great affection), "The thing I remember about her was that if I would frown she would look at me and say, 'Dad, I don't like that face,' and I would smile, and she'd say, 'That's better.'" JonBenét was the one who picked him up when he was down, the one who made him smile. John was hinting that he was secretly depressed and that he was using JonBenét to "pick him up," a common phenomenon in families in pain, families in which hurting members selfishly use another family member to temporarily relieve their suffering.

Patsy immediately followed John's remark in the CNN interview by adding, "She loved her daddy. She loved her daddy. She was Daddy's girl . . . . She's such a happy, spiritual child. She would ask me, 'Mommy, what's the difference in a day and a daydream, and how do you know if a day is real?'" Thus Patsy underscored JonBenét's role as "Daddy's girl," the one in charge of picking him up. But as Patsy told us, JonBenét also expressed confusion about the inordinate pressure placed on her to rescue her parents when she asked her mother if all this was real or just a dream, hinting at JonBenét's difficulty taking in reality. Surely a child who has to express her frustration by encopresis (because she can't say it any other way) is having difficulty holding on to reality.

Patsy told a final story about JonBenét during the *Geraldo* show. According to her, not long before JonBenét died, she asked her mother, "How much do you love me?" When Patsy replied that she loved JonBenét more than anything in the world, JonBenét immediately rebuked her by saying that she was only supposed to love God and Jesus that much. JonBenét was telling her mother that she loved her too much, that she was too close to her. Intuitively JonBenét understood that she was a pawn being used by her mother and her father.

The stories we have from JonBenét reveal that she was very confused and divided, which matches the details of the family dynamics as revealed in the ransom note. JonBenét understood that being sexually abused by her father greatly traumatized her, but she recognized that her father didn't know he was hurting her. At the same time, JonBenét's equally unaware mother joined the abuse by failing to protect her from the pain and by unconsciously encouraging JonBenét's sexual involvement with John. JonBenét questioned her mother's love and reprimanded her for not providing the necessary boundaries between the two of them—for "loving her too much" and not giving JonBenét her own life.

JonBenét probably experienced unconsciously her participation in beauty pageants in the same way she did her father's sexual abuse: more roses, more exploitation, more pain. Despite her pain, JonBenét's terror of being separated from her father drove her to allow the inappropriately bonding. But her burdens became so great that they almost overwhelmed JonBenét's sense of reality. Her parents' behavior was driving her crazy.

Living under such tumultuous circumstances, JonBenét began speaking out through her behavior: first by increased bedwetting and then, in desperation because she was not heard, by soiling. Her body joined with her and began breaking down, further communicating how much all of this pressure was destroying her. But no one was listening. Not her mother. Not her father. Not her pediatrician.

Sexual Acting Out

During their interview with Michael Tracey, the Ramseys underscored the sexual acting out that had taken place between John and JonBenét—the trigger that set off Patsy's murderous rage.

In response to a question he certainly would have expected about sexually abusing JonBenét, John stuttered, "I—I—I don't know how to say it any stronger . . ." John double-blinked every time he explicitly and vehemently denied sexually abusing JonBenét, twice on the word "absolutely [not]" and once on "nothing [happened]." John's stuttering and double-blinking confirmed that he felt anxious, that he was trying to deny the truth by closing his eyes to it, which means he was not telling the truth in the interview.

Patsy's body language matched John's during the interview. Sitting by his side when he responded to the questions about sexual abuse, Patsy suddenly turned to face him as if to confront him ("Oh, yeah?!"). Patsy stuck her tongue out at John when he said, "Absolutely [I didn't do it]" and she closed her eyes after another of John's denials ("false") as if to say, "I don't see it that way. He's lying."

Not surprisingly, John denied ever knowing that JonBenét was a bed wetter, despite her having been a severe and chronic bed wetter for several years and often having to wear protective underpants. Patsy said that she changed JonBenét's sheets several times a week and threw them into a nearby washer before the housekeeper even arrived. JonBenét went to a doctor multiple times because of vaginitis and bedwetting, and she progressed to encopresis during the last few months of her life. Despite all of these obvious clues, John claimed to be completely ignorant of JonBenét's bedwetting problem. Rather obviously John appears to be lying in order to distance himself from anything having to do with JonBenét's private parts. It seems inconceivable he didn't know about his daughter's extensive bedwetting problems.

John used a more subtle message when he used a key analogy in stating, with obvious affection, that "JonBenét was the spark plug of the family." He implied she was the one family member who brightened everybody's day, just as he'd told during the interview on CNN a week after JonBenét's murder. John intuitively was explaining why he acted out with his daughter: In the midst of his and Patsy's pain and terror, JonBenét provided both of them with energy. Unfortunately, spark plugs can also cause explosions.

John's explanation provides a clue about why JonBenét would have been predisposed to go along with the sexual abuse longer than another child might. First of all, JonBenét would have unconsciously sensed her role as the family savior (and scapegoat) as "hero children" often do. She would have been remarkably attuned to the pain both her parents were experiencing. Additionally, John Ramsey traveled a good bit, which would have only intensified JonBenét's separation anxiety and would make her an even more compliant "savior" child when it came to "bonding with Daddy in a special way." JonBenét would have also been inclined to please her mother because of similar separation anxiety, which would motivate her to follow Patsy's unconscious instructions to bond with John. Like the ransom note said, "two gentlemen were watching over" their daughter.

Next, speaking in a high-pitched animated voice, a distinctive change from his normal speaking voice, John Ramsey challenged the slightest suggestion that Patsy and he had been involved in JonBenét's murder. He said, "Help me understand. People think we brutally assaulted JonBenét, then sexually molested her, strangled her, went to bed, got up, wrote a three-page ransom note, called the police, sat around for four hours, and then went downscares [sic] and found the body. I was able to act distraught [he double-blinks]. Patsy was able to make herself throw up because of gut-wrenching anxiety. I was faking it. Please help me understand."

By saying, "We brutally assaulted JonBenét," John hinted that both Patsy and he brutally assaulted JonBenét. Most theorists on the case who believe the Ramseys were involved have always thought one or the other was the primary murderer. But the ransom note indicates that both of them were involved. Patsy confirms the collaboration. She winced noticeably on two words in John's long list of events, thereby revealing what were for her the most difficult aspects of the crime. When he said "strangulation," she closed her eyes and winced, and when he said "wrote a three-page ransom note," she even more prominently winced twice with her eyes closed.

John's verbal response also confirmed the order of events, something that has puzzled investigators. The injury to JonBenét's head came first, then the strangulation. This also matches the order of events described in the ransom note. But John's response suggested a possibility that none of the investigators had mentioned: "strangled her, went to bed, got up, wrote . . . note." After strangling JonBenét, John and Patsy lay down for a while to collect their senses and cool off, which probably was necessary because they would have been terribly alienated from each other. This, too, matches the ransom note, which states, "I advise you to be rested."

Finally John's chronology of events revealed that going down the stairs to find JonBenét's body caused him unspeakable anxiety, so much anxiety that he was terrified of going down the stairs—thus his slip of the tongue, "downscares." John Ramsey had been up and down the stairs all day long, and the only reason he would suddenly be terrified of going downstairs was that he knew what was down there. He knew that from the moment he went "downscares" his life would never be the same. When police officer Linda Arndt instructed him to search the house, John's abrupt charge for the room where JonBenét's body was hidden further reveals how his anxiety had been building. All morning long John and Patsy had sat in a room one floor above their daughter's dead body, hoping that no one would discover it before they did. John had a lot of reasons to think of downstairs as "downscares."

John's describing the correct order of injuries to JonBenét, including the molestation, and his striking slip "downscares" adds credence to the suspicion that he had sexually molested her.

More Strange Stories

We have no idea how hard it was for Patsy to watch her husband strangle her daughter and for her then to have carefully composed the ransom note, coming up with a semiplausible scenario while trying to disguise her handwriting, most likely by writing left-handed, all while her mind was preoccupied with the reality of having just murdered JonBenét.

John said that when he discovered JonBenét was missing, his immediate reaction was "to call out the Russian army and close the airports." John was really saying, "I am a traitor and the murderer is a pilot, which fits me perfectly." John had attempted to arrange a private flight out of Boulder only thirty minutes after discovering JonBenét's body, which not only matches what he said but also suggests that his deeper intelligence was advising the police not to let him leave, which they didn't. Because John didn't say, "Russian Air Force," which would have made more sense, he was suggesting that something destructive had happened on the ground, not in the air. He possibly was referring to carrying out his part of the deed, the strangulation, on the ground floor of the house—the basement. By referring to a foreign terrorist—himself—John suggested using a "foreign faction" as the evil culprit in the ransom note was really his idea.

When asked to describe the worst moment of the night, John said it was when JonBenét was missing. Then he said how relieved he was to discover her body, even though it was obvious that she was dead. JonBenét was cold, stiff, blue, and not breathing. But John insisted that, above all, she was back home and that at least he knew where she was. Most fathers would not have this kind of reaction. Parents hope against hope that a missing child is still alive, and when they reach the point that the child has been gone for days or weeks, when his or her death seems certain, then—and only then—are they relieved to find the body. But no parent would be relieved to find his or her child's dead body only eight hours after discovering she was missing. That would only be true if you are the one who finds the body so you can carry out your plan to beat the police to it and disrupt the crime scene. That kind of relief makes sense only in that context.

John stretched the limits of credulity even further when he said that he had hoped JonBenét was just asleep when he carried her cold, blue, stiff body upstairs after finding her. Surely he knew she was dead. Her body was so stiff that he had to carry her with his arms outstretched, like he was bringing in a load of wood.

Throughout the interview with Tracey, Patsy's and John's deeper mind insisted on confessing, providing motives as well as several hidden confessions. It is possible that, if they had gotten appropriate therapy for their fear and grief beforehand, this crime might never have happened.

John Ramsey Underscores the Sexual Abuse

On November 8, 1999, during the WSMV-TV interview in Nashville, where Thomas Nelson publishing is located, the Ramseys described plans to write a book on the investigation of their daughter's murder. The book's title, *The Death of Innocence*, suggests that they once again are unconsciously confessing and secretly talking about what they did to JonBenét. Indeed "innocence died" when they murdered JonBenét, but they had destroyed her innocence in other ways long before she died. In describing how others have treated them, Patsy and John are really describing their own behavior toward their daughter.

During the interview, John's deeper intelligence underscored that he had been sexually molesting JonBenét, while at the same time he was consciously trying his hardest to conceal his deviation, trying to appear his most spiritually righteous. Instead, he vividly drew attention to his sexual abuse and explained it better than he had at any other time.

Interviewer: Can you understand the public's fascination with this?

John: Well, I think it's a little bit of voyeurism frankly. I think the media has created us into somebody they wanted us to be and that became an exciting soap opera that they didn't have to create.

John chose an example of sexual deviation (voyeurism) as if to remind us, "Think: sexual deviation." And he strongly suggests that sexual deviation is at the heart of JonBenét's murder by using a powerful analogy that is simply too great to be coincidental, and he emphasizes it by adding "frankly." John's pedophilia probably started with voyeurism—observing JonBenét. John described perfectly how it must have unfolded from there: He created JonBenét into somebody he wanted her to be, a fantasy (a safe harbor from pain), and then "it became an exciting soap opera that they didn't have to create." In his brief but vivid response, John summed up the whole story, even touching on his regret: "I didn't have to do it, didn't have to create that fantasy."

> *Interviewer:* How often does it happen that you are recognized in public? And do you ever find yourself wearing disguises or making yourselves so you are not recognized?

> *John:* No, uh, we are recognized . . . We did discuss Patsy wearing a blond wig once, but thought, "That would be great. They'll see me with a blonde." We know where that would go.
>
> You know one of the things that's been comforting to me is that when we are out in public, anyone who has ever stopped us . . . "Don't I know you?" . . . "Aren't you the Ramseys?" Usually they say, "Aren't you JonBenét's parents? Aren't you JonBenét's dad?" I'll say, "Yes." Every time it's been an outpouring of compassion, caring, and sympathy. And that's really been uplifting for us.

Only six questions into the interview John Ramsey responded for the second time with a vivid sexual example, immediately after telling us he doesn't wear disguises and he is recognized. He tells a brief story of disguising Patsy in a wig, which leads him to talk about people seeing him with another woman, seeing him committing an infidelity with a blonde. But isn't this exactly what really happened? He got caught with a blonde, a blonde who looked like Patsy and was a substitute for Patsy, a blonde whom he was terribly unfaithful with. He is easily recognizable, and so is the blonde. He didn't have to tell us that Patsy wore a *blond* wig. It could have just been a wig or a red-haired wig or a hat. Secretly he was confessing to having sex with a blonde—a blonde named JonBenét.

He further confirmed the story by linking the story of the blonde to JonBenét, to being JonBenét's dad, and to needing someone to lift him up when he is down. Once more he conveyed his great need for comfort and sympathy in the face of loss. John grieves the loss of his daughter, JonBenét, but he also grieves the loss of the comfort she gave him when he was consumed by grief over his other losses. JonBenét temporarily lifted him up. For

John, JonBenét was Patsy in a blond wig. John Ramsey's deeper intelligence sums up in one phrase the essence of the sexual abuse. Being threatened by the loss of Patsy, he reached out to the closest substitute on the face of the earth—little Patsy (JonBenét Patricia Ramsey), Patsy with a blond wig.

John the Actor

During the same interview on the Nashville television station, John talked about how he had behaved since JonBenét's death.

Interviewer: One other thing he (Governor Bill Owens of Colorado) said, and I'll get off this. He said you weren't behaving the way he would if one of his children had been killed. He said, "I'd be at the police station saying, 'What can I do to help?'" And, you know, that may be something that people do struggle with when they talk about this case. You left the city; you went away. Can there be a perception that you're just not helping the police?

John: I take offense at anybody who says, "He didn't act right." I think I can write a book on how you act when you've lost a child. When you've lost a child, nothing else matters. You really don't want to be. You're rendered as low as you can possibly be without dying. And our focus was on laying JonBenét to rest properly, and that's really all that mattered during that period of time.

During his marketing efforts for his and Patsy's forthcoming book and in response to the accusation that he isn't behaving like a normal parent who has lost a child, John says that he could write (another) book on how a person should act. Could he really be saying that the book he and Patsy have written is about acting? His brilliant deeper intelligence would reveal his true intentions by talking about a book, and he couldn't say it any plainer: "I think I can write a book on how you act when you've lost a child." Perhaps *The Death of Innocence* is all about how to act—how to strike a pose when you want the authorities to think you had nothing to do with the death of your child. Perhaps Patsy and John's book tells how to act like you're grieving, when you're really more worried about getting caught.

John provided several other revealing messages in this statement. "When you've lost a child [he says it twice], nothing else matters. You really don't want to be. You're rendered as low as you can possibly be without dying." This statement revealed how depressing JonBenét's death was for Patsy and him. He suggested they became preoccupied with "laying JonBenét to rest properly," which echoes the haunting threat in the ransom note: "You will be denied her remains for proper burial." John used a key ransom note word, "proper," and linked it to JonBenét's body and her burial to make sure everyone saw it and understood that he was describing what he felt the night when he decided he had to end JonBenét's life. He was talking about JonBenét, Patsy, and himself.

Self-protectively, he and Patsy were consumed during that period of time with one idea: properly laying JonBenét to rest by covering up the improper events of the chaotic evening. And that is exactly what they did. They placed her body in a "proper," fixed way when they staged the crime to cover it up. But not only did the proper child JonBenét die that night, but the proper family also died. Life as they had known it as proper, upstanding successful people was over, and they were trying to lay themselves to rest as painlessly as possible.

Something else went through his mind that night after Patsy's blow to the head had knocked JonBenét unconscious, before he strangled her. "Proper burial" is mentioned in exactly the same place in the ransom note—between the first and second assaults. When JonBenét lay hopelessly unresponsive on the floor before their very eyes, both Patsy and John soon realized they had lost her, that the JonBenét they had known and loved would never again be herself. Once she had been assaulted, the proper child, the perfect child, was no more. Her head trauma was so severe, that is was obvious that, if she lived, the best that they could hope for was that she would be a vegetable.

John seemed to saying, "Don't you understand? JonBenét was gone. As much as we hated it, as much as we regret it, we had lost her"—JonBenét was at that moment rendered as low as she could possibly be without dying. John Ramsey's vivid image of "as close to death as possible but not dead" fits so well with the sequence of events suggested in the ransom note and autopsy that it's too great to be coincidental. Of course, Patsy and John also didn't want to get caught, but John strongly implied that neither he nor Patsy felt that they could go on living if they had to face a damaged child, a child who would be at best a living shadow of her former self, and each time they looked at her face they would be reminded that they had killed their proper child, the real JonBenét. John was already living with the terrible trauma that his older daughter's body had been destroyed in a fatal car accident and that Patsy's body had been partially destroyed by cancer. Living with a brain-damaged JonBenét would be an ongoing reminder for both John and Patsy of their overwhelming personal terrors.

But Patsy and John also knew that the second they got help for JonBenét they would lose her, because if she lived, the authorities would take her away. JonBenét had vaginal bleeding and a head injury, and the authorities would have deemed both Patsy and John as unfit parents, which would mean they might also take Burke. Even if JonBenét died in the hospital, the authorities still might take Burke, and Patsy and John would face a horrible court battle to get Burke back after serving whatever jail time they had to serve. The court battle would most likely take its their toll on the marriage, and Burke would have nothing left to go home to. They saw no way out, which ex-plains why Patsy and John would have become fixated on laying JonBenét to rest properly, on telling their proper child good-bye.

Moments like these reveal how our unconscious deeper intelligence is really our friend when it confronts us with the truth. Consciously, John Ramsey couldn't reveal so poignantly why he abused JonBenét, and he was probably just as surprised by his impulses as anyone else. By connecting such an obvious sexual phrases to the powerful effect death had on him, John repeated the same story he and Patsy have told before. The patterns—the thoughtprints—are far too significant to be mere coincidence and answer his frequently repeated question in different interviews "Why did this happen?"

Another story about John Ramsey's sexuality fits in striking ways. As Lawrence Schiller reported in his book on the case, shortly after the Ramseys had met Lou Smit, John Ramsey wrote him a letter—in an obvious effort to manipulate him. In the letter, Ramsey confessed to having once committed adultery in his first marriage and told Smit that he wanted him to hear it from him and not some tabloid. At first blush, it seems that Ramsey wanted to come across as honest and forthright, but his deeper intelligence had an-other plan. John Ramsey is removing all doubts and confessing that he has a tendency toward acting out sexually. His impulsivity in immediately con-fessing tells us the same tendency is still present. Instead of demonstrating patience and waiting for Smit to bring it up (which would have then been the perfect moment to be forthright and add, "but that was years ago when I was young and foolish"), John Ramsey couldn't wait to tell Smit about his sexual indiscretions. In the process, he was socially inappropriate, which should have been another clue. You don't tell someone you've just met such personal information—especially in writing. Ramsey's behavior had guilt written all over it, and putting it in writing left no doubts about how much it was troubling him. Under the circumstances, between the lines, John Ramsey's excessive need to reveal his previous sexual sins strikingly confirms he acted out sexually with JonBenét.

CHAPTER 14
Friends and Family Talk

We human beings are amazingly perceptive. We pick up on the slightest nuances in relationships—nothing escapes us. That's what I was banking on when I talked to several people who knew John and Patsy Ramsey. And I wasn't disappointed. These people were each able to recall key stories, events, or communications from the Ramseys that pointed to secret emotions locked up inside the couple, emotions that could lead to an explosion.

Insight sometimes comes from the briefest of encounters. I coincidentally met one of John Ramsey's former limo drivers. The driver initially described him as being "polite and quiet." But I knew there had to be more. After some gentle prodding, the driver told me that John Ramsey was the least communicative person who had ever ridden with him. The driver recalled that Mr. Ramsey always liked to have his coffee ready for him, but after chitchatting for a very short time, Ramsey usually lapsed into prolonged silence. The driver also added that whenever he picked up John Ramsey, regardless of the time of day (often in the early morning) or the brightness of the sun, Ramsey had on sunglasses—and kept them on, despite being constantly surrounded by tinted windows. The driver often would look in the rearview mirror and was unable to tell if the silent man was asleep or awake. Trained not to intrude, the driver kept to himself, and he and Ramsey would ride for miles in utter silence.

Sunglasses and silence tell us some things about John Ramsey. If it is true that the eyes are the windows to the soul, then John Ramsey seemingly didn't want anyone to see his soul. John Ramsey was keeping, particularly from himself, some terrible secrets. Because he didn't like to talk, Ramsey had to communicate in other ways. As with any human being, what's inside must eventually come out.

Patsy's former good friend and professional photographer Judith Phillips, a Boulder resident, remembered the same silence. Judith knew the Ramseys both in Atlanta and Boulder. Her former husband, an attorney, did legal work for the Ramseys, setting up their wills and trusts, and also had previously worked with Patsy Ramsey. At times the Phillipses traveled with the Ramseys, and Judith even played on the softball team, "Moms Gone Bad," which Patsy started and Access Graphics sponsored. Other Boulder teammates included Susan Stine, Roxy Walker, Priscilla White, and Patti Novak (all familiar names in the JonBenét saga). Judith also photographed both Patsy and JonBenét.

Judith Phillips described how uncomfortable one-on-one John made her with his silence. Whenever she was seated next to him at a dinner party, he continually rebuffed her attempts to establish communication—answering questions with clipped responses, often with a simple "yes" or "no." He showed no interest in Judith and made no effort to engage her in conversation, which made two interactions with John Ramsey on two other occasions stand out like bizarre snapshots. These two incidents take us to the heart of JonBenét's murder and answer crucial questions about John Ramsey, about what kind of man was behind the sunglasses.

One year while in Boulder with her husband who was under the weather, Judith Phillips attended the Ramsey Christmas party alone. As she approached the front door, John Ramsey greeted her with a dramatic change in his demeanor, wide-eyed and distinctly looking her over from tip to top. He began raving over her, "Wow, Judith! Do you look great!" Judith was shocked by John Ramsey's suggestive once-over and his effusive praise. She'd had men fawn over her at times, but John Ramsey's marked change and look was excessive. She knew that kind of look.

What he did next was even more revealing. Immediately, he dragged Patsy over, as he once again raved over Judith. "I want you to see this," he told Patsy. "Doesn't Judith look great?" This made Judith even more uneasy. She felt that John Ramsey's fawning over her in such a way was a put-down to Patsy, particularly coming from a man who rarely handed out compliments. In the briefest of moments, John Ramsey showed what he was hiding: an intense sexuality that could overpower him, even to the point of being inappropriate, and the need to demonstrate this sexuality to Patsy, at the same time both putting her down and confessing. John Ramsey implied that, given the right circumstances, he could be sexually inappropriate and would subtly flaunt it enough to get himself caught.

However, Patsy's reaction surprised Judith almost as much as John's had. Patsy joined John in praising her friend's looks and did it in such an excessive manner, as though they were toying with her, that Judith felt even more like a sex object. Upon reflection, Judith thinks Patsy was, on some level, aware of her friend's discomfort and vulnerability as a woman alone, and cruelly added to Phillips's being treated as a sex object. A few minutes later, Patsy pushed her friend to sit on Santa's lap and have her picture made, which Judith experienced as more inappropriate sexual behavior on Patsy's part. The experience was so disconcerting, Judith left the party early.

Through her behavior, Patsy was asking her friend to play the uncomfortable role of the sex object—the sexual woman—most likely repeating with Judith what she did with JonBenét. Patsy revealed her inclination to push women onto men, especially her husband, as a way of managing her own uncomfortable sexuality (underscored by her sexual dysfunction, frigidity). For their parts, John Ramsey and JonBenét seemed to have gotten the message.

Some time after that, in the fall of the year, Judith dropped by Patsy's house at 7:30 one morning to measure a wall for several of Judith's photographs, which Patsy intended to hang. She had walked the few blocks to the house, but the weather was cool, and John Ramsey asked Judith if he could drop her off at home on his way to take JonBenét to school. Patsy had already left to take Burke to school, so Judith accepted John's offer. He was driving a small Jeep, which had only two doors and a tiny back seat. Assuming JonBenét would get in the back, Judith waited on her to enter first, but JonBenét had no intention of sitting anywhere but up front next to her father. Surveying the scene, Judith couldn't believe what she was seeing. She stood and stared at John and JonBenét for a moment. Neither of them moved; they just sat there looking at the waiting woman. Any responsible adult would have insisted his child get in the back, but not John Ramsey. JonBenét was announcing where her place was, declaring powerfully through her actions that she was taking the adult seat and that she wasn't about to move. Judith has never forgotten having to squeeze past JonBenét to get into the small back seat.

Although not a word was said, John and JonBenét's actions shouted loudly what was going on in the family: JonBenét was John's little queen, "his girl" who was used to displacing anyone else who came along. This was a role her father obviously had groomed her for. Once again, John Ramsey's actions blatantly confessed to his misdeeds. Is there any doubt that Patsy would have gotten the same messages and had experienced JonBenét displacing her with her husband on other occasions? And she unconsciously would have been encouraging the dysfunctional enmeshment and confusion of roles.

Abundant hints exist that show Patsy and John Ramsey were repeating dysfunctional family patterns—secret, disturbing "incestuous" love triangles that were also described in the ransom note. Here are strong hints of the forces lurking in John Ramsey and of the distinct roles that he and his youngest daughter were caught up in. Certainly these are not sufficient to take to court on their own, but they do provide another piece of the puzzle, validating precisely what the ransom note tells us.

The same roles are apparent in family photographs, none more so than in the well-known Christmas 1994 photo in which Patsy sits up front (in the dominant role) wearing a huge, shiny cross around her neck, while Burke is off to her left. Behind her back on the right, John and JonBenét sit so closely together they appear to be merged as one. All that can be seen of John Ramsey are his face and hands, which are in overly familiar places, nearly touching JonBenét's genital area. The photograph implies, "Look at what's going on behind Patsy's back."

The Friendship: Judith and Patsy

Judith Phillips saw the charming fun, side of Patsy Ramsey and, as time went on, she saw her other side, too. Seeing her friend in a bad light didn't come easily for Judith. Like Patsy's other friends, Judith was protective of Patsy (and even of John). At first, she simply couldn't fathom either parent being involved in the murder, but slowly the pieces started to fall in place. Immediately after the murder, the Ramseys began blaming all their friends as possible suspects. Then Patsy essentially cut off her friendship with Judith, allowing herself to be controlled by Susan Stine, at whose home they were staying after the murder. Susan Stine had become possessive of Patsy and spoke for her, and for whatever reasons, wouldn't let Judith near Patsy. (Patsy later reported in her book, *The Death of Innocence*, that Judith had come to visit her only to get her to sign releases for pictures of Patsy, but Judith said she simply had gone to comfort her grieving friend.)

Several times Judith had seen Patsy unpredictably and suddenly cut people off from her friendship without batting an eye. Judith had experienced it herself. One time Judith's husband, who had worked with Patsy at another company in Atlanta, had corrected her about an error she had made in preparing a brochure. Basically Patsy didn't get her way, so (while never overtly protesting) Patsy simply ceased speaking to Judith. Just as suddenly, four months later at a party, Patsy introduced Judith and her husband to someone as "our best friends." Patsy also made it plain that she wanted Judith at her beck and call, both as a friend and a photographer, and when Patsy's demands were impossible to meet, she once again distanced herself from Judith. These sudden swings in Patsy's temperament helped convince Judith that Patsy could abruptly turn on anyone and that she possessed the necessary rage to carry out a murder. This is precisely how the Ramseys behaved toward Judith after the murder, later painting her in their book as a distant acquaintance.

Patsy dominated and used people. Judith laughed at Patsy's (and John's) claim that they were minimally invested in their daughter's beauty pageants. She knew about JonBenét's elaborate outfits—outshining her competitors in even the most minor of pageants—and about Patsy currying favor by giving the judges gifts. Patsy would also come to daytime social events extremely overdressed, effectively putting other women down. On one occasion, Patsy bought a large diamond ring and flaunted it, dramatically holding her ring next to her face. Patsy selected for friends women who would put her on a pedestal, women who would concede how lucky they were to be "Patsy Ramsey's friends," sounding as if they were back in junior high school. For the most part, Patsy's cadre of friends were women who lacked her glamour and social skills and who seemed grateful just to be around her. Many of these same women later became her ardent defenders, "Patsy's Pit Bulls," according to Judith.

Patsy apparently got her mile-wide competitive streak from her mother, Nedra. Nedra had reinforced Patsy's success and had pushed her into beauty pageants but, as Judith witnessed on more than one occasion, Nedra spewed biting put-downs of Patsy, so shocking that Judith was completely surprised that Patsy didn't speak up for herself. Of course, Nedra delivered the knife in the back subtly "Southern-belle style," between the lines, but effectively. For example, Nedra once said, "Patsy loves to spend John Ramsey's money. As long as he makes it, she's going to spend it. Now there's nothing wrong with it, but *I* wouldn't do it." An unkind, critical comment delivered ever-so-politely, barely recognizable that one Southern belle had just stabbed another one in the back. When you cut somebody's throat, do it with a smile. And Nedra's little snippets at Patsy were quite frequent.

Nedra is a mother who is deeply divided about her daughter. On the one hand, she praises her to the high heavens, but on the other, she brings her down faster than you can say "jack rabbit." It's no wonder Judith Phillips repeatedly experienced Patsy as the mirror image her mother, capable of subtle but extreme anger and sudden betrayal. Patsy Ramsey had good reason to demonstrate the same behavior toward her own daughter. Judith observed Patsy becoming overly critical of JonBenét.

Nedra demonstrated the same mixed messages toward Patsy's father. Surely he was her man—but, just as surely, she must have pushed Patsy toward him. When John Ramsey moved to Boulder to form Access Graphics and took his family with him, Nedra stayed in Atlanta while her husband, Don Paugh, followed the Ramseys west. He had been instrumental in helping John Ramsey get his business going, and Paugh continued to work for him. For more than six months, Patsy's father lived with them in a relatively small condo in Boulder while they were finding a house. Nedra intensely disliked Boulder and stayed in Atlanta with her other two grown children. John Ramsey was frequently out of town on business, so Patsy and her father were left in Boulder, living with her two children in the condo.

Here was more than meets the eye. First of all, Patsy had selected John Ramsey as her mate—a divorced man with three children who was thirteen years older than she. John was remarkably like her father in both personality and profession, clear hints that she had married a father figure. Years later in Boulder, Patsy and her father were symbolically recreating the "family romance" fantasy, in which the little girl marries her father, and in this case, with the mother's encouragement. Judith Phillips observed that Patsy and her father were extremely close, and that of his three daughters, she was clearly his favorite.

One particular incident stood out to Judith. One night Judith and her husband had invited Patsy and John over for dinner, but Patsy and her father showed up instead. John had unexpectedly gone out of town, and without discussion, Don Paugh became his substitute. In its own way, this is duplicated by JonBenét and her father.

I am not implying that something overtly sexual was going on between Patsy and her father, nor that he ever overtly sexually abused her. But there is strong evidence that Patsy Ramsey was sexually abused in some way. Patsy had major sexual problems—she was frigid. Sexual problems like this don't just come out of the blue. Something powerful caused her to shut down sexually, to deny strong natural sexual impulses. For some reason, Patsy linked her sexual impulses with dire consequences, because frigidity is always fear-based. Judith Phillips saw Patsy's need to shut down sexually as she recalled an occasion when a group of women were discussing oral sex. Patsy was extraordinarily naïve, causing Roxy Walker to tell Patsy, "Quit being such a Pollyanna." Finally, Patsy acknowledged that she didn't engage in sexual relations often, and never in oral sex.

Later, in her frustration, Patsy would reach out to her housekeeper, Linda Hoffman, for sexual advice. As Judith noted, this is the last person she would have expected Patsy to consult—a matronly lady who cleaned houses. But upon reflection, it seems obvious that Patsy was strongly suggesting what was behind her frigidity. While Patsy may have been embarrassed to discuss it with friends, by seeking counsel from a kind mother figure who greatly admired her, Patsy, in a sense, may have been seeking permission for her sexuality. Every young girl needs her mother's approval of her sexuality, and often frigidity is viewed as a denial of sexuality so as not to displease the mother. In Patsy's eyes, Linda Hoffman would have represented the perfect mother, someone safe and non-competitive, someone perhaps the opposite of Nedra Paugh, who, Judith observed, was not a "huggy" person.

For years, many clinicians have believed that two of the primary sources of frigidity are (1) a young girl being overstimulated sexually and (2) then becoming afraid of her impulses—afraid of losing control, afraid of guilt, and afraid somebody else (namely a mother figure) is going to punish you. It's not hard to see how both conditions fit Patsy Ramsey. If she got too emotionally close to her father, she could easily have been sexually stimulated.

Patsy's parents suggest personality splits in themselves. Judith Phillips never noticed Nedra making frequent sexual comments other than an occasional off-the-wall statement such as, "Women watch what you eat; your body is the most important thing you have to give a man." Similarly, she never picked up on Don Paugh making sexual comments or being out of line. But, from reports at their jobs, both Nedra and Don Paugh could be sexually inappropriate at times. One female employee at Access Graphics described Don's crude staring, and Nedra and her youngest daughter Polly bragging with employees at Access Graphics about the size of young Burke's penis. On another work occasion, Polly provocatively asked a man how he felt about oral sex. When her boss Jane Stobie confronted her, Nedra intervened, telling in graphic detail about why oral sex was sinful. Polly and Nedra saw nothing wrong with their bizarre and inappropriate behavior.

Nedra is unaware of her sexual inappropriateness, even as she rails against it, thus showing and denying it at the same time. She obviously passed the same message onto one daughter, Polly. Wouldn't Patsy have gotten the message, too—encouraged to show her sexuality and at the same time to deny it? Wouldn't this begin to explain her frigidity and her life as a beauty pageant contestant? Might not Patsy have had good reasons for passing the same unspoken message onto JonBenét? Beauty pageants are perfect vehicles for living out such sexual confusion, which explains why JonBenét's sexual exploitation in pageants was glaringly obvious to everyone—everyone but the Ramseys. Like mother, like daughter, like granddaughter. All in all, Nedra points to a huge split in her own sexuality and to the same turmoil in Patsy.

The evidence suggests Patsy Ramsey grew up in a sexually confused family, which could easily have frightened young Patsy, the oldest child. Also with two sisters following closely on her heels, Patsy and her father could have formed a special bond out of both their needs for attention, particularly with Patsy being his unquestioned favorite. For her part, Nedra could have unconsciously been pushing Patsy at an early age toward her father (liked she pushed Patsy to shine in pageants) and, at the same time, not liking their closeness one bit. Nedra once remarked that men only had one thing on their mind, even suggesting her own dislike of sex to some degree. Did she push Patsy to be the premier sexual object—Miss America—while at the same time saying, "Look, but don't touch"? Patsy's frigidity suggests that her take-home message was "be the sex object, but shut it down after that."

Patsy must have incorporated all those mixed messages and confusion. On the one hand, she was the special daughter, the special female with the seductive charm that could get all the votes. She must have seen herself as enormously sexually powerful, which also meant that she was in dangerous waters, considering how Nedra would knock Patsy's feet out from under her just as quickly as she would exalt her. Under these conditions, a girl would head to "La-La Land," to "Pollyanna Land." She would play as dumb as dumb can be, and, above all, she would shut down sexually. That's the only safe place to be, which is why, years later when she's looking for somebody to show her the way out, she searches for the kindest, safest mother figure she can find, somebody who will give her permission to be a woman—somebody like Linda Hoffman. But deep down she's been keeping score herself, and she doesn't like it one bit that she's missed out on something. She's hurt, angry, confused, afraid—in short, one big, walking time bomb, even before she gets cancer.

One of the hallmarks of dysfunctional families is the lack of clear boundaries, the lack of each member being a distinct individual. Under such conditions, everyone becomes the other's pawn, constantly playing a prescribed role. In Patsy's family we see boundary problems galore. The daughters become the extension of the mother, who insists on having beauty queens to shine for her. And one beauty queen lives out her unconscious wish to take the lead female's place and win over the father, most likely accomplishing something Nedra herself couldn't in an earlier time. We see Patsy's over-attachment to Nedra when she won't stand up to her mother, but still calls her long-distance ten times a day, running up huge phone bills.

At the same time, Patsy's father encourages Patsy to cross the boundaries by becoming over-attached to him even in her adult life, still enacting a "let's play house" fantasy with her father. This is the same father who works for her husband and who helped get his business started. (In fact, the whole family works for John Ramsey—another sign of co-dependency and the failure of family members to be individuals.) Patsy seemed to have repeated the same pattern with JonBenét, pushing her on stage and toward her father as a way of solving her own problems. If she couldn't be adequate as a woman, she would do the next best thing to control the situation—send in the substitute of her choice, groomed by her, so much a part of Patsy that JonBenét was almost an extension of Patsy herself.

And John Ramsey played his part. Growing up with a distant, controlling father in a dysfunctional family of his own, John had some of the same issues. He seemingly had a tendency toward infidelity—in high school (where he had one popular girlfriend and a party girl on the side), through his first marriage (his affair ended the marriage), and continued this pattern in his second. As the oldest son, perhaps he had been encouraged to try to meet his mother's emotional needs and, like Patsy, got too close emotionally to the opposite-sex parent. It wouldn't be unexpected with such a cold father. His father had his own boundary problems, marrying John Ramsey's ex-mother-in-law within three months of losing his wife, John's mother, to cancer.

Everywhere one turns, the boundaries are defective, and in a high-spirited, competitive, hard-driving family like the Paughs—a family one Access Graphics employee called "the meanest people I've ever met" and another describes as "evil"—you have the makings of a dangerous situation. Add to that a cold ruthlessness from the Ramsey side (John Ramsey's father was so dominant they called him "Czar"), and indeed you have a recipe for a huge explosion. Throw into that mix a life-threatening event like Patsy's cancer, and the potion becomes even more potentially lethal.

Patsy Ramsey apparently had been running from one activity to another all her life, hopping from one stage to another, hoping her performance could finally quiet the demons. However, as Judith Phillips observed, after her cancer, Patsy went into overdrive. Busy before, she became busier and busier, which her Christmas letters reflect, as if believing cancer can't hit a moving target. (The length of the ransom note reflects the same energy.) But the faster she goes, the more she is in danger of losing control.

Another Viewpoint: Jane Stobie, Employee

Jane Stobie has already provided us a look at Nedra's shadow side (her primitive sexuality), which surfaced more clearly in her work environment, away from her social life. Jane saw the same shadow side in John Ramsey and Don Paugh, perhaps explaining why John Ramsey was notorious for keeping his personal and business life separate, almost never socializing with his employees. Jane Stobie worked at Access Graphics both in Boulder and Atlanta for four years, beginning in 1990. She worked for John Ramsey and Don Paugh and was supervisor over John's in-laws, Nedra and Patsy's sister Polly, in Atlanta.

As one of the few employees who's spoken out, Jane has been characterized by the Ramseys as a disgruntled former employee and, therefore, was often ignored by the press. Instead, I found her to be a bright, capable person who, for a variety of reasons, was trying to tell the truth. In her unusual book, *JonBenét's Gift*, Jane talks of being a medium and of the deceased JonBenét speaking through her as a channel. However, she also clearly describes her association with the Ramseys and the Paughs, and she presented compelling reasons to explain why both of the Ramseys could have been involved in the murder—something she had presented publicly long before she wrote her story.

In 1990 after going to work at Access Graphics in the marketing department, Jane discovered that the business environment John Ramsey had created spoke volumes about him. Two attributes stood out to her immediately: the unpredictability and the need to blame. She eventually noticed a particular pattern to the unpredictability. Different people would be selected as the golden boy or girl, would be praised effusively, and then, without warning, their star would fall as fast as it had risen if something displeased John Ramsey, who often fired people on a whim. Without ever knowing why, these employees would discover that responsibilities had been taken away or they would be fired. John Ramsey and his father-in-law needed people to play that particular role: golden boy gone bad. Secrecy and a lack of communication were hallmarks of the unpredictability. John Ramsey also left the firing of employees—the dirty work—up to others, often to his father-in-law Don Paugh, known by some as the "Hatchet Man."

A corporation, particularly a small one the size of Access Graphics, takes on the personality of its leader. The secrecy and the failure to communicate reflect the a man who himself hides behind sunglasses in silence or who sits next to a dinner guest without conversing. The need to split others into good or bad and the sudden unpredictable abandonment tells us precisely what was going on inside of John Ramsey. Something had caused him to feel extremely insecure and on the verge of sudden abandonment, and whatever this was, it triggered enormous guilt in John Ramsey, which he was trying to cover up.

It's not difficult to understand that the powerful personal losses—his mother, his daughter, his father, and his wife (almost and possibly still)— had left him psychologically bordering on catastrophe, and had filled him with guilt, much in the way that trauma victims react. Having to live constantly under the cloud of "the other shoe," Ramsey must have felt that the storm that was sure to drop on him. He needed others to share his burden.

For a non-communicator like John Ramsey, someone who tries to stand as far away from himself as he possibly can, it's a given that he would act out his trauma. Likewise, Patsy, who was too busy to stop and think, would enact her own version of the same story, by also suddenly and unpredictably abandoning people for the slightest reasons. John acts out in his world (business) and Patsy acts out in hers (social circles).

Patsy and John were like peas in a pod even as they tried to cover-up their pain. Upon reflection, Judith Phillips thought Patsy loved "her things" so much that she would find it easier to dispose of JonBenét after the head injury than to confess and lose her "stuff" by being sent to jail. Jane Stobie thought John Ramsey was obsessed with having the young, beautiful people around him. (Access had a disproportionate number of these "beautiful people," and older people and minorities were the first to be let go.) In other words, externals would solve their problems—keeping focused on the outside keeps the pain and guilt buried inside. Or so they thought.

If Patsy and John couldn't own their guilt even before the murder, how much less could they admit it after? They were desperate to blame the murder on someone else. Why would it be any different when it came to blaming JonBenét? People who can blame innocent adults are only one step away from blaming innocent children. This explains how Patsy would have been prone to blame JonBenét for the sexual abuse. Jane Stobie felt, after knowing the Ramseys' capacity to shift the blame, that after the murder they would each blame the other, as well as JonBenét, for what happened. Jane felt certain they had convinced themselves that JonBenét had caused this with her seductiveness or other behavior. Jane Stobie had experienced how Patsy's mother, father, and sister so unreasonably blamed her for firing them when she was just following orders. As a result, she saw how Patsy had been groomed to deny responsibility. After all, Miss America candidates must be perfect. And later they live with their perfect husbands in perfect towns like Boulder.

Stobie observed other strange behaviors in John Ramsey. From time to time, he would suddenly disappear for a few hours without even his secretary knowing where he was—highly unusual behavior for a CEO. Where had this secret man gone? He had tried to keep his sexual behavior secret, both in his home and in his first marriage. Did his secret behavior at work involve sex? Like Judith Phillips, Jane had observed John Ramsey staring at women, but she had heard of only one incident that implied sexual impropriety, and she herself had observed none. (Similarly, a Ramsey maid reported that once when Patsy was out of town, she found long, red hairs on Patsy's side of the bed, which clearly appeared as though someone had slept there.)

Along with others in the corporation, Jane Stobie noticed a change in John Ramsey after his oldest daughter's death in January 1992. He became greedier and more sinister. Even his defender Jim Marino, a long-time friend whom John Ramsey had rescued from unemployment after an injury, discussed with Jane how John had changed. Repeated financial irregularities arose, many of which favored the Ramseys. Nedra Paugh, who worked for Access in Atlanta, took off for two weeks at John Ramsey's request to babysit JonBenét and Burke, and she later falsified time cards, indicating she had worked those two weeks. Access Graphics/Lockheed also paid for extensive, personal, long-distance phone calls from Patsy to her mother in Atlanta. Stobie was instructed to ignore this fact. Don Paugh lived in the company condominium for 18 months, paid for by Access Graphics, and he never paid the required income tax on the benefit. John Ramsey's private airplane hangar at Jeffcoat Airport was paid for by Lockheed, which had bought out Access. Eventually, when others in the company (including Jane Stobie and Jeff Merrick) noticed the deceit, John Ramsey moved some company records to his hangar to justify Lockheed's paying the bill. Jane insisted, "Jeff Merrick knows John Ramsey's evil. We talked about it." Some in the company called it the "Evil Empire."

Jane Stobie had an up-close and personal look at the nepotism and the boundary problems in Access Graphics. Not only did she see John Ramsey's ruthless side, she also witnessed first-hand the tremendous manipulation of Patsy's mother Nedra and her sister Polly. Jane had been transferred to Atlanta to work on closing the division in which Nedra and Polly worked. Reportedly, John Ramsey had come to the conclusion that the nepotism didn't look good. Nevertheless, when Jane confronted Nedra with her pink slip, Nedra became demanding and threatening. Later Polly, who was pregnant, had her baby prematurely, something the Paughs blamed on Jane. Finally, Don Paugh, who had sent Jane Stobie to carry out his orders to revamp the Atlanta office, rebuked her unmercifully upon her return for doing the very thing he had requested. Entitlement and payback are everywhere, including at the heart of the ransom note, in which the killers tell us they are entitled to do what they are doing because of the injustices inflicted upon them.

Was Jane Stobie telling the truth about John and Patsy Ramsey—and about Patsy's family? Was she a capable observer or someone who jumped on the Ramseys when they were down? Her observations suggest she is one of the few people who experienced the shadow side of the Ramseys—so much so that she wasn't shocked when she picked up a newspaper and read about JonBenét's death. Her immediate reaction was to think that this was an inside job—an interesting testimony of its own.

The Story in One Word

The mainstream media, typified by *Newsweek* writer Dan Glick, says it can't find anything to suggest that the Ramseys had a shadow side, that they could never do such a thing. Obviously, they either didn't do their homework (by interviewing those who knew otherwise), or they chose to ignore the facts, or they simply don't understand human nature.

The story, from beginning to end, can be summed up in one word: splits. Huge splits in personalities. Only such splits could explain how two seemingly loving parents could kill their daughter. Two people with courage enough to face such a possibility are Judith Phillips and Jane Stobie, both of whom have witnessed these splits.

Patsy Ramsey loved JonBenét, but used her. Patsy Ramsey was frigid, but possessed strong sexual impulses. Patsy Ramsey pushed her daughter as hard as she could toward John, but resented the daughter's success.

John Ramsey loved his daughter, but used her. John Ramsey, loving and morally upright father with two daughters, became overwhelmed by his own pain and violated his baby girl. John Ramsey, quiet and socially withdrawn, could be ruthless in business and possessed a primitive sexual streak. Even John's first mother-in-law described his split self: controlled and stoic in the face of grief over the loss of his oldest daughter, then suddenly breaking into sobs alone in his room at night.

Only by facing such powerful splits in the Ramseys can we understand this murder. Here is the story of a child beauty, living in her mansion in magnificent Boulder, Colorado, a stone's throw from the Rockies, on

Christmas night, after a joyous time of gifts and family togetherness, topped off by a party with friends, returning home with her trophy parents—the beauty queen and the CEO—only to be murdered, most likely in her own room by her own parents, when their shadow side finally has its day.

Patsy and John Ramsey were caught up in a modern-day Greek tragedy, living out roles that had been thrust upon them—roles they chose to continue playing. Patsy Ramsey, overly attached to her mother, pushed into beauty pageants, pushed into an overly close relationship with her father (which possibly doomed her to frigidity), passed the mantle on to her daughter, who would repeat the cycle of the daughter taking the mother's place and living out the family romance fantasy while the mother simmers disapprovingly in the background. But this time the stakes were higher. Everyone's pain was greater, particularly the mother's and father's (Patsy and John), the key players. This time the mother had a very real possibility she indeed would disappear from the scene, and the daughter held the distinct possibility she might take over the dominant female role in the house. The father's pain was so great that he needed the daughter in the role full-force, because he was so terrified he was going to lose the mother (like he had lost his own mother, his father, and his oldest daughter) that he had to have someone right now.

Cancer had set the stage for the explosion that the entire family had been waiting on for generations. Exactly when it was going to happen nobody knew, but in a family so filled with fear, manipulation, greed, and entitlement, as well as the destruction of boundaries and people, one thing was certain: It was coming. When all the traumas came into alignment the night of December 25, 1996, everything fell into place. And just as sure as rain will fall from a thunderstorm, the remaining walls between Patsy, John, and JonBenét finally came tumbling down.

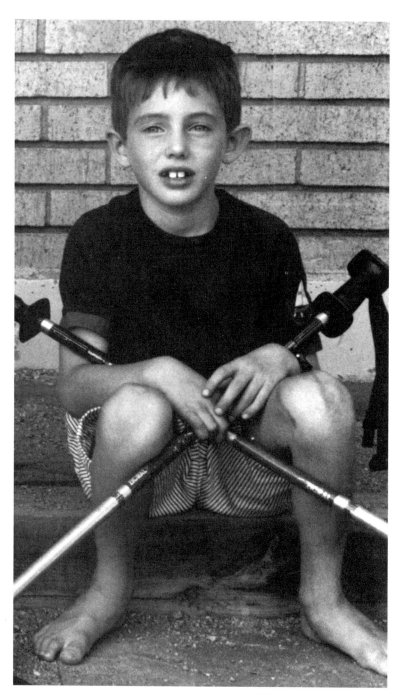

Burke Ramsey, circa 1994

CHAPTER 15
Burke Draws Attention to the Truth

"What we thought to be family secrets as Ackerman said turn out to be common knowledge but simply not spoken of. Children usually know more than their parents think they do. They also know what they're not supposed to talk about."

— *Family Therapy*, Nichols and Schwartz

Whether or not Patsy and John Ramsey killed their daughter, one thing is certain: Burke Ramsey knows the truth. He may or may not consciously know it. In fact, reports about his having been interrogated indicate he doesn't fully comprehend the truth. But just as sure as the sun comes up everyday, somewhere in his mind he knows the truth. We don't know exactly what the authorities learned from Burke's interviews with a child psychologist, but apparently it wasn't enough to point clearly to the Ramseys' guilt. Family members and friends were naturally relieved and use this as further evidence of the Ramseys' innocence and to justify their defense of them. But, for Burke's sake, they shouldn't be so quick to jump to conclusions.

For a long time we've known that when it comes to major events, deep down family members have no secrets from one another. We also know that the price for harboring secrets can be devastatingly high if the secret is toxic enough. If Burke Ramsey were hiding a secret (such as his parents murdering his sister) from himself, the effect would be powerful.

Not long after the murder, Burke gave us a window into his mind—four brief but striking glimpses, snapshots of his inner world. They are the only public knowledge we have about him. At first glance, his communications, not unlike the ransom note, seem insignificant. But a careful look reveals far more.

In September 1997, nine months after his sister was murdered and shortly after the family had moved back to Atlanta, during a church service Burke made a series of four drawings, which were later recovered by a tabloid. A psychologist analyzed the drawings for *The Globe*. Drawings have particular significance for those therapists who work with children. Often kids tell us things through drawings that they can't communicate in any other way. In their drawings, children in psychotherapy, like adult patients, will go over and over a trauma until they reach some sort of resolution. Their need to resolve their pain causes them to repeatedly think about the trauma. By leaving his drawings "in public" where they could (and were) discovered, Burke was making a public statement. He could have taken them home or he could have torn them up, but he left them behind, ostensibly for someone to find. As citizens, we are charged with the responsibility of protecting our fellow citizens in the name of justice, especially children, and as such, we are well within our rights to examine Burke's drawings. In fact, it's our duty.

There are certain essentials we know about his communications even before we examine them. First of all, we know that these illustrations are terribly important. We also know that Burke had a tremendous need to express himself, a need so strong that he couldn't contain it. Spontaneous drawings often reflect a compelling need to master troubling events. The church had "invited" the drawings as they placed a "Scribble Pad for Little Episcopalians" in every pew and Burke took them up on their offer. He was desperate to communicate. Feeling safe in "God's" place, he began to tell what he knew.

At a minimum he felt tremendously burdened by a number of stresses: a recent move, leaving his friends, a new school, the loss of his sister, his mother having had cancer, constant media attention, his parents preoccupied and under suspicion, and the threat that they could be jailed, guilty or not. At a maximum his stresses were overwhelming, particularly if, in reality, his parents were guilty. If this were the case, his drawings would unquestionably reflect it as the major event in his life, along with the fact that he now contained a terrifying secret. Under these conditions, his fears would be off the charts. Surely the terror that his mother and father could go to jail would be magnified, not to mention the possibilities that he might never live with them again. If they were charged, could his parents' marriage survive? Would they crack up under the pressure? Would either of them commit suicide, as both had alluded to? Worst of all, could they lose control again and kill him? As we can see, knowing he had information that could convict his parents was, to say the least, confusing—it was, at worst, terrifying. In the back of his mind, he would have all these questions and more.

Some of JonBenét's former classmates in Boulder had night terrors and feared they were going to be killed, simply because they knew her. Some even had a whistle pinned to their pajamas for a year and wouldn't go to bed without it. If this was true of these children, imagine what nightmarish scenarios wreaked havoc with Burke Ramsey's psyche. Not much is known about this child, but it is well-known that since JonBenét's murder, he has had several explosive outbursts at school. The fact that these outbursts occurred at school also tells us that he let his anger out where he felt safe. Who knows what he thinks every night as he lies down to go to sleep—in the same house with the two parents who killed his sister?

We may already have a good idea *what* he is going to tell us in his drawings, but we yet don't know *how*. We have a wonderful opportunity to see how he tells us and what kind of effect it is having on him. The event has greatly impacted him—and will for the rest of his life—so he has much to teach us. Through these drawings, we can "listen" and learn about what his inner world is really like. He should give us a unique view not only of what a family catastrophe does to the mind of a young, developing boy, but also of how living with certain secrets has affected him. Surely he will surprise us. Once more we also have an opportunity to validate that kids as well as adults have a very perceptive deeper intelligence, something his drawings should clarify. His drawings should show us that his sister's murder remains unquestionably the most important issue on the deepest level of his psyche.

Given the capability Patsy Ramsey's deeper mind demonstrated in the ransom note, we should expect no less from Burke. We would anticipate that each drawing would convey a key part of the story and that the four taken together show a major part of the story, at least from his viewpoint. We would expect to find matching thoughtprints in his art—ideas that repeat themselves—in order to demonstrate what he sees deep down.

The First Drawing

Not surprisingly, Burke quickly tells us something bizarre and disturbing is going on inside him. All of his drawings have a strange, primitive quality to them, which gets clearer and clearer, particularly in the second and fourth

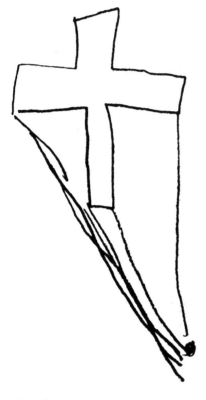

First drawing

drawings (See drawings on pages 206, 208, 211, and 213). In addition, there's a strange three-dimensional quality that he conveys by using sharp angles, as if he's telling us something powerful and immediate is about to overwhelm him. The drawings appear to be from a much younger child and reflect enormous inner disturbance.

The most obvious symbol is the cross, a large cross forming an equally large angular enclosure that comes to a sharp point, suggesting a dagger. Turned upside down, the drawing looks like a sword with the cross being the handle. The most loving force imaginable (the cross signifying supreme love) has turned into something dangerous and entrapping as the arms of the cross close and come together. The lower half of the drawing suggests what's going on unconsciously inside him. This drawing implies that on the surface, everything is religious and good; he sees only unconsciously that he is being threatened and that something violent has taken place.

The cross also suggests sacrifice and death, as does the dagger. Burke implies that deep down he views his sister as an innocent sacrificial victim of violence—and that the same thing is happening to him in his own way. The dagger also has several lines outside the point, suggesting that the violence is still uncontained and ongoing.

The sharp, angular figure suggests Burke is keeping a sharp and painful secret, an idea he repeats in three of the four drawings. He also hints that this secret is stirring up violent thoughts of despair in himself—no longer is he just an innocent good kid but now is facing violent anger of his own which he could turn on himself or others.

By changing the cross into three or four enclosed sharp triangles, Burke further suggests that his secret has to do with triangles that become sharp and dangerous. In three of the four drawings, he repeatedly draws triangles or diamond shapes (which themselves are two triangles, back to back) as if to confirm that triangles—relationships involving three people—are at the heart of his story.

As I mentioned earlier, Burke made these drawings at a church. Maybe the one place on the face of the earth he felt safe—in God's house, with the all-knowing Father (who knows the truth) looking down on him. The cross also hints at someone looking down and observing. The same idea will be repeated in the last three drawings, suggesting Burke is telling us about his observations.

Burke repeatedly adds the concept of communication to each of his drawings, drawing pairs of eyes or ears in the remaining three drawings, along with radio and television pyramid-shaped broadcasting towers in his fourth drawing, each of which conveys the same idea. Of course, a cross suggests prayer, communicating with God, and in the same drawing, the dagger pointing down suggests communicating with the devil. Once again Burke tells us he is getting mixed messages that are very dangerous and destructive—leaving him terribly divided and confused.

Another feature common to the first three drawings (and part of the fourth) is how they all seem suspended, as if everything is "up in the air." Burke seems to be saying he's not grounded, that the events in his life have left him completely up in the air. The drawings are each solo figures, indicating isolation, which tells us just how isolated he feels—that there is no place left to turn. The primary interaction suggested in the drawings is with God and to those to whom he is broadcasting his messages—particularly his parents and the authorities.

The Second Drawing

At first glance, the second drawing appears to be the clearest of the remaining three. It is certainly the most primitive. At first glance, we see a block head with a pair of eyes and no neck connected to a bent pair of arms with hands like claws. Each of the three remaining drawings have a distinct pair of eyes—far apart, as if he's telling us that he's seen something and that

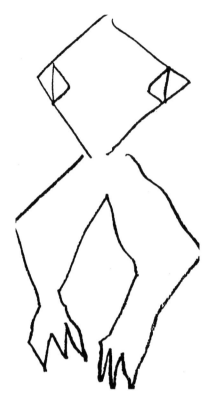

Second drawing

he sees everything. The great width also suggests the two eyes don't come together, as if he sees something and doesn't see it at the same time. In the second and fourth drawings, the eyes are also where the ears should be, suggesting that perhaps he's actually heard more than he's seen.

Clearly Burke is preoccupied with the murder of his sister—both the head injury and the strangulation. The block head strongly suggests a head injury of some sort. The primitive bent arms with the aggressive hands match perfectly with the strangulation the killer inflicted on JonBenét. The arms are bent away from the body and the hands do not come together, exactly as a strangulation with a garrote would occur (versus one carried out exclusively with the hands around the neck). The arms being in the lower half of the picture again suggests that Burke is only unconsciously aware of the full truth about the strangulation. One might wonder how someone would pick up on a family secret—how a person can only know something unconsciously. Communication takes place on so many levels—the stories we tell, whisperings we hear without realizing it, voice inflections, body language, slips. Our unconscious mind assesses all of these, and more, in a heartbeat.

We must ask the question, "Why is the body missing?" Burke is suggesting that the whole event was shattering to him and that he is trying to put it together. The trauma has clearly shaken his take on reality, so overwhelming that he views the murder as a strange and disconnected act—perhaps his wish to disconnect the act from anyone he knows. For his part, Burke suggests he is disconnected from his own rage—that he would like to personally strangle those responsible for his sister's death. (Without a doubt he views the killer as a monster.) Imagine how terrifying his own rage must be. He may be wondering if he, too, would lose control or if there would be retaliation from people far stronger than he if he expressed his anger. In this light, his reported hostile outbursts at school are not surprising.

The block head additionally suggests a nerd, "a square," a scholar, a bright student who studies all the time, like Burke would have been studying his parents. And he suggests in a striking way that he has put the puzzle together. Subtly, but distinctly, Burke tells us he is quite aware of the story behind both of his sister's mortal injuries.

A second look at the drawing reveals an entirely different picture—it is a drawing that can be read two ways. Now we see a picture of a headless, armless torso and legs, somewhat angular but clearly distinguishable. The length of the extremities certainly fits better with legs than with arms, as suggested before. Burke again projects a preoccupation with a beheading, which points toward both the crime scene and the ransom note. The missing arms also suggest not only the crime scene where JonBenét's arms were "missing" as they were tied above her head, but also her helplessness to do anything about the assault.

By creating two drawings in one (with both reflecting significant bodily damage to the head and neck), Burke is making sure we get the message that he knows what happened to his sister and is greatly disturbed by it. He shows this in one, last, crucial aspect to this highly creative and communicative drawing. The eyes in the first version of the drawing are the breasts in the second version of the same drawing. The exposed breasts and the wide-spread legs suggest an explicit sexual scene with an extremely vulnerable, helpless female. With the breasts doubling as eyes, Burke plainly implies, "I see that a sexual assault was behind this murder." By making the first message (the strangulation) of this two-faceted drawing easier to read, and then presenting the embedded sexual drawing, he not only shows us he knows the motives behind the crime, but he also wants to help the authorities get it straight.

The claws where the feet should be on this helpless headless figure suggest anger and a wild animal—on a woman's body—like a cat that is ready to fight despite her helplessness. Once again we find a striking link to the ransom note, which suggests indeed a "cat fight" was at the core of this murder. Perhaps, too, he is speaking for his mother, Patsy, who experienced both her cancer and the discovery of JonBenét's sexual abuse as a devastating assault on her feminine identity—prompting her rage when she "lost her head."

Beyond that, he is speaking for his sister JonBenét, who he knows has to be furious about what has happened to her. On yet another level, he is again describing his own anger over the murder and the assaults he has experienced, which have rendered him largely helpless and powerless, like a woman whose arms are tied behind her back. Surely the anger reflects his terror as to what could happen to him. We must interpret every drawing as suggesting a part of him or what could happen to him.

The Third Drawing

In this illustration, we see a picture of a distorted smiley face. Once again we find two eyes, wide apart. Burke sees what's going on—he has missed nothing. The face is the largest of the three faces in the drawings. The width and length of the large lips suggest the mouth is sealed or gagged. The right eye is connected to what appears to be a huge question mark with a closed loop. Burke suggests he has a huge question, and the closed loop and closed lips imply he is keeping the answer a secret: His lips are sealed. The size of the lips and the question mark convey an overwhelming urge to speak, the urge to admit to himself what has happened.

The numerous distortions of the head and face reveal part of his secret. The top of the head, the nose, and the chin are all missing. Not only does Burke feel that he has been personally damaged and that the events that surround him have distorted his view of the world, but he also tells his secret that someone's face has been incredibly damaged. First, the top of somebody's head has been knocked off, and the head has also been separated from the neck. The missing nose and gagged mouth suggest someone can't breathe and, along with the neck injury, these point to a strangulation. The closed question mark also suggests a noose or type of staff used to put around the neck of sheep or snakes. (Ironically, his noose matches the numerous disguised nooses the ransom note writer included in the note.) Burke clearly appears to be saying that a big part of his secret is that he knows who hit JonBenét in the head and who strangled her.

Above the left eye is a large, cylindrical, elongated object. The "eye" and object taken together suggest another punctuation mark, an exclamation mark. Two huge punctuation marks stand side by side. One eye sees a question, and the other eye exclaims definitively, "I know the answer!" The exclamation mark also suggests the idea of "a light coming on." Like the huge lips imply, Burke is shouting, "I know! I know! I know!"

But what exactly does he know? The coded answer is as plain as he could make it. On the right side of the drawing (as it faces the reader) he tells us he knows what happened. He draws an elongated object standing all by itself—a phallic symbol for all to see. To underscore his message, he has left two other disguised phallic symbols: curved lips and the enclosed question mark. The straight

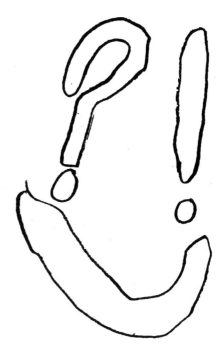

Third drawing

phallic symbol above the eye on the right side of the drawing suggests that we simply need to straighten out the other images—two more phallic symbols in the illustration—showing that behind this murder was a powerful sexual event. The huge lips in the bottom half of the picture are the most striking phallic symbol, again suggesting unconsciously that Burke was picking up on the story behind the murder.

Burke also repeatedly suggests that a threesome—a triangle—was behind the murder. This drawing contains three primary parts: the lips, the question mark, and the exclamation mark. Eerily, the exclamation mark matches Patsy's use of the same punctuation in the ransom note, a major characteristic of many of her writings.

Burke's third drawing seems to sum up the crime in a nutshell: three people, all about sex, and keeping his secret. There are also many disconnected pieces, like his family that is falling apart. And Burke Ramsey is pleading for someone to put it back together.

The Fourth Drawing

The illustration immediately suggests two things: communication and a stick figure with a large, isolated head. A significant number of messages appear in this drawing. Lines are running everywhere, suggesting both communication and confusion.

Both the large eyes and the long lines with converging center lines from top to bottom, shaped like a tower, suggest communication—messages being transmitted and received. Burke suggests he's broadcasting for all the world to hear. Along these lines, the drawing also suggests a kite—"flying" above it all and looking down at what's happening. Not only do the large eyes once again suggest that he saw everything, but also that he's also going to tell us what he saw if we keep "listening to" the drawing. The exceptionally wide-set eyes, along with the crossed lines running between them suggest that he's beginning to bring the two eyes together.

Between "the eyes" we see a distinct stick figure, a common way children draw people. The figure is once again headless, but the genital area is extraordinarily large and is clearly the center of attention. The "eyes" not only connect with each other but also with the genital area, which appears to be a large vagina. The vagina suggests enlargement by penetration of some type. Like the embedded image in the second drawing, the female figure appears not only headless, but this time her arms are outstretched in a crucifixion-type pose, tying together three out of the four drawings. Since the eyes are where the hands would be tied down, Burke suggests again that he clearly knows that sexual abuse and sacrifice were at the heart of the murder. The appearance and location of the eyes once again also suggest "breasts" like the embedded image in the second drawing, and being connected so strikingly to the genital area, Burke repeats the powerful message that at the heart of his sister's murder was a sexual event—when she was abused by an adult male. Breasts suggest once again that femininity is a major issue.

The three "sexual" circles along with the other numerous triangles in this drawing, particularly around the genital area, suggest a battle involving a threesome—three people—surrounded the murder. The repeated triangles announce over and over, "Family triangle! Family triangle! Family triangle!" The lines from the legs and vaginal area also form an embedded star suggesting not only sacrifice (JonBenét or a Christ figure) but a star looking down

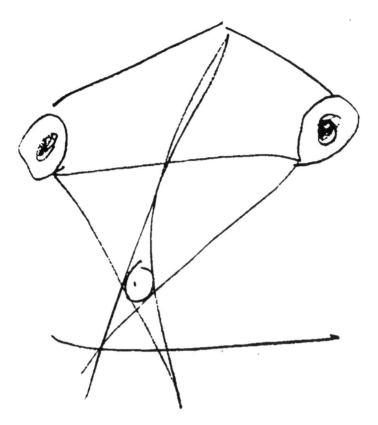

Fourth drawing

from the heavens, as well as a badge. Burke seems to be telling us that if the authorities put things together they can solve this crime and relieve everyone's pain, particularly his. He longs for justice.

The eyes not only point to the vaginal area below, but they also point up to the neck and the headless figure as though Burke again is connecting the sexual abuse with the head injury. More than that he uses these lines from the eyes to enclose virtually the entire drawing to tell us things are coming together and that this is his way of making sense of what's happened, his way of mastering his trauma.

In fact this is the first picture of the four that is grounded in any way, implying that his drawings, his form of communication, have already provided him some therapeutic benefit. He's trying hard to understand what's happened to him, trying hard to face the truth, and he's anchored now, though barely, as the legs of the stick figure are set slightly below the horizontal line at the bottom of the drawing implies. The structure looks to be quite fragile, indicating that he remains extremely vulnerable to falling apart.

At the same time, the fact that the legs form the bottom part of the star suggests he will be greatly relieved if the authorities would intervene and bring law and order to the situation so that he feels safe and anchored. In his own way, he is telling us that without justice and experiencing his parents being put back in the appropriate boundary of consequences, he will never be grounded. Because if they're not grounded, he won't be.

He further suggests that he's coming to terms with the reality himself of how his parents really treated his sister— and him. The lines of communication are opening up in this drawing, the secret is beginning to give way.

In several ways Burke suggests he is providing an overview of the crime— a star, a kite, a tower, even a cross all covey the idea of looking down and observing a situation from above. This is similar to the first drawing. Burke is not only telling himself what happened, but he's also telling the world— broadcasting the truth for all to hear. Most of all, he wants his parents and his extended family to hear. As the repeatedly sharp edges suggest, he still contains terrifying information, sharp secrets that are killing him. But the Ramseys are not listening to their only living child. While John and Patsy Ramsey are convinced that no good would come from confessing, Burke Ramsey knows otherwise. He is trying to tell them that the truth will set them all free, as free as they can get in this life.

The crossed lines in this drawing also symbolize a trap, a cage, and simultaneously a cross, as we see in the very center of this picture. He seems to be ready to accept that he might lose his parents to jail—to the trap—but that he would meet a true confession with forgiveness, and so would God. That's why he puts a cross in the very center of his vision, connecting his two eyes. This is the only way he can let himself see the reality of what happened as well. This would hold an impossible situation together.

Burke could live with the truth of a confession if he met it with faith and forgiveness—and holds up a model of hope for his parents. He could really begin to grow if such a confession occurred. He would finally have the only two things that would anchor him against the storm: the truth and the cross. Of course, that's where he began in his first drawing, in the very first thing he put down on paper: a cross. And by drawing in church, Burke was standing in the shadow of the cross the whole time, and in that place he finally found the courage to put everything down on paper.

It is amazing how much like the ransom note these drawings are, down to the very last message. Patsy Ramsey implied, in her S. B. T. C ending, that "Saved By The Cross" was her only hope. Better than anyone else, Burke Ramsey knows the only way he'll ever have his parents and his life back is through forgiveness. Clearly, that's his prayer. And you can't have forgiveness without a confession.

PART IV
When Darkness Touches Light
Gullibility, Guilt, and Grace

CHAPTER 16
One More Death of Innocence

Once again taking matters into their own hands, the Ramseys began their public defense in March 2000. By continuing the same controlling and stage-seeking behavior, they relentlessly attempted to exonerate themselves. The release of their book, *The Death of Innocence*, was followed by appearances on *20/20* with Barbara Walters, *The Today Show* with Katie Couric, and *Larry King Live*. These three interviewers threw mostly softball inquiries, mixing in an occasional off-speed fast-ball question, and all tried to stay within the boundaries of the left brain—no reading between the lines. Each appearance was carefully orchestrated by the Ramseys. Patsy and John were dressed in all the right colors: Patsy in light blue and occasional pink, suggesting innocence, and John in his dark business suit and white shirt, suggesting believability and authority. At opportune moments during the *20/20* interview, Patsy casually brought attention to JonBenét's little pink glove that she carried with her without, of course, directly mentioning it. Barbara Walters "astutely" picked up on it, enabling Patsy to become tearful and to lean touchingly against John's shoulder. But, despite their best PR efforts, the Ramseys could not wash themselves of JonBenét's blood, still on their hands.

The Ramseys have been polishing their act for three and a half years, so the only place we're going to see the truth is between the lines. As I read their book, the centerpiece of their strategy, they often came across as grieving parents, fine Christian people who truly loved their child and who were the victims of circumstance. Initially it was difficult to believe that people who claimed such devout faith would lie in such an insistent fashion. But once again, they gave themselves away in the very book that pronounced their innocence, showing between the lines, the big lie and their continued confessions.

One of the central tenants of understanding the right brain is that every idea must be taken to be a part of the individual. Unconsciously the Ramseys vividly described their public relations campaign in a chapter title, "Tell It

Loud, Tell It Often." This is reminiscent of the famous Nazi strategy that people will believe any lie if it is big enough, is told often enough, and is told loudly enough—the Ramseys' strategy in a nutshell.

Naturally we are inclined to listen sympathetically, in a direct left-brain way, to two parents, responsible citizens who are clearly grief-stricken and who describe it poignantly. Often overlooked is the reality that even if they *did* kill their child, their grief would be enormous—doubled by the knowledge that they are the only ones who could have prevented the murder. Of course they were grieving parents. But we must also remember that whatever feelings of pity the Ramseys evoke, they are primarily linked to the left brain. To read between the lines, we have to look past their feelings and ours in order to see what's really happening.

As I read their book, I still found it hard to believe that two people could lie so boldly—until I once again realized what they were really doing. Unknowingly, they continued to confess between the lines as again they unconsciously elaborated on and clarified how the murder occurred. They validated conclusions we had already come to in our report (and I in my first book), and in fact even added rich, new observations and confessions. In the process, both parents demonstrated skewed logic. Their lawyers and advisors reportedly searched their manuscript for any possible clues to their guilt, but the right brain can't be hidden. If people talk, they will eventually tell the truth.

Throughout the book, the Ramseys point to their spin and cover-up. Both Patsy and John mention a unique part of the Rockies that surrounds Boulder, The Devil's Thumb, and they allude to Satan's evil presence nearby. They repeatedly mention deceit—the Judas syndrome—in regard to friends who have betrayed them and who have financially profited from JonBenét's death. (This is an interesting accusation coming from parents who received a $750,000 advance for their book.) They also tell about a tour guide who embellished facts and repeatedly lied as he showed their home for the Boulder Parade of Homes. All of these stories about other people's deceit merely reflected their own deeper intelligence's take about themselves as deceivers.

At times the Ramseys even more directly linked deceit to themselves. For instance, they describe the glee they took in deceiving reporters, even to the point of enjoying how one reporter's wife had been set up by the Ramseys' friends to think her husband was having an affair. You would think that if the Ramseys were innocent of deceit, they would have attempted to shut off any such thinking early on in their book. John Ramsey himself labeled two incriminating observations from the Ramseys' CNN interview one week after the murder as "twisting his words." First, someone had seen hidden jealousy in Patsy's insistence that JonBenét was a daddy's girl, and second, someone noted John's striking comment that he wanted to find out *why* JonBenét was killed as opposed to *who* killed her. Even in his denial, John himself reinforces these valid observations and presents a major clue about where to look to find the truth.

Conspicuous in the Ramseys' book was their failure to mention the work of my colleagues or myself, while attacking every other known theorist on the case, even the most obscure. They attacked Donald Foster, the linguist from Vassar; Darnay Hoffman, the attorney; and even Dale Yeager with his wild theory based on one Bible verse. The Ramseys characterized all those who thought them guilty as mindless robots controlled by the media, incapable of independent thought. But when three forensic professionals—two psychiatrists and a psychologist—feel certain enough about their guilt to generate a solidly endorsed seventy-page report on the ransom note alone, there's nary a peep from the Ramseys. (Also conspicuously absent was any mention of Jane Stobie, who worked for John Ramsey and with both his and Patsy's relatives for more than four years and who knew them well.)

However, when they thought psychology would help them, they played the card. For example, they informed the public that John Douglas, who exonerated them, was not only an expert criminal profiler but also had a doctorate in psychology. Along these same lines, Patsy's comment on *The Today Show* about the tabloids deserving an A in creative writing fits hand-in-glove with her ransom note, as well as their book. So far Patsy has earned an A for her literary efforts designed to keep the authorities at bay. But judgment—being graded—is on Patsy's mind, and her final grade is not in. Out there somewhere is a prosecutor and a jury ready to give her work the grade it deserves.

The Mosaic

To appreciate the Ramseys' combined creativity, we must, as usual, pay close attention to the mosaic they are weaving with their stories—invaluable communication from their right brain. Like a criminal returning to the scene of the crime, they continually revisit the crime scene—each in his or her own way making plain their precise roles. Crucial stories abound.

Very early in the book, John Ramsey describes his special relationship with JonBenét. On different occasions she gives him gifts. On the very last day of her life, JonBenét excitedly gave John for Christmas a shiny, red gumball machine filled with jelly beans, which he dearly loved. A red container filled with treats. A few weeks earlier, he had arrived late to what would be JonBenét's last child beauty contest, the All-Stars Christmas Pageant. When her father sat down beside Patsy, JonBenét took off the medal she was wearing around her neck—the one she had just won—reached over her mother, and gave her father the shiny award. He placed it around his neck. After the murder (as he told Katie Couric), he began wearing the medal daily and said it was his "touchstone," something which he would periodically feel to overcome his grief over losing her and to remind himself she was in heaven.

See the images? Two treats from JonBenét: First, pleasure from a container linked to JonBenét, which harkens back to the ransom note and getting some valuable out of her little bank. Second, a gift from JonBenét— a gift he touches in order to ward off the ominous sense of death and loss. A gift linking her body with his. In short, John once again links "touching" with JonBenét. This suggests the same story—that when she was alive, he used her as a "touchstone" even then, to ward off terrible feelings of despair.

But he is not through. He next makes a connection between her neck and his neck. Something around his neck makes her death somehow better. From neck to neck. In psychiatry we call this "undoing"—when someone attempts to magically right a wrong by performing a certain act, often a symbolic one. For example, a son who greatly conflicted with his father when he was alive might wear his deceased father's coat as if to say, "See? We were really buddies."

Just for good measure, John repeats this act of undoing. When JonBenét was buried just outside of Atlanta in Marietta, Georgia, family members placed different items that had special significance to each of them in her coffin. When John Ramsey's turn came, he "tucked a scarf around her like a blanket." Scarves go around necks. Once again, John Ramsey is preoccupied with JonBenét's neck after her death. Does he not strongly, eerily hint, "Now I'm going to protect your neck like I didn't do before"?

On Larry King's show, immediately after releasing their book, John Ramsey tells the story of his involvement with JonBenét in another way. He describes how the tragedy affected him and his marriage. "One thing that does happen is you become very focused on yourself, your self-pity. You're as down and as needy of help and support as you have ever been, and your spouse can't give that to you, because she's in the same place." At first he appears to be talking about his marriage with Patsy after the loss of JonBenét, but he also takes us back to another time of great loss.

Wasn't he in an identical situation immediately after Patsy was diagnosed with ovarian cancer—filled with self-pity? Reeling from the catastrophic losses of his oldest daughter and father in 1992, John must have gone over the edge with the ominous prognosis of Patsy's cancer in 1993. Understandably, with Patsy now engulfed by her own world of pain, he would have been strongly inclined to turn to where the energy was in the family, to the family "spark plug"—to JonBenét, who picked him up when he was down. (See Chapter 13, page 171.) Surely, John Ramsey is answering his own question about why all this occurred. (Just as surely he must communicate his vulnerability to his daughters and elicit a protective response from them, as he amazingly recalls how his oldest daughter Beth used to worry about him.) Even without Patsy's illness, John Ramsey would have had a strong urge to bond with JonBenét in a special way in order to make up for the loss of his oldest daughter, Beth. Now his burden was tripled. With Patsy's cancer, the pressure on him to look to a female who could undo both losses would be magnified. As we will see him tell us himself, John Ramsey sees JonBenét as the perfect choice because she was available, he could control her, and she was almost guaranteed not to die on him. And she had the energy—the pick-me-up—he so desperately needed.

JonBenét herself points to the role she was in. In an excerpt from a beauty pageant interview not long before the murder (shown on the same *Larry King Live* show), JonBenét says she wants to be a doctor or a nurse when she grows up—unconsciously suggesting her role in the family. Family heroes and spark plugs also become family doctors and nurses—people who rescue hurting family members. But when asked what kind of doctor she wanted to be, JonBenét's response—"a pediatrician"—tells us even more. She herself needed a doctor, one who would rescue her because her pediatrician was missing the clues about the sexual abuse (twenty-seven visits in three years) and even her own mother kept secret JonBenét's encopresis (soiling)—the girl's most blatant cry for help.

Not to be outdone by John, Patsy revisits the crime scene in her own way. In their book, she describes experiencing a panic attack a month after JonBenét's death, an incident in which she became extremely short of breath, "As if someone were *strangling* me. I desperately gasped for air." I have treated hundreds of patients with panic attacks who get shortness of breath, but I've never heard one of them describe it as being strangled. Patsy cannot stop herself from linking a tremendous fear of being strangled with JonBenét's death. In the book, Patsy also describes a poignant moment after the murder when she looked at a cross she was wearing, one which contained an image of the Virgin Mary. Patsy "had this immediate empathy" with Mary because "she watched them kill her child." Strikingly, Patsy links herself with a mother who witnessed first-hand the murder of her child—a "messiah child" who carried the sins of others. Patsy suggests in the strongest way that she indeed witnessed JonBenét being strangled—just as John Ramsey suggested he was the one who did it (exactly like Patsy told us in the ransom note).

Even Patsy's casual story about a woman who received a shocking, unexpected phone call about her husband having an affair points to the trigger for her own rage—the unexpected realization of her husband's sexual impropriety in their own home. Impressively, John and Patsy—each in his or her own way—through stories and symbols vividly point to the same story we find in the ransom note. They continually fill in the tiles of the mosaic with each interview, statement, letter, and story.

Not only did John Ramsey hint at his participation in and reasons for the murder, but he also implied in several ways that he was lying, as did Patsy. In a fascinating sequence in their book in which he says he suspects the killer was a pedophile, swears that they were intent on finding the killer, and describes the interrogation of both Patsy and him at Assistant District Attorney Peter Hofstrom's house (where they had agreed to be interviewed privately), John Ramsey refers to two situations involving people who are lying—and Patsy refers to one. First, he discusses the tour guide in charge of showing people through the Ramsey's home, who lied about the past, saying that things happened much more recently than they really had. Then Patsy told a story about lying to her kids when a young puppy was dying and she secretly substituted another puppy, because the children were nearly overwhelmed with the loss of their half-sister Beth and possibility of losing their mother. Obviously John endorsed the deceit, making plain that in the face of death both would lie. Confessing that not only did they think their children couldn't handle another loss, but they also couldn't deal with it. Finally, in the middle of describing his interrogation, John recalls a story Hofstrom told about working with jailed criminals in a classroom setting, about how they often fooled judges into thinking they could be rehabilitated, and about how one criminal faked a crime by coming into the classroom through a window rather than through the door. (He was "just staying in practice.") The main idea—a seeming break-in through a window—never really occurred. It was faked to make a point. In short, the Ramseys' stories about lying suggest (1) that he lied to authorities about events taking place in the house, (2) that when it came to protecting someone from death, they both would lie, and (3) that he lied about an alleged break-in through a window. (He borrowed Hofstrom's story to make that particular point.) Additionally, John Ramsey stresses in his story his opinion that criminals don't reform. John's deeper mind, and Patsy's also, appears to be selecting key events in the crime and then tells stories that convey the real truth of each particular event.

A book is a perfect vehicle for giving the Ramseys' right brain/deeper intelligence an opportunity to speak. They choose, in an uninterrupted fashion, what to talk about, often spontaneously selecting stories—and stories access the right brain like nothing else. Their choices of stories and events to tell about in and of themselves are extremely enlightening. One of the most important revelations in *The Death of Innocence* was just how much death surrounded the Ramseys. It was no coincidence that "Death" with a capital *D* is the first major word in the title. Patsy made plain that she had a 95 percent chance of dying from her cancer and felt strongly that she wouldn't live to see JonBenét as a teenager. How close those odds are to those in the ransom note: 99 percent. After being diagnosed with cancer, she was deeply concerned about her husband being overwhelmed by her illness. Patsy knew John was still deeply grieving the loss of his oldest daughter, and even his father. Many times John Ramsey links the death of JonBenét with the loss of Beth, and in one memorable phrase says, "The loss of Beth softened my character." Indeed it did. In the book, death is everywhere.

But investigators still fail to see the motives staring them in the face. During Larry King's interviews with the Ramseys on March 27-28, 2000, following the release of their book, legal analyst Greta Van Susteren once more notes that no one has established a possible motive for the Ramseys' losing control. Yet, interview-by-interview, chapter by chapter, the Ramseys are weaving the mosaic, continuing to validate their motivations. When Barbara Walters, during an interview a few days earlier, raised the possibility of Patsy snapping during a bedwetting struggle with JonBenét, Patsy immediately came back at her. "Let me tell you something," said Patsy. "I'm a stage-IV cancer survivor and [in that light] bedwetting is totally insignificant." Once again, when discussing motive, Patsy unconsciously stresses the terror of her cancer, implying once again, "It's the cancer, stupid, [that set me off]" as she makes the clear connection between her battle with cancer and the trigger for the murder while overtly demonstrating how she can snap. Once again linking ideas is one of the key ways the unconscious mind says "these two ideas are connected."

Patsy also makes another striking revelation in her book when she tells us for the first time about her "premonition" of JonBenét's death. On Christmas Eve, she was wrapping the special look-alike Twinn doll for JonBenét. As she opened the box, for a moment Patsy had a striking image of JonBenét lying in a coffin. Patsy further revealed that that year she had decorated the Christmas tree in purple—for the first time ever—symbolic of Christ's death and atonement, because she had been struck by that color during the previous Lent season. Her own explanation for this incident was that she had unconsciously been psychic about JonBenét's impending death. However, a far more logical explanation exists: Murder was unconsciously on Patsy's mind as her rage toward JonBenét and John grew. Her fear of JonBenét's death was actually a forbidden wish. This is classic psychoanalytic theory, validated by years of experience. The conscious mind disguises a secret impulse, the wish, as a fear in order to make it acceptable. And note how clearly Patsy Ramsey points us to the unconscious mind, showing us that deep down she was picking up on everything. Her premonitions must be understood, not in terms of some strange psychic phenomenon, but as deep-seated wishes for JonBenét's death, held in her unconscious mind.

Patsy also tells about burying JonBenét on her birthday: "My fortieth birthday: A landmark in anyone's life, a tombstone in mine. The pain overwhelmed me. Why had I lived to be forty? Why would God do this to me? I had survived what should have been terminal cancer." As she now specifically links cancer to turning forty—itself symbolizing being "over the hill"—Patsy unknowingly tells us that in her vulnerable state, her fortieth birthday symbolized a tombstone to her even before JonBenét's death. This is why she slipped and called it her "acute birthday" in her 1996 Christmas letter, just two weeks before the murder.

These incidents validate the motives revealed in the ransom note and elsewhere. Clearly the Ramseys' book substantiates the tremendous pressure the Ramseys were under prior to the murder—pressure caused by cancer, death, and sexual secrets.

Miscellaneous Revelations

Now we can better understand Patsy and John Ramsey's behavior after the murder. John tells us that he asked himself a million times what he could have done to have prevented the murder, and we must take him at his word. Not only would he have wondered why he had crossed the boundaries with JonBenét and thus, in that sense, prevented her death, but he also must have been deeply puzzled by the sudden chaotic circumstances of that last night. Why hadn't he been able to see it coming? Why couldn't he see how out of her head with rage Patsy was? Could he have somehow gotten between Patsy and JonBenét and deflected the blow? Wouldn't anyone in his shoes have played that event over and over in his mind—even if he was caught molesting his daughter? Sexual assault is one thing, but the finality of murder is another matter altogether. Ask John Ramsey.

A close look at John Ramsey's logic also reveals it to be chock-full of holes. He insisted that all parents who assaulted their children had a record of previous assaults and were previously known to protective agencies, but Patsy herself contradicted him on national television. Susan Smith was a sterling example of someone, much like the Ramseys, with no prior record—and there are plenty of others. Why, he challenges, if he were the killer would he give the police a notebook containing the killer's practice ransom note? Because criminals are notorious for making mistakes in order to unconsciously confess to their crimes, something he continues to do every time he opens his mouth. He suggests it made no sense for him to stage the crime scene and then pick up JonBenét's body when, in fact, his disruption of the crime scene and trace evidence is the only thing that has saved him from incarceration. Logically, by staging her body, he left himself an out in case the police found the body before he did.

While we're thinking logically, let's consider that a loving father wouldn't have moved his child's body. He'd have been too scared about hurting her further or he would have immediately begun administering CPR, careful not to waste valuable time moving her. Not only would her cold, stiff body have told him she was dead, but so would the smell. Decomposition starts at six hours after death, and when John Ramsey "discovered" her body, it already had the distinct odor of death, as Detective Linda Arndt testified.

Furthermore, John wants us to believe that a kidnapper would leave a note asking for a ridiculously small ransom and then not even take the body with him. My colleague Patrick Callahan has spoken with a document analyst with a strong academic background in logic who examines forensic documents for internal consistency. The analyst unequivocally stated that the ransom note was filled with inconsistencies and was, therefore, not an authentic ransom note.

In the book, the Ramseys also give us a closer look at some of the important players in this drama, particularly Lou Smit. Now we can see how Smit invited himself to be manipulated by being so overly friendly with the Ramseys typified by inviting the Ramseys to hold hands with him and pray while sitting in his van during their very first meeting—in front of the very house where JonBenét was killed. The Ramseys willingly obliged as Smit deludes himself by doing shoddy detective work, failing to understand that when he started praying with them and bonding in this way, his objectivity was compromised. We have to question the prosecution's strategy of allowing Smit (along with Trip DeMuth) to be one of the two primary interrogators of John Ramsey when he finally agreed to be interviewed 18 months after the crime. As I have discussed, Smit had his mind made up long before that meeting.

Interestingly the Ramseys present a different version as to who initiated the contact with Smit. Schiller reports that Patsy called Smit asking him to look after their house while they were out of town and that he agreed to do so in an effort to get close to the Ramseys as "the good cop." Reportedly, the Ramseys then took advantage of the opportunity and met him when they knew Smit would be there. However, the Ramseys tell us they heard that Smit would come the house on his own, stopping to pray for guidance and reflect on the case and thus Smit indirectly suggested the meeting. Schiller reports that the Ramseys were waiting on Smit when he came by the house the first time, and the Ramseys tell us that Smit was already there when they drove up.

One other pressure on the Ramseys subtly emerges in their book—success. John Ramsey tells us that his company went over a billion dollars in sales and that he never envisioned himself running a billion-dollar company. Instead, he saw himself as a little guy just trying to make a living. Success puts inordinate pressure on people and magnifies whatever pressure they are under. This suggests another reason Patsy Ramsey sang Patsy Cline's "Crazy" at the Access Graphics Christmas party where they were celebrating the company's growth: Success was driving them crazy.

Also, we see the split in the Ramseys continuing. John Ramsey's harshness with himself stands out as he frequently insists in their book and during interviews that the public and the media are 100 percent sure he's guilty, that the killer is a monster, a madman, and "the worst evil imaginable," a man who is "boiling" inside. At the same time, the Ramseys cleverly point the finger at others, flippantly claiming God is on their side and manipulating their son in the worst possible way as they continue the charade that the killer is "out there." They went to great lengths to protect Burke—having him constantly observed at school, putting in an alarm system at the school, never letting him out of their sight. Appearing to be protective, loving parents, they terrorize his already-vulnerable psyche as, day after day, their overprotectiveness delivers to him the message, "Any moment, you could be next."

Finally, during the Ramseys' two interviews with Larry King, John Ramsey repeatedly referred to the garrote as a "gawrote," pronouncing it in such a way that it rhymed with "wrote," "note," or "throat." Patsy parroted his unique mispronunciation. Were the Ramseys finding yet another creative way of telling us that the voice of JonBenét was not silenced by that garrote the night of the murder as they subtly pointed us to the most crucial evidence in the case? The ransom note describes the garrote in word and in picture (see Appendix B, page 257). The Ramseys' mispronunciation—their voice, their "throat"—links their interviews and book with the murder and the crime scene (wrote, note, throat). They are suggesting that their book was another "garrote," another effort to silence JonBenét and those who would speak for her.

CHAPTER 17

In a Fog—The Ramseys Put on Piety

"The heart is the most deceitful thing there is, and desperately wicked. No one can really know how bad it is."

Jeremiah 17: 9 (TLB)

Two months after they had escaped the grand jury's indictment by the skin of their teeth, Patsy and John Ramsey attended a marketing meeting at Christian publishing house Thomas Nelson's modern headquarters in Nashville to go over plans for their soon-to-be-released book that would "tell their side of the story." As the meeting was getting underway, Patsy Ramsey spontaneously and unpredictably pulled out a bottle of shampoo. She then explained that the shampoo had made promises of a better, happier life but hadn't lived up to them telling her audience, "It's not true. That's not the way life turned out for me."

The people at the meeting were taken aback. Patsy's story seemed off the wall, and to everyone's left brain, it was. But listening to right brain/deeper intelligence communication, Patsy Ramsey's message was unmistakable— another confession in a long line of confessions.

What does shampoo do? It washes and cleans, but this particular shampoo Patsy had used didn't get the job done. However, marketing was the purpose of the meeting, so in Patsy's deeper mind, that was the real subject she was talking about. She's really communicating, "Something being marketed was supposed to clean things up, but it failed." It's not difficult to see that she is talking about the book, which itself is nothing more than a futile attempt to wash away their sins and cleanse their soul, which is destined to fail. How picturesque our deeper intelligence is. Patsy knows intuitively that "this isn't going to wash." But that's not what they had hoped for when they approached Thomas Nelson in the first place.

The Ramseys (as they had done everything else) had carefully selected the largest religious publisher in the world, Thomas Nelson Publishers, to be their spokesman. Apparently lacking in the street wisdom of Jesus, the founder of their faith, to be "as crafty as serpents," Thomas Nelson rolled out the red carpet for the Ramseys and took them at their word. The mega-publisher bought the Ramsey spin, hook, line, and Bible verse.

Ignoring those people who had seen through the Ramseys despite their marketing hype and victim role, Thomas Nelson's publisher Rolf Zetterstein vociferously defended the Ramseys. The marriage between heaven and hell wasn't going to be cast asunder by anything trite like justice or hypocrisy when economics were at stake. A Judeo-Christian standard found in every Bible Thomas Nelson published—"Avoid the appearance of evil"—was out the window. The Ramseys could speak the Christian language, making it convenient for the publisher to speak up for the "underdog and the persecuted." Whether it is true or not, the Nelson deal smelled to "high heaven" and appeared to be driven by economic consideration.

Interestingly, in 1994 Thomas Nelson published my book *The Deeper Intelligence*, in which I explained the breakthrough to the deeper mind and showed how it was linked to our spiritual nature. In it, I described how psychology and true religion—far from being bitter enemies—are ultimately allies ("psyche" in Greek means "soul"), two parts to the same picture. As with the Ramsey book, placing their imprint on *The Deeper Intelligence* would imply some endorsement of the material contained in its pages. If the people at Nelson had understood my book, they wouldn't have been so puzzled by what seemed like strange behavior on Patsy Ramsey's part at the marketing meeting. They would have seen the red flag in her message.

Patsy's deep heart tells us that when the hype from the book dies down, she is going to run head-on into her guilt again. Like Lady Macbeth whose hands will never be clean, Patsy Ramsey's guilt won't be washed away until she chooses her only route out—confession.

From beginning to end, JonBenét's murder is intertwined with religion. JonBenét was killed on Christmas Day, wearing a gold cross around her neck. After the murder the Ramseys continually announce their faith in God. Lou Smit boldly tells us God is his partner on the case. Writer Jeff Shapiro feigned interest in converting from Judaism to Christianity in order to get near the Ramseys at their church. And the Ramseys dramatically left their church after JonBenét's memorial service.

Both John and Patsy had Christian backgrounds, and Patsy's basic identity was that of a "good girl" desperately seeking the virginal Miss America crown. After marrying John, Patsy was civil-minded, a striver and a doer, and was actively involved in church. In Atlanta the Ramseys attended Peachtree Presbyterian. In Boulder, Patsy threw herself into the community, and the Ramseys joined St. John's Episcopal Church where Patsy was more involved than John. Even so, Judith Phillips, who knew them both in Atlanta and Boulder, never noticed any particular spiritual bent in either person until very recently.

Patsy's spiritual focus took a dramatic change after she was diagnosed with ovarian cancer in July 1993. Faced with an ominous prognosis, Patsy turned to the same place people in foxholes always have–to God. She sought not only medical treatment, but also a supernatural spiritual healing. Following a dramatic healing service involving her minister Rol Hoverstock, Patsy shortly thereafter received a clean bill of health from her physician. Of course, she had been treated with megadoses of chemotherapy, but Patsy attributed her healing to God and the healing service. The 118th Psalm became her favorite after reading *Healed of Cancer* by Dodie Osteen, who encouraged cancer patients to look to this particular Psalm for their healing. Several verses in this psalm stand out, but none more so that verse 17: "I shall not die, but live, and declare the works of the Lord." To Patsy Ramsey, the 118th Psalm was a guarantee from God that she had been healed. It was her lifeline, and the Bible in the Ramseys' bedroom was always open to this psalm. Her friend, Judith Phillips, noted that during this time Patsy began frequently referring to the Bible.

Patsy experienced a renewal of her faith as a result of her cancer (faith that seemingly continued for the next three years) – supporting her wholesome former Miss West Virginia image. One can only wonder what Patsy Ramsey, the "good girl," thought when she looked at herself in the mirror those moments after she had lashed out at JonBenét, suddenly for all practical purposes looking at JonBenét's corpse. Did she realize that for the first time in her life she had really lost it and was as bad as a person can be? Just a short twelve hours later, she dramatically brings her faith into the crime scene as she kneels down, facing her daughter's stone-cold body that John Ramsey had just brought up from the basement, crying, "Jesus, you raised Lazarus from the dead! Please raise my baby!" Mostly drama, without question, but also partly utter desperation, hope against hope that God would hear her. But God said, "No."

Patsy Ramsey had set the stage for what was to come. Publicly, God was going to be a big part of their defense. The Ramseys had already started the public relations campaign that very morning when they called their minister. The charade started even as the pastor stood there in the living room when John "found" JonBenét.

Three days later on December 29, 1996, the same minister presided over JonBenét's memorial service at their church. Patsy sat on the front row being comforted by John on her right with his left arm around her. This left Patsy room to maneuver. During the service Patsy periodically raised her left hand as a sign of praise to God. Genuine, perhaps, but also quite effective to show herself as a deeply spiritual person, one who couldn't have killed her daughter.

She and John continued wearing their spiritual masks on CNN seven days after the murder. Patsy sprinkled her talk with God here and God there, emphasizing that they were a Christian family, parents who loved their children and who were so spiritually devoted that they had sent JonBenét to a Christian pre-school. Patsy was clearly adopting the same tactics as Susan Smith, who upon drowning her two children immediately took to the airwaves, proclaiming that God was her witness and that she had nothing to do with the murders. And that would continue to be their story, too—Patsy and John Ramsey continued to spin the lie, without hesitating to invoke God's name in their defense.

People frequently are talking about themselves when they think they're talking about other people. On May 1, 1997, during an interview in Boulder, Patsy looked into the camera and said, "God knows who you are, and we will find you." While again claiming allegiance with God, Patsy's deeper self—the part of her that believes in right and wrong—made an accurate prediction: that the truth would come out. Patsy Ramsey may want us to think she's talking for God, but most likely she's accurately predicting the future, telling us that the God-part of her will bring about some type of confession.

During the same interview John Ramsey added his part, stating it was his "sole mission" to personally find the killer. Actually, he is on an even deeper "soul mission," which is to eventually tell the truth.

As the late Dr. Maurice Levine, one of the pre-eminent psychiatrists in the world, used to say, "The fifth commandment runs deep: 'Honor thy mother and father.'" So do the other nine, particularly if your heritage is Judeo-Christian, because all of the Commandments are really about honoring the Father. And if He's saved your or your wife's life from death in this world (and also, if you believe, in the world to come), then your entire well-being ultimately rests with God. If you are honoring Him with your trust, then the reverse is true—dishonor brings disowning. The Ramseys have dishonored God not only by breaking the commandment "thou shalt not kill," but they have also broken more. They have lied ("Thou shalt not bear false witness.") and continue to do so, even in the name of God ("Thou shalt not take the name of the Lord thy God in vain."). "Thou shalt have no other gods before me" has been broken by the Ramseys in that they have worshipped other people's opinions, their social standing, their "good people" image, their "freedom" more than the truth. And, before they killed her, in their own way they worshipped JonBenét. When people violate their basic integrity in this way, it eats them alive. It becomes their deeper mind's "soul mission" to tell the truth. You can see it in each of the Ramseys if you follow their thought-prints about God.

Patsy Ramsey is sometimes easier to read than John and usually has done more of the talking or the writing (particularly in the beginning of their cover-up). She follows her May interview with a spontaneous telephone appearance on *Larry King Live* the following September. She impulsively calls him to join his other callers in berating the evil paparazzi who "killed" Princess Diana. At the time, she told her mother that God would give her the words to say, and indeed He did. (See Chapter 4, page 31.)

During her next public interview, on *Geraldo*, November, 1997, Patsy casually told a story about how she had failed God and had loved JonBenét too much—her only public reference of any kind to failure. She insisted at the time that "JonBenét, she knew the truth" (that you weren't supposed to love anyone more than God). God and truth continue to be on her mind, the implications being that the truth will be known, that her conscience, growing more burdened daily, will one day confess.

Six weeks later, Patsy wrote the 1997 Ramsey Christmas letter, replete with hidden confessions and the pressure of time—the day approaches, seeing the light, hearing the music—and closing with a strong emphasis on the Grace of God's (her caps) love. If ever anybody needed grace—forgiveness—and love, it was Patsy.

Next, 1998 came and went with the Ramseys still on the edge of their seats, uncertain if an indictment is on its way. In July, during the infamous Ramsey infomercial—the Tracey interview—Patsy again makes several references to God, including, "God knows the truth—and God's not talking." Simple decoding reveals she's the one not talking. Again, Patsy Ramsey's words suggest that God—or someone—may one day talk.

That Christmas Patsy writes the briefest of letters and a much more private one to their Internet supporters. (See Appendix C, page 325.) Patsy's deepest concerns shine through. JonBenét is still very much on Patsy's mind and she is still speaking for her when Patsy writes that JonBenét "lives on." Like her Christmas letter from the previous year, Patsy is still so guilt-ridden she has to refer to JonBenét as a spirit instead of as a person. But JonBenét now lives in eternity. Patsy's use of "insure" between two references to the next world "eternity" and "short life on earth" suggests she is seeking "insurance" for the next life. Patsy shows she is concerned about gaining entrance into the next world—that one's life should have "great meaning for goodness and love"—suggesting Patsy is secretly worried about her eternal future. As the murderer of her daughter, and as one who continues to live in the lie that she's innocent, Patsy intuitively knows she is sorely lacking in goodness and love.

But if Patsy's "goal is to do our best to insure that our short life on earth will have great meaning for goodness and love," then it's not hard to imagine the Ramseys turning to a religious publisher less than a year later. In doing so, they hope to find respectability and to give their life some semblance of meaning—and to find a means by which they can tell us how much they love God.

The "Born Again" John Ramsey

John Ramsey echoes Patsy's religious spin and even orchestrated his own share of it. Less vociferous than Patsy, John has "Godprints" on his mind that go deeper than he's aware—but with the same relentless progression toward confession. He joined Patsy's God chorus on CNN one week after the murder, but then slowly branched out on his own. Taking offense to a Boulder artist's work portraying JonBenét as "Daddy's Little Hooker," John Ramsey wrote a "private letter" in response. The letter was released not by

John Ramsey but by his then-attorney, Mike Bynum. In it, Ramsey repeatedly defends JonBenét's goodness, at one point stating, "was very religious," even here covering his story with a patina of religiosity.

Then, in July 1997, John Ramsey takes another risk. After consulting with former profiler John Douglas, Ramsey released his profile of the killer, which among other things includes the expectation that the killer "may have turned to religion"—exactly what John and Patsy did, both publicly and privately. John Ramsey banged the drum of his Christian faith for all the world to see, but privately he also sought God's comfort. Every Tuesday morning he attended a Bible study at a private home in an exclusive Atlanta neighborhood with a group of Christian businessmen. He began reading Christian books, even at one point sending one to former *Globe* reporter Jeff Shapiro, who had apologized to Ramsey for thinking he was guilty. But Ramsey ended his Christian witness to Shapiro by continuing to blame those in the media who "persecuted him," stating "the evil is out there."

Having one foot in God's world and one foot in a lie makes a person spin as hard as he can in God's name. It's a game that cannot be won. As a result of him feeding his Christian conscience every week, John's guilt began to bite back. By September 1998, following outspoken Christian Lou Smit's public declaration of the Ramseys' innocent, John Ramsey in his own public letter can hardly contain himself as he becomes more outspoken about God—and the need for forgiveness. "To the killer, I would say that we can and will find you. You have the opportunity to do one good thing in your life by turning yourself in to the authorities and confessing."

Once more John predicts one day a confession will come. He offers a reward if the killer confesses, and then links the confession's value to the killer's mother, spouse, child, and friend: "Help them and help yourself." In the back of his mind, he is thinking of who and what would motivate John himself to confess: He wants to see his mother again; he wants to apologize publicly to Patsy for causing this; he wants to apologize to JonBenét and his other children; and he wants to apologize to his friends. Unconsciously, he sees what is best for him.

He continues advising himself, suggesting what he needs to do after confessing: "Turn yourself in and ask for God's forgiveness. Your fellow man will be grateful and our family will be grateful." After a confession, John's only hope would be to ask for forgiveness. But as he makes plain by his own appeal to "turn yourself in," he can't ask unless he first confesses. John has saved God until the end of the long letter, setting Him off and putting Him in a category all His own. John Ramsey can see that everything hinges on confession. He tells us then, and only then, will there be gratitude from his fellow man—and from the Ramsey family. Unconsciously John recognizes that his continual lies to the public have damaged his fellow man—the last in a long list of people he has harmed. But most importantly, he sees how grateful he will be when he confesses, as he spontaneously connects gratitude over a confession to his family—and to himself.

Obviously John Ramsey had become increasingly convicted about his continued lies and cover-up. We see this as, in the name of God, he becomes more and more confrontational toward the killer. He reveals his guilt in yet another striking way. At what should be one of his most freeing moments, having just been deemed innocent by Lou Smit, Ramsey speaks his loudest for God—and unknowingly, his strongest against himself by confessing once more through throughprints—his choice of words, which betray him: "The loss of JonBenét was a crushing blow" and a "lynch mob hiding behind authority." The pattern continues to emerge: as he advises the killer (himself) to confess, he does exactly that, suggesting once more he has been secretly talking about himself all along.

Three months later in December 1998 John Ramsey confesses in yet another way, telling on himself when he attacks a Boulder photographer. His inappropriate overreaction provided a living snapshot that confessed, "Not only am I capable of exploding into a rage, I am doing so because I need to show you how guilty I am." Christmas time would evoke not only the anniversary of his daughter's death, but would also be a distinct reminder of God.

In December 1999, following the grand jury's decision to hand down no indictment, John Ramsey makes another strong statement of his guilt. On Nashville television as he plugs his forthcoming religious book with Thomas Nelson, he simultaneously confesses more clearly than ever (between the lines) that he sexually abused JonBenét with his ideas and stories of sexual deviants (voyeurs) and an extramarital liaison with a blonde, which he links to JonBenét through the double entendre "laying her" (see Chapter 16, page 219). Driving his confession are his two goals: "to recapture the good name of our family to the degree we can" and "to find the killer of our daughter." Again he underscores that the only way to restore his good name is to confess. Just for emphasis, John Ramsey ends the interview with, "Our intent is not to let it [the case] fade away. We intend for it to be solved."

At an earlier publishers' sales meeting, John Ramsey told the gathering, "We believe we will find the killer." A major hidden part of himself truly plans to solve this murder, which means either he or Patsy, or both, will break.

Patsy added her own vow on Nashville television: "If the publicity for this book keeps it hot, keeps it on the minds and the forefront of the public, great, because somewhere out there is a killer. And we're going to find out who it is." Indeed both the Ramseys are on a "soul mission." Deep down, they really do intend to find the killer.

Imperfect Murder, Imperfect People

When it comes to their religious faith, John and Patsy Ramsey are swimming upstream. The Judeo-Christian heritage has never bought into the idea of perfect people, perfect town, or perfect anything else in this world—with one exception: God, which includes God's son Jesus in the Christian faith. But at the heart of both the Jewish and Christian faiths is atonement. The Old Testament symbol of atonement is a sacrificial animal—often a scapegoat. JonBenét served as the family hero who became the family scapegoat. In life, she carried the Ramseys' dreams, as well as their abuse. In death, she carried the Ramseys' evil—their sins.

In life, she carried—as they loaded her down with it—their terror of death. Beauty, youth, and sex are opposite of death, so she was the most logical family member to carry this burden. She carried or was the recipient of her father's manipulative addictive sexual behavior, and her mother's as well, being encouraged to shine on stage and in the bedroom—in her mother's place. She was made to carry her mother's fear of and guilt over sexuality, her mother's inadequacy and self doubt as a woman, and both her mother's and father's destructiveness—as she unknowingly joined in the destruction of family boundaries.

In death, JonBenét carried their shame, their false pride, their hypocrisy, their lack of love, their selfishness, their own past abuse, their failure to take responsibility, their rage, and especially their murderous impulses—in short, all their guilt and all their lies. JonBenét was a carrier, a momentary messiah. The problem was Patsy and John Ramsey had the wrong messiah. In their blindness they settled for a temporary solution that blew up on them—and part of them continues blindly following the same dead-end path. They will not be able to deny who they are forever, and, from all indications, not for very much longer. They need a permanent solution to their problems. This is why they insist they will find the killer. The killer is still killing—murdering themselves with guilt.

Despite what many people may think, the Ramseys can still preserve some dignity. They can preserve something valuable that still exists in their good name—they can tell the truth. Then and only then can they ask for forgiveness–and it's available to them. They can then give up their own secret roles as messiahs, where they continually wear the masks of perfect people and are thereby enslaved to carrying their guilt and others'. They know that everyone except their blind followers can see the truth and their guilt, and their continued lies invite the scorn of the world. As such, they continue to offer themselves as objects of ridicule.

Of course, if they confess there will be a fresh round of ridicule, but they would be free to admit how foolish they were to believe they were ever perfect. Instead of plastic, perfect people, they could serve as role models of people who need understanding and mercy. They could then be mercy carriers, which might invite ridicule of a different kind. But they would be in good company. Moses, David, the Apostle Paul, dominant Old and New Testament figures, were all murderers, too. In fact, David and Paul were guilty of premeditated murder. And God forgave them and they found peace. As T.S. Eliot once said, "Humiliation is good for all of us." Then we can see who we are and own up to it, and give up the myth of perfection.

Christians, which the Ramseys profess to be, should know better. The prophet Jeremiah described the human heart as possessing such inordinate potential for self-deceit that "no one can really know how bad it is" (17:9, TLB)—certainly not a popular idea, but at moments a chillingly accurate observation as the Ramseys reveal. Jesus agreed, stating, "From the heart come evil thoughts, murder . . . lying and slander" (Matthew 15:19, TLB). The Apostle Paul repeated the same message that the heart was "full of every kind of wickedness . . . greed, hate, envy, murder . . . gossip" (Romans 1: 29, TLB). Even a modern thinker such as the depth psychologist Freud wouldn't disagree with the latent potential for hostility in everyone—he saw the shadow side of man, which explains in part why he was not the most popular of men himself.

Contrast this with various statements from Ramsey supporters. The Ramseys' friend and attorney Mike Bynum said that he wouldn't dare ask them if they had killed JonBenét because "The Ramseys are . . . absolutely incapable of murder and incapable of harming that child." Don't ask, don't tell. Detective Lou Smit likewise insisted that he could size up human beings and that the Ramseys couldn't have done it. A neighbor who knew them summed it up for a lot of people, "If it turns out they killed their child, I'll lose all my faith in the human race."

Good people, bad people, the idealists or the realists? Or is the truth somewhere in between, in the shadows? The Ramseys are vivid reminders that man has a shadow side. Maybe it's time we lost some faith in the human race—time for humility and for walking around with our hat in our hand. Since humility is a prerequisite for being open-minded, we could listen a lot better—to ourselves, to each other, and to God. Maybe then people like Mike Bynum and Lou Smit would quit speaking for God, and let God speak for himself.

For better or for worse, religion is at the heart of this case. Rarely has the public had such a good look at how peoples' religion is interwoven with a murder, how they try to use it as a cover-up, and how their faith—including their need to tell the truth—overpowers them while at the same time offering them hope. The Ramseys and their supporter Lou Smit have given us a marvelous look at religious hypocrisy—compelled to do so out of their tremendous fear. But they unconsciously recognize what they are doing in their "right brain"/deeper intelligence—in their soul—and confess while they appear to be blaming others.

The Ramseys have given us a particularly marvelous look at their own religion, Christianity, from the vantage point of what their faith actually teaches versus how they have tried to manipulate it. The Old and New Testaments bear witness to the existence of a subconscious mind that knows more and sees reality more clearly—much more clearly—than our conscious mind. The Scriptures teach that we all possess a deeper wisdom, an innate sense of right and wrong, as well as instinctive knowledge of fair play and particularly of basic needs such as autonomy—the need to do things for ourselves and take responsibility for our actions. On the deepest level yet, Christian heritage teaches that everyone unconsciously knows God exists—even if consciously they are atheists. And the Ramseys, beyond a shadow of a doubt, have demonstrated these basic tenants of their faith in their repeated promises in the name of God, and in John Ramsey's insistence that he was on a "soul" mission. They both are desperately trying to cleanse their souls.

The Ramseys also provide us with a rich example of something else Christianity teaches—that we are all secretly looking for a scapegoat on which to unload our sins, a savior if you will, even in our daily interactions in this world. This explains both the constant blaming of others or the self-punishing behavior we witness in one form or another on a daily basis, often displayed no better place than in the television soap operas. Certainly, we can see the hope such a religion might offer to people like the Ramseys who have absolutely nowhere else to turn. The Ramseys even point us toward the next world as they talk about their desperate need to have done something good, something that will preserve their good name.

One can understand how such an atonement that Christianity claims to offer would indeed be the truth that could set them free, really the only truth. Because by anyone's account, the crucifixion of Jesus was no light slap on the wrist, no walk in the park, and if any two people in recent times have deserved such an atonement it is Patsy and John Ramsey. The fresh start their own faith offers them is the only way they conceivably can preserve their good name—if they confess and are punished (or someone in their place)—because none of us will be satisfied with just a confession. There must be restitution beyond whatever jail time they might serve. Many would want them to suffer like JonBenét suffered, precisely where substitutional atonement comes in. Of course those who struggle with capital punishment might have some problems with this type of atonement, but the Christian church holds out no such brief when it comes to the ultimate atonement of sin.

Noted writer and theologian C.S. Lewis once wrote that when you mix light and dark (i.e., truth and lies), you get fog. Herein lies the Ramseys' current problem. They can't see the truth they are constantly telling themselves and others between the lines because their lies cloud their vision. Yet unquestionably the Ramseys deep down yearn to tell the truth. And if they do, they will then see more clearly their need for a savior who offers forgiveness, a real Prince of Peace instead of the false princess of peace, JonBenét, whom they created and at whose altar they worshipped.

CHAPTER 18

Truth and Consequences—An Open Letter to John and Patsy Ramsey

"And you know that no murderer has eternal life abiding in him."
1 John 3:15 (NKJV)

John and Patsy,

Whatever your reasons are, you think what you're doing to hide the truth of your daughter's death is best for all. In spite of your determined efforts to continue the cover-up, in your private moments you've had thoughts about confessing, perhaps one of you more than the other. Your unspoken messages make that clear to someone with a trained eye for seeing hidden truth.

Of course, the longer you go on, the harder it becomes to confess. Now it seems all but impossible, and you've probably pushed the idea out of your conscious mind. But, above all, we must come back to what's best for you—and for those you love, particularly Burke and your other children.

If you truly believe in basic honesty and in your faith, you know that it's best to tell the truth, no matter what the consequences may be. To live in a lie is to live in a false reality and to encourage others to live in it as well. When you bury the truth, you bury a part of yourselves, an important part. You tell yourselves and others that the cost of facing the truth is too high—and then everyone lives in the lie. When that happens, there are consequences for everyone.

Actions always have consequences—and to tell someone they don't is to live a lie. We have seen some of those consequences. Your friends tell you the police are evil. Innocent people are labeled as suspects. Anger and suspicion grow. You foster the distrust of police and undermine law and order. You join with others in the belief that facing the truth about friends, family members and oneself is simply too painful to consider.

Without realizing it, you give testimony to the very opposite of your faith—perpetuating a myth that there are perfect people or nearly perfect people in this world, that is it acceptable to place blame outside ourselves and not own who we really are: broken, imperfect souls. Most of all, you tell those who love you that you don't believe they would continue to love you if they knew the real you. And, of course, they'll believe the same thing about your love for them, that it is entirely conditional. Is this the kind of love you believe in? A very conditional love, a love that is diametrically opposed to the central tenant of your faith: God's unconditional love that has been the driving force of true Christian faith for 2000 years?

You encourage your children to live in this false world with you—when a part of them constantly needs the truth, whatever it might be. Burke is in great turmoil, as his drawings reveal, because of your insistence on perpetuating a cover-up. A part of him knows the truth and wants to face it. Without it he will constantly be battling himself—confused, divided, and frustrated, constantly faced with breaking down. Because of his loyalty to you, he is paying a huge price. The pressure on him to live a lie and continue to protect you will take its toll on him. If the turmoil doesn't overtly destroy him, he will spend his life living a lie and defending you, never having a free life of his own—unless you tell the truth. He will remain living in fear that he is about to get it, too, all because he will never have the luxury of the truth: that JonBenét's death began as a freak event that had nothing to do with him. He also will have more than his share of guilt to deal with simply because he is the survivor. He will not have an easy life, but you can choose to add to his burdens or you can give him significant relief.

Your other children will have some of the same battles. You may have decided that you can't lay your shame on them. Living in a lie is worse than living in shame because lies always destroy—but there's a cure for shame.

Without realizing it, your friends perpetuate the same myth that the truth is simply too hard to face, perhaps because they, too, can't face the truth about themselves. All of those people who blindly support you aren't doing you any favors. Lou Smit, your Boulder friends, your attorney friend Mike Bynum, they're not telling you the truth when they imply that it's best to go on lying. None of them even had the courage to ask if you lost control that night and went over the edge. They don't want to get too close to your vulnerability behind JonBenét's death because that puts them too close to their own weaknesses—having to face their own fears. In the end you or anyone else who believes that it's better to continue the lie has been gullible and has believed a lie.

But every moment is a new day. You can abandon living a lie—and embrace telling the truth today. "Life is but a vapor" should be a familiar teaching to both of you, and you have lived long enough to know how true that is. Neither one of you will live that much longer, even if you life out your full life expectancy. What will you do when that last breath comes? Would you regret having told the truth then or would you be glad you continued the cover-up?

I understand that you may tell yourselves that you couldn't stand the embarrassment of a confession or you would have made one. But is what you're doing to your son and your family any easier? You only *think* you couldn't stand it, but the truth is that you can—you are strong enough to handle the truth. You will even be grateful that you did as you, John, pointed out in your public letter to the perpetrator. Then you would be free in a new way.

One option is not really available to you: to think you've privately confessed and that you're forgiven and to believe you don't have to publicly confess, thereby continuing to perpetuate untruths. Once again as you pointed out, John, the perpetrator needs to make a public confession and apologize to his fellow man. You have hurt more people than just JonBenét and you must own up to what you've done.

With a confession, you still have a chance to be a hero to your son. He would have at the core of his identity the idea, the fundamental building block, that his parents, against impossible odds, told the truth and stood up to the lie that the family's love for one another couldn't stand failure. Your son will fail plenty of people in his life, like us all, and he would know that love will see him through. Your son would know that not many people could do what I'm asking you to do—what I've heard you tell me you really want to do: to tell the truth.

Your faith teaches that it's never too dark nor too late to tell the truth. Your faith tells those who think they are superior to throw the first stone. The people who truly care about you will keep caring about you. People who are really honest will understand that under certain conditions they could lose control, too. No one knows the pain you were under that led to this murder. Do you think you are alone, that other people, countless thousands haven't found themselves in circumstances where they lost it, where a situation got the best of them? We've all been there.

Both of you have repeatedly said that the most important thing is your faith, just as you told the story on the *Geraldo* show, Patsy, about how JonBenét said it was wrong to love anything or anybody more than God. In the final analysis, we must look at everything from that vantage point. Surely, your faith teaches that indeed you are not alone, that everyone needs forgiveness—deep forgiveness. Yes, there will be those who would ridicule you if you confess, those who won't understand, those who must scapegoat you. But people who have halfway faced themselves know "there, but for the grace of God, go I."

Tell the truth. Certainly many will understand that you didn't want to admit what happened because you really did love your child—and you didn't want to hurt her brother. We know your having to live with her murder is the worst punishment possible, and we believe that you wouldn't kill again. But it's not enough. You must own what you have done and let circumstances take care of themselves. Forgiveness is a very real thing. The question is: How real do you want it to become for you? You do have a lot to be forgiven for—and it mounts up each day. But if your faith is true, then God is available to meet your humble confession with—as you said, Patsy, in your 1997 Christmas letter—the grace of His ever-present, unconditional love. Remember that Jesus taught that he who is forgiven much, loves much.

You have a chance to do some good things—to shine in a way you never have. Very few people who have come as far down the road as you have, could do what the truth asks you to do—confess now. You would be an example to many who feel they can't change or they're too bad to own up to what they've done, who feel it's too late, who feel they can't face everyone. You would serve as a marvelous example, pointing to the grace of God that your faith teaches, that He awaits honest hearts, ready to meet contrition with a fresh start. That's the central message He's trying to get across according to what you believe.

Doesn't your own faith also teach that He is not surprised at anything, that He knows what is in the hearts of all people? Your faith teaches that He's a realistic God, that He has never lived with the illusion of your perfection. Your faith is a tough faith—prepared for the worst events in life. While God doesn't excuse you, He does understand. Better than anyone, He knows the avalanche that hit both of you. He understands far better than you do why you acted as you did.

But as the Christian faith espouses God is also a tough God. He takes lying extremely seriously—it is the very opposite of Who He says He is. Lying offends Him to the core and He cannot and does not look with favor on what you are doing. You are in very dangerous waters. If you continue down the same path you are on, you run the great risk of exhausting His mercy—particularly as you claim His support in your cover-up.

So you must decide how you want to live the rest of your lives. You can speak to the question of why God allows bad things to happen. You can balance the books and show that often bad things happen because imperfect people make wrong choices—but on the other side is a loving God. That when all is said and done that Love surrounds the universe. That Love is at it's core about forgiveness which is far greater than our imperfections.

And, strangely enough, you could have credibility with many. If you tell the truth and find out how freeing that is, then others could follow your example. Think of how a man like Chuck Colson has turned his life around by telling the truth—stepping down from the White House to prison.[1] There were plenty who doubted that his faith was genuine, but look at all the good he has done: ministering to people in jail after he knew what it was like to be there. Who could have foreseen that when he confessed and lost all his prestige and went to prison that he would come out on the other side with more genuine prestige than before—and with more peace. He didn't let his fear of prison control him. Many other people in history have handled prison well, including the Apostle Paul who spoke the truth from his heart when he knew he would land in jail. You would be in good company. There are worse things than prison.

You have the power to write your own future. Will it be a continued cover-up, a possible jury trial some day, more wasted time and energy protecting a false image? Or will you draw the breath of fresh air that will nurture your soul that comes with the truth? The truth will free you up to face without dread that day of accountability we all must face, knowing that you

---

[1] Charles Colson was a notoriously hard-nosed White House aide under Richard Nixon who confessed to participating in the Watergate cover-up knowing full well when he did that he would end up in prison. While there, he experienced a Christian conversion. After he was released he founded what is now an international organization to reach out to those in prison.

have already owned what you've done and who you are—warts and all—and then you will be received into the heavenly kingdom to once again be reunited with JonBenét who waits for you with the open arms. You can take a chance and continue to live a lie, uncertain of what the consequences might be. Because of your pride, you may find that on that day you might not be welcome.

Patsy, you yourself said it—that you hope you will be with JonBenét in heaven. The only hope that you have comes through truth. Although you corrected yourself and said you *will* be with JonBenét in heaven, your first response was what you truly feel. You aren't certain at all of what the next world has in store for you. As your faith teaches, you can change that at any moment—with a confession. You then can receive mercy because your pride, the one thing that keeps people away from God, will be done with. It is only false pride in the end, because you can take true pride in the only thing you have left—telling the truth, owning who you are.

Of course, what you have suggested repeatedly to yourselves—confess—will not come easy. You will not—cannot—do it (as your faith makes plain) without God's help. As C.S. Lewis said, "It takes a good man to repent, and we're all bad men." Indeed you have an impossible mission before you, but an even more impossible mission waits down the road if you don't find the willpower to confess. Step out on faith—the one you claim to believe—tell the truth, and you will find rest. And with it I believe you will make an incredible impact for good, far more than you can ever imagine.

What will it be? Your perfection or God's? To open your soul or hide it? To rely on forgiveness or pride? Oneness with light and truth or continued cover-up? Every minute of every day, you make a choice. There is only one good choice left. As the Scriptures say, "Today is the day, now is the time."

APPENDIX A:

The Ransom Note
An Overview, Outline, and Additional Insights

Overview of Entire Note

The ransom note is a product of an amazingly organized and highly creative mind, and it has a striking structure. The note is organized into three paragraphs on three pages and includes both a salutation and a signature. To demonstrate the killer's extraordinary ability to communicate in a variety of ways, we will review the note from several angles. It is important to keep in mind the basic validating methodology we use: letting the killer's thoughtprints (ideas) guide us to (1) develop a hypothesis of the crime and (2) to verify the messages by repeating the thoughtprints. This enabled Drs. Callahan, Groesbeck, and myself as investigators to make predictions, which if we were on the right track, the killer's deeper intelligence would confirm. We remained open throughout the process and, as a result, the killer's mind continually surprised us with its additional messages.

Art in the Note

(See Conclusions in the complete report, Appendix B, page 308)

Numbers in the Note

The Number 18

Everyone has been puzzled as to the meaning of $118,000 in the ransom note: why the killer selected such an odd number and what it tells us. Understanding the nature of the unconscious mind and the ways in which the deeper intelligence repeats its messages reveals that the answers to these questions are in the note itself. The number 118 or 18 occurs when the numerical code regarding 8 and 10 is deciphered. All numbers are derivatives of the digits 1 through 10, a crucial principle in understanding the cryptology of numbers, which necessitates ignoring zeroes. Thus, the writer clearly was preoccupied with the numbers 8 and 10—repeating both numbers three times in various forms, with the 8 usually mentioned first as in the $118,000 amount being before $100,000 (or 8 before 10 reduced when derivatives above 10 are ignored). Along the same line, it will help to keep in mind specifically that 18,000: 8,000 + 10,000 (8 + 10); and 118,000: 18,000 + 100,000 (8 + 10) are the same basic numbers.

The key to understanding any encoded message, including numbers, is the context that the writer herself defines. In this case, it is the crucial idea of the life-threatening, narrow time frame "between 8 and 10." The writer gives us the code for 8 and 10—it means time is short or limited with life hanging in the balance, and is specifically limited to the exact amount of 2, another crucial number. (Earlier in dividing $18,000 into $20 bills, the writer underscores in another way the importance of the number 2 and its connection to the number 8.)

The writer next connects numbers in the note to survival percentages and the same idea of a life-and-death time pressure, further suggesting the numbers 8 and 10 are linked to these percentages. With her stage IV ovarian cancer, Patsy Ramsey had between an 8 and 10 chance of dying, which translates into only a 20 percent survival rate. This would explain her preoccupation with the numbers 8 and 10. In the note the writer connects the number 118 (the ransom) with warding off the death of JonBenét, suggesting the writer herself sees the number as having magical properties—just as Patsy Ramsey viewed the 118th Psalm as magically undoing the pressure of her death. In other words, the special number 118 overcomes the deadly numbers of 8 and 10.

Now we can understand why the number 118 would have such special meaning for her as a lifeline, reminding her of the 118th Psalm, which magically undoes the pressure of "between 8 and 10." Thus, the writer's preoccupation with the number 118, along with 8 and 10 (and 2), uniquely fit Patsy Ramsey and offers its own testimony, pointing to her being the author of the ransom note.

We find yet another fit in the numbers: Death can also be prevented by dividing up the valuable money ($118,000) into smaller pieces ($20 bills) until only remains are left. This suggests another strong connection with the "valuable" JonBenét who was "divided up" and the 118th Psalm where the bound scapegoat (sacrifice) prevented death. Once more the writer, Patsy Ramsey, suggests JonBenét was like a sacrificial lamb for her.

The Number 3

The three pages and three paragraphs themselves suggest 3 is an important number to the writer. This is further confirmed by other embedded threes in the note: (1) the writer adhering to the three-part structure of a salutation, body, and closing; (2) three parts to the salutation (including the comma); (3) three parts to the first sentence, including the prominent exclamation mark; (3) prominent threes on both lines of the closing, dividing up "Vi ctory !" into three parts, the last line into three parts considering "S. B.T.C" with the gap between the "S" and "B" and the missing period at the end; additionally the note ends with three initials together ("B.T. C") set apart from the "S;" (4) three words on the last line to the note; (5) ending the second page with three words "Follow our instructions;" (6) using "instructions" three times; (7) using "delivery" three times (not counting the cross-out); (8) only vertical message of three words "I am delivery;" (9) directions about changing containers three times (bank to attaché to paper bag); (10) $118,000 divided into $100,000 and $18,000 making a total of three large sums of money along with the money being divided a third time; (11) $118,000.00 itself having three parts counting decimal (thousands, hundreds, cents); (12) three distinct exclamation points; (13) three overt cross-outs or corrections; (14) using "John" three times; and (15) using "don't" three times on the last page. The writer also suggests the meaning to the number three in the distinct reference to three people—two gentlemen watching over JonBenét—implying the murder is about a horrendous conflict involving three people, which the writer has continually suggested.

Once again the key to understanding the numbers in the note is the context that the numbers themselves suggest. This is precisely how the human mind works in therapy (and life), as a person will often tell one meaningful story after another until he or she can see the context of his or her life that is disruptive. For example, patients with a serious illness will often want to deny how much their illness is bothering them, all while telling one story after another about bodily damage. In other words, the unconscious mind will repeat an idea in an effort to help people understand themselves.

Prominent Thoughtprints: An Outline

Five major thoughtprints that show up in the ransom note may be organized as follows:

Thoughtprint A: Instructions, hidden messages
Thoughtprint B: JonBenét already dead (before note written)
Thoughtprint C: Trigger motive—sexual abuse
Thoughtprint D: Deeper motive—damaged femininity because of cancer
Thoughtprint E: John Ramsey involved in murder instruction

[Author's note: Sections of the ransom note are coded below in brackets according to which thoughtprint is being communicated.]

I.   Salutation: John Ramsey linked to the crime [E]
II. Paragraph One (page 1):
    A. Opens by providing police key to case: "Listen" [A]
    B. Establishes JonBenét already dead: two slips ("un harmed" and "pose") [B]
    C. Numerous references to female suggest killer a woman [D]
    D. Suggests trigger motive: writer angry with John over sexual matter [C]
    E. Begins to establish deeper motive behind murder (possessed, enslaved) [D]
    F. Predicts there are clues/instructions in the letter: establishing motive [A]

Hypothesis: The primary killer was a walking time bomb—a damaged woman who already felt personally entrapped and physically damaged by some disease. She became enraged after catching John Ramsey sexually abusing the victim. More clues follow that will elaborate on motives. If this hypothesis is fulfilled, then it indicates we are accurately decoding the writer's messages.

III. Paragraph 2: (page 1 to top of 2)
    A. Elaborates on deeper motive: devastated femininity due to medical problem [D]
    B. Suggests writer has been assaulted by female form of cancer [D]
    C. Describes writer's psychotic rage: most chaotic sentence in note appears here [C + D]

    D. Clarifies trigger motive: rage over discovering sexual abuse [C]

    E. Reveals JonBenét is dead and why: "Hence" = conclusion [B +E]

Hypothesis: Further validation is evident by the end of the second paragraph. The writer strongly confirms the same story, adding to the picture of how the writer/killer momentarily went insane upon discovering the sexual abuse and how this was the final blow to her already severely damaged identity as a woman. The rest of the note should give more details.

IV. Paragraph 3 (page 2):

    A. Describes in four sentences order of events night of the murder [C]

    B. Describes trigger motive in four sentences: John Ramsey's misbehavior [C]

    C. Describes more clearly deeper motive in sequence of three ideas: terror of cancer [D]

    D. Links John Ramsey to "killing": bold statement about 99% chance of killing daughter [E]

    E. Confirms JonBenét already murdered: repeated references to death [B]

Hypothesis: Further confirmation of story is evident in this paragraph with the writer elaborating in an extremely organized fashion, and in more detail, showing how the two motives came together—and most clearly of all, linking John Ramsey to the murder: "a 99% chance he killed his daughter."

V. End Paragraph 3 (page 3):

    A. Describes deeper motive again, links it to Patsy Ramsey for first time [D]

    B. Closes with five personal comments to John Ramsey, suggesting personal crime [C+ E]

    C. Describes in four ways witnessing explicit sexual scene: trigger motive [C]

    D. Describes why she killed JonBenét instead of John: felt displaced by JonBenét [C]

    E. Refers to "killing" JonBenét, suggesting she's dead [B]

    F. Describes more plainly that John Ramsey strangled JonBenét [E]

Hypothesis: Here is the rich confirmation of the writer's command to "follow instructions" with the writer elaborating on the trigger motive like no where else in the note, shocking the reader as she was shocked—with explicit, crude sexuality. [A] Also the writer explains why she killed JonBenét instead of John: because of competition, a cat fight. The writer also links Patsy Ramsey to the story for first and only time, specifically to her terror of her cancer reoccurring. Finally the writer makes boldest statement yet—that John Ramsey strangled JonBenét.

VI. Closing
    A. Matches "Vi ctory" in embedded message with "Listen carefully"
    B. Describes ransom note as a story about a six-year-old
    C. Tells a sick story of abuse and violence and a sick story
       about cancer
    D. Tells again about her anger at John and describes trigger motive
    E. Shows how badly she needs a victory over cancer [D]
    F. Reflects final wish: forgiveness
    G. Reveals uncertainty about how story will end

Hypothesis: The closing confirms that the ransom note is a story and that it repeats the same story in its own way, using messages, offering powerful validation that ransom note reveals the thoughtprints of the killer.

Additional Insights

The salutation "Mr. Ramsey" brings John Ramsey into the crime and, because it is addressed to him, allows the writer to make disguised, personal comments to John throughout the note. The writer immediately instructs the reader to "listen" for hidden messages and indicates when to pay extremely close attention for particularly important messages by using certain message markers (e.g.,"Listen") that emphasize communication.

The second sentence informs us that the writer and accomplice are going to be speaking for JonBenét. Then the writer goes on to begin to establish the killer's deeper motive for the crime: The killer is disrespected, is entrapped, in servitude, and is most likely a woman experiencing significant concerns herself of bodily harm. Through two disguised sexual references connected to a crucial slip, disrespect for John Ramsey, the writer also suggests a trigger motive for the murder: She caught John Ramsey not minding his business and sexually abusing JonBenét. The killer through "un harmed" hints that JonBenét is already dead at the time the note was written. At the end of the first paragraph the killer makes a bold prediction that the note will guide the police clearly to the motives of the killer and that they must follow the "instructions to the letter." Thus, in the introductory paragraph the killer has accomplished a great deal.

In the second paragraph, which runs through the rest of the first page and briefly onto the second page, the killer elaborates on her deeper motive. By arranging for two tasks to be going on simultaneously—money being divided up and then being changed from one container to a progressively weaker container—the killer paints a picture of her deeper motive. She repeats the ideas about the money being divided up three times and the container being changed three times to convey that she is changing and being eaten up inside (divided up surgically) by a force, almost certainly a disease, that is inflicting great damage on her identity as a woman. She repeats the word "delivery" four times to convey her preoccupation with her femininity. She uses another idea—missing periods (punctuation marks)—to underscore her decline and to convey that she is no longer fertile. Additionally, through the use of the medical concepts of "monitor," "delivery," an exhausting delivery, and advice to get rest, she confirms that she has a major medical problem. In short, she elaborates in great detail about her deeper motive: her declining femininity and life.

At the end of paragraph two, in the most important single sentence in the note, she makes seven slips of the pen, including a large chaotic cross-out of "delivery," replaced by "pick-up" and ending in "daug hter"—all to explain why and when JonBenét was killed. She informs us between the lines that John Ramsey had been molesting JonBenét—through such ideas as (1) preoccupation with "early," used four times and linked to John Ramsey, suggesting an unexpected event set her off; (2) the idea of John Ramsey sexually abusing JonBenét, gratifying himself by "getting some" out of the bank, which links to JonBenét's bank; (3) the crucial slip of the cross-out "delivery," which if read the way it was originally written tells us that John Ramsey had the money *and* JonBenét; (4) chaotic writing when "delivery," symbolizing JonBenét (and feminintiy), is destroyed and changed into a "pick-up."

The writer then presents a series of clues that she was temporarily insane at that moment: (1) the totally misplaced mid-sentence period before the special word "hence," suggesting "conclusion" or "this is what happened;"

(2) the huge, chaotic cross-out of "delivery," (3) replaced by "pick-up" as she turns two words into one; and (4) misspelling a word she spelled correctly earlier in the sentence. At the very end of this sentence. she describes in one word the outcome of her discovery and the ensuing chaos: "daug hter"—she has hit her daughter. Overall, in paragraph two the killer has greatly defined her deeper motive and has vividly described what set off her rage that night.

Paragraph three begins almost at the top of page three. This comes after the killer describes her chaos and rage in a prominent place: at the top of the second page. This third paragraph is strikingly organized. The first four sentences describe the sequence of events: (1) a sudden attack on JonBenét (the head injury); (2) JonBenét is unconscious and terminal, nothing but remains; (3) both parents who have been or will be provoked are watching over her unconscious body lying before them; (4) JonBenét is then strangled (beheaded). Following this crucial sequence is another sequence of four ideas, all of which suggest JonBenét died as a result of John Ramsey being caught secretly abusing her. Thus, the third paragraph starts with the killer picking up where she left off in paragraph two and validating her trigger motive: the event that set her off.

Toward the end of the second page, the killer shifts back to her deeper motive while simultaneously linking it to the trigger motive and presents four consecutive sentences conveying that she had cancer: scanners finding defects that mean certain death, countermeasures failing, and survival percentages (mentioned twice).

On page three, still a part of the lengthy third paragraph, the writer once again confirms her deeper motive with one last reference to survival percentages and cancer: being under constant scrutiny. Finally, the writer returns to the explicit sexual scene she witnessed that drove her temporarily mad as she presents repeated sexual imagery. The writer closes by suggesting again that John Ramsey strangled JonBenét at the very end. The closing confirms this sad story.

For Validation of Major Message Markers as Internal Predictors, see Appendix B, "Conclusions," page308.

APPENDIX B

The Official Report to Michael Kane

A PSYCHOANALYTIC DECODING OF THE UNCONSCIOUS
CONTENT IN THE RAMSEY RANSOM NOTE

This reconstruction is submitted to Mr. Michael J. Kane, Deputy District
Attorney for the city of Boulder, County of Boulder, State of Colorado in the
criminal matter of the death of JonBenét Patricia Ramsey, a human being.

By Andrew G. Hodges, M.D.
Patrick J. Callahan, Ph.D.
C. Jess Groesbeck, M.D.

April 14, 1999

Introduction and Methodology

The homicide of six-year-old JonBenét Ramsey seemingly occurred in
her Boulder, Colorado, home late the night of December 25 or early the
morning of December 26, 1996. Only the victim, her parents, Patsy and
John Ramsey, and her nine-year-old brother, Burke, were home the night of
December 25. The victim attended a Christmas party with her parents and
brother that evening, and the family arrived home around 9:30 p.m. The
parents told the police that the victim had become sleepy on the way home
and they had immediately put her to bed. The parents reported they last had
contact with the victim around 10 p.m. The victim's brother reportedly last
saw her before the parents put her to bed.

Patsy Ramsey reported finding a ransom note shortly after 5:30 a.m.
December 26. She found the note on the stairs outside the couple's third-
floor bedroom. Patsy and John immediately contacted the police who searched
the house but did not find the victim. John Ramsey discovered the victim's
body in the house around 2 p.m.

The victim's body was found partially bound and gagged, in rigor mortis, with some evidence of possible sexual abuse. The victim had suffered a severe head injury across the entire right side of the cranium with a compressed skull fracture posteriorly, but the cause of death was reported as ligature strangulation. The parents denied participating in any way in the victim's death. They further reported that the victim's brother, Burke, had slept through the entire night and could not have killed the victim by himself.

The alleged "ransom note" is a major piece of evidence that virtually cannot be contaminated because it is an unchangeable document. It has come under much suspicion because there was in fact no kidnapping and no one demanded money. While the note alleges a kidnapping for ransom, the victim's body was found in the house with no evidence of an abduction, which appears to contradict the intent of the note. This raises the question of the real purpose of the note—who wrote it and why. The circumstances suggest the note was part of the staging of the crime.

The ransom note is addressed to Mr. Ramsey, but a practice note, found by police in Patsy Ramsey's kitchen notebook later the morning of December 26, was addressed to Mr. and Mrs. Ramsey. Why did the writer change his/her mind? The wording in the "revised" note suggests multiple clues about why the writer chose to exclude Patsy Ramsey. The note also suggests the identity of the writer and the motive for the homicide.

A number of forensic experts on communication have examined the ransom note. Handwriting experts reportedly have ruled out John Ramsey and Burke Ramsey as the writer. Conflicting reports exist about the possibility of Patsy Ramsey being the writer, but one expert stated there was a 90 to 95 percent chance the handwriting was hers. Dr. Donald Foster, a linguist from Vassar, examined the note using an attributional method and, according to some reports, found several striking similarities in Patsy Ramsey's writings and the ransom note.

We have analyzed the ransom note using a longstanding method of psychodynamic reconstruction that applies principles of psychoanalytic theory. According to these principles the human mind works simultaneously on two levels—the conscious and the unconscious, and the mind observes and communicates both consciously and unconsciously. Recent studies have revealed that the unconscious mind is more perceptive and more communicative than previously recognized. The unconscious observes truth in far more detail than the conscious mind, and it communicates its observations in words and ideas that reveal a strikingly honest, deeper train of unconscious thought that occurs simultaneously with conscious thought. In a second level of communication the unconscious mind communicates unconscious messages amid conscious thought.

We have examined the ransom note for its communications from the writer's unconscious mind. In determining what the writer's unconscious mind may be revealing about the crime, every word, punctuation mark, and phrase in the note must be analyzed for the multiple ideas it contains, which means that the words and phrases must be examined symbolically as well as literally. Then each idea the writer presents must be considered as either a self-perception or a perception of someone involved in the crime. The communications from the writer's consistently honest unconscious mind give clues about what really happened the night of the murder as well as why the victim was murdered and who murdered her and where it happened.

The Document

The ransom note contains three paragraphs. The brief opening paragraph describes the alleged kidnappers, the reason for the kidnapping, and warnings to John Ramsey to carefully follow the "kidnappers'" instructions. All that is necessary for a ransom note—and more—is contained in the first paragraph. The slightly longer second paragraph gives very specific instructions about how John Ramsey is to obtain and deliver the ransom money—information that could have been communicated in a phone call or in a much shorter way than a long paragraph. The long final paragraph, which runs one and a half pages, contains multiple warnings to John Ramsey to follow the kidnappers' instructions without any deviation if he wants the victim to live.

Significant words, or "message markers," in the ransom note signal unconscious intent in communications from the writer's mind. The ransom note contains what appears to be a large number of message markers, which itself implies that the note contains a significant amount of unconscious communication.

Message Marker 1: "Listen"

The ransom note opens with *"Listen carefully!"* This strong signal at the beginning of the note suggests paying close attention to the whole note and reading between the lines for the real story. It also suggests paying particularly close attention to the ideas that immediately follow the message marker "Listen" because these ideas are a crucial part of the truth about the homicide. This means we must also pay attention to such things as the slip of the pen in "carefully" that makes the "ll" look like a capital "V" as well as to the exclamation point, which is the first symbol after the message marker—for both may have significance. Exclamation points signify drama, excitement, and strong communication. The writer is suggesting that the deeper story in this note—the story beyond the alleged kidnapping—will stand out in dramatic fashion.

The first idea that follows *"listen carefully"* is *"we are a group of individuals that represent a small foreign faction."* Here the writer strongly implies that more than one person is involved in the crime. The writer also strongly suggests that the group can be broken up into individuals, or every person for himself.

The next idea is *"we . . . represent a small foreign faction."* The writer's conscious intent was to imply that the kidnappers are connected in some way to something powerful but small and foreign, such as a terrorist group. These words also suggest that the writer unconsciously perceives a small foreign part of himself/herself that is terrorizing him/her, and this small foreign part is also terrorizing anyone else who might be involved in the crime.

Since "small foreign faction" immediately follows the message marker "Listen," this idea probably has a particularly personal and important meaning for the writer. It could be a major clue to the writer's identity as well as the central motive for the crime.

Based on knowledge of the unconscious mind and studies of serial killers, "foreign faction" suggests it refers to a powerfully abusive and probably life-threatening experience that terrified the writer. "Foreign faction" also implies that the writer is expressing or has expressed aggression to a much stronger degree than is normal for him/her, to a degree that is "foreign" to him/her—a degree that is also "foreign" to any other participants in the crime. Past traumatic experiences often become a powerful "foreign" part of a murderer's psyche and precipitate violent acting out. Studies show that some murderers who have unresolved issues revolving around rage and killers inflict on their victims the pain that they themselves experience.

"Foreign faction" may also refer to the victim, JonBenét, whose French name and young age make her a "small foreign entity." The writer is indirectly suggesting that "we, the kidnappers, represent—speak for—the victim," a revelation that suggests the writer may be expressing guilt about his/her actions toward the victim. This also suggests that the ransom note may be confessional in nature and that it may be an attempt to represent the victim's best interests.

Message Markers 2 and 3: Two Slips of the Pen—"don't" and "bussiness"

"We ["don't" crossed out] respect your bussiness [misspelled] but not the country it serves." These two slips of the pen suggest that the writer's unconscious mind is revealing how the writer unconsciously saw the crime and the motive(s) behind it. These slips also imply that the writer is experiencing chaos and confusion and that what is being written has a particularly personal meaning for him/her. The two slips in one sentence further imply that the writer is under such great pressure that his/her deeper, unconscious mind is overpowering his/her conscious intent.

Both slips reflect the writer's unconscious hostility toward John Ramsey. The crossed-out "don't" suggests that the writer is secreting his/her true feelings. This attempt to deny any personal hostility toward John Ramsey's business—and thus to John himself—suggests that in truth the writer does resent John Ramsey because of what his business symbolizes to him/her: success, authority, power, and competition.

In alleging respect for John Ramsey's business but resentment toward the United States, the writer implies that he/she has deeply divided feelings about John Ramsey. The writer has reinforced his/her suggestion in the previous sentence that he/she is a very divided person by stating a more overt reference to a division and to anger, which suggests more specifically that the writer is unconsciously torn between being respectful and feeling angry. The clearly stated idea of dividedness further implies that the writer is unconsciously very angry and has the potential for violently acting out, and that unconscious anger is indeed a major "foreign" part of his/her personality. The writer's emphasis on respect suggests a major split in his/her personality—he/she is consciously respectful but is unconsciously filled with hostility.

The crossed-out "don't" also strongly suggests that the writer is the one who resents John Ramsey and that the writer is the one who feels disrespected. The writer's unconscious mind is communicating his/her own perceptions and not allowing the writer to simply write down what someone else—perhaps another person involved in the crime—could be telling him/her to write.

This sentence also implies that unconscious resentment is a prime motive for the crime. The writer connects this resentment to two key ideas: respect and servitude. This strongly suggests that the writer is personally dealing with these two issues, and the writer unconsciously feels disrespected and in servitude. These ideas suggest that some foreign force in the writer—possibly rage as a result of traumatic pain—has erupted out of deep resentment caused by a sense of feeling disrespected and controlled.

The writer's attempt to link the crime to a "foreign faction"—a terrorist group—implies an attempt to mislead the authorities by staging a kidnapping. People who commit homicides occasionally stage crime scenes in order to conceal their identity and true motives. The murderer(s) in this case did not complete the kidnapping, which reinforces the suggestion that the "foreign faction," the terrorist group, is part of the staging to conceal the real reasons behind the victim's murder.

The writer suggests that his/her resentment is directed at the country that John's business serves, the United States, which symbolizes the government, the military, the military-industrial "big business" complex, the land of plenty, and the All-American persona of motherhood and apple pie. These concepts imply that the writer resents John Ramsey for his connection with the American dream.

By linking "country that it serves" to the misspelled word "bussiness," the writer suggests his/her true motive. "Buss" brings to mind a number of other words and ideas such as kiss, bust, bustle, busyness, and bossiness that are used in reference to women and power. The misspelled "bussiness" changes the concept of John Ramsey's business from an aggressive, masculine-oriented entity to a nurturing feminine-oriented entity. This misspelling also implies that the writer is the "boss"—specifically a female boss.

The misspelled "bussiness" also suggests that the writer wants John Ramsey to serve him/her. To conduct business with the kidnappers, John Ramsey must passively follow their very specific orders and allow them to be in control. These ideas imply that the writer feels he/she has the power, at least for the moment, to change John Ramsey's primary identity from an aggressive in-charge male to what is characterized as a passive controlled female.

The misspelled "bussiness" also suggests that the deep-seated resentment the writer feels about being controlled is related to gender issues; authority issues, which John Ramsey symbolizes, and success issues, which again John Ramsey symbolizes. These ideas imply that the writer of the ransom note is a victimized woman who wants to control John Ramsey.

By writing "the country that [John's bussiness] serves" rather than "the country you serve," the writer suggests that he/she wants to excuse John Ramsey from any culpability in the crime—it's not him or his "bussiness" that is at fault, it is his country. The writer's blatant attempt to excuse John Ramsey implies that John Ramsey indeed was involved in the crime.

[*A closer look at this sentence and the slip "bussiness" and the cross-out "don't" suggest that the writer is deeply divided about John Ramsey and that he/she does and doesn't respect him. Specifically, the slip "buss" implies most clearly kiss/romance/sex and that the writer doesn't respect John Ramsey when his business involves sex, pointing to a sexual event the night of the murder. The writer further suggests in a crude fashion becoming upset with John Ramsey when he was discovered "serving his country" as in "cunt ry" or "cunt." (Later, we will see the writer use similar double entendres to shock the reader, which offers strong confirmation of the writer's intent.) The writer suggests by using two sexual references in a row that John Ramsey's sexual behavior wherein he degraded a woman making her "a cunt" would explain why the writer might resent him and want power over him, "degrading" him by feminizing his business as retaliation for his mistreatment of women. The writer unconsciously appears to be laying the groundwork for the motives behind the crime, and already suggests a powerful sexual event was behind this crime.*][1]

---

[1] Italicized comments in brackets were additional insights gleaned from the ransom note after the report to Michael Kane. Here the writer establishes earlier than we previously appreciated a powerful sexual trigger motive, which she clearly confirmed later in the note.

Message Marker 4: Another Slip, "posession"

"At this time we have your daughter in our posession [misspelled]" suggests that a young/little female/woman is entrapped. The misspelling draws attention to "posession" and suggests that this idea is a key part of the true story of the victim's death.

The misspelling also suggests that the writer feels possessed, which reinforces the suggestion that the writer feels greatly entrapped. It also strongly implies that the writer feels so anxious about being entrapped that he/she turned "posse ssion," into "pose ssion," which relates the word to "posse" and "pose." The writer is implying that he/she is anxious about being pursued by a posse, such as the police and other law enforcers, as well as about holding a "pose," which includes the staging of the crime and the continued cover-up. This sentence also links "daughter," female gender, to being possessed, which reinforces the suggestion that gender plays a key role in the writer's feelings about being controlled and entrapped. [*The slip "pose" also suggests staging as in "we have your daughter in our pose." Once more the killer reflects a need to confess, here informing the police that indeed they had accurately concluded that the crime scene was staged.*]

Message Marker 5: A Word with Disconnected Syllables

"She is safe and "un harmed" brings in a new idea. While "safe" introduces the idea of potential bodily harm, the spacing between the syllables of "un harmed" suggests that the victim is actually disconnected, damaged, and perhaps even dead by the time the ransom note was written.

The idea of bodily harm follows the idea of being controlled or entrapped—servitude and possession, which suggests that the writer unconsciously perceives himself/herself to be in physical danger. The two words referring to bodily harm—"safe" and "un harmed"—are followed by a threat that the victim will die, "if you want her to see 1997." The inclusion of three references to bodily danger in one sentence suggests that the writer was overwhelmed with his/her own fears of being harmed. These three references including the overt threat connected to the victim also suggest that she is already dead.

The writer uses two female references in this sentence—"she" and "her." This reinforces the suggestion that gender, and specifically female gender or femininity, may be a major issue for the writer.

Message Marker 6: "Instructions"

"If you want her to see 1997, you must follow our instructions to the letter" links "instructions" to the "letter"—implying the ransom note itself. "Instructions" is a significant message marker that strongly implies that there is a hidden roadmap in the ransom note to help identify the killer. This is reinforced by the idea of "to the letter"—pay particular attention, look closely which further suggests look deeper. "Follow our instructions to the letter" suggests that there are hidden instructions in the ransom note that if properly, strictly followed—"to the letter"—would allow the victim to "live," to "speak" for herself. This further suggests that a confession—instructions—hidden within the note speaks for the victim and points to who the writer and killer is, what happened the night of the murder, and why.

Three references to bodily damage in one sentence linked to the message marker "instructions" implies that the writer is unconsciously communicating a key part of the true story. The writer suggests she/he is experiencing significant fears of bodily harm and may perceive this to be a central motive for the murder.

The explicit threat that the victim would be killed—"if you want her to see 1997"—linked with the particularly important message marker "instructions" also suggests that the writer may be the killer. The feminine pronoun "her," used instead of the victim's name in this crucial phrase, reinforces the suggestion that the writer is a woman.

Message Marker 7: A Decimal Point

"You will withdraw $118,000.00 from your account. $100,000 will be in $100 bills and the remaining $18,000 in $20 bills" comes immediately after the clue to pay particularly close attention to the instructions. The concept of (1) something valuable being withdrawn fits with (2) bodily harm, (3) being disrespected, (4) being controlled—servitude and possession, and (5) small foreign faction. These five ideas strongly suggest the writer's identity and the motivation for the crime: Something valuable has been withdrawn from the writer, the writer feels physically endangered, threatened by a seemingly small entity or event, and he/she feels controlled to the point of entrapment which also causes her to feel disrespected.

Linking these five ideas with the idea of a large amount of money being divided into smaller and smaller amounts—following three specific references to bodily harm highlighted by the crucial message marker "instructions"—suggests that a small foreign force is terrorizing the writer's body and making the writer feel smaller and smaller. This sequence of ideas also suggests that the writer's health has been severely threatened and that he/she either has had a surgical procedure that withdrew a valuable body part or he/she is suffering from some type of debilitating medical illness, something small and foreign but powerful. Based on the knowledge that criminals often inflict on their victims the pain that they themselves are feeling, the essence of this crime—parents suddenly losing a child—reinforces the suggestion that the writer himself/herself has suffered a sudden, major, life-threatening loss related to bodily damage. The idea of kidnapping itself suggests something valuable being taken away which further suggests the writer's staging the crime as a kidnapping reveals the writer's motives.

The writer instructs John Ramsey in detail about the "ransom" money, including the exact number of $100 and $20 bills. The writer includes a decimal point in the total amount to be withdrawn, $118,000.00, but not in the smaller amounts—$100,000, $18,000, $100, and $20. This detailing and the idea of a large sum of money being divided into smaller and smaller amounts reinforces the suggestion that the writer is unconsciously observing a small but significant force that makes him/her feel smaller and smaller, to feel diminished as a person. The decimal point in $118,000.00 is so different and small that it serves as a message marker to reinforce the suggestion that the writer unconsciously perceives himself/herself becoming smaller and more insignificant.

The decimal point message marker also implies that the idea of small is particularly important in the true story, and it also reinforces the idea of listening carefully for small details. "The remaining" is yet another concept of smallness and suggests that the force that possesses and controls the writer also creates a deep sense of taking something valuable from him/her so that only a small part of the writer is left—remains. Even the ransom demand is small—another suggestion that the writer sees himself/herself as small and insignificant. The somewhat low and odd amount of the ransom—$118,000.00—also suggests that it has personal meaning for the writer.

The concept of a large amount of money becoming smaller and smaller, the deliberate inclusion of a small decimal point, and the idea of "remaining/remains" fit with the idea of a "small foreign faction"—which implies once again that a small alien force in the writer's body is destroying him/her. The decimal point and the repeated idea of smallness along with the other patterns in the note suggest that the writer is not simply taking down dictation from another person. The writer is composing the note to reveal his/her personal concern with smallness, a deep sense of being diminished/depleted, and the recognition of something large becoming smaller until there are only "remains."

"Remaining/remains" reinforces the suggestion that some force has caused the writer to experience great bodily harm to the extent that a part of himself/herself has been withdrawn, causing him/her to feel deep emotional pain as though he/she is possibly dying and only remains are left. Deep emotional pain can cause people to become enraged and explode in violent behavior, which reinforces the suggestion that the writer is also the killer.

Studies of murderers indicate that two motivating factors precipitate murder: deep enduring emotional pain/"the time bomb motive" and a cataclysmic event/"the trigger motive" that causes the murderer to lose control and inflict deep pain on a victim. The ransom note suggests both deep emotional pain and an event that triggered a rage serious enough to kill.

"Make sure that you bring an adequate size attaché to the bank" implies that the writer has a controlling nature so strong that he/she is compelled to remind John Ramsey, who is a highly functioning CEO, of a most minute detail. This parental, controlling tone reinforces the suggestion that the writer feels hostility toward John Ramsey by its attention to the specifics of the transaction.

This sentence also reinforces the suggestion that the writer is preoccupied with size, in particular the size of a "container," an attaché, and especially concerned that a container might be inadequate. This is the writer's fifth general reference to size and the fourth in a row—small foreign faction, the money being divided up into smaller amounts, the small decimal point, and remaining—which reinforces the suggestion that the writer is concerned about how small and inadequate he/she feels. The concepts of size and container linked with the concept of money being changed from one container to another with the adequacy of the container questioned implies that the writer is concerned about a container changing—and the ability of the container to hold valuables.

"The bank" as a valuable container suggests a woman's primary identity as someone who contains and protects valuable life in a small container deep within her. This idea is reflected in the analogy that a bank is where people keep their nest eggs and the idea of a woman's purse. In addition, a bank vault within a large bank building suggests an even stronger image of a woman whose body contains a small valuable vault or container. Medically, the vaginal canal is referred to as the vaginal vault.

All of these related ideas reinforce the suggestion that the writer is concerned about a damaged, diminished, depleted feminine identity. They also suggest that the writer has experienced a direct attack on a woman's femininity, most likely a life-threatening female medical condition or at the very least a major physical assault unique to a woman. The idea of a container being damaged, diminished, and/or depleted of its valuables suggests a woman who has lost her ability to bear children, something that threatens her feminine identity. This reinforces the suggestion that the writer is concerned with a sexual identity issue, specifically "a woman's femininity has been made small and inadequate because her container has been damaged, diminished, and/or depleted."

"When you get home you will put the money in a brown paper bag" contains another controlling comment—"you will"—linked with two feminine references to containers "home" and "brown paper bag." Something very valuable, the large sum of money, is being sequentially changed from a larger container to a small one: from a bank to a small attache to a brown paper bag. This progression, downward in size, suggests that the change in a feminine identity has left the writer feeling small, plain, and dead or dying—the color brown reflects death. The downward progression from a solid bank, to a less-solid attache whose adequacy the writer questions, to a thin brown paper bag suggests that the writer feels deeply vulnerable.

Valuable containers may symbolize femininity or a woman's uterus, which is shaped like a thin paper bag held by the neck—with a large container and a much smaller neck. Of all the containers the writer mentions in the ransom note, "brown paper bag" specifically suggests a woman's uterus. The idea of valuables being in a paper container also implies that the writer is observing a feminine identity becoming "paper-thin" and therefore vulnerable.

The number of feminine references and the number of references to various containers, including the "brown paper bag" which may be seen as uterus-shaped, suggest that the writer is concerned about something devastating that has happened to a woman's uterus and thereby has diminished her feminine identity. This concept of "change" strongly suggests that the writer has experienced "The Change"/menopause in a sudden way, as the result of a hysterectomy due to a life-threatening medical problem, one that left a woman feeling deeply emotionally depleted. Very few diseases besides cancer affect the uterus in a life-threatening way, which strongly suggests that the writer herself has experienced a female form of cancer, which fits with the idea of a "small foreign faction," a very accurate description of cancer. The instructions that the money change containers twice—to progressively weaker and smaller containers—along with the money having to be divided twice provides two strong suggestions that a dramatic deteriorating change is going on within the writer himself/herself.

The ideas of emptying the brown paper bag and exchanging the valuables inside it for the life of the victim suggests that the valuables the writer wants are connected to the victim. This further suggests a personal relationship between the writer and the victim.

This depletion of the brown paper bag, which is the image of a uterus, suggests the delivery process or giving birth. Moving a large amount of money, "the valuables," four times from one container to progressively smaller containers—withdrawals from a bank mentioned twice to an attaché to a brown paper bag—suggests not only a declining feminine identity but also a repeated "delivery" of the valuables, a fantasized repetition-compulsion[2] revealing the urgent pressure the writer is unconsciously feeling. This delivery suggests that the writer is trying to compensate for a lost femininity and the extreme vulnerability of the loss of the ability to deliver a child symbolized by ordering "deliveries" on demand. It also suggests that the writer feels empowered by repeatedly ordering a male, John Ramsey, to symbolically carry out a birth or rebirth process, "delivering" the ransom money. All of these ideas imply that the motive for the crime lies in the deep sense of declining femininity the writer is experiencing.

---

[2] Repetition-compulsions occur when a person unconsciously arranges certain situations to repeatedly occur as a way of attempting to master painful emotions. It represents an attempt to recreate a familiar painful situation in hopes of "getting it right this time," and thereby undoing the pain.

"Home" is the strongest symbol of nurturing environments, and "when you get home" suggests that the writer is looking for comfort and relief. This fits with the other suggestions in the note—the alleged group of kidnappers can be separated, specific instructions are hidden in the note to reveal the true story of the crime, the repeated pattern of declining femininity and bodily damage as a motive—that point toward the writer wanting to unconsciously confess in order to find some comfort and relief from their criminal participation.

The significant number of feminine references including the specific references to a container shaped like a uterus and the repeated ideas suggesting delivery of a child strongly suggest that a physically and emotionally distressed female wrote the ransom note. Therefore from this point on in the analysis of the note, the writer will be considered to be and will be referred to as a woman.

Message Marker 8: "Call"

"*I will call you between 8 and 10 am tomorrow*" implies that the writer is feeling the pressure of time. "Between 8 and 10 am" represents a narrow time window, and it is the second reference to time and pressure—"if you want her to see 1997" is the first. This window suggests that the writer feels time is running out because of some physical harm/condition and also because of impending entrapment once the ransom note is discovered. The word "tomorrow"—the third reference to time—also suggests that the writer was already feeling the pressure of the investigation that would be certain to take place.

"I will call you" suggests that the kidnappers intend to make the parents wait helplessly until the kidnappers choose to call them. The idea of keeping a vigil also suggests that the writer herself feels helpless because of having to wait to receive some information about a life-threatening situation, which gives the reader a fourth reference to time and pressure. These four references imply that time and pressure are of great concern to the writer.

The writer deliberately put a small decimal point in the figure $118,000.00 but did not put periods after "a" and "m" in "a.m." This makes "a.m." read "am." "Am" is always used with "I," which suggests that "I/the writer am" personally connected to this particular time frame. The writer suggests that she unconsciously left out the periods in "a.m." to link it with "am." Since

"I" is so strongly associated with "am" and there is an "I" directly above the "am" in the sentence, the writer is suggesting that the words be read vertically—the only direction with any apparent meaning using the word "am" and the only meaningful vertical message in the note. The vertical "sentence" reads "I am delivery," a very powerful message that implies "I am woman." This message infers again that the writer is a woman facing crucial issues with her femininity.

The message marker "instruct" comes a few words after "am" in the line below and is connected to "delivery," further signaling that this is a very important sentence and also further encouraging the vertical reading of "I am delivery." By leaving out the periods in "am" in conjunction with "delivery" the writer is implying in another way that she has a problem with her femininity—she is missing her periods.

"I will call you . . . to instruct you on delivery" suggests a medical doctor calling a patient to discuss her impending delivery. This reinforces the repeated suggestion that the writer is dealing with a serious medical matter related to her femininity.

The use of the word "tomorrow" additionally suggests that the writer is writing the note during the night of December 25. This strongly suggests that if the victim was already dead by the time the note was written, the victim would have been killed before midnight.

The message marker "call" precedes "between 8 and 10 am," which signals that this is an important communication from the writer's unconscious mind. The writer's repeated use of the number 118 ($118,000.00) or 18, as in 8 and 10 adding up to 18, suggests either number—118 or 18—or both could have some significance for the writer. The two numbers 8 and 10 also suggest the possibility that a significant event took place between 8 and 10 the night of the murder.

Message Marker 9: Another "Instruction"

"*I will call you between 8 and 10 am tomorrow to instruct you on delivery*" suggests that at least briefly the writer feels in control: Don't call me— I'll call you. "Instruct you on delivery" again suggests a doctor giving instructions about childbirth, which is at the heart of many women's feminine identity—the unique thing that only a woman who is a mother can do. "Delivery" itself, following numerous more indirect references to femininity, even more strongly infers the writer's preoccupation with childbirth. This emphasis on the word "delivery" strongly suggests that the writer has experienced something connected with her ability to deliver a child, a concept which fits with the writer's preoccupation with diminished femininity and power, feelings of deep emotional pain, and the demanding "powerful" tone of the note.

This is the first time the writer uses "I," which suggests in yet another way that the idea of "delivery" is part of her personal identity. The writer uses the word "delivery" no less than four times in the next three sentences, which further reinforces the suggestion that the writer is preoccupied with issues related to femininity and childbearing.

The multiple references to delivery, container, and bodily harm could suggest that the writer suffers from the deep pain of severe sexual abuse or a physical assault that resulted in a hysterectomy. But these ideas don't fit well with ideas of a declining feminine identity, being under the pressure of time, and dealing with a small foreign faction.[3]

"The delivery will be exhausting so I advise you to be rested" is the second reference to childbirth in two sentences, which suggests that whatever is threatening the writer's feminine identity is exhausting her. It also suggests that the writer is very tired both emotionally and physically and wants to rest. In addition this reference implies that the motive for the crime has a lot to do with the writer's exhausted body: She is exhausted not only from being up most of the night participating in the crime but also from the effects of dealing with a life-threatening female health problem.

The reference to the exhausting feminine medical procedure of delivery and the recommendation "I advise you to be rested" suggest a physician advising a patient to "get plenty of rest," which again reinforces the suggestion that the victim's death is connected in some way to a medical condition.

---

[3] The possibility of a sexually abused woman replicating her abuse as in a repetition-compulsion by a horrendous sexual and physical assault on a victim doesn't fit with this crime scene. The victim's body reportedly was not displayed in a degrading fashion. Also, the items reportedly found with the victim's body reflected a woman's nurturing touch: two blankets—one of them covering the victim, her favorite nightgown and a suitcase by the window containing a Dr.Seuss book. In addition a heart had been drawn on the palm of one of the victim's hands. The crime scene combined with all of the feminine references in the ransom note suggest that the writer is a woman who deeply fears a life-threatening disease that has attacked her female body parts and thereby has diminished her feminine identity.

This reference to exhaustion also suggests that the writer was exhausted the night of the murder and rested for a brief time after the murder—before "tomorrow" came.

"I advise" is the second of only three times the writer uses "I," which implies the ideas in this sentence have particularly strong personal meaning for the writer. "I advise you to be rested" strongly suggests that the writer is exhausted from attempting to be delivered from a disease. This reinforces the suggestion that the writer is a cancer victim and that she is exhausted, probably both from the treatments and the emotional stress of dealing with this life-threatening disease. And if her medical prognosis had a low survival percentage, her level of stress and physical and emotional exhaustion would be intensified. This sentence further suggests that the writer is frustrated that her ability to deliver is exhausted and she no longer has the female ability to reproduce.

"Exhausting" also suggests that the killing was an attempt for the writer to find rest or relief. A threatened woman who gains victory over a less powerful female such as a child would experience temporary relief as well as a sense of renewed power, the type of momentary relief and power that rageful murderers many times experience.

The idea of being "rested" also suggests that the writer will be able to find relief when she no longer has to hold a "pose" or worry about a "posse"—when the true story of what happened the night of the victim's murder, the identity of the killer(s), and the motive is finally revealed. This reinforces our suggestion that the ransom note may be confessional in nature, an attempt by the writer to unconsciously cast off the exhausting "pose" and find relief from her guilt by finding the place of psychological truth.

Message Markers 10-19: "Monitor," "Call," Five Slips, Two Preoccupations, and "hence."[4]

"*If we monitor you getting the money early, we might call you early to arrange an earlier delivery of the money and hence.* [sic] *a* [sic] *earlier* ["delivery" crossed out] *pick-up* [sic] *of your daug hter* [sic]" is the longest sentence in the note, and it breaks the rhythm of short sentences allegedly given by demanding

---

[4] Message Markers 9-18, all in this one sentence, will be explained out of sequence because of the unique features of this sentence and for a logical flow of ideas.

kidnappers. This sentence contains ten distinct message markers: #10 "monitor," #11 "call," #12 "early/earlier"—used two times each, #13 "delivery"—used for the third time, #14 "hence," #15 the misplaced "psychotic period," #16 "a earlier"—a grammar error plus a misshapen "a," #17 "delivery"—crossed out, #18 "pick-up," and #19 "daug hter." This sentence contains that most message markers of any sentence in the note, which underscores the importance of this sentence—the writer gave repeated signals that it contains crucial information about the crime.

Along with the three message markers of "monitor," "call," and "hence," there are five slips of the pen—the crossed-out word, a mid-sentence period, a grammatical error, connecting two words with a hyphen to make a word that is spelled without a hyphen, and putting a space between the two syllables of "daug hter." In addition the idea of early is repeated four times—both "early" and "earlier" are used twice—and "delivery" is used once and crossed out once after being used twice in the two previous sentences. The numerous slips suggest that the writer's mind is in chaos and she is having an extremely difficult time holding on to her thoughts.

The five slips of the pen are linked with the powerful message marker "hence"—"therefore" or "in conclusion"—which suggests that the writer is overwhelmed as she relives in her mind the events that led to the conclusion that it did that night, the murder of the victim. This degree of the writer's personality disintegration here also suggests that the writer was personally involved with the murder, making this "a crime of passion" versus a killing by an impersonal, detached murderer.

The original sentence, before the writer crossed out the word "delivery" and changed it to "pick-up," reads "If we monitor you getting the money early, we might call you early to arrange an earlier delivery of the money and hence. a earlier delivery of your daug hter." This suggests that the one who is going to deliver the money—John Ramsey—is also the one who is going to deliver, not pick up, the child, which further suggests that the murderer(s) is a family member—John or Patsy Ramsey, or both working in concert.

The repetition of the idea "early" strongly suggests that something happened early in the crime scenario, earlier than the writer expected. The fourth reference to early—a the second "earlier"—comes right before the "delivery" that is crossed out by a chaotic black mark, which strongly suggests that the murderer got caught off guard, startled and perhaps acted without pre-meditation or conscious intent, killing the victim in a moment of chaos.

Message Markers 14 and 15: "Hence" and the Psychotic Period

The word "hence" indicates "conclusion," which suggests that the writer is going to reveal how the deep pain and stress she felt, the "time bomb motive," merged with the events of the evening, the "trigger motive," and led to the victim's murder. "Hence" is followed by an out-of-place period, which reinforces the suggestion that the writer's mind is in chaos at this "point." A period is used to mark the end of a declarative sentence, which reinforces the idea of conclusion or end. The word "period" suggests a number of ideas: the completion of a cycle or action, the end, an interval of time, a single cyclic occurrence of menstruation, a stage in development, and one of the divisions of playing time in a game. All of these ideas reinforce the suggestion that a woman, the writer, is describing the conclusion of an event or interval of time.

The finality indicated by the use of a period and its insertion in the middle of the sentence directly after a word that means conclusion, "hence," strongly implies that some event was unexpectedly completed or concluded before the end of "its time." The out-of-place period also implies that the writer observed an event that led her to become chaotic to the point of experiencing a temporary break with reality. After this psychotic "period" comes "a [sic] earlier," a grammatical error that reinforces the suggestion that the writer's mind is in chaos. This error is immediately followed by the most chaotic slip in the note where the writer blatantly crosses out "delivery." This large black mark reinforces the suggestion the writer is overwhelmed and in chaos—the third such suggestion in a row.

The idea then of "hence" linked with the psychotic period, the grammatical error, and the crossed-out "delivery" together are strong evidence that at the time these words were written, that the writer's massive confusion and loss of touch with reality led to the homicide.

The crossed-out word "delivery" is followed by another message marker "pick-up," which is immediately followed by another message marker—"daug hter"—one word divided into two. Taken together "pick-up" and "daug hter" suggest the event that triggered the writer's chaos and confusion—and thus the murder.

Message Marker 17: The Crossed-out "Delivery"

The bold, blatant crossing out of the word "delivery" suggests that the writer is not only capable of but already has expressed significant aggression. The literal destruction of "delivery," a word the writer repeatedly suggests symbolizes femininity, fits with the idea of destroying a female victim. It reinforces the suggestion that the victim is already dead and also strongly suggests that the writer was the one who attacked and destroyed her. The cross-out or destruction of the word "delivery" also suggests that the writer's femininity was unexpectedly assaulted prior to the murder.

Message Marker 18: "Pick-up"

The crossed-out "delivery" is replaced with "pick-up." The writer used a hyphen to link two words—"pick" and "up"—to make the word "pick-up," which is spelled without a hyphen—"pickup." This draws attention to the word and suggests that it has particular meaning for the writer. "Pickup" is often used to refer to a prostitute,[5] another distinct albeit negative reference to feminine identity. The writer clearly links the victim to both the crossed-out "delivery" and to "pick-up" since the victim is the one being delivered or picked up. Conceptually these three ideas together—destruction, femininity, and being replaced by a pickup—suggest that the victim was destroyed when the victim was changed from a respectable little woman into a pickup. The writer is suggesting that she was shocked when she discovered the victim being sexually abused, prostituted—which the autopsy also suggests.[6]

The writer further suggests that this change in the victim from respectability to being debased destroyed the writer's femininity and provoked uncontrollable psychotic rage in the writer that pushed her into chaos and out of control. The writer suggests that this rage led to the murder and explains a major part of how the events of the night culminated—concluded—in the homicide.

---

[5] "Pickup" also is used to refer to trucks, but here "truck" would not fit with the context of the sentence. A truck is an inanimate object and the writer suggests she is unconsciously describing events occurring between people. Also the writer repeats the idea of the victim being prostituted in several ways.

[6] The autopsy points toward both acute and chronic sexual abuse of the victim, and the ransom note suggests that sexual abuse fits with the evidence found at the crime scene.

Certainly for the writer to react in this chaotic way suggests that her feminine identity was deeply threatened by the victim being prostituted, and it further suggests that the writer was personally involved with both the victim and the perpetrator of sexual abuse.

The next words in the sentence suggest even more clearly who the prostitute was: "pick-up of your daug hter" points to the victim, John Ramsey's daughter, as the "prostitute" who threatened the writer's feminine identity. "Early pick-up" suggests "a young pick-up," which reinforces the suggestion that the writer unconsciously viewed the victim as the prostitute.

To consider an innocent six-year-old, particularly a helpless murder victim, a prostitute is offensive to almost everyone. However, the writer suggests she is graphically portraying the way she experienced the victim's abuse to convey the painful emotions that overpowered her. The writer suggests that the idea of the victim being prostituted was such an offensive thought to her that it overwhelmed her abilities to think and act rationally.

Message Marker 19: "Daug hter"

The writer separates the syllables of the word "daug hter," essentially breaking it into two words—"daug" and "hter," after she gives the message marker "hence," which very strongly suggests that the conclusion is that the victim has been murdered, "broken," "separated" from life. By placing "daug hter" in such a key place in the sentence—the very last word and the natural conclusion—the writer suggests again that she is unconsciously describing in this sentence the sequence of events that led to the writer's chaos and the victim's murder.

The chaos and destruction seen in the crossed-out word "delivery" and in the split word "daug hter" reinforce the suggestion that the writer's chaos led to rage and that she was the killer, not just an accomplice. The boldly crossed-out word "delivery" suggests that the night of the murder both the writer's femininity and the victim's femininity was completely shattered—literally and figuratively. The writer suggests that she was emotionally shattered and then she destroyed. This extreme reaction on the part of the writer also suggests that she was deeply personally involved with the victim and that she was also deeply threatened by discovering the victim being sexually abused.

The writer suggests that she was so deeply involved with the victim that an assault on the victim was an assault on the writer. But the writer's chaos and rage was directed at the victim, which suggests that the writer had deeply conflicting feelings about the victim. The writer suggests that she was extremely upset when she saw the "daug hter" being abused but simultaneously she was also extremely angry at the "daug hter." This reinforces the suggestion that unexpectedly finding the victim being sexually abused was the "trigger" motive that caused the writer to lose control and assault the victim in a rage the night of the murder.

A person who would feel this degree of simultaneous protectiveness and betrayal would have to be an extremely close female family member, a mother or less likely a sister. This increases the likelihood that a powerful family triangle relationship is a key factor in the death of the victim. It also suggests that the writer is the victim's mother.

The "hter" of "daug hter" strongly suggests the idea of "hit her"—even more so since "hter" is higher on the page than "daug," which suggests "hit her from above." Together the split word suggests "daughter—hit her" or "hit her daughter," reinforcing the idea that the writer is confessing that she is the victim's mother.

With "daug" strongly suggesting "dawg" or "dog," the split word also suggests "hit her dawg" or "hit her daughter the dog." This implies that the writer is confessing how badly she mistreated the victim. The writer's words in this sentence match the autopsy findings: The victim's body shows evidence that the murderer(s) "treated her like a dog." The autopsy findings show that someone hit the victim in the head with a severe blow,[7] which suggests a rage murder. The writer suggests by referring in such a degrading fashion to the victim as a dog that again she is conveying the depth and primitive nature of her rage and how overpowered she was by her emotions.

The sequence of ideas in this sentence also strongly implies that the writer viewed the victim as a threat and lost control when she experienced the ultimate betrayal "by the victim" in relationship to someone else very

---

[7] The autopsy revealed that the victim suffered an extremely severe head injury over the entire right side of her cranium most likely secondary to a blunt object. The injury almost certainly would have been fatal if the victim had not been strangled.

close to the writer. The original sentence, before "delivery" was crossed out, strongly suggests that the one who was to deliver/had the money was also the one who was to deliver/had the "daug hter." This striking slip suggests that John Ramsey was involved with the victim as a "pickup." And "pickup of your daughter"—or "your daughter, the pickup"—is addressed to John Ramsey, which reinforces the suggestion that he picked up his own daughter. The original sentence also reinforces the suggestion that the murder involved a powerful family triangle.

The next sentence includes "immediate execution of your daughter," which suggests confirmation that the "pickup," the victim, is already dead. In addition the sequence of these ideas continues to suggest that the writer became chaotic, lost control, and became enraged when the victim became a little pickup and replaced her—further threatening the writer's already precarious feminine identity. These concepts reinforce the suggestion that the deep pain the writer felt because of her damaged feminine identity would predispose her to lose control if she experienced another major threat to her femininity, a threat the writer suggests she experienced the night of the murder. Thus, in this half of the sentence alone, the writer has suggested both the "time bomb" and the "trigger" motives as well as the sequence of events, all of which fit with the forensic evidence in this homicide.

Message Marker 16: "A Earlier"

The unconscious mind sometimes communicates in rhyming words, and the grammatical error "a earlier" instead of "an earlier," which the writer had written correctly previously in the sentence, subtly links "a" earlier/young and unexpected pickup with the pronunciation of the victim's name, "Jon-Ben-ay." The word "attaché," used earlier in the ransom note, refers to a small, valuable fancy-sounding container and also rhymes with JonBenét. And like JonBenét, "attaché" has a fancy accent on the last "e." The writer made the dot of the "i" in "earlier" look like an accent mark, which suggests that she is again unconsciously referring to JonBenét and that she is personally involved with her.

Message Markers 12 and 10: "Early" and "Monitor"

The first part of the sentence, before the "psychotic period," contains three references to the idea of "early" plus the message marker "monitor." In the context of this sentence "monitor" means "secret observation" or "secret"—the "kidnappers" would be secretly monitoring John Ramsey; he would not be able to see them monitoring him. The ideas related to "monitor" suggest that this part of the ransom note contains the secret/true story of what happened the night of the murder. The writer suggests that she "monitored," clandestinely observed, someone—John Ramsey—withdrawing money/valuables from a bank, a feminine container as the writer suggests, early or unexpectedly. In other words the writer unconsciously observed John Ramsey "getting some," or "gratifying himself."

"Bank" again in this note particularly implies a feminine reference and the money withdrawn from the bank will be exchanged for the victim, which links the particular bank John Ramsey is getting valuables from, with the victim. It is John Ramsey who is to deliver the money/valuables as well as to "pickup" the other valuable, the victim.

The word "early" suggests several interpretations: John Ramsey was secretly dipping into the victim's valuable "early/before-her-time/young" bank, and the killer had unconsciously been observing John Ramsey "early/unexpectedly" gratifying himself. This suggests that the night of the murder John Ramsey went to the victim's "bank" to "gratify himself"—and the writer secretly monitored him doing so. This abuse suggests the "trigger" motive for the writer's rage and resulting chaos.

"Monitor" also suggests that the writer herself is being observed for any secrets, specifically for any hidden medical problems. This suggestion also reinforces the previous suggestion that the writer is greatly concerned about her health and that she is being monitored for the return of the "small foreign faction," a symbol for cancer.

Message Marker 11: "Call"

"If we monitor you . . . we might call you early to arrange an earlier delivery" suggests that the writer had played a part in arranging for the delivery of the valuables—the victim. In dysfunctional families, which externally can appear healthy, parents often unconsciously encourage their children to participate in aberrant, deviant behavior so that the children express the forbidden desires—foreign parts—of the parents.

If the writer had played a part in the sexual abuse of the victim though, why would she be so devastated and become enraged when she observed it taking place? The writer would be enraged if she "knew about it but didn't know it," if she unconsciously encouraged the secret activity for her own reasons but became overwhelmed and out of control when she consciously saw it taking place.

The sequence of ideas in this sentence suggests that the writer was someone who was involved with both the victim and John Ramsey, someone who in some way helped the victim become a "pickup"—and at the same time someone who lost control when she consciously acknowledged the sexual abuse. The sentence suggests that the writer was unconsciously monitoring John Ramsey, paid an unexpected "call" on him, and consciously discovered his abuse of the victim.

The writer is arranging for the delivery of the money and for the delivery of the child, which turns out to be a disaster—the crossed-out "delivery"— because the child has become a pickup. "Call" also suggests that the writer would call to arrange for a "delivery"/ woman/ "call girl," another common term for prostitute, which suggests "prostituting" the victim. This reinforces the suggestion that the writer is personally involved with both the victim and John Ramsey and in turning the victim into a "pickup."

Message Marker 13: "Delivery" Repeated

The repetition of the word "delivery" suggests that the writer was secretly bolstering her damaged femininity by unconsciously arranging for the "valuable" relationship to take place as she "delivered" the child. This further suggests that the writer unconsciously saw the victim as living out the writer's secret desires. This temporarily restored the writer's feminine power because she identified with the victim who had the ability to attract a man, which made her a "powerful woman." This suggests that, because of her own sexual inadequacies, the writer pushed the victim toward adult sexuality.

The original wording "earlier delivery of your daughter" literally suggests a birth process. This "delivery" reinforces the suggestion that the writer unconsciously experienced delivering the child victim to her sexual abuser as a temporary victory over her deficiencies as a woman—it gave the writer "new birth as a woman."

It also suggests that introducing the child victim into adult femininity/ sexuality gave the writer a vicarious sense of satisfaction as a woman. But the boldly, chaotically crossed-out word "delivery" suggests that when the writer consciously observed the abuse that she had contributed to, she was overwhelmed and had to destroy the "little woman" she had delivered. The chaotic crossed-out "delivery" also suggests that the writer destroyed her own feminine identity as a nurturing woman when she destroyed the victim.

The chaotically crossed-out word "delivery," the divided word "un harmed," the divided word "daug hter," and the repeated implications in the note that the writer felt extremely threatened and thus had a powerful reason to erupt in rage all reinforce the suggestion that the writer of the ransom note assaulted and murdered the victim.

When taken as a whole, the sentence suggests a broader understanding of the "psychotic period": The writer was overwhelmed by the sexual abuse and interrupted it, suddenly putting an end to it. The conscious discovery of the sexual abuse along with the writer's medical problems were unconsciously experienced as a sudden and premature ending to her femininity—"my periods are over/my feminine identity ceases to exist/my value as a woman is finished." Both the writer's observation of the sexual abuse and her medical problems contributed to her externalizing her rage the night of the murder.

Message Markers 20 and 21: "Instructions" and "Result"

"*Any deviation of my instructions will result in the immediate execution of your daug hter [sic]*" is a particularly important sentence in the ransom note for three reasons: It contains the key message marker "instructions," it is the first sentence in the last paragraph of the note, and it links the ideas of instructions and result. The word "instructions" appears three times in the note, which means that it is a particularly important idea for the writer. The writer suggests that the note is confessional in nature, and she unconsciously repeats the idea of "instructions" to call attention to "instructions" on how to catch her. The first sentence of the last paragraph implies that the rest of the note contains specific information about who the writer is and how she can be apprehended.

The linking of the word "instructions" with "result" further suggests that the writer is giving information about the "end" or "conclusion" of some event. This sentence warns of the "immediate execution of John Ramsey's daughter," which suggests that the writer is giving information about the murder—why the kidnapping "resulted/ended" with the victim's death.

The other two references to instructions are to "our" instructions; this time the writer says "my" instructions, which suggests specific instructions from the writer herself, an "individual," not from the "kidnappers" as a group. This sentence suggests that a "deviation" occurred—that John Ramsey "deviated" from specific instructions given by the writer and the result was the victim's immediate execution. "Deviation" suggests "deviant," which implies that a deviant act resulted in the victim's sudden death—the conclusion of the matter.

This sentence also suggests that John Ramsey, as a result of his deviation from the writer's instructions, participated in the "immediate execution" of his daughter. "Immediate" suggests the ideas of (1) direct, (2) independent of other factors, (3) derived from a single premise, (4) next in line or relation, (5) near at hand, (6) occurring without loss or interval of time, (7) near to or related to the present time, (8) current, and (9) directly touching or concerning a person or thing.

The word "deviation" in the sentence slants slightly downward, which implies that the deviant act depressed the writer. The next line, which contains the word "result," shows the most inconsistent handwriting in the note—the line literally goes up and down, which implies that at this point in writing the note the writer is experiencing chaos and significant mood swings at this point. This mood swing reinforces the suggestion that the writer was personally involved with John Ramsey and the victim at the time of her death and also that the writer was personally responsible in some way for the victim's death. It also reinforces the suggestion that the victim had already been murdered by the time the note was written.

"*You will also be denied her remains for proper burial*" gives two additional references to the victim's death: "remains" and "burial." The writer is suggesting that if any deviation occurs on John Ramsey's part, he will be denied the victim's body "for"—for the purpose of—someone else giving her a proper burial. This suggests that the writer wants to get the victim's body away from John Ramsey because his behavior toward her has not been proper. "Proper" burial is another feminine and somewhat elitist word, which reinforces the suggestion that the writer is a "proper" woman.[8]

---

[8] The ransom note fits with the crime scene, which evidences a "proper burial" with blankets and a nurturing woman's touches.

By threatening to deny John Ramsey his child's body, the writer is suggesting that some event has denied her, the writer, a body. This reinforces the suggestion that the writer has experienced a life-threatening event or an event that "denies" her the female ability to produce a new "body."

Message Marker 22: A Proofreaders' Mark and the Left-out Word "Not"

"The two gentlemen watching over your daughter do not [inserted with a proofreaders' mark, a caret, or "v"] particularly like you so I advise you not to provoke them" contains another proper word, "gentlemen," that fits with "proper burial" and "attaché," "particularly," and "advise." This reinforces the suggestion that the writer is appearing to be a proper woman. In addition, the caret, a proofreaders' mark, suggests that the writer has an editorial background.

The writer's slip of the pen "do particularly like you" instead of "do not [inserted] particularly like you" suggests that the writer has a particular affinity for John Ramsey. This slip follows a reference to "your daughter," which suggests that the writer also has a particular affinity for the victim, JonBenét.

The word "not" written inside the arms of the proofreaders' "v" mark suggests the shape of a heart, which reinforces the suggestion that the writer particularly likes—even loves—the victim. The image of a "heart" "inside the arms" of the "v" implies the ideas of "motherly caring," an emotion of the heart—a place where hot blood flows. In this graphic, pictorial way the writer is suggesting that the original sentence—without the inserted "not"—was correct: She particularly likes the victim. A heart-shaped drawing on the victim's left palm reinforces the link between the victim, the story told in the note, and the writer. The drawing also reinforces the suggestion that the writer loved the victim.

The "heart" shape that appears in the ransom note also suggests that the writer has artistic ability, which further suggests that the writer herself drew the heart on the victim's palm. This is consistent with other feminine "touches" found at the crime scene.[9] The "heart" in the words also suggests the possibility that the writer has hidden other significant graphic art, "pictures," in the ransom note.

---

[9] Also marking the victim's body, as with tattoos and/or "tagging," suggests possession and points toward the killer being very close to the victim. For example, gangs "mark" their territory with graffiti.

"Two gentlemen" strongly implies that at least two people participated in the crime. "Gentlemen" strongly implies that the people who are "watching over" John Ramsey's dead daughter are "proper" people who were provoked the night of the crime. Two proper people linked with "your daughter" reinforces the suggestion that the crime is connected to a love triangle.[10] "Watching over" not only reinforces the suggestion that the victim was already dead when the note was written but also that two killers stood "over" and looked down at the victim's body on the floor.

The writer's original sentence, before the insertion of "not," also suggests that both the proper people watching over the victim were fond of her. If that is true then the "heart" shape in the note suggests that both killers were fond of the victim, which reinforces the suggestion of a love triangle. A love triangle further suggests that one of the two people who greatly cared about the victim was a female nurturer who drew a heart on the victim's palm, while the other one saw the victim as a little "valentine," a love object.

The inserted word "not" is not clearly written, which suggests chaos in the writer's mind. This reinforces the suggestion that the murder was related to a chaotic power struggle involving a threesome in which the victim was the love object.

The writer suggests this same idea by spacing out the letters of the word "your" in this sentence. "Your daughter" appears six times in the ransom note, but this is the only time the letters of "your" are distinctly spaced farther apart, which suggests that the writer is coming apart—she had difficulty writing and thinking when she thought about assaulting someone she loved. The increased spacing of the letters in "your" also suggests "our," which draws attention to the fact that there is only one letter difference between "our daughter" and "your daughter." This suggests that the writer felt divided about "your/our daughter." "Our daughter" also reinforces the suggestion that John and Patsy Ramsey were the two people who were provoked and then watched over the body of the daughter that both of them truly loved.

The slip of the pen and the afterthought of inserting the word "not" with the proofreaders' "v" also suggests that the writer has divided feelings

---

[10] The autopsy revealed two severe injuries to the victim. This fits with the suggestion in the ransom note that two people participated in the murder, with each inflicting what would have been fatal injuries had the victim had time to die from the initial head injury.

about the victim: One side of the writer deeply cared for the victim, but the other side was so provoked by some event that the writer killed the victim. This reinforces the suggestion that the murderer was personally involved with the victim.

Message Markers 23 and 24: "Speaking" and "Result"

"Speaking to anyone about your situation, such as Police, F.B.I., etc., will result in your daughter being beheaded" includes another major reference to the victim's death: "beheaded." This fits with the autopsy results, which show that the victim suffered a severe head injury from which she would have died had she not been strangled. "Beheaded" also fits with both the head injury and the ligature strangulation. "Result" suggests that the conclusion—the same concept as "hence"—of the matter is that the victim has been already been killed with injuries to her head area.

"Speaking to anyone about your situation . . . will result in your daughter being beheaded" contains the message markers "speaking" and "result." These message markers imply the ideas of a secret communication between John Ramsey and "one" other person. These markers also imply the writer's ability to observe that communication no matter how hidden John Ramsey may try to keep it. It also suggests that an attempted private communication with the victim by John Ramsey has caused the head injury and death of the victim.

"Police, F.B.I., etc." suggest not only law-enforcement authorities but also the "enforcing" role the writer played in the relation to John Ramsey and the victim. The writer is suggesting that she was responsible for enforcing the "boundaries of society"—proper family boundaries—and while doing so she discovered John Ramsey "speaking" or "communicating" with "someone," an act he tried to hide. The writer then suggests that a private meeting of John Ramsey and the victim, who indirectly is connected to "someone," caused the writer to physically lose control and fatally assault—"behead"—the victim.

The writer strongly implies that she was secretly "policing" John Ramsey's communications with the victim and that John Ramsey's attempted private "communications" with the victim enraged her. The writer further suggests that the rage she unleashed on the victim was the equivalent of a significantly powerful "police" force.

This first mention of the police and the FBI implies that by this point the ransom note contains enough "instructions"—clues or evidence—for the law enforcers to identify the writer. "Speaking to anyone" and "Police and F.B.I." suggest that the writer is "speaking to the police and F.B.I., and if they hear her she will be beheaded herself—as in convicted or "strung up." Capitalizing "Police" and "F.B.I." suggests that the writer sees these law enforcers as very powerful and capable. The extremely accurate punctuation of "F.B.I." and "etc.," suggests that the writer is a highly organized bright individual who has experience in writing and possibly editing.[11]

The unconscious mind often repeats stories and sends the same message in two or more ways. The idea of police authorities who would be taking control of the investigation suggests two different communications from the writer's unconscious mind: (1) the writer's own powerful punishing tendencies in relationship to the victim and John Ramsey, and (2) law authorities as being terribly powerful—she capitalized Police and F.B.I.—in their pursuit of the writer/killer. These ideas reinforce the suggestion that the writer had been "monitoring" John Ramsey and the victim and that a deviant act provoked her powerful rage that night. These ideas also reinforce the suggestion that the writer is deeply frightened of the law enforcers (the "posse") who will pursue her.

The word "beheaded" fits with the idea "early." Following the head injury, someone had to go ahead and strangle the victim, kill her "early" or unexpectedly, in order to have a body to hide. If the victim had been left to die slowly after the head injury, she possibly could have lived for at least another eight to ten hours.[12]

The ransom note suggests that the perpetrator(s) did not have a great deal of time and that's why the victim had to die "early," "ahead of time,"

---

[11] Some investigators, including Clinton Van Zandt, who formerly worked for the FBI Behavioral Sciences Unit, have suggested that the writer borrowed these sentences from Dirty Harry movies or books. That does not really matter because the writer's unconscious mind would still choose particular sentences and where to use them. The writer's unconscious mind shaped all the words—including any borrowed words—in very personal ways to communicate the observations of his/her unconscious mind.

[12] According to Robert Brissie, M.D., Chief Medical Examiner, Jefferson County, Birmingham, Alabama, and Professor of Pathology and Director of the Division of Forensic Pathology, University of Alabama at Birmingham School of Medicine.

"before her time." The "kidnappers" were also not inclined to either leave behind an unconscious victim or take her with them. The two injuries and the victim's dead body at the crime scene suggest that the ransom note and alleged kidnapping are a ploy, part of the staging or "posing" to cover up the identity of the murderers.

"Immediate execution" and "beheaded" suggest two different deathblows, which the results of the autopsy confirmed. "Immediate" suggests something sudden, which further suggests that the strangulation was the "immediate execution" and the second injury, which brought about instantaneous death— the victim was still alive after the "beheading," the head injury. "Beheading" more clearly suggests the victim's head area, and the fact that the writer lists it as a separate entity suggests that it was an act separate from "the immediate execution." The fact that the writer mentions "beheading" second in the murder sequence also suggests that the head injury was "lingering behind"— that the victim had not yet died from the head injury.

The writer links "beheading" with "Police" and "F.B.I.," which suggests her participation in this part of the crime. This further suggests that the writer feels much more vulnerable when talking to the law authorities about the victim's head injury.

The murder sequence suggests that the writer participated in the head injury and a second person participated in the strangulation, which resulted in two people "watching over" the victim's body. The head injury, the "beheading," came first, but the writer lists the strangulation—"the immediate execution"—first, which implies that she is trying to shift the blame for the murder to the second participant. This reinforces the suggestion that the second injury[13] was necessary for the cover-up to begin because the victim could have lived at least eight to ten hours after the initial head injury.

Two severe assaults on one victim in one night also suggests that two people participated in the murder since a "proper" person who cared about the victim would have a great deal of difficulty inflicting the two life-threatening injuries. The autopsy strongly suggests that whoever the killer was who strangled the victim had emotional difficulty carrying out the

---

[13] The autopsy revealed a severe blow on the right side of the cranium eight and one-half inches long from front to back with a compressed skull fracture posteriorly. However, the cause of death was officially determined to be a ligature strangulation. According to Robert Brissie, M.D.

strangulation,[14] which reinforces the suggestion of two killers, each inflicting one of the injuries.

Message Marker 25: "Talking"

"If we catch you talking to a stray dog, she dies." "Talking" suggests the idea of communicating and specifically John Ramsey communicating with another being—even an insignificant being, "a stray dog." The writer's emphasis on "catching" John Ramsey interacting in a one-to-one communication reinforces the suggestion that John Ramsey was secretly interacting with the victim.

This sentence also introduces the concept of a stray dog, which suggests several other ideas. "A stray dog" implies someone who is vulnerable compared to the very capable man John Ramsey. "A stray dog" also implies someone who has strayed and is lost, homeless, not where they are supposed to be. It further implies that the dog has not been properly cared for—is unloved and perhaps not far from death. "A stray dog" can also be a frightened or dangerous dog.

The writer previously suggested a link between the victim and a dog with the use of the divided word "daug hter," "dawg hter." "Stray" also rhymes with JonBenét, which reinforces the suggestion that the daughter, JonBenét, was "lost" and had been abandoned because of inadequate supervision, and the writer had "caught"—as in "catch you talking"—John Ramsey with her. This reinforces the suggestion that the parents had abandoned the victim, JonBenét. It also supports the suggestion that the writer is emotionally involved with both the victim and John Ramsey, and it strongly suggests that the writer is, in fact, the victim's mother, Patsy Ramsey.

"She dies" immediately follows "stray dog," which strongly suggests that when the writer "caught" John Ramsey and the "stray dog" she killed the "dog"—the victim. Because every idea in the note must also be considered a part of the writer—a projection of her unconscious mind—the idea of "stray dog" also suggests that the writer herself is "a stray dog," a woman who feels abandoned and frightened. This fits with previous inferences that the writer is a woman who feels depleted of her femininity, a woman who is severely damaged physically and emotionally and perceives herself to be on the verge

---

[14] According to Robert Brissie, M.D.

of death, much like a stray dog who is at the mercy of external control-ling forces.

This sentence is the first of a series of four that end with the words "she dies." The writer is not only strongly suggesting that the victim is dead, but she is also suggesting that she herself is very concerned about dying. "She dies" then implies the writer's concerns about dying from a life-threatening medical condition as well as her concerns about being apprehended by law enforcers and as a result dying, as in "If the police understand I am a 'stray dog' and why, I am as good as dead."

The concept of "catch you" also implies that the writer is very concerned with the authorities being alerted and with being caught. "Catch you" is linked to "talking," which reinforces the suggestion that the ransom note contains significant clues—the writer "talking" or confessing—that will help the authorities "catch" the writer.

Message Marker 26: "Alert"

"*If you alert bank authorities, she dies*" not only suggests authorities in general, but it also suggests authorities who specifically understand banks—people who know about valuable containers. The ideas of bank authorities and John Ramsey suggest and link several other ideas: John Ramsey, a blood bank, a woman's "bank/container"—female body parts, and the writer moni-toring John Ramsey's interaction with female body parts. It further reinforces the suggestion that when the writer saw John Ramsey "getting" something from a bank—specifically the female victim's "bank vault"—she killed the victim. This is the second consecutive sentence that implies John Ramsey's behavior resulted in the victim's death.

"Bank authorities" suggests experts who "monitor" female body parts such as physicians, and "monitor" is a commonly used medical word. This rein-forces the suggestion that a female medical problem carrying a very uncer-tain prognosis is on the writer's mind and that it played a role in the events leading up to the murder of the victim. It also reinforces the suggestion that the ransom note contains a clue for law enforcement: A woman participated in this crime.

"If the money is in any way marked or tampered with, she dies" sug-gests that if the writer secretly observes John Ramsey tampering with or marking the valuable in the slightest way, the victim dies. This reinforces the suggestion that the writer did catch John Ramsey tampering with his valuable little daughter and as a result exploded in rage and killed the daughter, as the repeated "she dies" implies. The words "tampered with" slant downward, which suggests that this idea depresses the writer.

The writer's choice of the two words "marked" and "tampered" suggests that John Ramsey not only tampered with the victim's body—sexually abused her—but also that he "marked" it or did physical damage. This idea reinforces other suggestions in the note that John Ramsey strangled the victim, which further reinforces the suggestions that two people physically assaulted the victim: the writer who lost control and hit her in the head area and John Ramsey who marked the victim's body by strangulation.

"Marked" and "tampered" also imply that the writer unconsciously sees herself as a marked woman whose body has been tampered with, an experience that has left the writer very concerned about bodily harm and death. "She dies" suggests a verdict, prediction, or medical prognosis that applies to the writer herself, something that relates to the "small foreign faction," probably cancer.

Message Markers 27 and 28: "Scanned" and "Electronic Devices"

"You will be scanned for electronic devices and if any are found, she dies" suggests that a "scanner," a sophisticated electronic device, will be used to detect something hidden on or about someone's body. A scanner is used for electronic surveillance or detection in a number of settings including the medical field. "Electronic devices" in this sentence implies the smallest defects or entities.

"Found" is used frequently in medical settings and particularly with cancer patients as in a "finding" of cancer. A cancer patient undergoes procedures where her/his body is scanned to find the smallest evidence of a life-threatening disease. The concepts of being scanned and of the slightest defect being "found" reinforces the suggestion that the writer is very concerned with the smallest particle of evidence of cancer being found in her own body.

Scanning to detect for the slightest hidden or foreign defect also suggests a connection to "small foreign faction" and further confirmation that the fear of cancer was on the writer's mind from the beginning of the letter. This sentence is an outstanding example of how the writer's fictional ransom note reveals her motives. It simultaneously reinforces the suggestion that the note is a pseudo-ransom note because kidnappers almost never have a face-to-face meeting with the victim's family as they would have if the kidnapper(s) "scanned" John Ramsey.

"She dies" implies that if the smallest defect is found, someone—the victim and/or the writer herself—will die. The concept of bodily defects causing death comes immediately after the idea in the previous sentence of the writer being a tampered with and marked woman. The sequence of ideas in the two sentences further implies that the writer exploded and tampered with the victim's body, marking or damaging it by her own hands just as her life-threatening disease had marked her. Also, when people die they are "marked" for identification by the hospital, coroner, or funeral home.

A number of communications in the ransom note from the writer's unconscious mind imply that her life-threatening medical condition is cancer. The note suggests that the writer is very concerned with a body being scanned for the smallest of defects/"a small foreign faction", feminine containers/female organs being withdrawn (hysterectomy), a body being brutally assaulted until eventually nothing but remains are left, someone living under the constant threat that the slightest deviation or abnormality results in death, and a body being tampered with and marked. These images further imply how much pressure the writer was under—she was alive, but she unconsciously viewed herself as good as dead and in the process of deteriorating to nothing.

"She dies," "she dies," "she dies," "she dies" repeated four times in rapid-fire fashion strongly suggests the writer's deep sense of destruction and damage. The staccato chant "she dies" suggests a "time bomb" motive: The writer is suffering from a virulent disease and acted out her own fear of being destroyed by destroying another person, which explains why a "proper" person could commit murder. A "proper" person living with the terrifying reality that she might die at anytime from a life-threatening medical condition would be vulnerable to exploding in rage, and she would be particularly vulnerable to any unforeseen traumatic situation that intensified the helplessness she was already experiencing.

The writer's unconscious mind is symbolizing and encoding these clear messages, which suggests that the writer was in denial about the extent of her health concerns and would not consciously know how terrified she felt, no matter how hopeless her medical prognosis was. She then would most likely present the front of a "proper" person who was very organized, in control, and used to giving orders. The sheer length of the ransom note coupled with the writer's ability to write such a lengthy highly organized note immediately after participating in a murder suggests that the writer is a very determined person. It also suggests that the writer "contains" the terror of her life-threatening medical condition by repression and denial.

"Scanned" also suggests that John Ramsey has a secret in regard to his body—he had been covertly interacting sexually with another person. This assertion reinforces the suggestion that the writer discovered John Ramsey's secret interaction with the victim.

This is the fourth consecutive sentence that implies that John Ramsey's secretly observed misbehavior results in the victim's death—a strong suggestion that his deviant behavior with the victim precipitated the killer's rage. In this sentence the writer gives the most vivid picture yet of how the two motives came together the night of the crime: Her deep pain "time bomb" motive—the cancer that was destroying her body—and the continued suggestion of a "trigger" motive—John Ramsey's illicit behavior. The writer is reinforcing the implication that her primary motive for the murder was the deep terror caused by her fear of dying from cancer, and this terror caused her to explode in rage when she discovered the victim being sexually assaulted by John Ramsey.

Message Marker 29: Countermeasures and Tactics

"You can try to deceive us but be warned that we are familiar with Law enforcement countermeasures and tactics" implies that John Ramsey will not get away with any attempts of deception because the writer knows "countermeasures and tactics" and has used them previously to see past John Ramsey's attempts at covering up his acting out. The writer has seen past John Ramsey's "disguise" as a law-abiding citizen. The word "familiar" suggests "family," which links John Ramsey's attempted deception to the family. This sentence also implies that John Ramsey knows how law enforcers gather evidence and has tried to apply that knowledge in the staging the cover-up of the crime with the pseudo-ransom note.[15] "Law enforcement countermeasures" also suggests countermeasures to law enforcement.

---

[15] The police found a copy of *Mind Hunter*, by former FBI agent John Douglas, next to John Ramsey's bedside.

"You can try to deceive us" also implies the writer's strong attempts at denial and projection. The writer states that she possesses great capacities for outsmarting law-enforcement agents even though they possess powerful methods—even "undercover" methods—to detect deception. By capitalizing the word "Law," however, the writer is suggesting that she is in denial of her fear and is projecting it onto someone else: Unconsciously the writer sees herself as very vulnerable in relation to the authorities. She is projecting onto law enforcers what she knows to be true about herself—that there is a force greater than herself, "Law enforcement," that can detect her attempts at covering up, that can uncover the psychological truths that are hidden in the ransom note. This reinforces the suggestion that the writer has given law-enforcement agents enough information to "see/uncover" her true identity and the truth about the murder by "reading between the lines" of the ransom note.

Since the writer is trying to deceive law-enforcement agents by writing a cover-up ransom note, she is suggesting that they apply "countermeasures and tactics" specifically to the note and decipher the hidden messages. The writer implies that law enforcers need to "see" the note through the perceptive eyes of the writer's unconscious mind. "Familiar with Law enforcement" also suggests that the writer, as well as John Ramsey, knows how law enforcers gather evidence and that unconsciously she has carefully presented enough information for them to uncover who she is and what really happened the night of the murder. This implies a second meaning to why the writer capitalized "Law": She feels the information in the ransom note would be effective in a court of law.

The word "countermeasures" itself suggests several ideas. It implies that measures taken against a powerful force will not work. It also relates to the concepts of counting and measuring and that such efforts will fail. "Counting and measuring" is exactly what scanners do, and in medical settings they direct where to apply countermeasures—forces against—cancer. This reinforces the suggestion that the writer is being regularly monitored with a scanner and that unconsciously she feels certain that even though a scanner may measure or find defects she is helpless to defeat her life-threatening disease—the countermeasures will fail.

Message Marker 30: "Instructions"

"You stand a 99% chance of killing your daughter if you try to outsmart us. Follow our instructions and you stand a 100% chance of getting her back" gives survival percentages, which reinforces the suggestion that the writer is a cancer victim and has been given a survival percentage herself. The writer gives these specific numbers and survival percentages after she has introduced the idea of "countermeasures"/counting and measuring, which reinforces the suggestion that the writer unconsciously is concerned about being constantly measured with scanning equipment. This also relates to the idea of the ransom money being counted and measured into smaller and smaller parts, which reinforces the suggestion that the writer's is being diminished/destroyed by cancer.

The 100% chance of survival for both the victim and the writer follows the message marker "instructions," a signal that this sentence contains crucial clues about the writer's identity and about the events the night of the murder. This sentence also suggests that law-enforcement agents have a 100% chance of identifying the writer if they follow the "instructions" communicated by her unconscious mind in the ransom note.

This is now the third time the writer uses the word "instructions," and it is remarkably similar to the first time it is used: "if you want her to see 1997, you must follow our instructions to the letter." These two references to "instructions" are linked to the threat that the victim could be killed, and a number of other sentences in the ransom note suggest that the victim died before the note was written. Taken together these two ideas—the hidden "instructions" and the victim being deceased— strongly suggest that the writer is speaking for the deceased victim. The writer says to "listen carefully" to what she is really saying in the note because it will be the same thing as "listening" to the victim herself telling the true story of the murder. By following the "instructions" and listening carefully there is "a 100% chance" of the victim coming "back" to life and telling the true story of what happened, who did it, and why.

Like the heart shape formed by the word "not" inserted in the proofreaders' "v" earlier in the ransom note, the percentage symbols in these two sentences appear to be graphic art: someone's eyes and long nose. These images suggest two ideas: "sniffing out" the motive and "looking down your nose at someone," which the killer did to the victim. The writer further suggests that she has "a 100% chance" of being caught if the law enforcers "sniff out"—detect—the hidden/true meaning of the survival percentages. The two "pictures" of a face come right next to the survival percentage numbers, which suggests that the writer's unconscious mind is trying to highlight the link between cancer and the motive.

The writer also suggests that she has a "99% chance of dying"—that she herself is living with a fear of death and that this fear is linked to the motive for the crime. It further suggests that the writer is "99%" certain that her efforts at deceiving the police will eventually fail.

"You stand a 99% chance of killing your daughter" strongly links John Ramsey to the victim's murder, and "99%" suggests that it's not just a "chance" but a very strong probability that John at least participated in the killing. It also implies that there is a 1% chance someone else could/did kill the victim, a subtle suggestion that two people participated in the victim's death.

This sentence further implies that John Ramsey will be held responsible for the victim's death if he tries to outsmart the writer. This reinforces the suggestions that the writer is intimately involved with John Ramsey and that his efforts to deceive the writer caused the victim's death. Each of these suggestions depends on which person the writer's unconscious mind is perceiving at any given moment—the writer in relation to her illness, the writer in relation to law-enforcement agents, and/or John Ramsey.

Message Marker 31: "Scurtiny [sic]" and Chaos

The slip of the pen in *"You and your family are under constant scurtiny [or scartiny or scortiny; (sic)] as well as the authorities"* reinforces the suggestion that the writer's mind is in chaos. It also strongly suggests that the victim's family was involved in the murder.

The writer's unconscious misspelling of "scurtiny" suggests that the idea of "constant scrutiny" is very uncomfortable—she misspells it to the point that it is not completely legible. This suggests that the writer wants to avoid the issue—"scurt" or "skirt the issue."

Linking "the authorities" with the idea of scrutiny suggests that the writer is very apprehensive of law enforcers and she once again is projecting the idea of being scrutinized onto them. It also suggests that the scrutiny is so pervasive that everyone in the family is under intense observation.

The misspelled word could also be read "scartiny," which suggests that the writer has been scarred by being under constant scrutiny. This reinforces the suggestion that the writer was living under constant scrutiny before the murder and that this pressure was a "time bomb" motive for the crime.

"Constant scrutiny" suggests a progressive event, such as a life-threatening disease, rather than a one-time physical assault. "Scar" also strongly suggests a medical procedure and links several ideas: The writer has been scarred symbolically by a medical condition and also literally by a medical procedure and, as a result, is under constant scrutiny. This interpretation also fits with other suggestions in the ransom note that the writer is a cancer victim. "Scar" suggests both "scan" and "scare," which also link to cancer.

"And your family" is the first reference in the ransom note to Patsy Ramsey and the Ramseys' son, and it links one or more of them to being under constant scrutiny and to having cancer. Since this description particularly fits Patsy this implies that Patsy is the writer and that unconsciously she is describing her own motives. It also suggests that Patsy, and not the son, had been closely scrutinizing events going on in the family—particularly the suggested sexual abuse of the victim by John Ramsey—and that she is telling us about the "trigger" motive that led to the murder. The reference to "family" and thereby to Patsy Ramsey comes a few words after "100% chance" of the victim "speaking again," which reinforces the suggestion that Patsy Ramsey is secretly confessing and speaking for the victim.

In numerous previous sentences, including the chaotic sentence with the crossed-out "delivery," the writer implied that the "trigger" for the rage killing was a sexual event between John Ramsey and the victim that the writer secretly observed. This sentence reinforces that suggestion. The word "scurtiny" also suggests the word "scortiny/score tiny/tiny score." This further reinforces the suggestion that John Ramsey has made a "tiny score" in his secret "communications" with the victim —and that the writer witnessed it.

The repeated suggestion of a sexual event "trigger" motive in conjunction with the writer's third use of the message marker "instructions" points back to the first "instructions" message marker because the writer implies strongly in both instances that she is speaking for the victim. "If you want her to see 1997, follow our instructions to the letter" contains the subtle sexual suggestion "if you want her"—which further suggests that John Ramsey was sexually involved with the victim, that he "wanted her." The writer could have written "if you want to see her" or "if she wants to see" or many other variations, but she chose to write "if you want her."

Message Marker 32: "Brain"

"*Don't try to grow a brain John*" is a command similar to "Listen carefully!" This very specific personal reference to John, rather than John Ramsey, strongly implies that the writer has an extremely close personal relationship with John. This personal reference comes at the end of the ransom note, the point where the writer may be tired and more inclined to let her defenses down and make an even clearer confession than earlier in the note.

The writer is suggesting that "I am on a first name basis with John." This very personal comment follows "you and your family," the first reference in the note to Patsy, which strongly suggests that this sentence has to do with how John relates to Patsy. "Don't try and grow a brain John" is a negative statement that reinforces the suggestion that the writer personally resents John Ramsey.

The letter "a" next to the word "brain" looks like an arrow that is pointing downward—another piece of graphic art the writer has hidden in the note that also suggests a natural break in the sentence. Dropping the word "brain" makes the sentence read "Don't try and grow John," which has the strong sexual connotation of commanding John to not get an erection. An arrow is sometimes interpreted as a phallic symbol, and the writer has graphically reinforced her command to John that he not get an erection by "drawing" a "down" or nonerect phallus.

"Brain" is a message marker that implies "think"—particularly about the context of "brain" in this sentence. Since a message marker always suggests to pay particular attention to ideas connected to it, the writer gives us another reason to look at "don't try and grow" on its own, which reinforces the sexual connotation.

The sentence taken as a whole offers a third suggestion with sexual connotations: The main idea is instructing John not to get the big head or grow a big head. The brain is often referred to as the "primary sexual organ," and one of the links with the brain and sex includes the common idea that the "little head" controls the "big head" or men think with their little head.

"Don't grow a brain" also comes a few words after the message marker "scurtiny [sic]," which implies that the writer has been scrutinizing John Ramsey's sexual behavior closely and that it has created a great deal of chaos in the writer, which is reflected in the chaotic, misspelled word "scurtiny." Linking the two ideas of scrutiny and instructions not to grow a brain reinforces the idea that the writer witnessed a secret "communication" between a sexually aroused John Ramsey and the victim and that this observed explicit sexual scene shocked the writer so greatly that it caused a cataclysmic crisis and sent her into a chaotic, psychotic rage.

The writer is also suggesting that John Ramsey not use his brain, that he be "brain-dead," an idea that can be interpreted in several ways. The writer is alluding to how foolish it was of John Ramsey to get involved with his young daughter. The writer's continued preoccupation with the head and the brain also suggests another reference to the victim who was most likely strangled after she was believed to be "brain-dead"—and the writer's wish that John would join the victim and be out of the picture, and an even deeper wish that John had never existed and caused this whole problem.

A "growing brain" implies cancer because brain cells do not grow, they do not duplicate themselves. This reinforces the suggestion that cancer plays a major role in the writer's relationship with John Ramsey, one reason she resents him, and the "time bomb" motive for the crime.

"Don't try and grow a brain John" relates to several other ideas. It suggests that John Ramsey may try to outsmart a hidden authority or force, which is an "instruction"/clue for law enforcers. It also suggests that John Ramsey was not able to outsmart the writer in their personal contest and that the writer was deeply insulted when John tried to outsmart her. It further suggests that when the writer uncovered John Ramsey's secret "instructions"/communications with the victim and lost control, she unconsciously perceived that her rage was a victory over him. It also relates to the previous sentence and "constant scrutiny": The writer is reminding John Ramsey that she has outmaneuvered him by constantly scrutinizing him.

Message Marker 33: "Think"

"*You are not the only fat cat around so don't think that killing will be difficult*" contains the message marker "think," which suggests to think deeply about what is being said here. "Think" links two ideas—"fat cat" and the killing will not be difficult. The overtly negative statement "fat cat" reinforces the suggestion that the writer has an intimate relationship with John Ramsey and that she is angry at him because he acted like a "fat cat." By linking "fat cat" and "killing" the writer is suggesting that seeing John behave like a "fat cat" precipitated her rage that "concluded" in the murder of the victim.

The writer is suggesting that John Ramsey became "fat" and cocky in his attempt to dominate. A male "fat cat" suggests someone who abuses his power and behaves with contempt. In the previous sentence the writer commanded John "Don't try and grow," and here she commands "Don't get fat," which reinforces the suggestion that the writer is referring to John's sexuality and telling him "Don't, John." This suggests that John Ramsey had greatly offended the writer in an explicit sexual way and she is now rebuking him.

Another name for cat is "pussy," which has strong sexual connotations. It suggests that the writer was angry at John Ramsey for arrogantly becoming involved with another woman, a "fat pussy." While this degrading sexual term is particularly offensive when it is related to an innocent six-year-old victim, nonetheless it is important to consider because the ransom note must be "read" through the eyes of the writer/killer. The writer suggests that she is unconsciously explaining just how threatened she felt by the victim and how angry she was at the victim as a way of explaining how great her rage was and how she could murder someone she greatly loved. The writer further suggests that she wants to shock and offend whoever reads the ransom note just as she was shocked and offended when she observed John Ramsey sexually abusing the victim.

This is the second of three sentences in a row and the only times in the note where the writer uses the word "don't," and all three "don'ts" refer to John Ramsey. In two of the three sentences she uses the familiar "John" instead of his full name—commanding him "don't" in a very personal way.

Referring to John Ramsey as a "fat cat" because of his wealth and position suggests that the writer feels deeply threatened by him. This reinforces the suggestion that the writer resents John's "bussiness [sic]." The idea that John Ramsey is not the only "fat cat," the only prominent person "around," reinforces the suggestion that the writer feels left out, abandoned, and depleted.

The writer links the idea of a "fat cat" to the victim's death and the ideas of competitiveness and resentment, which implies that the writer was in direct competition not only with John Ramsey but also with the victim as there was more than one "fat cat around." A catfight, which often occurs when one cat realizes another one is "around," may be interpreted as an intense fight or argument between two women, which reinforces the suggestion that the writer and the victim were in fierce competition. The idea of a catfight in this case strongly implies the death of one cat, the victim, and the other cat's—the writer's—sheer brutality.

A "fat cat" can also be a pregnant cat, which reinforces the suggestion that femininity is a major concern for the writer. The link between "fat cat" and the idea of being insulted and ignored reinforces the suggestion that the writer experienced the victim's involvement in the sexual abuse as deeply threatening to the writer's femininity—as though another "fat cat" tried to insult or degrade her as a woman.

The concept of another person being the "only fat cat" around suggests that the writer, whose femininity had been damaged, viewed the victim as the only "real" woman between the two of them who could potentially— one day—get pregnant, which would make the victim even more of a threat to the writer. The writer's brutal comment linked specifically to the murder suggests the "trigger" motive for the murder. The sentence taken as a whole can be read as the writer's comment to the victim explaining the writer's rage: "You are not the only fat cat around so don't think that killing will be difficult." This reinforces the writer's suggestions in previous sentences that she was closely scrutinizing John Ramsey and other family members. It also reinforces her command in the preceding sentence for John not to grow.

The writer doesn't mention the victim in any direct way in this sentence but refers only to "killing" rather than "killing your daughter." This suggests that the killer is so personally involved with the victim that she needs to distance herself from her extreme aggression toward the victim even as she brags about it. Denying that the killing will be difficult—"Don't think killing will be difficult"—but distancing herself from the victim implies that killing the victim indeed had been difficult for the killer, which reinforces the suggestion that the writer/killer is personally involved with the victim.

The writer uses the word "killing" only twice in the ransom note. The first time is when she warns John Ramsey that he had a "99% chance of killing" his daughter, and the second is in reference to herself, the writer, "don't think that killing will be difficult." This strongly suggests that there were two killers—the writer and John Ramsey.

"Don't underestimate us John" is the writer's fourth personal first-name-only comment to John Ramsey in a row, her third straight major negative comment to him, and the third "don't" in a row. "Don't underestimate us" suggests that two or more people feel they have been insulted and over-looked by John Ramsey, which reinforces the idea of a triangle relationship. The ransom note includes several suggestions of a triangle relationship: Two gentlemen have—are "watching" over—the victim, John Ramsey speaking to police and FBI, the killers watching John talk to a stray dog, and the killers watching John talk to bank authorities. This strongly suggests that a threesome is part of the true story of the murder of the victim.

The "us" in "don't underestimate us" suggests that John Ramsey insulted two or more "fat cats." It further implies that he has been aggressive and that he has hurt not only the writer but also at least one other person—the victim, which suggests that John Ramsey's sexual assault on the victim dev-astated the writer—and certainly the victim. This reinforces the suggestion that a threesome, a triangle relationship, is at the center of the crime.

The apostrophe in "don't" in "don't underestimate us" looks like an ac-cent mark, suggesting once again JonBenét's name and further suggesting the condensed message "Don't underestimate JonBenét" as though the writer is speaking for her.

The writer is suggesting more clearly why she experienced such chaos when she discovered John Ramsey sexually molesting the victim. She suggests that she felt betrayed by and enraged at both John Ramsey while simultaneously she loved the victim and identified with her as someone who was also underestimated, ignored, and insulted by John Ramsey.

The writer implies in the second sentence in a row that she has been greatly insulted by the events of the night. She follows up the idea of being ignored and set aside in a competitive love triangle involving John Ramsey and the victim with the idea of being underestimated. This reinforces the suggestion that the event that triggered the writer's rage and the killing of the victim is related to a competitive triangle involving John, the victim, and the writer. The writer was extremely vulnerable to exploding because her life-threatening medical condition had created a deep sense of being degraded, underestimated, and unimportant, and her attack on the victim was "triggered" by her experiencing the sexual abuse simultaneously as a betrayal and insult by both John Ramsey and the victim. The attack on the victim was characteristic of a personal assault by someone who knew the victim: a severe head injury in the victim's home on a major holiday.

Message Marker 34: "Sense"

The direct command *"Use that good southern common sense of yours"* is a very personal comment that contains a partial compliment, which reinforces the suggestions that the writer has a personal relationship with John Ramsey and that she feels very divided toward him.

"Common sense" linked to the idea of "southern" suggests someone who knew John Ramsey, who is a Michigan native, during the time he was in "tlanta—someone who would view him as Southern. This suggests that the writer is not Southern, because Southerners typically do not refer to each other as Southerners, but she may have met John when he lived in Atlanta.

"Southern common sense," which is an unusual phrase compared to the more common "Southern charm," implies that the killer sees John Ramsey as an intelligent, logical person and respects his judgment. In this sentence the writer appears to be encouraging John to use his brain, but three sentences earlier she encouraged him not to "grow a brain," which implies that "don't try and grow a brain" refers to ideas other than "mind" or "intelligence"—namely "sexuality." By not using "Southern charm," which connotes love and romance, but instead "good southern common sense," the writer is suggesting that the "good" part of John is his mind and not his sexuality. It also suggests that John has now become "good" because he is now using his brain in the cover-up part of the crime.

"That good southern common sense of yours" also suggests "common" as in "base" or "crude," which implies an entirely different command: The writer is encouraging John to express his base desires. [*Southern common sense also implies his "below the belt" or sexual instincts.*] "Use" also suggests that John Ramsey was a "user," which the writer suggests she partially wants to control by telling John what part of himself to use.

Message Markers 35 and 36: "John" and the Last Sentence, the Last Word, the Conclusion

The writer ends the ransom note with one last personal comment: *"It is up to you now John!"* The letter starts with "Mr. Ramsey" but ends with "John," which reinforces the suggestion that the writer has a personal relationship with John Ramsey. This is also the fifth very personal comment in a row, coming after introducing the idea of John and his family. This reinforces the suggestion that the writer is a family member.

In this sentence the writer suggests that John is back in control, everything is "in John's hands." This reinforces the suggestion that John participated in the crime, and it implies that it was John who strangled the victim. Ending the note with the striking idea that all the responsibility is on John implies that he also had the final responsibility for what happened to the victim. The strong personal ending with the implied message that the matter is in John's hands "now" suggests John's participation at the end of the crime but not necessarily before. The repeated references to John's involvement in the crime and the personal references to him strongly suggest that the killing was a family matter and that John was the one who actually ended the victim's brief life.

"John" is often used to refer to both a prostitute's customer and a toilet. The idea of a "john" fits with the idea of "pickup," which reinforces the suggestion that John Ramsey was caught prostituting—sexually abusing, using—his daughter. It also suggests that the writer perceives the events on the night of the victim's death to be as disgusting and dirty as a toilet, which further suggests that she wishes everything could be washed—"flushed"— away as if it didn't happen. This reinforces the suggestion that the writer wants to confess and start over "clean."

Leaving out two words in the middle of the sentence—"to you"—makes the last sentence read "It is up . . . now John!" An exclamation point conveys excitement and could symbolize an erect phallus. The word "up" is distinctly set apart in the sentence as if the writer wants to call particular attention to it, just as she used an arrow pointing downward earlier to suggest "down." "Now John" is also a very personal comment, and it subtly suggests sexual activity and links it to John Ramsey—as in "now is the time to consummate sexual activity."

Combining the commands in the last five sentences gives "don't John" three times followed by "use it" along with "now John," which implies that the writer has given John conflicting messages around his sexuality. She first instructed John to "keep it down" and then instructed him to "keep it up," which reinforces the suggestion that the writer has divided sexual feelings about John. It also reinforces the suggestion that the writer was enraged at John's sexual activity with the victim and at the same time encouraged it. The repeated vivid sexual imagery in the note implies that a central part of the writer's trauma the night of the murder was that she witnessed John Ramsey having an erection when he was with the victim.

The writer suggests that we read the sentence without the "to you" in "It is up . . . now John!" by the unusual configuration of the word "to." This "to" looks like a knot or noose, which almost makes the word hard to read or comprehend and illegible when read by itself. This "to" also suggests the picture of an anchor, which symbolizes sailing, boats, and the Navy and links this word to John since he had been in the Navy and was a sailor. The noose-like/anchor-like "to" reinforces the suggestion that John Ramsey strangled the victim.

The only similar "to" out of the eleven the writer wrote in the note is the very first one, which comes at the end of the first paragraph next to the first use of the message marker "instructions." This "to" stands out prominently at the end of the line—which suggests that both of these uses of the word "to" are significant and that they are unconscious instructions on how to identify the murderers. The "d" in the first use of "daughter" in the first paragraph is also shaped like a hanging noose, which reinforces the suggestion that the writer meant for the "to" to look like a noose. The "d" in "advise" of "I advise you not to provoke" in the third paragraph also looks like a noose and is again specifically linked to the victim and to the idea of the killers being provoked.

In the last sentence of the ransom note—"It is up to you now John!"—the writer implies that she has again unconsciously described John Ramsey's participation in the murder: His sexual abuse provoked the writer's rage and caused her to inflict the head injury and then John strangled the victim.

The writer's statement to John Ramsey that everything rests on his shoulders along with her previous hostile threats imply that she is unconsciously blackmailing John Ramsey and is holding his abusive sexual behavior over his head while also acknowledging that he has valuable information. This further suggests that the writer's string of controlling comments directed at John Ramsey unconsciously were designed to remind him of the knowledge that she held over him—she advised him that he shouldn't try to outsmart or underestimate her because she could cause "fat cat" John Ramsey great harm. This reinforces the suggestion that the writer was the primary killer and that John Ramsey knows it, but both the writer and John Ramsey know that he was responsible for triggering the writer's rage killing because of his sexual behavior.

The last two words of the note, "now John," suggest a subtle confrontation as well as an intimate reminder that the writer has information that would harm John Ramsey. Ending the note in a sexually suggestive way implies that the writer was reminding John Ramsey precisely what information about him she possessed. The ending also fits with the idea that the killers were a small group of individuals who each have separate interests that can potentially be exploited by law enforcers to break up the group.

Message Marker 37: The Signature

"*Vi ctory [sic]!*" suggests that the victim's murder unconsciously represents a powerful victory for the writer. A woman who felt deeply defective and on the verge of complete deterioration—death—as well as deeply insulted by the victim and John Ramsey would feel a sense of power over her helplessness and victory over her rivals after participating in a "successful" murderous rage.

The idea of victory reinforces the suggestion that the writer is a highly competitive woman. It also reinforces the suggestion that the writer is a woman who was desperate for a victory in her ongoing battle with a life-threatening medical condition, which the note implies is cancer. Cancer victims often talk about "victory over cancer" or "defeating cancer."

This suggestion is reinforced by the very first words, which are the first message marker, of the ransom note: "Listen carefully!" The "ll" in "carefully" looks like a capital "V" followed by a lowercase "y" and an exclamation point. "Vy!" suggests "Victory!" which relates to the "Victory!" at the end of the note. From the beginning of the note to the end, the writer unconsciously suggests that if the reader listens carefully the note tells the dramatic story of a perceived or hoped for victory.

There is a significant space between "Vi" and "ctory," and the "c" in "ctory," unlike any other "c" in the note, has a long flowing tail that gives the impression of a reversed "s," which suggests the word "story." "Vi" is the Roman numeral "six," which suggests that the ransom note is the "story of a six-year-old."

The "V" in victory can also be read as an angular "S," which then makes the signature read "Si ctory" or "Sic" story, which suggests "sick story." The killer also runs the last two letters in "victory" together creating effectively a six-letter word that can be read "victoy" or "victom" or "victim." "Victoy" also suggests a victim who is someone's toy. These ideas suggest that the murder is the sick story of a six-year-old victim who was used like a toy, which matches the story the writer tells in the body of the ransom note.

After "Victory" comes the note's third exclamation point, which unlike the first two exclamation points is set apart from the word by several spaces. Both of the earlier exclamation points follow specific comments to John Ramsey, and the previous exclamation point is directly next to "John," which suggests that the use of exclamation points relates to John Ramsey.

The writer's placement of "Vi ctory" between two exclamation points makes the end of the ransom note read "John! Vi ctory!" This strongly links the idea of "victory" with a "victory over John." This reinforces the suggestions throughout the note that the writer feels hostility and resentment toward John, a condescending "fat cat" who "underestimates" the writer.

"John! Vi ctory!" also implies that by using his daughter sexually John Ramsey himself had a temporary victory over his own pain and helplessness. This suggests that John Ramsey was intimately involved with the writer and was greatly affected by the writer's life-threatening disease and inadequacy as a woman—and he turned to the victim for relief.

"S. B.T.C" includes a significant space between the "S" and the "B," which divides the letters into two words "S." " B.T.C" with no period after C. The "second word" including the two periods becomes a five-letter word with the larger period after "B" suggesting the word "BiTC" or "bitch." Combining this with "S." gives "S. BITC" or "son-of-a-bitch." This suggests that the writer's victory was over that SOB John who was responsible for this "sick story of a victimized six-year-old."

It also suggests that the writer is desperately looking for a victory over another foe—cancer, the "Big C," which is the last letter in the note. The writer suggests that her powerful rage gave her a temporary victory over the helplessness of cancer, which may be characterized as a "bitch" in reference to the severity of the disease. The writer concludes the ransom note by suggesting that the killer John was a son-of-a-bitch, cancer was a bitch, life was a bitch—the whole thing was a bitch.

"SBTC" also suggests "Saved By The Cross," which suggests that perhaps unconsciously the writer deeply wishes for forgiveness—her only hope at this point.

The Conclusions

1. A woman wrote the ransom note.

Numerous messages from the writer's unconscious mind suggest that a woman wrote the ransom note. The note contains many female-gender references. The misspelling of "bussiness" has strong feminine connotations and in the context of the sentence suggests a victimized woman. "Proper burial," "two gentlemen," and "attaché" give the note a refined, sophisticated feminine tone. "Use that good southern common sense" has a "mothering" connotation.

The multiple references to various containers that hold valuables—"bank," "attaché," and "brown paper bag," and especially a container that resembles a uterus, "brown paper bag"—strongly suggest a female writer. The numerous references to "delivery" also strongly suggest a female writer especially since "I" is linked to two uses of the word "delivery."

The missing periods in "a.m." makes the word read "am," and when read with the word immediately above and immediately below it gives the vertical message—the only meaningful vertical message in the note—"I am delivery" which suggests "I am woman"—another indicator the writer is a woman. The missing periods in "a.m." and after the "C" at the end of the note subtly suggest missed menstrual periods as well as a woman who can no longer have periods. The out-of-place, chaotic, "psychotic" period after the word "hence"—conclusion—suggests that the writer's period/menstrual cycle ended prematurely and "concluded" that part of her feminine role in life, which resulted in her diminished femininity and self-esteem. Even the word "pickup" refers to feminine identity and suggests that the writer's femininity was greatly assaulted when the victim was sexually abused. Taken together these messages reinforce the suggestion that female issues are very much on the mind of the writer, that female issues/femininity played a key role in the victim's murder, and that a female wrote the ransom note.

2. The writer is a cancer victim.

Numerous messages from the writer's unconscious mind suggest that she is living under the life-threatening effects of cancer. The note contains multiple references to bodily damage, including "safe," "un harmed," and threats that the victim won't "see 1997."

The note describes two sequences of change that strongly suggest cancer: The ransom money is to be divided twice into progressively smaller amounts, and the money is to be "withdrawn" from its container twice and placed in progressively weaker containers—"bank," "attaché," and "brown paper bag." These ideas suggest surgical removal and deterioration of female body parts, and "brown paper bag" specifically suggests a weak paper-thin dead container—a defective uterus.

The messages in the note link the diminishing amounts of money to the idea of "remaining," which strongly suggests that the writer feels a destructive force within her that is attacking her feminine container and progressively dividing and withdrawing her valuable femininity until there are only remains. These ideas strongly suggest a female form of cancer because virtually no other life-threatening disease that causes total deterioration would necessitate a hysterectomy, and no other feminine disease destroys femininity so thoroughly.

The writer used the word "delivery" four times but crossed out the fourth reference—she "destroyed" it—which strongly suggests that her femininity has been destroyed and that this issue played a key role in the murder. The use of the medical word "monitor" and the writer's suggestion that she is exhausted are linked to the ideas of "delivery" and femininity. "Delivery" from cancer—surgical removal of diseased organs and chemotherapy—are "exhausting."

The references to survival percentages and the idea of being under constant scrutiny reinforce the suggestion that the writer is living under the threat that the slightest deviation or abnormality will result in death. The reference to being scanned, specifically connected to the idea of a bodily defect, strongly suggests that the writer is undergoing cancer diagnosis and treatment—her body is being scanned to detect the smallest traces—"electronic devices"—of the disease.

The references to being "marked or tampered with" also suggest cancer. These words follow the message marker "instructions," which reinforces the suggestion that these words apply to the writer—they are messages from the writer's unconscious mind about herself and her motives. The twin ideas of "99% chance" of dying and how easy killing someone is further reinforce the idea of imminent death—another link to cancer.

The writer's command to John Ramsey that he not "grow a brain," a common place for cancer to spread, suggests cancer because brain cells don't grow—cancer cells, however, do grow in the brain. Throughout the note the writer's unconscious train of thought strongly suggests that she feels entrapped and that she is terrified by a disease. She is not respected but rather is in servitude, possessed, depleted, and assaulted, all of which are linked to the idea of a "small foreign faction" or force that destroys, an accurate description of cancer.

The decimal point in $118,000.00 followed by instructions about dividing the money suggests that the writer is observing herself being divided up into the smallest parts and being divided by a small fraction—the decimal point—which suggests "a small foreign faction." The "psychotic period" after "hence" suggests that the writer feels a great deal of pressure from the idea of cancer prematurely ending her life.

The missing period after the "C" in the signature at the end of the note suggests that the writer is frightened of endings and doesn't want her story—her life—to end. "Want her to see 1997" and the narrow window of time between 8 and 10 reinforces the suggestion that the writer feels the pressure of time. The last sentence of the note, "It is up to you," reinforces the suggestion that the writer is under the pressure of time.

The note includes multiple references to "delivery," and it starts and ends with "Vi ctory," two words that cancer patients use to express their deepest wish—victory over and delivery from cancer. [Finally, the suggested Roman numeral "vi" in "Vi ctory" also points to ovarian cancer, which is categorized by stages I to IV described in Roman numerals. The reverse of "Vi" is "IV" and would have been a familiar number to Patsy Ramsey who had stage IV ovarian cancer, the most advanced type, carrying the worst prognosis.]

3. The writer is a killer.

Numerous messages from the writer's unconscious mind suggest that the writer is capable of hostile actions. In the third sentence, the writer describes a split in her personality—she is respectful but hostile. Her slip "bussiness" reflects significant disguised hostility. The boldly, aggressively crossed-out word "delivery," which symbolizes the victim, suggests that the writer not only is capable of but also has acted on her hostility toward the victim. The divided word "daug hter" reinforces the suggestion that the writer has assaulted the victim. The word "my" used with the message marker "instructions" suggests that the writer is personally connected to "immediate execution," "denied her remains," "beheaded," "she dies," "she dies," "she dies," "she dies," "99% chance of killing," and "don't think killing will be difficult."

The link between "my" and "instructions" also suggests that the writer's unconscious mind was accurately describing the sequence of events the night of the murder: a sudden execution, the victim ready for burial, two killers who had been provoked, and a beheading. Throughout the note the writer suggests that she was personally involved with the victim, and she describes both the "time bomb" and the "trigger" motive for the murder (see below).

4. The writer identifies the unconscious deep pain/"time bomb" motive for the murder.

Numerous messages from the writer's unconscious mind reinforce the suggestion that she was a terrified cancer victim, which further suggests that cancer played a key underlying role in the murder. The first message marker "Listen" links "small foreign faction," an accurate description of cancer, to the motive. "Listen carefully" with the "Vy!" embedded in the word "carefully" also suggests a wish for a victory over cancer, which is reinforced by the "Victory!" at the end of the note.

The first "instructions" message marker suggests that the writer's terror of bodily harm identifies her as the killer and reinforces the suggestion that the life-threatening fear of cancer became a powerful "time bomb" motive. The last "instructions" message marker suggests the same deeper motive with two references to survival percentages—hallmarks of cancer patients. The deep-seated terror of cancer is linked to the "trigger" motive (see below) in a sentence that suggests the writer has "scanned"—a medical procedure used to detect cancer—John Ramsey and caught him in a deviant and secret communication with the victim.

5. The writer identifies the "trigger" motive for the crime.

Numerous messages from the writer's unconscious mind suggest that she is personally involved with both John Ramsey and the victim. The writer loses control, graphically emphasized by her aggressive crossing out of the word "delivery," when she is writing about the victim being changed into a "pick-up." In the four consecutive sentences that follow "pick-up," the writer suggests that secretly observing John Ramsey's misbehavior with the victim resulted in the victim's death—which is emphasized in "she dies" repeated four times. The writer slipped up when she wrote that the "two gentlemen kidnappers" particularly liked the victim and she had to use a proofreaders' "v" to insert the word "not," which forms the shape of a heart and further reinforces the suggestion that the writer both loved and hated the victim—and that a powerful love triangle existed between the writer, the victim, and John Ramsey.

By linking a picture of a powerful sexually explicit triangle—the killer, John Ramsey, and the victim—to the brutal personal statement "don't think killing will be difficult" the writer suggests that she experienced the victim as a competitive "fat cat" in a battle with her for John Ramsey's love and affections, which the killer also experienced as a catfight to the death. The note contains multiple references to the ideas of envy, power, diminished self-esteem and femininity, neglect, and being insulted. The alternating personal threats and affection in the last few sentences of the note reinforce the suggestion that an event involving John Ramsey and the victim triggered the writer's rage and prompted her to kill—even though she loved both John and the victim.

The chaotic sentence that contains ten message markers strongly suggests the conclusion of the events the night of the murder: The writer became psychotically enraged when she unexpectedly observed the victim being turned into a "pickup." The multiple use of the word "early" reinforces the suggestion that the events of the evening caught the writer off guard. The writer repeatedly suggests that she secretly observed John Ramsey with the victim and that seeing them in a sexually explicit act triggered her killing rage. The crucial message marker "think" in "don't think that killing will be difficult" reinforces this suggestion.

6. John Ramsey was caught sexually abusing the victim the night of the murder.

Numerous messages from the writer's unconscious mind suggest that John Ramsey was sexually abusing the victim the night of the murder. In the chaotic sentence containing "hence" implying conclusion the writer suggests that the victim had been turned into a "pickup" and a "call girl" by John and that he was gratifying himself in the victim's little bank—he was "getting some." "You want her," another sexually suggestive phrase, is also linked to the first crucial "instructions" message marker, which points to the killer, and it is also specifically linked to John Ramsey and the victim.

[*The writer's crude suggestion that she was angry with John Ramsey and disrespected him over a sexual matter when his "buss-iness" became "serving cunt" is emphasized not only by a slip ("bussiness") but by a cross-out ("don't"), the second most blatant sign of chaos in the note. Additionally the writer repeats the same crude message in the third paragraph, confirming her intent to reveal the trigger motive was a sexual one.*]

The writer also suggests that a "deviant" John Ramsey caused the victim's death. The writer suggests that she had been unconsciously monitoring John Ramsey's secret "communications" with the victim and that when the writer consciously saw John sexually engaged with the victim she erupted in a killing rage. The proofreaders' "v" with the inserted word "not" looks like a heart or a "valentine," which strongly suggests a "love triangle"—John, the victim, and Patsy—as does the sentence that originally stated that the two "kidnappers" particularly liked the victim.

The first and only mention of Patsy Ramsey is linked to a personal reference to John Ramsey and four shocking suggestions that the writer witnessed explicit sexual abuse: "Don't try and grow John," "It's up . . . now John!" the implied command "don't get fat," and the degrading idea of "fat pussy." The writer uses a number of exclamation points close to John's name, and exclamation points suggest phallic symbols. Also, the repeated idea of a "john" fits with the idea of "pickup," which reinforces the suggestion that John was caught sexually abusing his daughter—using her and in that sense prostituting her.

7. The writer unconsciously encouraged the victim's sexual involvement with John Ramsey.

Numerous messages from the writer's unconscious mind suggest that she participated in turning the victim into a "pickup" or "call girl." "We might call you early to arrange an earlier delivery [crossed out] pick-up" suggests that unconsciously the writer not only knew about the sexual abuse but was also encouraging it. "I will call you between 8 and 10 am tomorrow to in-struct you on delivery"—the first time "I" is used in the note—reinforces the suggestion that the writer was encouraging the sexual abuse. The writer's suggestion that she had unconsciously arranged for the victim to be deliv-ered to John Ramsey between 8 and 10 the night of the murder also reinforces this suggestion. The writer's command to "use that good southern common sense" also suggests that John use his most common or base instincts, which again reinforces the suggestion that the writer was encour-aging John's sexual abuse of the victim.

The writer's repeated use of the numbers 18 or 118—or "8 and 10," which add up to 18, are linked to the idea of delivery, which strongly suggests that she viewed the victim as a sacrifice—she was delivering the victim up to John Ramsey and eventually to her own rage and terror. The repeated use of 18 fits with Patsy Ramsey's reportedly favorite Psalm, the 118th, which speaks of binding the sacrifice with cords in reference to Abraham binding and sacrificing his son Isaac. Reportedly Patsy Ramsey used this Psalm as her "protection" against cancer reoccurrence, which links the deep pain "time bomb" motive with the "trigger" motive. [*Further understanding of the number 118 or 18 occurs when the numerical code regarding 8 and 10 is deciphered.* (*See Appendix A, "Overview of Note," page 249.*)

The fact that the murder occurred on Christmas Day suggests even more strongly that Patsy Ramsey saw the victim as a "Christ" figure, a scapegoat, and in its own way Christmas Day further suggests an unconscious confes-sion that Patsy Ramsey, with her specifically Christian sensitivities and her desperate need for sacrifice—someone else to carry her fear and pain—was the murderer.

The murder occurring on Christmas Day also has great significance be-cause of the similarities between Christ and the victim: Both were innocent scapegoats who were punished at others' expense; both were bound; both deaths were associated with a ransom—"Christ died to ransom many;" both suffered head injuries but died from bodily injuries; and both had a "proper" burial in a rich man's tomb—just like Christ's body, JonBenét's body was wrapped (in a blanket) and it was buried in the most tomb-like room in her wealthy parents' house.

The victim was further identified with Christ by (1) having a gold cross around her neck; (2) having a new Christmas bracelet inscribed with her name and 12-25-96; (3) John Ramsey carrying her body up from "the grave of the basement" to the upstairs living room where, (4) Patsy Ramsey reportedly made a further connection between Christ and JonBenét by crying out words to the effect of "Jesus, you raised Lazarus from the dead—please raise my baby," thereby herself linking the basement to a tomb: (5) both parents insisting that JonBenét's death be listed on her tombstone as 12-25-96, which matches her bracelet even though her body was not discovered until December 26.

All of this suggests that the deepest meaning of "S.B.T.C" is "Saved By The Cross" because it reflects Patsy Ramsey"s unconscious wish for forgiveness and her continuing search for someone to atone for her murderous rage. It also reflects John Ramsey's needs because he too was looking for a sacrifice in the victim as he sacrificed her innocence. In a strange way the Christian symbols repeatedly connected to the victim at the crime scene identify both Patsy and John Ramsey as her parents and her murderers.

[*Months after this report, the Ramseys unconsciously confirm the scapegoat role JonBenét served for them in the title of their book* The Death of Innocence.]

8. The note suggests there were two killers.

Numerous messages from the writer's unconscious mind suggest that two people participated in the victim's murder. "We are a group of individuals" immediately follows the first message marker "Listen," which suggests from the beginning of the ransom note that more than one person was involved in the murder.

The writer's frequent use of "we" and "our" reinforces the suggestion of two murderers as does "two gentlemen watching over" the victim. The writer particularly suggests that two murderers—two gentlemen—were provoked.

The writer uses the word "killing" only twice and both times in the context of brutality: John Ramsey has a "99% chance of killing" the victim, and the writer does not "think killing will be difficult." In the sequence that follows the chaotic "conclusion" ("hence") sentence, the writer mentions two explicit and separate acts of murder: "immediate execution" and "beheading," which strongly suggests two separate lethal assaults (strangulation and the head injury).

"It is up to you" in the final sentence suggests "it is in John's hands" and that he was the one who strangled the victim. The "to" shaped like a noose in "It is up to you now John!" suggests in a pictorial way that John Ramsey strangled the victim. The first "to" in "follow our instructions to the letter" has the same appearance, which suggests the writer was conveying the hidden confession that John Ramsey strangled his daughter—giving the authorities "instructions" on who to apprehend.

"To" also suggests "two" for two murderers. This "to" also suggests a U.S. Navy symbol or a sailing symbol, which links to John Ramsey who was a former Navy pilot whose hobby is sailing.

The writer ends the note with the idea that all the responsibility is on John, and this third reference to John in the context of the victim's death reinforces the suggestion that John had the final responsibility for the victim's death.

9. Patsy Ramsey wrote the note, and she participated in the murder.

Numerous messages from the writer's unconscious mind suggest that the writer was personally involved with the victim and with John Ramsey and witnessed John sexually abusing the victim, an event that triggered her chaotic rage the night of the murder. The writer's chaos and destructiveness in the crucial sentence that points toward the victim being turned into a "pickup" suggests extreme personal involvement and rage at the victim. The repeated suggestion that the writer caught John Ramsey secretly involved with the victim followed by a string of brutal comments—"sudden execution," "remains for burial," "beheaded," and four repetitions of "she dies"—points even further to passionate involvement with the victim. The inserted word "not" that forms a heart-shaped image along with "two gentlemen" who actually like the victim but are provoked suggests a powerfully competitive family triangle.

The part in the note that describes the writer's rage reaching its peak "don't think killing will be difficult"—is linked to the first and only reference to Patsy Ramsey—"family." The writer's additional suggestion that at the peak of her rage she was simultaneously intimate and enraged with John Ramsey is indicated by five consecutive personal, first-name comments/

commands to him, all of which come after the first and only reference to Patsy Ramsey.

The note suggests that the writer has approached the primitive emotions behind the crime—explicit sexuality, envy, betrayal, and rage—in a deeper and more personal way by repeatedly linking them to "John." The reference to southern common sense has a feminine tone that suggests a woman who met John Ramsey during the time that he was in Atlanta but who is not a southerner herself.

The writer repeatedly suggests that the killer is a woman whose femininity has been severely damaged by a life-threatening form of cancer and her treatment included a hysterectomy, which left her feeling depleted as well as in a constant state of terror that the cancer would return. This description fits Patsy Ramsey who is a stage-four ovarian cancer survivor and had an unplanned "sudden" hysterectomy.

The proofreaders' "v" used to insert the word "not" suggests that the writer has an editorial background: Patsy Ramsey majored in journalism in college. The specific amount of the ransom money strongly suggests that the writer had very personal information about John Ramsey's bonus. The crime scene and autopsy fit the profile of a nurturing murderer, a mother. The note contains graphic art, and Patsy Ramsey is an artist.

Messages throughout the ransom note lead to the conclusion that Patsy Ramsey wrote the ransom note and that Patsy assaulted her own daughter in a rage killing by inflicting a severe blow to her head most clearly suggested in "daug hter" meaning "hit her daughter." Although as the autopsy revealed this injury would have eventually ended the victim's life, the cause of death was strangulation from a second violent assault on the victim that suddenly and immediately ended her life.

In the ransom note, particularly in the last sentence, Patsy strongly suggests that a second person, John Ramsey, inflicted the second assault. Patsy also suggests by leaving her name out of the greeting versus the practice note, which included "Mr. and Mrs. Ramsey," that she wanted to shift the focus away from her since the note reveals her significant culpability.

10. The victim was dead before the ransom note was written.

Numerous messages from Patsy Ramsey's unconscious mind suggest that the victim had been fatally assaulted before the ransom note was written.

The divided word "un harmed" linked to the threat that the victim will not "see 1997" suggests that the victim has already been harmed.

The divided word "daug hter" comes a few words after the message marker "hence," the out-of-place period, and the crossed-out word "delivery," which strongly suggests that the conclusion of the chaotic events was the murder of the victim. The crossed-out word "delivery," which is a strong reference to femininity and is clearly linked to the victim, suggests that the victim had been destroyed. The sequence of threats following "daug hter" suggests confirmation of her death: "immediate execution," "denied her remains," "beheaded," "she dies," "she dies," "she dies," "she dies," "99% chance of killing," and "don't think killing will be difficult." The intensity of these threats suggests that the murder was a rage killing and that Patsy wrote the ransom note as part of the cover-up, the "pose," or the staging of an alleged kidnapping.

11. The ransom note is a confession.

From the beginning of the note to the end, Patsy Ramsey suggests she is speaking for the victim—"we represent a small foreign faction"—or entity links the note to JonBenét's "foreign" name. The writer suggests there are hidden instructions in the note that if followed will point to the murderers as though the victim herself could speak from the grave. In the last "instructions" message marker, the writer virtually guarantees—"100% chance"—the murderers will be caught if the note is "carefully listened to."

Patsy's note suggests both a deep pain/"time bomb" motive and a "trigger" motive as well as who was involved in the murder and even what type of cover-up the murderers will use. Patsy's note suggests looking for "two gentlemen"—two proper people. She even suggests the entire note is the sick story of a "six-year-old victim"—and the story of a physically sick murderer.

12. The murderer(s) will be relieved to be caught.

Patsy Ramsey's specific instruction "I advise you to be rested" following the idea of an exhausting delivery suggests the writer particularly longs for the charade, the "pose," to be over. The writer's preoccupation with "delivery" also suggests she wants to be delivered from her lies. The extensive confession in the note suggests Patsy unconsciously has a great need to tell the truth.

13. The writer and comurderer has artistic skills.

Numerous messages from the writer's unconscious mind appear as graphic signs in the ransom note, which links the writer's artistic skills with Patsy Ramsey, the artist. The heart formed by the word "not" inserted in the proof-readers' "v" suggests the Patsy's love/hate relationship with both John Ramsey and the victim. The two percent signs appear to be faces with long noses, which suggests "sniffing out" or searching for the motive. When viewed side-ways in one direction the "Vi" of "Vi ctory" appears to be a face with a furrowed brow. The aggressively crossed-out word "delivery" artistically suggests chaos and destruction of femininity—both Patsy's and the victim's. An "a" drawn as an arrow pointing downward graphically emphasizes the writer's command that John Ramsey lose his erection, which reinforces the words "don't grow." Patsy uses exclamation points to suggest phallic symbols, and an exclamation point reinforces her statement that "It is up . . . John!"

The first and last "to" in the note suggest a knot or noose, which can also be seen in other letters at important points in the note such as the "d" in both "daughter" in the first paragraph and "advise" in "I advise you not to provoke." The image in the last "to" also looks like an anchor, which sug-gests a U.S. Navy symbol and suggests that the victim is anchored, tied down, still, not moving—dead. The anchor, knot, or noose also reinforces the sug-gestion that the victim was strangled.

The horizontal and vertical spacing between the syllables of "daug hter" suggests that the victim was dead when the note was written and that she had been hit from above. The writer left wide spaces between letters and words to convey important messages in a number of places, including the word "un harmed" and in both lines of the signature. The writer also used an out-of-place period, missing periods, and a decimal point to draw attention to important messages in the note.

In the closing, Patsy uses a space between "Vi" and "ctory" in "Victory" and the unique shaped of "ctory" to suggest the "story of a six-year-old victim"—matched with the "Vi" looking like a face with a furrowed brow. Additionally Patsy reveals an artist's ability to use symbols to convey several messages at the same time such as the crossed-out "delivery" followed by "pick-up."

14. The message markers serve as valid predictors of valuable unconscious messages and rich new information.

Numerous messages from Patsy Ramsey's unconscious mind support the validity of using message markers in the ransom note as key words in understanding the actual events the night of the victim's murder. Patsy's opening message marker "Listen carefully!" suggests that the note is rich with these messages, and it is. "Listen carefully" also fulfills its suggested prediction that "small foreign faction" will have great importance for understanding the murderer's motives, as does the "Vy!" for victory embedded in the word "carefully." The message marker "hence" is followed by a striking sentence that suggests a cohesive series of events pointing toward a logical "conclusion" that matches the crime scene.

The message marker "our instructions," which is used twice, suggests two logical ways of identifying the murderers and speaking for the victim: Patsy has suffered bodily damage, her valuable feminine container has been damaged and removed, and she has cancer—all of which suggest a deep pain motive for the murder; and John Ramsey had a "99% chance of killing his daughter"—an explicit suggestion that he did murder the victim, a suggestion that comes after Patsy's seven suggestions that he was sexually abusing the victim.

The two similar message markers "instruct" and "my instructions" suggest clarification of Patsy Ramsey's mixed motives: Unconsciously she "instructed" John Ramsey that she was delivering the victim to him for abuse, but consciously she was enraged that he would deviate, a message that is emphasized by Patsy's use of "my" instructions.

The crossed-out "delivery," the most blatant message marker in the note, strongly suggests the chaos and destruction that is confirmed in the rest of the sentence, and the message marker "pick-up" provides significant meaning to the rest of the sentence. The message marker "daug hter" provides a logical conclusion to the events leading up to the murder—the victim has been hit, broken into, and killed.

The twin message markers "scanned" and "electronic devices," both used in the same sentence, point to both Patsy's "time bomb" motive, her deep pain caused by her life-threatening, femininity-diminishing cancer, and her "trigger" motive, her rage triggered by being betrayed by both John and the victim. "Pick-up" and the other nine message markers in the chaotic sentence that points toward a sexual abuse trigger motive are confirmed in the rest of the note, including the references to sexual abuse that Patsy gives at the end of the note.

The message marker "Vi ctory" points to the note being a "story"—a story of a six-year-old victim. This suggestion is strongly validated by the cohesive story of the murder of JonBenét Ramsey as told by messages from Patsy Ramsey's unconscious mind in the ransom note she wrote to cover-up her rage killing.

The Summary

The writer had it right—the ransom note is a story. The cohesiveness of the story from the writer's unconscious mind, unveiled between the lines, and compared with the crime scene offers persuasive evidence of its validity. The writer consistently presents two key motives for the crime, the mostly unconscious deep pain—the fear of her cancer returning—which terrorized her and the horrible experience of witnessing her young daughter being sexually abused by her husband, which triggered her murderous rage. The ransom note suggests the devastating effects a female form of cancer carrying a poor prognosis with its accompanying medical procedures, particularly the sudden hysterectomy and chemotherapy, can have on a young woman's feminine identity and how vulnerable it left her to any further insult to her femininity.

Patsy Ramsey also elaborates in detail about the circumstances that might cause a mother and a father to assault their child. The ransom note presents a clear explanation of how and why two parents could have carried out the murder and then a cover-up. The two severe injuries to the victim found on autopsy point to two separate acts and suggest two separate killers as does the ransom note. As the autopsy suggests, the victim would almost certainly have died from the head injury, but the murderers did not wait for that to happen. As the note suggests, the parents were operating under a narrow time window and after the severe head injury needed a body to proceed with the cover-up.

The idea of marked or tampered with money leading to the victim's death suggests the idea of a damaged valuable, linked with the victim, leading to a death—and thus further suggests that neither parent could have lived with the reality of having a brain-damaged child, which would have been the case had the victim survived the head injury. In refusing to get the victim medical help, Patsy Ramsey again enacted her helplessness on her daughter, as unconsciously Patsy perceived herself as beyond medical help.

The observed sexual abuse that Patsy Ramsey unconsciously suggests in her ransom note was explicit and shocking, along with the distinct suggestion that unconsciously she knew it was going on and even encouraged it. This again matches the findings on autopsy, which strongly suggest acute and chronic sexual abuse. The sexual abuse explains an event powerful enough to drive Patsy Ramsey into a brief experience of psychotic rage. As the ransom note suggests, Patsy Ramsey identified with her daughter so greatly that witnessing JonBenét being sexually abused was so intolerable that Patsy completely lost perspective as the core of her feminine identity was destroyed.

At the same time, Patsy Ramsey's feminine identity was so precarious that she was deeply threatened by her daughter being the recipient of John Ramsey's affections. Patsy attributed her daughter's sexual abuse to her own inadequacy as a woman, and she struck out at her daughter, instead of John Ramsey, to destroy the person she perceived to be her rival and to protect her own feminine identity. John Ramsey's sexual abuse of JonBenét leading to Patsy Ramsey's explosion explains why he would be motivated to carry out the "second act of murder"—the strangulation and the cover-up.

Furthermore, Patsy Ramsey's note suggests that unconsciously she was closely scrutinizing both herself and John Ramsey and that both of them had been living with a great deal of terror. Additionally, the obsessive focus on money and the anger at "fat cats" suggest that both Patsy and John Ramsey were uncomfortable with their extreme monetary success. Also, Patsy Ramsey suggests that John Ramsey's sexual abuse of JonBenét was precipitated by his own deep sense of potential loss connected to Patsy. The consistent observations and communications from Patsy Ramsey's unconscious mind reflected in the ransom note she wrote match in striking ways the powerful emotional stresses experienced by both Patsy and John Ramsey.

Opinion

Based upon the reconstruction of the unconscious content of the ransom note, we opine that Patsy Ramsey is the author of the note, that she wrote it after she had participated with her husband, John Ramsey, and caused the death of their daughter, JonBenét Ramsey. It is further opined that there were two motives, a primary and a secondary motive: (1) the first motive being that Patsy Ramsey went into an uncontrollable rage precipitated by the observing of sexual activity between her husband and her daughter, JonBenét; (2) and secondarily because of Patsy Ramsey's unresolved fear and anger over her diagnosis and treatment for ovarian cancer. This resulted in two independent acts of violence against JonBenét that ultimately caused her death. It is further opined that while the conscious purpose of the note was to create a cover story that an intended kidnapping of JonBenét had occurred rather than her being the victim of a rage murder, in fact, the unconscious motive of the writer was to tell the story of the crime and its aftermath, and was an attempt to relieve the note's writer of her guilt as well an attempt to understand why she had acted as she did.

Additional Information Following Report

Further reflection and additional information obtained suggest more confirmation of our report. In his book, *JonBenét,* Steve Thomas tells of an important conversation Patsy Ramsey had with Detective Linda Arndt shortly after the murder. Waiting with Arndt while Burke was being interviewed, Patsy spontaneously broke into tears as she revealed how grief-stricken she had been by her hysterectomy because she could have no more children. She went on to tell Arndt how lost she felt with Burke going back to school and John going back to work while she had nothing. Additionally, she recalled being saddened that her chemotherapy treatment "vied for the family's attention with her younger sister's pregnancy." Patsy's stories precisely match the thoughtprints in the ransom note (and elsewhere): connecting competition with a fertile younger woman to her cancer, being devastated by her nest/container being removed with the ensuing infertility—further aggravated by an empty nest syndrome.

Also, one striking aspect to the crime scene has been largely overlooked. The killer left one of the Ramseys' suitcases containing a blanket and a Dr. Seuss book at the scene—obviously a part of the staging. What did it mean? The empty container and blanket suggest unconsciously Patsy Ramsey was once again pointing to her empty container with the blanket also suggesting femininity as well as cover-up. The suitcase and two items also suggest something juvenile, contrived, and fantasy-like, something a child would pack who was going to pretend running away. But most striking was the Dr. Seuss book—a written communication of pure fantasy—suggesting the other writing at the crime scene, the ransom note, was likewise a fantasy. In a nutshell, the Dr. Seuss book is a perfect picture of the ransom note and another striking unconscious confession.

APPENDIX C:
The Christmas Letters

1995 Ramsey Christmas Letter

Twas a week before Christmas with a million things to do,
And wouldn't you know it, Mom came down with the flu!

Fortunately the gifts were all gotten and under the tree,
But the Christmas cards didn't make it—as you can well see!

So we'll take this opportunity to extend the Holiday Cheer
And be the first to wish you a Healthy & Happy New Year!

We've finally given in to the computerized form letter! What better way to keep the high-tech industry in business!? Speaking of business, John and Access are going great guns. Europe has been successfully conquered with offices in every country except Norway! Mexico & Canada opened too. (Can you believe this grew out of our garage on Northridge?) Anyway, John was rewarded by parent company, Lockheed-Martin, by being elected an officer of the company.

All work and no play makes John a dull boy, so he leaves plenty of time for the latter. This year John, John Andrew, and Melinda took the crew of the Miss America (our sailing sloop) to victories in the NOOD Races in Chicago and a 4th place division finish of the Chicago-Mackinac Island Race. Seventy-knot winds in the Mac race really made the finish line look pretty good! John Andrew is a freshman at CU here in Boulder, and Melinda is due to complete her Nursing Degree from MCG [Medical College of Georgia] in Augusta next June.

Burke is busy in his third grade year at a new school named High Peaks. It is a Core Knowledge school which accesses high academics and personal achievement. He loves it! He continues with Boy Scouting and the piano. This winter he is the tallest guy on his basketball team. Summer on Charlevoix was spent taking golf and sailing lessons each day. Burke is quite the sailor!

JonBenét too had a busy summer in Charlevoix. She was crowned Little Miss Charlevoix in a pageant in July and spent the rest of the summer riding in convertibles in various hometown parades throughout Michigan. She performed a patriotic tap & song for her talent. She and Burke both won ribbons in several decorated bicycle contests. In October, JonBenét became Little Miss Colorado, she rode on the "Good Ship Lollipop" float during the Boulder Christmas parade. (Grandpa Paugh built the float!) She waved and sang all along the parade route! She also takes piano, violin, and drama classes. Busy little Pre-kindergartener! [sic.] (Busy Mom hauling her around!)

I continue to have good check-ups at NIH in Bethesda, MD. God has surely blessed me with energy and the ability to return to raising a family. I thank Him every morning when I wake up and see the sunrise reflecting on the Flatirons over Boulder. Please continue to keep us in your prayers.

Hope your Christmas was merry and here's to 1996! By the time you read this we'll be cheering on the Buffs at the Cotton Bowl in Dallas and then on to the Fiesta Bowl in Phoenix! Thanks to everyone who visited us in Colorado or Charlevoix this year. Please come see us in 1996! Love to you all!

The Ramseys

1996 Ramsey Christmas Letter

Dear Friends and Family.

It's been another busy year at the Ramsey household. Can't believe its almost over and time to start again!

Melinda (24) graduated from the Medical College of Georgia and is working in Pediatric ICU at Kennestone Hospital in Atlanta. John Andrew (20) is a Sophomore at the University of Colorado.

Burke is a busy fourth grader where he really shines in math and spelling. He played flag football this fall and is currently on a basketball binge! His little league team was #1. He's lost just about all of his baby teeth, so I'm sure we'll be seeing the orthodontist in 1997!

JonBenét is enjoying her first year in "real" school. Kindergarten in the Core Knowledge program is fast paced and five full days a week. She has already been moved ahead to first grade math. She continues to enjoy participating in talent and modeling pageants. She was named "America's Royale Tiny Miss" last summer and is Colorado's Little Miss Christmas. Her teacher says she is so outgoing that she will never have trouble delivering an oral book report!

John is always on the go traveling hither and yon. Access recently celebrated its one billion $$ mark in sales, so he's pretty happy! He and his crew were under way in the Port Huron to Mackinac Island yacht race in July, but had to pull out mid way due to lack of wind. (Can you believe that?) But, his real love is the new 'old looking' boat, Grand Season, which he spent months designing.

I spend most of my "free time" working in the school and doing volunteer work. The Charlevoix house was on the home tour in July and will likely appear in one of the Better Homes & Gardens publications in 1997. On a recent trip to NYC, my friend and I appeared amid the throng of fans on the TODAY show. Al Roker & Bryant actually talked to us and we were on camera for a few fleeting moments!

We are all enjoying continued good health and look forward to seeing you in 1997! One final note .... thank you to all my "friends" and my dear husband for surprising me with the biggest, most outrageous 40th birthday bash I've ever had! We'll be spending my acutual [sic] birthday on the Disney Big Red Boat over the new year!

Merry Christmas and much love,
The Ramseys

1997 Ramsey Christmas Message

With the Christmas season upon us and the anniversary of JonBenét's death approaching, we are filled with many emotions. We, as a family, miss JonBenét's presence among us as we see the lights, hear the music, and recall celebrations of Christmases past. We miss her every day—not just today.

On the one hand, we feel like Christmas should be canceled. Where is there joy? Our Christmas is forever tainted with the tragedy of her death. And yet the message rings clear. Had there been no birth of Christ, there would be no hope of eternal life, and hence, no hope of ever being with our loved ones again.

As the day of the birth of our Lord and Savior approaches, we thank all across the nation and around the world for your continued prayer of concern and support. It is those prayers that sustain us. We ask that as you gather with your families and loved ones this Christmas, be joyful in the celebration of the birthday of Christ, knowing that this is truly the reason of the season. We must continue to celebrate the birth of Christ for our hope of life together ever after.

Thank you for all you meant to her and mean to us.

With blessing and prayer for a Joyful Holiday and the Grace of God's ever present love for the New Year,

John, Patsy, John Andrew, Melinda, and Burke

APPENDIX D:

Biographical Information on Dr. Hodges, Dr. Callahan, and Dr. Groesbeck

Andrew G. Hodges, M.D., is a former Assistant Clinical Professor of Psychiatry at the University of Alabama at Birmingham School of Medicine, a Diplomate of the American Board of Psychiatry and Neurology, and in the private practice of psychiatry in Birmingham, Alabama. His psychiatric residencies were done at the University of Cincinnati and Emory University. He has published professionally and is the author of two books on the unconscious mind. He has developed a model of analyzing forensic documents for unconscious communication applying Robert Langs's work with unconscious perception and communication.

Patrick J. Callahan, Ph.D., is a Diplomate of The American Board of Psychological Specialties with a specialization in Forensic Psychoanalysis and a Diplomate in Forensic Examination. He is in the private practice of Forensic Educational and Neuropsychology and Psychoanalytic Psychotherapy in Orange, California. Dr. Callahan has been a consultant in both civil and criminal cases and is an expert in medico-legal death investigation and psychological autopsy. He has presented on forensic cases nationally and internationally.
(P.O. Box 831, Yorba Linda, CA, 92886)

C. Jess Groesbeck, M.D., is a Certified Psychoanalyst of the American Academy of Psychoanalysis and a graduate of the C.G. Jung Institute in San Francisco. He is an Associate Professor of Psychiatry at the University of Utah College of Medicine and the University of California-Davis, Sacramento and a Diplomate of the American Board of Psychiatry and Neurology as well as a Diplomate of the American Board of Forensic Psychiatry. He is also in the private practice of clinical and forensic psychiatry in Sacramento, California. He has published extensively and consulted in both civil and criminal cases including capital murder cases where he has applied Lang's work with unconscious communication.

(2025 "P" Street, Sacramento, CA 95814)

BIBLIOGRAPHY

Colorado Woman News. Excerpt from "Beating Breast Cancer With a Little Help From Angels." December, 1994.

Darden, Christopher. *In Contempt*. New York: Regan Books/Harper Collins, 1997.

Green, Chuck. *The Denver Post*. Excerpts from various articles regarding the Ramsey case in 1998 and 1999.

Lewis, C.S. *Mere Christianity*. New York: MacMillan, 1952.

Langs, Robert. *A Primer of Psychotherapy*. New York:Gardner Press, 1988

_____. *A Technique of Psychoanalytic Psychotherapy*. Volume I. New York: Jason Aronson Publishers, 1973.

Newsweek. Excerpts from "Innocents Lost," and "Why Parents Kill." November 14, 1994.

Nichols, Michael P. and Schwartz, Richard C. *Family Therapy*. 4th edition. Needham Heights, Maine: Allyn & Bacon/Viacom Company, 1998.

Osborn, Albert S. and Osborn, Albert D. *Questioned Document Problems*. Patterson Smith series in Criminology, Law Enforcement, and Social Problems Publishers, 1991.

Ramsey, John and Patsy. *The Death of Innocence*. Nashville: Thomas Nelson Publishers, 2000.

Schiller, Lawrence. *Perfect Murder, Perfect Town*. New York: Harper Collins, 1999.

Singular, Stephen. *Presumed Guilty*. Beverly Hills: New Millennium Press, 1999.

The New Yorker. Quote from "Justice Boulder Style." January 19, 1998.

Thomas, Steve. *JonBenet*. New York: St. Martin's Press, 2000.